Association for Computing Machinery

Advancing Computing as a Science & Profession

ISPD'14

Proceedings of the 2014 ACM
International Symposium on Physical Design

Sponsored by:
ACM SIGDA

Technical Co-sponsored by:
CAS and IEEE Circuits & Systems Society

Supported by:
Altera, ATopTech, Cadence, IBM Research, ICScape, Intel, Mentor Graphics, Oracle, Synopsys, and Xilinx

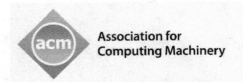

Association for Computing Machinery

Advancing Computing as a Science & Profession

ISBN: 978-1-4503-2592-9

Additional copies may be ordered prepaid from:

ACM Order Department
PO Box 30777
New York, NY 10087-0777, USA

ACM Order Number: 478145

Phone: 1-800-342-6626 (USA and Canada)
+1-212-626-0500 (Global)
Fax: +1-212-944-1318
E-mail: acmhelp@acm.org
Hours of Operation: 8:30 am – 4:30 pm ET

Printed in the USA

Foreword

On behalf of the organizing committee, we are delighted to welcome you to the 2014 ACM International Symposium on Physical Design (ISPD), held at the Sheraton Sonoma County Petaluma, California. Continuing the great tradition established by its twenty-two predecessors, which includes a series of five ACM/SIGDA Physical Design Workshops held intermittently in 1987-1996 and seventeen editions of ISPD in the current form since 1997, the 2014 ISPD provides a premier forum to present leading-edge research results, exchange ideas, and promote research on critical areas related to the physical design of VLSI and other related systems.

We received 40 submissions from all around the world. After a rigorous, month-long, double-blind review process, the Technical Program Committee (TPC) met face-to-face to select papers to be included in the technical program based on about 200 reviews provided by 20 TPC members and 10 external reviewers. Finally, the committee accepted 14 papers to be presented in the symposium. These papers exhibit latest advancements in a variety of topics in placement, routing, 3D integration, clocking and power-grid planning, and design for manufacturability, and applications of physical design in cyber-physical systems.

The ISPD 2014 program is complemented by two keynote addresses as well as nine invited talks, all of which are delivered by distinguished researchers in both industry and academia. Serge Leef, Vice President, New Ventures and General Manager of System-Level Engineering Division at Mentor Graphics will present in the Monday keynote speech challenges and opportunities in hardware cyber security from a physical design perspective. Rob Aitken, R & D Fellow at ARM will present in the Tuesday keynote speech impacts of FinFET technology on physical design. A commemorative session on Tuesday afternoon pays a tribute to Dr. Bryan Preas. His collaborators will share with us Dr. Preas's exceptional contributions, both to EDA research as well as community, including his contributions to the first Physical Design Workshops and first EDA contest/benchmarks, and his services to Design Automation Conference and ACM SIGDA, and for his pioneering effort in electronic publication of proceedings of EDA conferences. Dr. Preas will conclude the commemoration session with a talk entitled "Smart Matter Systems: An Introduction Through Examples." Other invited talks will be interspersed with the presentations of accepted papers. The topics of invited papers range from emerging technologies such as 3D ICs and carbon nanotube computers, to modern challenges of place & route for FPGAs and structured ASICs, and applications of EDA algorithms in cyber-physical systems.

Since 2005, ISPD has organized highly competitive contests to promote and advance research in placement, global routing, clock network synthesis, and discrete gate sizing. This year's contest is on detailed routing-driven placement and is organized by Mentor Graphics. Specifically, the contest evaluates the quality of placement using a commercial detailed router in order to motivate research to address significant complexity of routing-design rules in advanced technology nodes. The contest results will be announced by the ISPD Contest Chair, Ismail Bustany, on Wednesday morning. Continuing the tradition of all the past contests, a new large-scale real-world benchmark suite will be released in industry-standard formats including LEF, DEF, and Verilog description in ISPD website: http://www.ispd.cc

We would like to take this chance to express our gratitude to the authors, the presenters, the keynote/invited speakers for contributing to the high-quality program, and the session chairs for moderating the sessions. We would like to thank our program committee and external reviewers, who provided insightful constructive comments and detailed reviews to the authors. We greatly appreciate the exceptional set of invited talks put together by the Steering Committee, which is chaired by Cheng-Kok Koh. We also thank the Steering Committee for selecting the best paper. Special thanks go to the Publications Chair Young Fung Yu and the Publicity Chair Mustafa Ozdal for their tremendous services. We would like to acknowledge the team organizing the contest led by Ismail Bustany. We are also grateful to our sponsors. The symposium is sponsored by the ACM Special Interest Group on Design Automation (SIGDA) with technical co-sponsorship from the IEEE Circuits and Systems Society. Generous financial contributions have also been provided by (in alphabetical order): Altera, ATopTech, Cadence, IBM Research, ICScape, Intel, Mentor Graphics, Oracle, Synopsys, and Xilinx. Last but not least, we thank Lisa Tolles of Sheridan Communications for her expertise and enormous patience during the production of the proceedings.

The organizing committee hopes that you will enjoy ISPD. We look forward to seeing you again in future editions of ISPD.

Cliff Sze
ISPD 2014 General Chair

Azadeh Davoodi
Technical Program Chair

Table of Contents

Welcome and Monday Keynote Address
Session Chair: Cliff Sze *(IBM Research)*

Session 1: Placement
Session Chair: Jackey Yan *(Cadence)*

Session 2: Routing
Session Chair: Igor Markov *(University of Michigan)*

Session 3: 3D Integration
Session Chair: Markus Olbrich *(University of Hannover)*

Tuesday Keynote Address
Session Chair: Patrick Groeneveld *(Synopsys)*

Session 4: Clocking and Power-Grid Planning

Session Chair: Yu-Yen Mo *(Oracle)*

Session 5: DFM

Session Chair: Mustafa Ozdal *(Intel)*

Session 6: Commemoration for Dr. Bryan Preas

Session Chair: Cliff Sze *(IBM Research)*

Session 7: CAD for Cyber Physical Systems

Session Chair: Dwight Hill *(Synopsys)*

Session 8: Contest

Session Chair: Bill Swartz *(TimberWolf Systems)*

ISPD 2014 Symposium Organization

General Chair: Cliff Sze *(IBM Research)*

Technical Program Chair: Azadeh Davoodi *(University of Wisconsin - Madison)*

Past Chair: Cheng-Kok Koh *(Purdue University)*

Steering Committee Chair: Cheng-Kok Koh *(Purdue University)*

Steering Committee: Charles Alpert *(Cadence)*
Yao-Wen Chang *(National Taiwan University)*
Jason Cong *(UCLA)*
Jacob Greidinger *(Mentor Graphics)*
Prashant Saxena *(Synopsys)*

Program Committee: Laleh Behjat *(University of Calgary)*
Ismail Bustany *(Mentor Graphics)*
Azadeh Davoodi *(University of Wisconsin - Madison)*
Stephan Held *(University of Bonn)*
Dwight Hill *(Synopsys)*
Tsung-Yi Ho *(National Cheng Kung University)*
Marcelo Johann *(Universidade Federal do Rio Grande do Sul)*
Charles C.C. Liu *(TSMC)*
Guojie Luo *(Peking University)*
Malgorzata Marek-Sadowska *(UCSB)*
Yu-Yen Mo *(Oracle)*
David Newmark *(AMD)*
Markus Olbrich *(University of Hannover)*
Tom Spyrou *(Altera)*
Bill Swartz *(TimberWolf Systems)*
Atsushi Takahashi *(Toyko Institute of Technology)*
Natarajan Viswanathan *(IBM)*
Jackey Yan *(Cadence)*
Evangeline Young *(The Chinese University of Hong Kong)*
Cheng Zhuo *(Intel)*

Publication Chair: Evangeline Young *(The Chinese University of Hong Kong)*

Publicity Chair / Webmaster: Mustafa Ozdal *(Intel)*

Contest Chair: Ismail Bustany *(Mentor Graphics)*

Additional Reviewers:

Sarvesh Bhardwaj
Jonathan Bishop
David Chinnery
Salim Chowdhury
Duo Ding
Sergei Dolgov
Houle Gan
Ryoichi Inanami
Ivan Kissiov
Chikaaki Kodama
Yukihide Kohira
Alex Korshak
Michael Leonard
Yan Luo
Chi-Yu Mao

Pavlos Mattheakis
Rush Mehta
Sergey Mikhaylov
Tarun Mittal
Ming Ni
Rajendran Panda
Manoj Ragupathy
Joseph Shinnerl
Valeriy Sukharev
Yasuhiro Takashima
Dean Wu
Yue Xu
Guo Yu
Xueqian Zhao

ISPD 2014 Sponsors & Supporters

Sponsor:

Technical Co-sponsor:

Supporters:

Hardware Cyber Security

Serge Leef
Mentor Graphics
8005 SW Boeckman Road
Wilsonville, OR, USA 97070
+1 (503) 685-7000
serge_leef@mentor.com

ABSTRACT

The attacks targeting hardware range from IP piracy to data theft to intentional hardware compromise and sabotage. Of particular concern are systemic, or combined, attacks that include both software and hardware elements: as the secure computing architectures, such as Intel TPM or ARM TrustZone, become more common, their hardware-based trust anchors will become attractive targets for hardware-based attacks whose goal is to create a vulnerability in the supposedly secure software.

Design of the trusted IC requires awareness of the security needs at every step of the physical design flow to combat this wide range of threats. Some of the security needs can be served by the EDA (Electronic Design Automation) tools specifically targeting threat detection and verification of design security and integrity. Other threats can only be resisted using special design elements and properties, such as on-chip encryption and trust verification. Designing these secure elements, as well as protecting them from hardware attacks, will also require specialized EDA tools.

Categories and Subject Descriptors

K.6.5 [**Security and Protection**]: Authentication – *detection, characterization, countermeasures.*

General Terms

Security, Design, Reliability, Standardization, Verification.

Keywords

Counterfeiting, recycling, trusted manufacturing, hardware Trojans, bus hijacking.

Short Bio

Serge Leef serves as the Vice President of New Ventures, responsible for identifying and developing product opportunities for systems markets adjacent to EDA.

Before joining Mentor Graphics in 1990, Serge was responsible for design automation at Silicon Graphics, where his team created revolutionary high-speed simulation tools to enable design of high speed 3D graphics chips that defined state-of-the-art in visualization, imaging, gaming and special effects for a decade.

ISPD'14, March 30–April 2, 2014, Petaluma, California, USA.
ACM 978-1-4503-2592-9/14/03.
http://dx.doi.org/10.1145/2560519.2565868

Prior to 1987, Serge managed a CAE/CAD organization at Microchip Inc. From 1982 to 1987 he worked at Intel Corp. developing functional and physical design and verification tools for major microcontroller and microprocessor programs. Serge holds a BSEE and MSCS from Arizona State University.

1. INTRODUCTION

Focus of cyber security is starting to shift toward hardware. In complex electronic systems, hardware structures can be modified, intentionally or unintentionally in a variety of ways. These modifications can lead to system behaviors that are different from those intended by the designers and expected by the consumers. Unwanted hardware behaviors and structures can represent independent threats to system operation. They can also be exploited by software that is aware of their existence.

These weaknesses fall into two broad categories: design time and manufacturing time vulnerabilities.

2. DESIGN TIME THREATS

Many modern systems are actually systems on chip (SOCs). The basic architecture of these devices is common and well understood. One or more bus structures support multiplexed communications among function blocks in the system. A CPU typically controls the bus which connects to the memory subsystem and hosts a number of peripherals. These peripherals (referred to as IP blocks) perform specific functions ranging from controlling links to the outside world to graphics processing.

Design of modern SOCs is all about selection and integration of appropriate IP blocks into the system. These blocks can have many origins. Some are home-grown and re-used from a previous generation SOC. Others are obtained from commercial vendors or open source repositories. The barrier to entry for designers of IP blocks is quite low, which results in existence of an unregulated ecosystem of suppliers and consumers of these blocks.

When an IP block is acquired from outside the company doing the design, it is typically subjected to verification. The buyer runs the test suites (provided by the IP block supplier) through simulation to confirm that the IP block actually does what it is supposed to do. Sometimes additional, independent tests are developed and executed to further validate the block's purported functionality.

This approach does nothing to ensure that the IP block does not contain functionality outside the specification. In other words, the IP blocks can contain features and functions that are not accessible to the provided test suites and are very difficult to find via code inspection. These features and functions can contain malicious capabilities that may be triggered by software or some other external or internal events.

Several approaches have been contemplated for better examination of the incoming IP blocks. These include improvements of test suites and use of formal methods to check for some levels of logic equivalency. The test suites can potentially be enhanced to look for behaviors outside of spec – for example, trying to reach otherwise unreachable states in the state machines. Formal verification methods where the design is mathematically compared to the specification have also been considered. Neither approach proved promising as manual test suite expansion is very time and effort intensive and does not guarantee even minimal coverage, while formal approaches are limited in comparing design intent to implementation.

Increasingly the focus is shifting to run-time detection. The basic premise is that we have to accept the fact that nothing can be done to block the viruses from entering the designs when they are brought in by contaminated IP hosts and instead look for malicious behaviors when the chip is operating. This approach presents interesting questions, for example: how to represent legal and illegal behaviors, how much silicon real estate would such countermeasures require, what power and performance costs they will carry, and what to do if a malicious behavior is detected at run time.

3. MANUFACTURING TIME THREATS
As majority of modern designs are manufactured externally, several additional dangers emerge. Devices can be over-produced by the contract manufacturer and find their way in volume to the black market causing commercial damage to the IP rights holders. ICs can be removed from recycled PCBs and sold as new, exposing the system integrator to potentially severe reliability issues. Parts can be manufactured to mimic physical appearance of the genuine products while containing different implementation of the expected function along with added malicious circuits that could open these chips up to future hijackings.

Several approaches have been proposed that would lead to improved confidence in security of the chip contents. The most commonly accepted concept is the use of a "Trusted Foundry". In order to achieve this status, a foundry must meet numerous criteria to be certified. A result is that there are very few such facilities and their services are viewed as expensive.

Another approach is called split manufacturing. Here different foundries manufacture different layers of the chip, thus removing tampering opportunities from any single party. This approach, while conceptually simple, is logistically challenging to implement as it measurably impacts commonly accepted post-layout methodologies and flows.

Far more promising approaches fall into a design tool category that goes by names of logic encryption and circuit obfuscation. The designs are automatically modified via insertion of a small number of strategically placed logic gates wired to a register containing the activation key. In the absence of correct bits in the key register, the chip will not function correctly. The activation key is not known to the manufacturer and is only inserted after the chip has been delivered to the IP rights holder. There are numerous technical challenges in this area ranging from identification of good key gate injection sites to key management, to resistance to side channel attacks to post production key insertion, etc. There are also significant issues with respect to post-layout flows that may necessitate re-thinking manufacturing testing strategies.

4. CONCLUSIONS
Hardware security is an exciting area for application of existing and new EDA technics. Current security guidelines that dictate use of "Trusted Fabs" to achieve higher levels of silicon security is dated and unnecessarily expensive because it does not take into account on-chip countermeasures that are now possible as a result of academic and industry research activities.

While no DFS (Design for Security) tools can promise or deliver fully secure silicon, they can be used to dramatically increase confidence in security of the ICs and systems that incorporate them.

Effective use of DFS tools enables system companies working on national security applications to produce secure chips without incurring high costs of "Trusted Fabs."

5. ACKNOWLEDGMENTS
My thanks to ACM SIGCHI for allowing me to modify the template they had developed.

6. REFERENCES
[1] Jarrod A. Roy, Farinaz Koushanfar, Igor L. Markov, "EPIC: Ending Piracy of Integrated Circuits," Design, Automation & Test in Europe Conference & Exhibition, pp. 1069-1074, 2008 *IEEE/ACM Design Automation Test in Europe Conference*, Munich, Germany, 2008

[2] Jeyavijayan Rajendran, Ozgur Sinanoglu, Ramesh Karri and Youngok Pino, "Logic Encryption: A Fault Analysis Perspective", *IEEE/ACM Design Automation Test in Europe Conference,* Dresden, Germany, 2012

[3] John Villasenor, "Compromised By Design? Securing the Defense Electronics Supply Chain," Brookings Institution Paper, November 2013

Cell Density-driven Detailed Placement with Displacement Constraint

Wing-Kai Chow, Jian Kuang, Xu He, Wenzan Cai, Evangeline F. Y. Young
Department of Computer Science and Engineering
The Chinese University of Hong Kong
Shatin, N.T., Hong Kong
{wkchow,jkuang,xhe,wzcai,fyyoung}@cse.cuhk.edu.hk

ABSTRACT

Modern placement process involves global placement, legalization, and detailed placement. Global placement produce a placement solution with minimized target objective, which is usually wire-length, routability, timing, etc. Legalization removes cell overlap and aligns the cells to the placement sites. Detailed placement further improves the solution by relocating cells. Since target objectives like wire-length and timing are optimized in global placement, legalization and detailed placement should not only minimize their own objectives but also preserve the global placement solution. In this paper, we propose a detailed placement algorithm for minimizing wire-length, while preserving the global placement solution by cell displacement constraint and target cell density objective. Our detailed placer involves two steps: *Global Move* that allocates each cell into a bin/region that minimizes wire-length, while not overflowing the target cell density. *Local Move* that finely adjust the cell locations in local regions to further minimize the wire-length objective. With large-scale benchmarks from ICCAD 2013 detailed placement contest [7], the results show that our detailed placer, *RippleDP*, can improve the global placement results by 13.38% − 16.41% on average under displacement constraint and target placement density objective.

Categories and Subject Descriptors

B.7.2 [**Integrated Circuits**]: Design Aids — Placement and routing

Keywords

Detailed placement, legalization, displacement constraint, cell density

1. INTRODUCTION

Modern placement process involves global placement, legalization and detailed placement. Global placement produces a placement solution with minimized target objective,

which is usually wire-length, routability, timing, etc. Legalization removes cell overlap and aligns the cells to the placement sites. Detailed placement further improves the solution by relocating cells.

Traditionally, the major objective of placement is to minimize the total wire-length. However, as VLSI technology advances, wire-length is no longer the only objective. Modern placement is usually an optimization problem with multiple objectives, including wire-length, routability, timing, and power, etc.. One of the hard constraint of the placement problem is non-overlapping and placement site alignment. However, satisfying such constraint during the global placement stage is very complicated. Therefore, legalization is usually applied to the global placement solution to satisfy these constraints. Detailed placement is then applied as an independent step to further optimize the design objectives like wire-length.

In recent decade, many works have focused on the global placement problem. Different approaches have been proposed, including analytical placement [3][5], force-directed placement [13], partitioning-based approach [1] and simulated annealing-based approaches [14]. After global placement, we can assume that the global placer has already distributed the cells over the placement region well, such that the target objective is minimized. Therefore, the following legalization process should target at legalizing the solution with minimum perturbation, i.e., to minimize the cell displacement from the global placement solution.

In contrast to global placement, there are much less work in detailed placement. Although almost all placers have deploy detailed placement step, many of them share common detailed placement technique and even the same independent detailed placer. mPL6 [3], FengShui [1], NTU-Place [5] shares the same techniques of sliding window-based cell swapping; FastPlace [15], SimPL [8], MAPLE [9], Ripple [4] directly use FastPlace-DP [12] as the detailed placer.

Recently, Li et al. [10] proposed a mixed integer programming models to optimize detailed placement. Although it can achieve high quality, the run-time is too long and it is not flexible for other additional objectives. Liu et al.[11] proposed an routability-driven placement optimizer that can improve the placement solution in terms of wire-length and routability.

However, the previous works on detailed placement do not consider the impact of cell movement to the global placement solution. As most of the modern global placers target at multiple objectives, in detailed placement stage, the placer should either target at the same set of objectives or minimize the perturbation to the solution. Since integrating different objectives into the current detailed placer is difficult, we believe that a detailed placer that have minimal impact to the global placement solution can be more flexible and thus more useful to modern placement problem.

In this paper, we proposed a novel way of detailed placement, that can minimize wire-length while maintaining a specified target placement density, under constraint of limited perturbation to global placement solution.

The main contributions of our work includes:

- A legality-maintaining framework that keeps the solution legal throughout the detailed placement.

- A displacement-constrained *Global Move* to allocate each cell into a bin such that the total density-aware scaled wire-length is minimized.

- A displacement-constrained *Local Move* to finely adjust the cell positions to further minimize scaled wire-length.

- An extension to the algorithm in [12] that optimally solves *fixed order single segment placement problem*, to also consider placement density and maximum displacement constraint.

The rest of the paper is organized as follows: Section 2 gives the formulation of the detailed placement problem as well as the objective. Section 3 provides a detailed description of our approach to solve the problem. Section 4 shows the experimental results and Section 5 concludes the paper.

2. PROBLEM FORMULATION

Beginning with a legalized placement with all macros fixed, our detailed placement algorithm move the standard cell legally to minimize the total wire-length in terms of half perimeter wire-length (HPWL) defined as in (1), with consideration of user-specific placement density and maximum displacement constraint.

$$\text{HPWL} = \sum_{n \in N} (\max_{i \in n} x_i - \min_{i \in n} x_i + \max_{i \in n} y_i - \min_{i \in n} y_i) \quad (1)$$

2.1 Maximum Displacement

In most detailed placement algorithm, cell displacement is not constrained. However, unless the target objective in detailed placement is the same as that in global placement, detailed placement could ruin the optimized objective of global placement, such as timing and global routability. Therefore, detailed placement should perform local optimization instead of re-placing the cells globally. In our proposed algorithm, we consider displacement as a constraint, so that the resulting solution has similar cell distribution as in global placement, while the detailed placement objective is also optimized. Our placer formulate maximum displacement constraint D_{disp} as:

$$D_{disp} \geq \max_{c \in C} (|x_c - x_{c0}| + |y_c - y_{c0}|) \quad (2)$$

where C is the set of all movable cell, (x_c, y_c) is the current position of cell c, (x_{c0}, y_{c0}) is the original position of cell c in the given global placement solution.

2.2 Average Bin Utilization (ABU)

In [9], the author proposed the concept of *Average Bin Utilization (ABU)* as a metric to evaluate placement density. ABU_γ is defined as the average area utilization ratio of the top $\gamma\%$ bins of highest area utilization ratio. Following the metric of the ICCAD 2013 placement contest, overflow is defined as (3). Our placer formulates the overall placement density overflow as a weighted sum of $overflow_2$, $overflow_5$, $overflow_{10}$, $overflow_{20}$, and it is considered as a scale factor in evaluation of the wire-length. The objective of our placer is to minimize the scaled half perimeter wire-length (sHPWL) as defined in (5).

$$overflow_\gamma = \max(0, \frac{ABU_\gamma}{density_{target}} - 1) \quad (3)$$

$$scale = \frac{\sum_{\gamma \in \Gamma} w_\gamma overflow_\gamma}{\sum_{\gamma \in \Gamma} w_\gamma}, \Gamma = \{2, 5, 10, 20\} \quad (4)$$

$$\text{sHPWL} = (1 + scale) \cdot \text{HPWL} \quad (5)$$

In our implementation, we use $w_2 = 10, w_5 = 4, w_{10} = 2, w_{20} = 1$. Unlike other placers that formulate cell density as sum of area utilization overflow, we give higher weight to the bins with higher area utilization ratio. Therefore, for two solutions with the same value of total utilization overflow, the one with higher peak value results in higher scaling factor in our metric.

In summary, our placer formulate the detailed placement problem as follow:

$$\begin{aligned} min \quad & \text{sHPWL} \\ s.t. \quad & D_{disp} \geq \max_{c \in C}(|x_c - x_{c0}| + |y_c - y_{c0}|) \end{aligned} \quad (6)$$

3. OUR PROPOSED ALGORITHM

3.1 Overview

Algorithm 1 shows the flow of our placer. We first divide the whole placement region into regular rectangular bins. The resulting bins are the basic unit in evaluating placement density. In the first stage, *Global Move*, we try to move each cell to another bin to reduce the scaled half perimeter wire-length (sHPWL), while the bin should be within the range of maximum displacement constraint. We don't care the precise position in a bin at this stage and will randomly place the cells in the selected bins. The scaled wire-length will monotonically reduce throughout the process. We iteratively repeat Global Move until the improvement of an iteration is below a threshold.

In the second stage, *LocalMove*, we locally move the cells to the nearby placement sites. This stage composes of three sub-steps: *Vertical Move*, *Reordering*, and *Compaction*. Vertical Move targets at reducing the sHPWL, and it moves cells vertically within several rows above or below. Reordering also targets at reducing the sHPWL, and it changes the cell order within a few neighbouring cells horizontally. Compaction targets at reducing the HPWL without increasing the placement density overflow, and it adjusts cell positions horizontally without changing the cell orders. We iteratively repeat the three steps until the improvement of an iteration is below a certain threshold.

Before we go into details of our algorithm, we need to introduce a key operation in our algorithm called *Legalized Cell Move*.

Algorithm 1 Detailed Placement Algorithm

Detailed Placement
1: **Input**: Legal global placement solution
2: **Output**: Legal detailed placement solution
3: Let C be the set of all movable cells
4: Partition placement region into rectangular bins
5: **repeat**
6:     GlobalMove(C)
7: **until** $improvement < threshold_g$
8: **repeat**
9:     VerticalMove(C)
10:    Reorder(C)
11:    Compact(C)
12: **until** $improvement < threshold_l$

3.1.1 Legalized Cell Move

In many detailed placers, cell move is simply moving a cell to a position aligned to placement site, but the site may already be occupied by another cells and cell move can cause overlapping. They usually deploy an explicit legalization step to the resulting solution to remove overlaps by spreading the cells out. However, we found that such approach is harmful because of the following reasons: 1) Legalization usually increases wire-length; 2) Spreading can harm placement density; 3) It can bring a cell further away from its original location in the global placement solution, and violate the maximum displacement constraint. To resolve these issues, we proposed a novel technique of Legalized Cell Move. The idea is to keep our intermediate solution legal after every cell movement. To facilitate such requirement, we have an efficient "legalizability" check to ensure that a specific cell move can be leagalized with an affordable impact to the result, and also gives a corresponding legalization to commit the cell move. Therefore, cell move in our algorithm may involve movement of multiple cells instead of moving just one single cell.

The concept of "legalizability" check is usually implicitly considered in other placers by calculating the whitespace remaining in the placement row and the amount of local whitespace near the target location. In contrast, our algorithm will capture the legalization impact more accurately and yet efficiently. The legalization impact is evaluated in our algorithm as the sum of cell displacement caused. When the sum of cell displacement caused by a cell move exceeds the limit, we consider the cell move is not "legalizable", and the cell move is discarded. Legalized Cell Move is used in Global Move and the Vertical Move step in Local Move, while the other steps do not need legalization as their results are always legal. The algorithm of Legalized Cell Move is shown in algorithm 2. To check if a cell move is legalizable only (without really moving the cells), we have another function named *IsLegalizable*, which is similar to *LegalizedCellMove* but without any actual cell move.

3.2 Global Move

Before the Global Move step, the whole placement region is partitioned into regular rectangular bins. In Global Move, we aim at moving each cell into the best bin that can minimize the sHPWL under the constraint of maximum cell displacement.

Algorithm 2 Legalized Cell Move

LegalizedMove
1: **Input**: Cell c_i, location (x, y) and width w_i of c_i
2: **Output**: True if the legalization is successful, False otherwise
3: Find the first cell c_l at the left of (x, y)
4: Find the first cell c_r at the right of (x, y)
5: Let c_l^L and c_l^R be the left and right boundary of cell c_l
6: Let c_r^L and c_r^R be the left and right boundary of cell c_r
7: Move cell c_i to (x, y)
8: $dist \leftarrow 0$
9: $L \leftarrow x - w_i/2$
10: **while** $c_l \neq \varnothing$ and $c_l^R > L$ **do**
11:    Move c_l leftward with distance $c_l^R - L$
12:    $dist \leftarrow dist + c_l^R - L$
13:    $L \leftarrow L - w_l$
14:    $c_l \leftarrow$ the first cell at the left of c_l
15: **end while**
16: $R \leftarrow x + w_i/2$
17: **while** $c_r \neq \varnothing$ and $c_r^L < R$ **do**
18:    Move c_r rightward with distance $R - c_r^L$
19:    $dist \leftarrow dist + R - c_r^L$
20:    $R \leftarrow R + w_r$
21:    $c_r \leftarrow$ the first cell at the right of c_r
22: **end while**
23: **if** $dist >$ impact limit OR any cell violate the maximum displacement constraint OR any cell is at illegal position **then**
24:    Restore all cell positions
25:    **return** False
26: **end if**
27: **return** True

We can estimate the resulting scaled wire-length for each cell movement by assuming that all other cells are fixed. The objective at this stage is to place every cell into the bin with the lowest cost. Instead of testing every bin to make the decision of movement, we select a set of candidate bins. The bin selection is based on two regions: "optimal region" and "max-displacement region". *Optimal region* is proposed by [12]. *Optimal region* of a cell c is defined as the region bounded by the median of the x- and y-coordinates of c's associated net's bounding boxes. *max-displacement region* is defined as the movable range of each cell under the maximum displacement constraint. The bins overlapped with both regions are selected as candidate bins. It is possible that the two regions do not overlap, especially when the maximum displacement constraint is tight. In such a case, we will consider the eight neighbouring bins of the bin containing the cell as candidate bins.

In this stage, the precise cell location is not important. For each candidate bins selected, we pick n random placement sites in the bin that can accommodate the cell without violating the displacement constraint ($n = 4$ in our implementation). We calculate the cost when the cell is moved into the bin, assuming that all other cells are fixed. The cost s_c^b of moving cell c into a candidate bin b is calculated with the following formula:

$$s_c^b = \text{sHPWL}_c^b + w \cdot \text{density}_b \qquad (7)$$

where sHPWL_c^b is the resulting scaled wire-length when cell c is moved to the random location in bin b. w is the weight of bin density, $density_b$ is the area utility of bin b after the cell movement.

The cost is a weighted sum of two parts. The first part is the sHPWL which reflect the resulting solution quality. The second part is the bin-density. The weight w in the second part is very small, such that the first term has much higher priority. However, the effect of the second term is still significant. It is because when there are several candidate bins that can produce similar sHPWL, the second term helps to evenly distribute the cell among the bins. It reduces the number of bins with critical cell density, which can cause overflow easily with a slight increase in bin utilization.

For each iteration, the above procedure is applied to each movable cell and it is repeated until the improvement in scaled wire-length is less than a threshold. In our implementation, the threshold is 0.2%. The overview of an iteration of Global Move is shown in algorithm 3.

Algorithm 3 Global Move

Global Move
1: Let C be the set of all movable cells
2: Let B be the set of all bins
3: **for all** $c \in C$ **do**
4:     Find optimal region R_o of cell c
5:     Find the max-displacement region R_d of cell c
6:     $B' \leftarrow \varnothing$
7:     **for all** $b \in B$ **do**
8:         **if** b overlap R_o AND b overlap R_d **then**
9:             Add b into B'
10:         **end if**
11:     **end for**
12:     **if** $|B'| < threshold$ **then**
13:         Add neighbouring bins into B'
14:     **end if**
15:     $s_{best} \leftarrow$ cost when cell c is at original position
16:     **for all** $b \in B'$ **do**
17:         **for** $j \leftarrow 1$ to 4 **do**
18:             Randomly pick a placement site (x_j, y_j) in b_i
19:             Calculate cost s of moving cell c to (x_j, y_j)
20:             **if** $s < s_{best}$ AND IsLegalizable$(c, (x_j, y_j))$ **then**
21:                 $s_{best} \leftarrow s$
22:                 $(x_{best}, y_{best}) \leftarrow (x_j, y_j)$
23:             **end if**
24:         **end for**
25:     **end for**
26:     **if** $s_{best} <$ original cost **then**
27:         LegalizedMove$(s_{best}, (x_{best}, y_{best})$
28:     **end if**
29: **end for**

3.3 Local Move

After Global Move, all movable cells are allocated to appropriate bins that can minimize total scaled wire-length. However, since the position of cells are randomly chosen, there still have room to finely adjust the position in order to further minimize the wire-length. Our Local Move stage consists of three sub-steps: Vertical Move, Local Reordering and Compaction.

3.3.1 Vertical Move

The objective of Vertical Move is to reduce the sHPWL. For each cell, we try to evaluate the resulting sHPWL when the cell is vertically shifted and aligned to the several nearby rows. Then we choose to move the cell into the row with the maximum improvement in sHPWL, while the maximum displacement constraint is satisfied. The cells are also moved with Legalized Cell Move proposed in section 3.1.1.

In contrast to a similar operation *Vertical Swap* in [12], we fix the x-coordinate of the cell being moved, instead of searching for different positions in another row. This ensure that the improvement in sHPWL is produced by the decision of allocating the cell in that row, instead of by cell shifting in horizontally. Figure 1 illustrates such a a situation. In figure 1(a), shifting the cell in the x-direction produces an incorrect information that row $i - 1$ is closer to the optimal location. In figure 1(b), fixing the x-coordinate when evaluating the direction of vertical movement can correctly identify the better row. Also, if we try a few more rows, we will not be blocked by wide cells or congested rows.

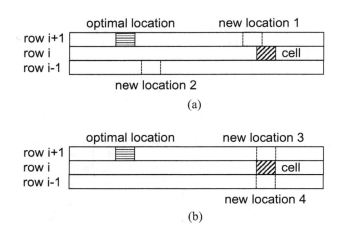

Figure 1: Example of incorrect row selection due to cell shifting.

Since Vertical Move only move vertically to the nearby rows, the sHPWL improvement is usually quite small. Therefore, when we apply Legalized Cell Move in this step, the impact of legalization may even be larger than the improvement. We could reduce the cell displacement limit, i.e., the *impact limit* in algorithm 2, to reduce this effect. To handle this issue robustly, we dynamically set the total cell displacement limit in Legalized Cell Move for Vertical Move, such that larger improvement in sHPWL of a cell move can afford larger legalization impact, i.e., impact limit. In our implementation, the legalization impact limit is set to be $1.2 \cdot \Delta sHPWL$ where $\Delta sHPWL$ is the improvement in scaled wire-length.

3.3.2 Local Reordering

After Vertical Move, the cells are located in a better row than before. The next two sub-steps horizontally shift the cells to further minimize wire-length. Many detailed placement algorithms use an approach of examining all permutation in a window to minimize wire-length. The idea of local reordering proposed in [12] is similar but it is restricted to all permutation of ordering three consecutive cells within the same placement segment. We use the similar approach: For every set of three consecutive cells, we try all six possible permutations of the cell order to find out the best order with minimum sHPWL.

3.3.3 Compaction

In Compaction, we try to move cell to optimal position while maintaining the cell order in a row. The problem is defined in [12] as *fixed order single segment placement problem* and it is optimally solved. However, as we have to consider placement density and the maximum displacement constraint for each cell, the original algorithm does not apply. In this paper, we extend the algorithm to consider maximum displacement and bin density.

The algorithm proposed in [12], [2] and [6] base on the fact that the HPWL wire-length function of the x-coordinate of a cell is a convex function. However, the sHWPL function of the x-coordinate of a cell is not convex due to the formulation of the overflow factor. Therefore, the objective in Compaction is different from that of the previous sub-steps. It now minimizes wire-length in HPWL instead of sHPWL, while the bin density overflow is maintained independently.

For each cell c in a segment s, we find two sets of values: *optimal region range* and *displacement range*. *Optimal region range* is found with the method proposed in [12], which represents the bounds on the x-coordinate that will result in the minimum wire-length. *Displacement range* is the bounds on the x-coordinate of a cell that is within the maximum displacement constraint within the segment. For all bins overlapping with the segment, we identify the set of critical bins that will have cell density overflow when the whole target segment is fully occupied by cells. The bins with such property are referred as *critical bins*, which means that moving cells into these bins may worsen the placement density. Therefore, moving cells into these bins should be restricted. Although this will constrain the wire-length improvement, it is necessary to guarantee that the primary objective of sHPWL does not get worsen.

Since we should not move cells into the critical bins, the actual movable range of a cell is not simply the displacement range. The next step is to find out the *actual movement range* of a cell c. It is found by removing the parts of the displacement range that overlap with the critical bins. However, moving a cell within a fragmented movable range is running time expensive, we will only keep the part that overlaps with the cell's x-coordinate, while other disjointed parts will be discarded. With the fact that the density overflow is usually very low in the Local Move stage, and we have tried to minimize the number of critical bins in the GlobalMove stage by equation 7, the quality loss due to this is not large. The procedure is visualized in figure 2. In the figure, the cell can move within the x-coordinate range of $range_{disp}$ without violating the maximum displacement constraint. bin_2 and bin_4 are identified as critical bins and the two bins span in range of $range_{cbin2}$ and $range_{cbin4}$. The subtraction of these from the displacement range results in two discontinuous parts (red and blue) and only the part overlapping with the cell's x-coordinate remain (red). This results in the actual movement range of the cell shown in the figure as $range_{actual}$.

The pseudo-code of the Compaction step is shown in algorithm 4. In Compaction, we shift every cell horizontally to its optimal location, i.e., a position in its optimal region range within the actual movement range. Placing a cell at any location within optimal region range produces the same

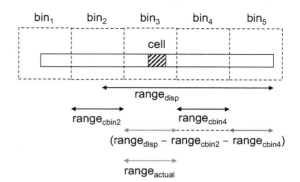

Figure 2: Example of actual movement range computation

optimal wire-length. In our implementation, we try to place the cell at the center of the optimal region. When the optimal region range and actual movement range do not overlap, we will shift the cell to the left or right end of its actual movement range that is closer to its optimal region. The resulting cell positions may overlap. If overlapping occurs, we will merge the overlapping cells to form a new supercell by abutting the cells in the original order. Then we will update the optimal region range of this super cell by considering all the pins on the cells within it. The actual movement range of this supercell is also updated based on the actual movement range of each individual cell inside. The above process is repeated until no new supercell or no cell overlap occurs.

When the segment has no critical overlapping bin, we can achieve the optimal solution with the given order of cells and the given maximum displacement constraint. The proof is shown as follow:

Theorem *Given a fixed order of cells, and given the maximum displacement constraint, the Compaction algorithm gives the optimal solution of minimum HPWL.*

PROOF. Our algorithm is similar to the approach in [6] and [12]. The only difference is the existence of movement range coming from the maximum displacement constraint that limits the movement of a cell. Consider the actual movement range R_x of a cell (or cluster formed by merging 2 or more cells) x. If R_x has overlap with the optimal region range Q_x of x, we can simply put x within the overlapping region $R_x \cap Q_x$ and the HPWL w.r.t. cell x is optimal. Otherwise, since the wire-length function of x w.r.t. its x-coordinates (assumming center) is a convex function and we should put x within its movement range R_x closest to its optimal position Q_x to minimize HPWL. In this way, the HPWL w.r.t. cell x is also optimal. The correctness and optimality of the overall flow follow from [6] and [12]. $\square$

4. EXPERIMENTAL RESULTS

To validate our proposed algorithm, the algorithm is implemented in C++. The experiments were performed on a 64-bit Linux Server with Intel Xeon 3.4GHz CPU and 32GB memory, using the detailed placement benchmarks provided by ICCAD13 detailed placement contest [7]. Each benchmark includes a placement problem, a legalized global place-

Algorithm 4 Compaction

Compaction
1: **for all** $s \in S$ **do**
2:    Let C be the set of all cells within a segment s
3:    Let $Cluster$ be the set of all cluster
4:    $Cluster \leftarrow C$
5:    **repeat**
6:       Find the set of critical bin range B that overlap with segment s
7:       **for all** $c \in Cluster$ **do**
8:          Find optimal region range for Cluster c
9:          Find displacement range for Cluster c
10:          Find actual movable range for Cluster c by subtracting each critical bin range from the displacement range.
11:       **end for**
12:       **for all** $c \in Cluster$ **do**
13:          Shift each cluster c to a position within its actual movable range closest to its optimal region.
14:       **end for**
15:       **for** $i \leftarrow 1$ to $|Cluster| - 1$ **do**
16:          **if** c_i overlap with c_{i+1} **then**
17:             Merge c_{i+1} into c_i by abutting the two clusters.
18:             Remove c_{i+1} from $Cluster$
19:          **end if**
20:       **end for**
21:    **until** all cluster and cells are not overlapping
22: **end for**

---

ment solution as input, a target placement density and two maximum displacement constraints. One of the displacement constraints is tight, ranging from $150 - 220$, while the other one is more relaxed, ranging from $15,000 - 25,000$. Table 1 shows the information of all benchmarks being used in the experiments. In the table, *#cell* and *#net* denote the total number of movable cells and nets in the circuits; *Target Density* denotes the target density; *Overflow* denotes the weighted sum of overflow in terms of ABU; *HPWL* and *sHPWL* denote the wire-length and scaled wire-length of the given global placement solution; D_1 and D_2 are the two maximum displacement constraints specified by the contest.

4.1   On Placement Density

Table 2 and 3 show the detailed placement results under two different maximum displacement constraints. In the table, D_{max} and D_{avg} denote the maximum and the average displacement of the solutions. By comparing the overflow values in Table 2, 3 with the overflow values of given input global placement solution from Table 1, we can see that our detailed placer can effectively reduce the placement density overflow to nearly zero, while HPWL is also significantly reduced by 6.27% on average even under the tight displacement constraint, and 9.49% under the relaxed displacement constraint. In terms of sHPWL, the reduction is 13.38% under the tight constraint and 16.41% under the relaxed constraint.

4.2   On Maximum Displacement Constraint

We obtained the source code of the detailed placer FastPlace-DP from the author of [12]. FastPlace-DP does not consider maximum displacement and placement density. Therefore, we do the minimal adjustment to FastPlace-DP to make

it consider displacement constraint in *Global Swap*, *Vertical Swap*, and *Local Reordering*. Cell moves in these steps are permitted only when the cell movement can satisfy the displacement constraint or it can reduce the violation to the displacement constraint [1]. However, it is difficult to integrate such constraint in FastPlace-DP's *Clustering* and *Legalization* steps. To consider displacement in these two steps indirectly, we partition long placement segments into shorter ones with length at most double of the maximum displacement constraint. In this way, the maximum possible movement distance within a segment in these two steps will be reduced. However, it will still violate the maximum displacement constraint in their solutions.

We perform two experiments to compare RippleDP with FastPlace-DP. The first experiment is done without considering the placement density and displacement constraint, i.e., the traditional detailed placement formulation. In this test, FastPlace-DP works without any modification, while our placer works with setting of target density to 1.0 and maximum displacement of infinity. The result in table 4 shows that our detailed placer performs slightly better on average than FastPlace-DP with reasonable run-time.

The second experiment is done considering the displacement constraint. We found that no matter whether the maximum displacement is tight or relaxed, the modified FastPlace-DP still will violate the constraint for all benchmarks. In the experiment, the maximum displacement constraint is set as twice the tight maximum displacement constraint, so as to have less violations in the results of FastPlace-DP. Placement density is still not considered in this experiment. The experimental result is shown in Table 5. D_{cons} denotes the maximum displacement constraint for each benchmark. The modified version of FastPlace-DP can now consider maximum displacement constraint to a certain extent, although it still violates the constraint. FastPlace-DP can achieve 7.45% of improvement on average. In our detailed placer, larger improvement of 8.32% in wire-length is observed, while the cell displacement constraint is strictly satisfied.

5.   CONCLUSIONS

In this paper, we proposed a detailed placer targeting at optimizing the multi-objective modern placement problem. Unlike previous detailed placers, we consider placement density and also minimizing the perturbation to the global placement solution by integrating the maximum displacement constraint. Our two-step approach detailed placer composes of two stages: Global Move moves cells to bins to minimize the scaled half perimeter wire-length under the maximum displacement constraint. The Local Move stage locally adjusts the cell positions to further optimize the scaled wire-length. Vertical Move vertically move cells to different rows which produces lower sHPWL. Local Reordering locally find the best cell order to minimize the sHPWL. Compaction shifts cells to achieve the best cell locations under the maximum displacement constraint while maintaining placement density. Our experiments on large-scale benchmarks show that our proposed algorithm can effec-

---

[1]Violation of the displacement constraint is still possible since the movement restriction step we added is hard to be implemented in some steps of FastPlace-DP

Table 1: Details of ICCAD 2013 detailed placement contest benchmarks.

Benchmarks	#Cell	#Net	Design Utility	Target Density	Overflow (before)	HPWL (before)	sHPWL (before)	D_1	D_2
superblue1	765102	822744	0.347	0.51	9.92	339099616	372736183	150	20000
superblue5	677416	786999	0.372	0.50	16.38	395464608	460241360	160	20000
superblue7	1271887	1340418	0.578	0.74	7.23	478403584	513005419	200	20000
superblue10	1045874	1158784	0.313	0.53	6.17	610708992	648403031	220	25000
superblue11	859771	935731	0.403	0.64	8.40	394250528	427363458	220	25000
superblue12	1278084	1293436	0.435	0.63	5.14	340540256	358032046	180	18000
superblue16	680450	697458	0.458	0.55	6.63	305835392	326101664	150	15000
superblue19	506097	511685	0.491	0.68	7.11	167200288	179086438	150	15000

Table 2: Detailed placement results with tight maximum displacement constraint. D_{max} and D_{avg} denote the maximum and average cell displacement from the global placement solution.

	D_{max}	D_{avg}	Overflow (after)	Δ Overflow	HPWL (after)	Δ HPWL	sHPWL (after)	Δ sHPWL	Runtime (sec)
superblue1	150	39	0.02	-99.84%	321339488	-5.24%	321388935	-13.78%	107.71
superblue5	160	47	0.66	-96.00%	377410080	-4.57%	379885066	-17.46%	125.26
superblue7	200	49	0.00	-100.00%	443692544	-7.26%	443692544	-13.51%	283.36
superblue10	220	50	0.00	-99.94%	579638464	-5.09%	579660007	-10.60%	176.43
superblue11	220	49	0.03	-99.61%	371626432	-5.74%	371746638	-13.01%	169.19
superblue12	180	46	0.00	-99.98%	306118368	-10.11%	306121044	-14.50%	324.18
superblue16	150	44	0.00	-100.00%	286653216	-6.27%	286653216	-12.10%	82.07
superblue19	150	37	0.03	-99.63%	157406768	-5.86%	157447729	-12.08%	118.99
Average				-99.38%		-6.27%		-13.38%	

tively optimize placement solution under different maximum displacement constraints and target densities.

6. REFERENCES

[1] A. Agnihotri, S. Ono, C. Li, M. Yildiz, A. Khatkhate, C.-K. Koh, and P. Madden. Mixed block placement via fractional cut recursive bisection. *Computer-Aided Design of Integrated Circuits and Systems, IEEE Transactions on*, 24(5):748–761, 2005.

[2] U. Brenner and J. Vygen. Faster optimal single-row placement with fixed ordering. In *Proceedings of the conference on Design, automation and test in Europe*, DATE '00, pages 117–121, New York, NY, USA, 2000. ACM.

[3] J. Cong and M. Xie. A robust mixed-size legalization and detailed placement algorithm. *Computer-Aided Design of Integrated Circuits and Systems, IEEE Transactions on*, 27(8):1349–1362, 2008.

[4] X. He, T. Huang, W.-K. Chow, J. Kuang, K.-C. Lam, W. Cai, and E. Young. Ripple 2.0: High quality routability-driven placement via global router integration. In *Design Automation Conference (DAC), 2013 50th ACM / EDAC / IEEE*, pages 1–6, 2013.

[5] M.-K. Hsu, Y.-F. Chen, C.-C. Huang, T.-C. Chen, and Y.-W. Chang. Routability-driven placement for hierarchical mixed-size circuit designs. In *Design Automation Conference (DAC), 2013 50th ACM / EDAC / IEEE*, pages 1–6, 2013.

[6] A. Kahng, P. Tucker, and A. Zelikovsky. Optimization of linear placements for wirelength minimization with free sites. In *Design Automation Conference, 1999. Proceedings of the ASP-DAC '99. Asia and South Pacific*, pages 241–244 vol.1, 1999.

[7] M.-C. Kim. IEEE CEDA / taiwan MOE, ICCAD 2013 contest. Retrieved October 10, 2013 from http://cad_contest.cs.nctu.edu.tw/ CAD-contest-at-ICCAD2013/problem_b, 2013.

[8] M.-C. Kim, D. Lee, and I. L. Markov. Simpl: An effective placement algorithm. *IEEE Trans. on CAD of Integrated Circuits and Systems*, 31(1):50–60, 2012.

[9] M.-C. Kim, N. Viswanathan, C. J. Alpert, I. L. Markov, and S. Ramji. Maple: multilevel adaptive placement for mixed-size designs. In *Proceedings of the 2012 ACM international symposium on International Symposium on Physical Design*, ISPD '12, pages 193–200, New York, NY, USA, 2012. ACM.

[10] S. Li and C.-K. Koh. Mixed integer programming models for detailed placement. In *Proceedings of the 2012 ACM international symposium on International Symposium on Physical Design*, ISPD '12, pages 87–94, 2012.

[11] W.-H. Liu, C.-K. Koh, and Y.-L. Li. Optimization of placement solutions for routability. In *Proceedings of the 50th Annual Design Automation Conference*, DAC '13, pages 153:1–153:9, 2013.

[12] M. Pan, N. Viswanathan, and C. Chu. An efficient and effective detailed placement algorithm. In *Computer-Aided Design, 2005. ICCAD-2005. IEEE/ACM International Conference on*, pages 48–55, 2005.

[13] P. Spindler, U. Schlichtmann, and F. Johannes. Kraftwerk2 – a fast force-directed quadratic placement approach using an accurate net model. *Computer-Aided Design of Integrated Circuits and Systems, IEEE Transactions on*, 27(8):1398–1411, 2008.

Table 3: Detailed placement results with relaxed maximum displacement constraint.

	D_{max}	D_{avg}	Overflow (after)	Δ Overflow	HPWL (after)	Δ HPWL	sHPWL (after)	Δ sHPWL	Runtime (sec)
superblue1	19991	107	0.01	-99.94%	300900000	-11.27%	300918158	-19.27%	204.96
superblue5	19607	128	0.13	-99.24%	364778272	-7.76%	365234290	-20.64%	200.9
superblue7	19999	101	0.00	-100.00%	428872320	-10.35%	428872320	-16.40%	422.3
superblue10	25000	104	0.00	-100.00%	566647104	-7.21%	566648189	-12.61%	261.6
superblue11	24997	105	0.02	-99.79%	361081056	-8.41%	361145182	-15.49%	233.2
superblue12	18000	75	0.00	-100.00%	296077440	-13.06%	296077440	-17.30%	452.85
superblue16	15000	102	0.00	-100.00%	278006080	-9.10%	278006080	-14.75%	147.26
superblue19	15000	87	0.03	-99.52%	152526080	-8.78%	152578076	-14.80%	150.76
Average				**-99.81%**		**-9.49%**		**-16.41%**	

Table 4: Comparison with the original FastPlace-DP without any constraint.

	FastPlace-DP					Ours				
	D_{max}	D_{avg}	HPWL	Δ HPWL	Runtime (sec)	D_{max}	D_{avg}	HPWL	Δ HPWL	Runtime (sec)
superblue1	11019	164	300702240	-11.32%	189.24	33563	115	297145152	-12.37%	219.14
superblue5	16889	176	358064096	-9.46%	147.45	28640	140	355578496	-10.09%	175.58
superblue7	25327	169	421648896	-11.86%	334.72	31594	113	422021664	-11.79%	438.21
superblue10	19573	161	564782784	-7.52%	214.72	37981	115	560863744	-8.16%	247.94
superblue11	40207	151	358554720	-9.05%	188.88	41590	112	354556832	-10.07%	200.96
superblue12	24361	211	286595904	-15.84%	407.25	25009	100	288083072	-15.40%	721.18
superblue16	25511	138	274610464	-10.21%	108.29	24744	112	273619520	-10.53%	165.41
superblue19	22631	129	150141792	-10.20%	86.14	24000	100	148739280	-11.04%	189.42
Average				**-10.68%**					**-11.18%**	

Table 5: Comparison with the modified FastPlace-DP with displacement constraint. D_{cons} denotes the maximum displacement constraint specified in the experiments.

		FastPlace-DP					Ours				
	D_{cons}	D_{max}	D_{avg}	HPWL	Δ HPWL	Runtime (sec)	D_{max}	D_{avg}	HPWL	Δ HPWL	Runtime (sec)
superblue1	300	1199	72	318601280	-6.04%	140.90	300	55	314771776	-7.17%	136.43
superblue5	320	902	84	372861888	-5.72%	121.51	320	69	367689920	-7.02%	124.95
superblue7	400	1165	83	436650720	-8.73%	249.43	400	68	434180640	-9.24%	354.51
superblue10	440	1417	89	576288000	-5.64%	185.75	440	69	571392576	-6.44%	203.06
superblue11	440	1072	85	369094208	-6.38%	163.61	440	66	363791616	-7.73%	174.24
superblue12	360	1335	86	298825088	-12.25%	298.56	360	66	297952704	-12.51%	485.73
superblue16	300	934	77	282755712	-7.55%	156.05	300	62	280808032	-8.18%	116.44
superblue19	300	629	67	154998144	-7.30%	84.59	300	54	153431216	-8.24%	147.48
Average					**-7.45%**					**-8.32%**	

[14] T. Taghavi, X. Yang, and B.-K. choi. Dragon2005: large-scale mixed-size placement tool. In *Proceedings of the 2005 international symposium on Physical design*, ISPD '05, pages 245–247, New York, NY, USA, 2005. ACM.

[15] N. Viswanathan, M. Pan, and C. Chu. Fastplace 3.0: A fast multilevel quadratic placement algorithm with placement congestion control. In *Design Automation Conference, 2007. ASP-DAC '07. Asia and South Pacific*, pages 135–140, 2007.

MIP-based Detailed Placer for Mixed-size Circuits

Shuai Li and Cheng-Kok Koh *
School of Electrical and Computer Engineering, Purdue University
West Lafayette, IN, 47907-2035
{li263, chengkok}@purdue.edu

ABSTRACT

By modifying an existing Mixed Integer Programming (MIP) model for optimizing the placement of cells in sliding windows, we develop a detailed placer for large-scale mixed-size circuits. To make it possible to optimize the placement of larger sliding windows in reasonable time, we reduce the number of integer variables in the modified MIP model such that when compared with the original complete MIP model, the solution time is shortened greatly while the solution quality does not degrade much. Experimental results on DAC12 benchmark circuits show that our detailed placer manages to further reduce half-perimeter wirelength (HPWL) of the placement results generated by many other existing detailed placement techniques. Moreover, by making use of a commercial router, we also evaluate the routability of the placement results before and after the application of our detailed placer. Both the routed wirelength and the number of vias in routing solutions are reduced, while the number of design rule violations does not change much for most circuits, implying the routablity of placement results are not perturbed.

Categories and Subject Descriptors

B.7.2 [**Integrated Circuits**]: Design Aids—*Placement and Routing*

Keywords

Detailed Placement, MIP, Mixed-size Circuits

1. INTRODUCTION

In the placement of modern circuits, the locations of movable cells are determined with the objective of minimizing the wirelength of the circuit, usually estimated by the half-perimeter wirelength (HPWL). Besides, critical issues such as routability should also be considered in placement. The

---

*Supported in part by NSF CCF-1065318.

ISPD11, DAC12 and ICCAD12 routability-driven placement contests [1][2][3] were held in recent years to promote the development of routability-driven placers.

The problem of global placement, the first step of placement, is considered to be a continuous optimization problem, whose solution provides approximate locations of cells. Then the global placement solution is legalized so that cells are exactly placed into predefined sites without overlapping. Many research efforts have been spent on global placement. The development of analytical global placers has led to a great reduction in the HPWL of placement results. Furthermore, many effective routability-driven placers, like NTU-place4 [4], Ripple [5], [6], etc., were proposed. To avoid routing congestions, in global placement, they apply techniques like white space allocation [7], cell bloating [6], net-based movement [5], etc., and/or make use of new analytical global placement formulations that take wire density and/or pin density into consideration [4][8][9].

After global placement and legalization, the exact locations of cells are further optimized in detailed placement. Although it draws less attention, it has been demonstrated in [10][11] that detailed placement is also critical in generating placement results with good quality.

In [12][13], it is shown that the detailed placement of cells placed in a fixed order can be optimized in polynomial time. Cell swapping techniques are also usually applied in detailed placement, among which is the FastPlace-DP proposed in [14]. By implementing cell swapping globally with the guidance of cells' optimal regions, FastPlace-DP manages to reduce HPWL effectively. However, as illustrated in [5], the HPWL-driven detailed placer is likely to move sparsely-spread cells together and results in global routing overflows. Therefore, both Ripple [5] and SimPLR [6] made use of congestion-aware FastPlace-DP to avoid swapping cells to possible routing congested areas.

Another commonly used approach for detailed placement is the sliding window technique, an application of "divide and conquer". The whole circuit is partitioned into overlapping windows, and the placement of each window is optimized separately. In the simplest way, the optimal solution for a window can be found after the enumeration of all possible solutions. However, because the solution space of detailed placement is the factorial of the number of cells, and is also dependent on the window size, the enumeration approach is usually applied only on windows with no more than 6 cells [7][15][9]. To cope with larger sliding windows, a cell matching technique is applied in NTUplace [4][16]. Given a group of independent cells (cells that are not connected with each other), matching these cells to empty slots in a sliding window is formulated as a bipartite matching problem and can be solved quickly.

Mixed Integer Programming (MIP) is also applied to optimize the placement of larger sliding windows [11][17][18]. The single-cell-placement (SCP) model in [18] is the most efficient among all the existing MIP models. Also, experimental results show that a parallelized detailed placer based on the SCP model can reduce HPWL and routed wirelength of IBM version 2 benchmark circuits [19] effectively.

Compared with IBM Version 2 benchmark circuits, which contain only standard cells, most of the recent mixed-size benchmark circuits, including the DAC12 benchmark circuits [2], contain over 10 times more cells, plus a number of fixed macro blocks. Moreover, in the mixed-size circuits, the average cell width is larger, while the rate sites are occupied by cells is lower. As a result, sliding windows containing the same number of cells usually is composed with more sites in the mixed-size circuits. The number of integer variables in the SCP model, proportional to the number of sites, becomes larger, too, leading to a great increase in average solution time of the model.

However, in this paper, it is shown that even if a portion of the integer variables in the SCP model are ignored, we may still obtain a good feasible solution by solving the incomplete model. Although the solution quality may be degraded, the solution time is greatly decreased.

Based on the incomplete SCP model, we developed a parallelized detailed placer for mixed-size circuits. For DAC12 benchmark circuits, we applied the detailed placer on placement results generated by many effective placers introduced earlier in this section. Results show that HPWL are reduced effectively after the placement of larger sliding windows are further optimized.

Additionally, as in [15][20], we also obtained detailed routing solutions for all placement results before and after the application of our detailed placer, by means of a commercial detailed router. A comparison shows that for all the circuits, both wirelength and via count in routing solutions are reduced after the application of our detailed placer. Meanwhile, for most circuits, the number of design rule violations in routing solutions nearly stays the same, implying that our detailed placer does not perturb the routability much.

2. BACKGROUND

2.1 Mixed Integer Programming

In this paper, we refer to a Mixed Integer Programming (MIP) problem as a discrete optimization problem in which some variables are restricted to be integer while both the objective function and constraints are linear.

The basic approach to solving an MIP problem is to build a branch-and-bound tree. In general, the size of the tree is dependent on the number of integer variables in the problem. First, at the root of the tree, the MIP problem is relaxed and "solved" as a linear programming (LP) problem. The objective value of the LP solution provides a lower bound for the objective of the MIP, but probably the solution does not satisfy the requirement that some variables must be integer. If so, by restricting a particular integer variable into two different ranges, we branch the root into two child nodes, each of which corresponds to a subproblem of the original MIP. Next, the relaxed LP at both child nodes are solved

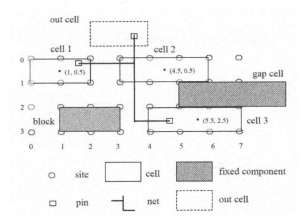

Figure 1: An illustration of a 3-row, 7-column window containing 3 cells.

and branching continues on both of them. Naturally, the branching on a leaf node terminates when the relaxed LP is infeasible, or the relaxed LP solution is an integer solution Also, if the objective value of the LP solution, the lower bound of the subproblem rooted at the node, is worse than that of the best integer solution found so far, the branching can terminate, too, because the pruning will not result in missing better integer solutions. When the branching across the whole tree terminates, the optimal solution to the MIP is determined.

The efficiency of solving MIP problems has been greatly improved in the past decades because of the maturity of the branch-and-cut technique. With branch-and-cut, after the relaxed LP at each node is solved, new constraints or *cuts* valid for the MIP but violated by the relaxed LP solution are added. Then, the relaxed LP is solved again. Because of the newly added cuts, the new solution usually provides a tighter bound, and pruning may take place as a result.

Branch-and-price is another popular technique for solving MIP problems [21]. It usually copes with the MIP problem derived from the original MIP problem by Dantzig-Wolfe decomposition [22]. The derived problem may have huge amount of variables, which makes the application of branch-and-price technique necessary. Even so, the derivation may still be worthwhile because the derived model is *tighter* than the original model, i.e., the objective value of its relaxed LP solution is closer to that of the MIP solution, which results in more pruning in the branch-and-bound tree.

2.2 MIP Models for Detailed Placement

In detailed placement of a sliding window, the window can be considered to be uniformly partitioned into a grid with rows of *sites*. A sliding window with 3 rows of sites is illustrated in Figure 1. *Cell*s of different width are restricted to occupy integer number of sites, and cannot overlap with each other. Only single-row cells are considered in this paper. All cells partially located in the window, called *gap cell*s, as well as blocks located partially or totally in the window, are always fixed. Two fixed components are illustrated in Figure 1.

A group of *net*s are related to the window, each of which connects a number of *pin*s located on cells inside the window. These nets may also connect to pins on other cells or

Table 1: Statistics of IBM Version 2 benchmark circuits [19], and the average number of sites (n.s.), average number of integer variables in the SCP model (n.v.) for 10-cell windows.

	n.c.	c.w.	o.r.	n.s.	n.v.
ibm01	12k	9.44	0.85	132.5	1025.1
ibm02	19k	8.51	0.90	117.0	898.6
ibm07	45k	8.32	0.90	109.8	855.3
ibm08	51k	8.01	0.90	108.2	827.3
ibm09	51k	8.14	0.90	123.0	941.9
ibm10	67k	10.67	0.90	140.4	1053.4
ibm11	68k	8.00	0.90	116.8	896.0
ibm12	69k	11.43	0.85	151.2	1138.6

Table 2: Statistics of DAC12 benchmark circuits [2], and the average number of sites (n.s.), average number of integer variables in the SCP model (n.v.), SCP_OR model (n.v.o.), SCP_ES model (n.v.e.) for 10-cell windows.

	n.c.	c.w.	o.r.	n.s.	n.v.	n.v.o.	n.v.e.
s3	833k	10.80	0.42	316.8	2816.4	1027.2	329.3
s6	919k	10.10	0.43	300.0	2709.8	850.8	223.7
s7	1272k	13.15	0.58	255.7	2143.0	1234.9	480.8
s9	789k	10.54	0.47	255.9	2219.6	1027.1	391.4
s11	860k	12.07	0.40	346.7	3075.7	1131.4	253.4
s12	1278k	8.69	0.44	220.6	1959.0	736.7	227.2
s14	568k	13.06	0.50	261.7	2190.1	1250.0	711.2
s16	680k	10.14	0.46	257.2	2254.3	949.7	364.9
s19	506k	10.04	0.49	232.7	2036.8	892.1	335.8

blocks. Accommodating pins of these nets, cells outside the window are called *out cells*. The basic objective of detailed placement is to place all the cells legally to minimize the summation of HPWL of all related nets.

In [18], three different MIP models for detailed placement of sliding windows are discussed. The S model is defined with binary site-occupation variables, p_{crq}, denoting whether a site located at row r and column q is occupied by cell c. The number of binary variables in the model is $O(|C||R||Q|)$, where C, R, and Q are the set of cells, rows, and columns, respectively. Constraints are included in the model to make sure each cell occupies the correct number of consecutive sites in the same row and cells do not overlap.

The RQ model is defined with row-occupation variables, $\bar{p}_{cr}$, and column variables, $\hat{p}_{cq}$, denoting whether cell c is placed in row r and column q, respectively. The number of integral variables is reduced to $O(|C|(|R| + |Q|))$. However, a much larger number of constraints must be added to the model to make sure cells do not overlap.

The SCP model is defined with binary single-cell-placement variables. Derived from the S model by applying the Dantzig-Wolfe decomposition, it is tighter than the original S model. Also, the number of integer variables in the derived model is still $O(|C||R||Q|)$. Thus, we need not resort to branch-and-price for its solution. It could be solved efficiently by the general branch-and-cut solver.

Besides the three models above, another model for detailed placement is proposed in [11]. We can also consider it to be derived from the S model by Dantzig-Wolfe decomposition. However, the number of integer variables in it is so large that it can only be solved by specific branch-and-price solver. So far, no efficient branch-and-price solver for

the model has been proposed. Besides, the model in [11] considers only uniform-width cells.

3. INCOMPLETE SCP MODEL

3.1 Characteristics of mixed-size circuits

Because of its efficiency, we choose to make use of the SCP model in our detailed placer for mixed-size circuits. In [18], a parallelized detailed placer based on the SCP model has already been proposed, and experimental results on IBM Version 2 benchmark circuits show that it can effectively reduce HPWL and routed wirelength.

However, compared with the IBM Version 2 benchmark circuits, which contain only standard cells, the size of the recent mixed-size circuits, including the ISPD11, DAC12 and ICCAD12 benchmark circuits[1][2][3], is much larger. As shown in Table 1 and Table 2, the number of cells (n.c.) in 7 out of 10 DAC12 benchmark circuits is over 10 times larger than that of ibm12, the largest among all IBM Version 2 benchmark circuits.

Moreover, sliding windows containing the same number of cells in DAC12 benchmark circuit are usually larger than those in IBM Version 2 benchmark circuits. For all the circuits in discussion, we have randomly extracted over 1000 4-row sliding windows containing exactly 10 cells, and the average number of sites (n.s.) in windows are given in Table 1 and Table 2.

On average, the 10-cell sliding windows in most DAC12 benchmark circuits have over 2 times more sites. There are two reasons for their larger size. First, the average cell width (c.w.), or the average number of sites occupied by each cell, are larger in most DAC12 benchmark circuits.

The second and the more important reason is the lower occupation rate of sites in DAC12 benchmark circuits. Calculated as the summation of cell area over the block-free area, occupation rate (o.r.) for all circuits are listed in the two tables. Given two sliding windows containing the same group of cells, smaller occupation rate implies a larger window with more empty sites unoccupied by any cells. The optimization of such a window is more difficult because of its larger solution space. For a 1-row window containing n cells and m empty sites for detailed placement is:

$$\frac{(n+m)!}{m!} = (n+m)(n-1+m)...(1+m)$$
$$= n!\frac{n+m}{n}\frac{n-1+m}{n-1}...\frac{1+m}{1} \geq n!(1+\frac{m}{n})^n$$

If occupation rate is below 0.5, m will be no less than the number of sites occupied by cells, and m/n will be no less than the average number sites occupied by cells, around 8 to 13, as is shown in Table 2. Thus, the solution space of the window is greatly larger than $n!$, the size of the solution space for a window with occupation rate equal to 1.0. For multiple-row windows with a fixed number of rows, larger window size means more sites in each row. The solution space of each row is thus larger, too, and so is the solution space of the whole window.

Specifically, the number of integer variables in the SCP model, $O(|C||R||Q|)$, is proportional to the number of sites in the window. Thus, as shown in Table 1 and Table 2, the average number of integer variable in the SCP model (n.v.) for 10-cell sliding windows in most DAC12 benchmark circuits is over 2 times larger.

With more integer variables in an MIP problem, typically a larger branch-and-bound tree must be built for its solution, leading to longer solution time. With the application of branch-and-cut, more pruning takes place, and the size of the tree may be greatly reduced. But even so, experimental results in Section 5 show that the variable count still has a great negative influence on the solution time of the MIP problems for detailed placement.

3.2 Incomplete SCP Model

To improve the efficiency of the MIP-based detailed placer so that it could cope with large-scale mixed-size circuits, we propose the incomplete SCP model:

$$\text{Min}\quad \text{HPWL} = \sum_{n\in N}(urx_n - llx_n + ury_n - lly_n) \quad (1)$$

subject to

$$llx_n \leqslant x_c + p_x \leqslant urx_n, \quad \forall(p_x, p_y, c)\in P_n, n\in N, \quad (2)$$

$$lly_n \leqslant y_c + p_y \leqslant ury_n, \quad \forall(p_x, p_y, c)\in P_n, n\in N, \quad (3)$$

$$\sum_{c\in C} p_{crq} \leqslant 1, \quad \forall q\in Q, r\in R, \quad (4)$$

$$x_c = \sum_k x_c^k \lambda_c^k, \quad \forall c\in C, \quad (5)$$

$$y_c = \sum_k y_c^k \lambda_c^k, \quad \forall c\in C, \quad (6)$$

$$p_{crq} = \sum_k p_{crq}^k \lambda_c^k, \quad \forall c\in C, \quad (7)$$

$$\sum_k \lambda_c^k = 1, \quad \forall c\in C, \quad (8)$$

$$\lambda_c^k = 0, \quad \forall k \text{ s.t. } |k - o_c| \bmod skip \neq 0, \quad (9)$$

$$\lambda_c^k \in \{0, 1\}, \quad \forall c\in C.$$

The model is derived by Dantzig-Wolfe decomposition. In the model, C, N, R, Q refer to the set of cells, set of nets, set of rows, set of columns, respectively. The objective is to minimize HPWL, which is calculated based on (llx_n, lly_n) and (urx_n, ury_n), the coordinates of the lower-left corner and the upper-right corner of net n's bounding box. Constraints (2) and (3) show that the bounding-box variables are determined by the coordinates of cell centroid, (x_c, y_c). In the constraints, P_n refers to the set of pins connected by net n, and each pin is denoted as (p_x, p_y, c), where c is the cell the pin belongs to, and (p_x, p_y) are the pin's coordinates w.r.t. the centroid of cell c.

Binary site-occupation variable p_{crq} denotes whether cell c occupies the site at row r and column q, and constraints (4) make sure cells do not overlap at any site.

As discussed in [18], after adding two more groups of constraints to make sure each cell c occupies exactly w_c consecutive sites in one row, we will get the S model for detailed placement. However, since the added constraints are independent for each cell, we can apply Dantzig-Wolfe decomposition and derive a tighter SCP model from the S model.

First, for each cell c, all the solutions satisfying the added constraints, or all the legal *patterns* to place the single cell in the window, are determined, the kth of which corresponds

to a constant vector recording the cell centroid and site-occupation variables:

$$(x_c^k, y_c^k; p_{c,1,1}^k, p_{c,1,2}^k, ...; p_{c,2,1}^k, p_{c,2,2}^k, ...; ......)$$

Then, a binary *single-cell-placement* variable, λ_c^k, is defined for each pattern, denoting whether the kth pattern is chosen or not. Constraints (8) make sure that exactly one pattern is chosen for each cell. Moreover, constraints (5)-(7) show that x_c, y_c and p_{crq} can be considered as middle variables dependent on the single-cell-placement variables.

Note that for simplicity, gap cells and blocks in the window are not considered in the model. Not much change need to be made to take them into consideration.

Additionally, different from the SCP model in [18], the objective of our model is the *within-window* HPWL rather than global HPWL. All the pins connected by nets in N but outside the window are projected to *pseudo pins* on the edge of the window, as shown in Figure 2. The coordinates of pseudo pins can be determined before optimization, and constraints similar to (2) and (3) are added for every pseudo pin. In this way, the net bounding boxes are always within the window.

Furthermore, the model ignores a portion of single-cell-placement variables. Given cell c occupying w_c sites, the number of binary variables for the cell, v_c, is:

$$v_c = |R|(|Q| - w_c + 1) = \alpha_c |R||Q|, \quad \alpha_c = (|Q| - w_c + 1)/|Q|$$

In most cases, w_c is not comparable to $|Q|$, and v_c is close to $|R||Q|$. In a window with more sites, the number of integer variables is proportionally larger.

Therefore, we choose to ignore some integer variables in the model. First, all legal patterns for each cell are numbered from left to right and from top to bottom. Take cell 1 in Figure 1 for example. All the single-cell-placement variables and corresponding vectors are:

$$\lambda_1^1 : \quad (1.0, 0.5; 1, 1, 0, 0, ...; 0, 0, 0, 0, ...; 0, 0, 0, 0, ...)$$

$$\lambda_1^2 : \quad (2.0, 0.5; 0, 1, 1, 0, ...; 0, 0, 0, 0, ...; 0, 0, 0, 0, ...)$$

$$\vdots$$

$$\lambda_1^7 : \quad (1.0, 1.5; 0, 0, 0, 0, ...; 1, 1, 0, 0, ...; 0, 0, 0, 0, ...)$$

$$\lambda_1^8 : \quad (2.0, 1.5; 0, 0, 0, 0, ...; 0, 1, 1, 0, ...; 0, 0, 0, 0, ...)$$

$$\vdots$$

$$\lambda_1^{13} : \quad (1.0, 2.5; 0, 0, 0, 0, ...; 0, 0, 0, 0, ...; 1, 1, 0, 0, ...)$$

$$\lambda_1^{14} : \quad (2.0, 2.5; 0, 0, 0, 0, ...; 0, 0, 0, 0, ...; 0, 1, 1, 0, ...)$$

$$\vdots$$

Then with constraint (9), we keep only one variable among every *skip* consecutive variables in the variable list. In addition, for each cell c, the variable corresponding to its placement pattern in the original solution, numbered o_c, is kept in the model, so that the solution to the incomplete model will not be worse than the original solution. For cell 1 in Figure 1, if *skip* is set to be 3, we will keep only λ_1^1, λ_1^4, λ_1^7, λ_1^{10}, λ_1^{13}, λ_1^{16}.

After a portion of variables are skipped, the exact locations of cells in the solution may not be optimal, but by setting *skip* properly, we make sure to consider all the per-

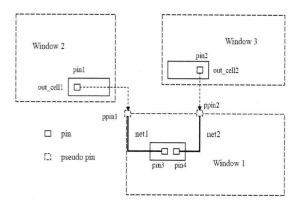

Figure 2: An illustration of pseudo pins and independent windows in the parallelized detailed placer.

mutations of cells in the window when optimizing the incomplete model.

First, we can set *skip* as the rounding of the reciprocal to the occupation rate (*ocp_rt*):

$$skip = \text{round}(|R||Q|/\sum_c w_c) = \text{round}(1/ocp\_rt)$$

The corresponding incomplete model is called the *SCP_OR* model. When *ocp_rt* is close to 1 and *skip* = 1, the model is just the SCP model. And based on $x - 0.5 < \text{round}(x) \leqslant x + 0.5$, we can get the bounds for v_c:

$$\frac{2\alpha_c}{2 + ocp\_rt}\sum_c w_c \leqslant \frac{\alpha_c|R||Q|}{skip} < \frac{2\alpha_c}{2 - ocp\_rt}\sum_c w_c$$

Even in a sparse window with *ocp_rt* close to 0, v_c is around $\alpha_c \sum_c w_c$, which is equivalent to the case of placing the same group of cells in a compact window without empty sites.

Second, we can calculate *skip* from the number of empty sites in the window:

$$skip = \text{floor}((1 - opt\_rt)|R||Q|/|C|) + 1$$

The obtained incomplete model is called the *SCP_ES* model. Similarly, when *opt_rt* is close to 1 and there are few empty sites in the window, the model is the same as the SCP model. And based on $x - 1 < \text{floor}(x) \leqslant x$, we can get the bounds for v_c:

$$\frac{\alpha_c}{1 - (1 - |C|/\sum_c w_c)ocp\_rt}|C| \leqslant \frac{\alpha_c|R||Q|}{skip} < \frac{\alpha_c}{1 - ocp\_rt}|C|$$

When the window is mainly composed of empty sites with *opt_rt* close to 0 and α_c close to 1, the difference in cell size can be neglected. Meanwhile, v_c is just around $|C|$, which is equivalent to the case of permutating $|C|$ uniform-width cells.

The average number of integer variables in the SCP_OR model (n.v.o.) and the SCP_ES model (n.v.e.) for the same 10-cell windows extracted from DAC12 benchmark circuits are listed in Table 2. Naturally, the solution quality to the incomplete models may be degraded because of fewer variables. However, the models can be solved more quickly than the original SCP model, as shown in experimental results in Section 5.

4. IMPLEMENTATION DETAILS

As in many other detailed placers based on the sliding window technique, the chip is firstly partitioned into fine grid. Tiles fully occupied by multiple-row macro blocks are ignored. Then, the remaining tiles are merged with their neighbors into overlapping sliding windows. Since in recent mixed-size circuits, occupation rate of sites is quite small and occupation rate across the chip varies a lot, the generated windows are set to be large enough so that they will not contain too few cells even in a local area with very low occupation rate. On the other hand, when there are too many cells in a window, it is further partitioned into sub-windows containing no more than a given number of cells.

The detailed placement of each sliding window is formulated into an MIP problem solved by CPLEX 12.1, a commercial MIP solver. General branch-and-cut techniques are applied in the solution of MIP problems.

Additionally, as in [17][18], the optimization of sliding windows are parallelized by applying Message Passing Interface (MPI). The parallelization is realized in a Master-Slave structure, with one master allocating *independent* windows to multiple slaves, and slaves optimizing the allocated windows simultaneously. As in [17], two windows are independent and can be optimized simultaneously if they do not overlap and do not accommodate pins of the same nets.

However, in our implementation, we find that as long as two windows do not overlap at any of the two dimensions, they are always independent. One example is given in Figure 2. pin3 in Window 1 and pin1 in Window 2 are connected by net1. But when optimizing Window 1, we are considering the pseudo pin ppin1. No matter how pin1 is moved in Window 2, its projection is always ppin1. Thus, the existence of net1 does not prevent Window 1 and Window 2 from being optimized simultaneously. On the contrary, since moving pin2 in Window 3 may influence the position of its pseudo pin ppin2, Window 1 and Window 3 cannot be optimized simultaneously.

The same conclusion can be drawn without pin projection. If Window 1 and Window 3 are optimized simultaneously, pin1 in Window 1 may be moved rightwards so that the HPWL of net2 is reduced. But pin2 in Window 3 may be moved leftwards for the same reason, too. If so, in reality, the HPWL of net2 may not be reduced at all. In contrast, for net1, no matter how pin1, pin3 are moved in their windows, the summation of HPWL reduction in both windows always equals the global HPWL reduction.

5. EXPERIMENTAL RESULTS

5.1 Effects of Incomplete SCP Models

Experiments are implemented on *superblue16*, a DAC12 benchmark circuit. 2-row and 4-row sliding windows containing different number of cells are randomly extracted from the circuit. Over 300 windows are extracted for each window size. The average number of sites (n.s.) in extracted windows is given in Table 3. The detailed placement of windows are formulated into different models and solved with CPLEX 12.1 on a PC workstation with 3.10GHz CPU. The average number of variables (n.v.), the average HPWL reduction (red.), and the average solution time (t(s)) in seconds for all windows are listed in Table 3.

Since the solution time for some large MIP may be extraordinarily long, a tolerance time, *tt*, is set and the op-

Table 3: Experimental results after the optimization of 2-row and 4-row sliding windows with different number of cells; for each window size, over 300 windows are randomly extracted from superblue16.

	n.c.	n.s.	SCP			SCP_OR			SCP_ES			ENUM	
			n.v.	red.	t(s)	n.v.	red.	t(s)	n.v.	red.	t(s)	red.	t(s)
2-row	8-cell	203.4	1058.6	9.7	9.2	531.0	9.7	0.85	195.4	5.9	0.22	4.2	48.8
	10-cell	240.6	2238.5	13.9	19.6	971.2	12.5	4.4	354.5	8.2	0.72	2.0	70.7
	12-cell	300.6	3406.7	23.8	113.3	1393.0	21.8	24.9	504.8	16.0	2.55	–	–
4-row	8-cell	247.6	1760.8	17.8	13.8	524.1	18.0	1.51	164.9	12.7	0.054	8.2	53.3
	10-cell	291.6	2623.1	24.2	30.6	868.3	22.7	4.35	291.3	13.7	0.213	4.1	76.3
	12-cell	318.4	3470.2	28.5	203.6	1230.6	25.0	32.9	419.9	17.0	2.03	–	–

Table 4: Routing solutions and HPWL of the initial placement results generated by our routability-driven placer for DAC12 benchmark circuits, as well as the further optimized placement results with the application of the MIP-based detailed placer.

	INIT						MIP						
	WL(e7)	VIA(e7)	VIO	T(m)	OF	HPWL(e7)	WL(e7)	VIA(e7)	VIO	T(m)	OF	HPWL(e7)	TP(m)
s2	6.626	0.833	333	105	1350	6.177	6.584	0.824	319	102	1317	6.133	582
s3	3.913	0.791	213	86	1219	3.244	3.876	0.782	218	90	1189	3.207	716
s6	3.864	0.843	83	101	1293	3.372	3.811	0.829	89	95	978	3.321	840
s7	4.709	1.244	56	148	1037	3.942	4.660	1.228	49	146	969	3.896	1274
s9	2.784	0.702	8	81	663	2.303	2.754	0.692	10	76	647	2.272	636
s11	3.856	0.752	202	107	8498	3.477	3.817	0.743	211	101	8193	3.438	580
s12	3.839	1.214	49	155	216	2.911	3.740	1.207	49	146	219	2.820	702
s14	2.648	0.517	10	70	515	2.298	2.617	0.511	9	66	463	2.270	662
s16	2.901	0.550	10	78	644	2.668	2.863	0.541	11	74	649	2.634	371
s19	1.667	0.423	46	56	688	1.467	1.647	0.419	48	56	729	1.448	246
Norm.	1.000	1.000	1.000	1.000	1.000	1.000	0.988	0.988	1.003	0.965	0.952	0.987	–

timization would terminate if no better integer solution is found in the past tt seconds. The tolerance times for 8-cell, 10-cell, and 12-cell windows are 40s, 60s, and 800s, respectively. With the given tolerance times, the MIP problems for over 70% 12-cell windows can be optimized with the SCP model, and for over 90% 8-cell and 10-cell windows, the optimization can be achieved.

First, the average solution time of the SCP model shows us how much influence the variable count has on the solution time of MIP problems. In [18], from ibm01, an IBM Version 2 benchmark circuit, hundreds of 2-row windows were also extracted and optimized with the SCP model. CPLEX was used in optimizing extracted windows, and the average solution time was provided in [18]. For 8-cell, 10-cell and 12-cell windows of 2 rows in ibm01, the average solution times are only 0.82s, 1.93s and 5.86s, respectively. In contrast, the corresponding data in Table 3 are 9.2s, 19.6s, 113.3s. The main reason for such a large increase in solution time is just the larger variable count in sliding windows of DAC12 benchmark circuits, as shown in Section 3.

Second, the SCP_OR model is shown to be a good compromise of the SCP model. On average, the SCP_OR model contains fewer than a half integer variables, and the average solution time is over 6 times shorter. Meanwhile, the average HPWL reduction is within 10% smaller than that of the SCP model.

Third, the SCP_ES model can be solved much more efficiently than the other two models. Because of the great reduction in variable count, it can be solved over 100 times faster than the SCP model, while the average HPWL reduction is still around 60% of that of the SCP model.

Finally, the enumeration approach (ENUM) is also applied on the same extracted windows, and the results are listed in the rightmost columns in Table 3. The same tol-

erance time is used for the enumeration approach. The results of 12-cell windows are not available because it would take extraordinarily long to get solutions for all windows. Since for fewer windows, placement can be optimized with the given tolerance time, the average HPWL reduction is even smaller than that of the SCP_ES model. On the other hand, to achieve optimal solutions for over 70% windows, as it is achieved with the SCP model, the run-time of the enumeration approach would be much longer. Note that the original placement results in experiments are generated by applying the enumeration approach on 4-cell or 5-cell sliding windows. And results show that it is ineffective to further reduce HPWL by enumerating solutions for even larger sliding windows with acceptable tolerance time.

5.2 Experiments on DAC12 benchmark circuits

The MIP-based detailed placer introduced in Section 4 has been applied on DAC12 benchmark circuits. Each circuit is partitioned into 2-row and 4-row overlapping sliding windows with no more than 10 cells. The SCP_ES model is used in the optimization of each window because of its high efficiency. The tolerance time for optimization is 10s. The detailed placement of each circuit is optimized until each sliding window in the circuit has been scanned for no less than 3 times. All experiments are implemented on a computer system with 32 1.87GHz CPUs. Although the solution quality is degraded with the SCP_ES model, the following results show that we may still achieve effective reduction in circuit wirelength.

Three groups of placement results are used as the input to the MIP-based detailed placer, including NTUplace4's, Ripple's placement results in DAC12 routability-driven contests [2], as well as the placement results generated by our routability-driven placer. The detailed placement of the in-

Table 5: Routing solutions and HPWL of NTUplace4's placement results in DAC12 placement contest, as well as the further optimized placement results with the application of the MIP-based detailed placer.

	INIT						MIP						
	WL(e7)	VIA(e7)	VIO	T(m)	OF	HPWL(e7)	WL(e7)	VIA(e7)	VIO	T(m)	OF	HPWL(e7)	TP(m)
s2	6.546	0.839	329	103	4411	6.114	6.519	0.831	311	102	4066	6.087	584
s3	3.857	0.805	204	86	3743	3.273	3.836	0.796	207	84	3551	3.253	445
s6	3.784	0.848	92	93	2841	3.305	3.760	0.835	75	91	2662	3.282	658
s7	4.658	1.250	48	146	2213	3.906	4.632	1.235	46	143	2018	3.881	830
s9	2.817	0.703	11	79	1166	2.370	2.801	0.693	8	87	1111	2.353	374
s11	3.765	0.753	202	108	17551	3.419	3.745	0.744	206	99	17586	3.399	437
s12	4.053	1.217	48	134	228	3.118	4.011	1.205	46	134	245	3.080	517
s14	2.552	0.524	11	70	1887	2.251	2.540	0.518	11	66	1680	2.239	246
s16	2.838	0.554	11	73	1014	2.616	2.823	0.545	9	74	965	2.601	260
s19	1.711	0.425	45	54	1882	1.504	1.698	0.420	44	54	1716	1.492	230
Norm.	1.000	1.000	1.000	1.000	1.000	1.000	0.994	0.988	0.962	0.987	0.964	0.993	−

Table 6: Routing solutions and HPWL of Ripple's placement results in DAC12 placement contest, as well as the further optimized placement results with the application of the MIP-based detailed placer.

	INIT						MIP						
	WL(e7)	VIA(e7)	VIO	T(m)	OF	HPWL(e7)	WL(e7)	VIA(e7)	VIO	T(m)	OF	HPWL(e7)	TP(m)
s2	7.000	0.881	317	102	1571	6.512	6.888	0.860	304	103	1640	6.405	600
s3	4.080	0.843	205	87	1714	3.343	4.033	0.823	200	84	1671	3.301	544
s6	3.901	0.873	93	94	1068	3.346	3.855	0.851	94	92	1167	3.302	682
s7	5.151	1.318	47	151	1390	4.231	5.086	1.287	49	147	1388	4.174	1348
s9	3.086	0.740	10	81	849	2.577	3.038	0.718	8	79	882	2.533	568
s11	3.908	0.784	204	104	15693	3.563	3.840	0.762	210	102	15687	3.499	656
s12	4.340	1.268	51	140	399	3.326	4.254	1.240	53	136	416	3.249	777
s14	2.617	0.540	10	71	845	2.274	2.586	0.527	10	68	857	2.247	577
s16	2.802	0.567	9	77	802	2.589	2.778	0.555	9	74	829	2.567	311
s19	1.796	0.445	55	57	1018	1.590	1.759	0.434	43	56	1124	1.555	235
Norm.	1.000	1.000	1.000	1.000	1.000	1.000	0.985	0.976	0.979	0.976	1.012	0.984	−

put results have already been optimized by different techniques introduced in Section 1. Specifically, in our placer, the enumeration approach is applied on 4-cell or 5-cell sliding windows to reduce wirelength in detailed placement.

All the input placement results are generated by routability-driven placers. To evaluate how much our detailed placer would influence routability, the routing solutions for both the initial placement results (INIT) and the results further optimized by our MIP-based detailed placer (MIP) are generated by a commercial router, denoted as Router X.

The translator proposed in [20] is used so that circuit netlist and placement results in Bookshelf Format are translated into input files to the commercial router. Unlike [20], 22nm design rules instead of 28nm design rules are used in the translation. The pitches of wire tracks at different routing layers are determined by the size of gcell and the capacity of gedge, which are provided in the .route file of each circuit. Also, as in the definition of routing resources in the .route file, metal layer 1 is always reserved and not used for routing.

As mentioned in [20], in the original definition of fixed blocks in DAC12 benchmark circuits, there are some overlapping pins and pins placed too close to make violation of design rules inevitable. Thus, for all placement results, design rule violations cannot be reduced to 0 even after the search and repair step of Router X. But even so, the variation of violation count still can tell us what effect our detailed placer has on routability.

Table 4 lists all the placement and routing metrics of the initial placement results generated by our routability-driven placer, and the placement results further optimized with our MIP-based detailed placer. First, 1.3% reduction in HPWL is achieved by the MIP-based detailed placer. Next, the detailed routing solutions show that both routed wirelength (WL) in micrometers and via count (VIA) are reduced by 1.2%. Comparing the number of design rule violations (VIO) before and after the application of the MIP-based placer, we can see that for most circuits, the variation of VIO is below 10. Also, the detailed routing solution time (T) in minutes is reduced by 3.5%, while the overflow in global routing (OF) is also reduced by 4.8%. The run-times of our detailed placer (TP) in minutes are also given in the table. Similarly, in the experiments introduced in [18], the placement of IBM Version 2 benchmark circuits were also optimized with the MIP-based detailed placer proposed in that paper on a 33-CPU computer system. And on average, HPWL was reduced by 1.66% within 110min to 480min. In our work, although most DAC12 benchmark circuits contains over 10 times more cells, and the average window size is over two times larger, still a 1.3% average HPWL reduction is achieved within 250min to 1300min.

Table 5 and Table 6 list the same placement and routing metrics for NTUplace4's and Ripple's placement results, respectively, as well as those of the further optimized placement results. For NTUplace4's results, the average reduction in HPWL and routed wirelength are both below 1%, but the average reduction in via count is 1.3%. For Ripple's results, the average reduction in HPWL, routed wirelength and via count are 1.6%, 1.5% and 2.4%, respectively. As for the design rule violations, the variation of violation count is within 10 for most placement results.

An obvious advantage of our detailed placer based on the sliding window technique is that it manages to reduce both HPWL and routed wirelength for all the 30 placement results without great perturbation of design rule violations. This is because by moving cells only within local areas, our detailed placer does not introduce great negative influence on the allocation of routing demands across the chip. Meanwhile, by means of MIP, our detailed placer is capable of optimize larger sliding window to further reduce wirelength. As a comparison, if the enumeration approach, instead of MIP, is used in our parallelized detailed placer, and the same amount of time is given to the updated detailed placer, the HPWL of our routability-driven placer's, NTUplace4's, and Ripple's placement results on superblue19 can only be reduced by 0.064%, 0.032%, and 0.12%, respectively.

6. CONCLUSION

Mixed Integer Programming (MIP) is applied in the detailed placement of mixed-size circuits. Recent mixed-size circuits contain much more cells. And because of lower occupation rate of sites, a sliding window containing the same number of cells usually has more sites. As a result, the single-cell-placement (SCP) model contains more integer variables, leading to an increase in solution time. However, our work shows that we can make use of the flexibility of the SCP model and ignore some integer variables in the model. With the incomplete SCP model, we may still get feasible solutions with high quality while the solution time is greatly shortened.

With the incomplete SCP model, we have developed an MIP-based detailed placer for mixed-size circuits. With the detailed placer, effectively we can further reduce the HPWL of the placement results generated by different other detailed placement techniques. Also, the detailed routing solutions generated by a commercial router for all the placement results show that our detailed placer has little negative influence on circuit routability.

7. REFERENCES

[1] Natarajan Viswanathan, Charles J. Alpert, Cliff Sze, Zhuo Li, Gi-Joon Nam, and Jarrod A. Roy. The ISPD-2011 routability-driven placement contest and benchmark suite. In *Proc. ISPD*, pages 141–146, 2011.

[2] Natarajan Viswanathan, Charles Alpert, Cliff Sze, Zhuo Li, and Yaoguang Wei. The DAC 2012 routability-driven placement contest and benchmark suite. In *Proc. DAC*, pages 774–782, 2012.

[3] N. Viswanathan, C. Alpert, C. Sze, Z. Li, and Y. Wei. ICCAD-2012 CAD contest in design hierarchy aware routability-driven placement and benchmark suite. In *Proc. ICCAD*, pages 345–348, 2012.

[4] Meng-Kai Hsu, Sheng Chou, Tzu-Hen Lin, and Yao-Wen Chang. Routability-driven analytical placement for mixed-size circuit designs. In *Proc. ICCAD*, pages 80–84, 2011.

[5] Xu He, Tao Huang, Linfu Xiao, Haitong Tian, Guxin Cui, and Evangeline F. Y. Young. Ripple: an effective

[6] Myung-Chul Kim, Jin Hu, Dong-Jin Lee, and Igor L. Markov. A SimPLR method for routability-driven placement. In *Proc. ICCAD*, pages 67–73, 2011.

[7] C. Li, M. Xie, C.-K. Koh, J. Cong, and P. H. Madden. Routability-driven placement and white space allocation. *IEEE TCAD*, 26(5):858–871, May 2007.

[8] K. Tsota, C.-K. Koh, and V. Balakrishnan. Guiding global placement with wire density. In *Proc. ICCAD*, pages 212–217, 2008.

[9] S. Li and C.-K. Koh. Analytical placement of mixed-size circuits for better detailed-routability. In *Proc. ASPDAC*, pages 41–46, 2014.

[10] S. Ono and P. H. Madden. On structure and suboptimality in placement. In *Proc. ASPDAC*, 2005.

[11] P. Ramachandaran, A. R. Agnihotri, S. Ono, P. Damodaran, K. Srihari, and P. H. Madden. Optimal placement by branch-and-price. In *Proc. ASPDAC*, pages 858–871, 2005.

[12] J. Vygen. Algorithms for detailed placement of standard cells. In *Proc. DATE*, pages 321–324, 1998.

[13] A. B. Kahng, P. Tucker, and A. Zelikovsky. Optimization of linear placements for wirelength minimization with free sites. In *Proc. ASPDAC*, pages 241–244, 1999.

[14] M. Pan, N. Viswanathan, and C. Chu. An efficient and effective detailed placement algorithm. In *Proc. ICCAD*, pages 48–55, 2005.

[15] Wen-Hao Liu, Cheng-Kok Koh, and Yih-Lang Li. Optimization of placement solutions for routability. In *Proc. DAC*, pages 153:1–153:9, 2013.

[16] Tung-Chieh Chen, Zhe-Wei Jiang, Tien-Chang Hsu, Hsin-Chen Chen, and Yao-Wen Chang. NTUplace3: An analytical placer for large-scale mixed-size designs with preplaced blocks and density constraints. *IEEE TCAD*, 27(7):1228–1240, July 2008.

[17] S. Cauley, V. Balakrishnan, Y. C. Hu, and C.-K. Koh. A parallel branch-and-cut approach for detailed placement. *ACM TDAES*, 16(2), March 2011.

[18] S. Li and C.-K. Koh. Mixed integer programming models for detailed placement. In *Proc. ISPD*, pages 87–94, 2012.

[19] X. Yang, B.-K. Choi, and M. Sarrafzadeh. Routability-driven white space allocation for fixed-die standard-cell placement. *IEEE TCAD*, 22(4):410–419, April 2003.

[20] Wen-Hao Liu, Cheng-Kok Koh, and Yih-Lang Li. Case study for placement solutions in ISPD11 and DAC12 routability-driven placement contests. In *Proc. ISPD*, pages 114–119, 2013.

[21] C. Barnhart, E. L. Johnson, G. L. Nemhauser, M. W. P. Savelsbergh, and P. H. Vance. Branch-and-price: Column generation for solving huge integer programs. *Operations Research*, 46(3):316–329, May - Jun. 1998.

[22] F. Vanderbeck. On Dantzig-Wolfe decomposition in integer programming and ways to perform branching in a branch-and-price algorithm. *Operations Research*, 48(1):111–128, Jan. - Feb. 2000.

A Study on Unroutable Placement Recognition*

Wen-Hao Liu[1,2], Tzu-Kai Chien[1], and Ting-Chi Wang[1]
[1]Department of Computer Science, National Tsing Hua University, Hsinchu, Taiwan
[2]Block Implementation, ICD, Cadence Design Systems, Taiwan
whliu@cadence.com, cakeboy1029@gmail.com, tcwang@cs.nthu.edu.tw

Abstract – To avoid producing unroutable placement solutions, many state-of-the-art routability-driven placers iteratively invoke global routers to evaluate their placement solutions and then perform routability optimization. However, using a global router to evaluate hard-to-route placement solutions may spend considerable runtime and it cannot guarantee that a placement is truly unroutable to any router. This paper presents an unroutable placement recognizer based on a window-based layout scanning algorithm, which can confirm some placements that are exactly unroutable among a set of hard-to-route placements. In addition, if a placement is recognized to be unroutable, the recognizer can point out unroutable regions and report a lower bound of total overflow for the placement. The experimental results reveal that the proposed recognizer can find out 16 placements that are definitely unroutable among 23 widely used hard-to-route global routing benchmarks.

1 INTRODUCTION

As technology advances, keeping the shrinkage of the feature size makes the routing problem become more difficult. To address the routing problem, two research directions are promoted from industry. The first one is to improve the capability of routing tools, and the second one is to develop routability-driven placement tools to generate easier-to-route placement solutions.

To motivate the routing research, ISPD07 and ISPD08 host global routing contests and release a set of global routing benchmarks [1]. As a result, many modern global routers [2-10] are developed to explore the high-quality routing results for these benchmarks. Recently, the placement solutions released by ISPD11 placement contest [11] are also adopted to be the routing benchmarks by the papers of [12, 13], and trigger a new global routing research direction. The major objective of global routers is to find an overflow-free routing result for the given benchmark (overflow will be defined in Section 2). However, for some hard-to-route benchmarks, no global router has been able to find out overflow-free results so far. One may ask whether existing global routers are not powerful enough to tackle these hard-to-route benchmarks, or whether identifying an overflow-free routing result for these benchmarks is impossible. This question is a general interest to the researchers in the global routing field. To answer this question, this paper analyzes the routability of the widely used global routing benchmarks. If no overflow-free result exists for a benchmark, this work regards the benchmark to be **unroutable**.

Considering routing information in the placement stage is another direction to address the routability issue. Recently, many routability-driven placers [14-18] invoke global routers to evaluate their placement solutions and then perform routability optimization. However, using a global router to evaluate a hard-to-route placement solution may spend considerable runtime. Moreover, if the global router routes the placement roughly for time saving, the evaluation result may be inaccurate. For example, given two placement solutions p_1 and p_2, the rough routing result of p_1 has a smaller total overflow than p_2, so one may think that p_1 has better routability than p_2. However, if the router takes longer time to route so that all overflows in p_2 are eliminated but some of overflows in p_1 are still unsolvable, then the actual routability of p_1 is clearly worse than p_2. This implies that developing an efficient tool to recognize unsolvable overflows can help the routability evaluation of placement solutions.

This paper presents an unroutable placement recognizer based on a window-based layout scanning algorithm, which can recognize some placements that are exactly unroutable among a set of hard-to-route placements and point out the locations of unroutable regions in the unroutable placements. Also, if a placement is recognized to be unroutable, the recognizer can report a lower bound of total overflow (LBTO) for the given placement. This implies that identifying a routing result with a smaller total overflow than the LBTO is impossible for the placement. In addition, in the global routing field, some placements are commonly used to be benchmarks for testing global routers. Once the LBTOs of these benchmarks are known, the capability of each router under test can be more accurately evaluated. For example, suppose global routers A and B respectively obtain the routing results with the total overflow values of 100 and 104 for a benchmark; one my think that the capabilities of routers A and B on solving overflow are similar. However, if LBTO=100 is known, one may agree that router A is more powerful than B to eliminate overflow because it achieves the LBTO for this benchmark. Thus, investigating the LBTOs for the commonly used routing benchmarks is important.

The rest of this paper is organized as follows. Section 2 introduces the global routing problem and the contributions of this paper. Section 3 presents the proposed unroutable placement recognizer. Section 4 shows experimental results. Finally, conclusions and future directions are drawn in Section 5.

2 PRELIMINARIES

In recent years, evaluating the routability of a placement by global routing is common to see [14-18]. This section first introduces how to model a placement into a global routing instance, and then introduces the contributions of this work.

2.1 Global Routing

In the 2D global routing problem, a placement solution is partitioned into a 2D array of global cells (g-cells), and then is modeled into a grid graph $G(V, E)$, where V denotes a set of g-cells, E denotes a set of grid edges (g-edges), and two abutting g-cells are connected by a g-edge. There is a set N of nets, each of which is composed of a set of pins located in V. The capacity c_e of a g-edge

*This work was supported in part by the National Science Council of Taiwan under Grant No. NSC-102-2220-E-007-012.

e denotes the number of routing tracks that can be legally used. The demand d_e of a g-edge e denotes the number of routing nets currently passing through e. The overflow of e is defined to be $max(d_e-c_e, 0)$.

The global routing problem is to find routing paths to connect all pins of each net in N. Typically, identifying an overflow-free routing result is the primary concern of the global routing problem. Therefore, if a placement is formulated into a global routing instance and no overflow-free routing result exists in the instance, we regard the placement to be **unroutable**. For easy description in the rest of this paper, this paper uses a term **layout** to represent the global routing instance of a placement.

2.2 The Contributions of This Work

The proposed unroutable placement recognizer has the following functionalities that can help researchers to better address the routability issue in the VLSI design flow:

- After the proposed recognizer processes a layout, it would report either "unknown" or "unroutable". If the recognizer reports "unroutable", we can guarantee that no overflow-free routing result exists in the layout and its corresponding placement is unroutable. If the recognizer reports "unknown", we cannot affirm that the layout is routable or not because the recognizer does not capture all the issues like pin access, via spacing, routing demand of overlong nets, etc.
- If a placement is unroutable, the recognizer can identify a set of unroutable regions in the placement. Guiding placers to move cells out of unroutable regions can improve the routability of the placement.
- If a placement is unroutable, the recognizer can identify a LBTO for its layout. Namely, we can guarantee that no router can identify a total overflow lower than the LBTO.

If the proposed recognizer can recognize more placements that are unroutable among a set of hard-to-route placements, we say that the recognizer has a better recognition rate. For different purposes, the proposed recognizer is tunable to trade off its recognition rate and runtime. When the recognizer cooperates with a placer to iteratively improve routability, the recognizer can be tuned to rapidly report unroutable regions but sacrifice a little recognition rate. On the other hand, to discover whether some hard-to-route cases among a set of placements that are widely used to be the global routing benchmarks are unroutable, the recognizer can be tuned to spend a longer runtime to yield a better recognition rate. This finding can help global routing researchers avoid wasting their time on looking for overflow-free routing results for the unroutable benchmarks.

3 UNROUTABLE REGION RECOGNITION

At first, let us define what an unroutable region is. Let $R_{x,y,w,h}$ denote a rectangular region that comprises a set of g-cells in a layout, where x and y respectively denote the x- and y-coordinate of the g-cell located at the bottom-left corner of $R_{x,y,w,h}$, and w and h respectively denote the width and height of $R_{x,y,w,h}$. A bridge edge of $R_{x,y,w,h}$ is a g-edge connecting a g-cell in $R_{x,y,w,h}$ to a g-cell not in $R_{x,y,w,h}$. If a net has at least a pin in $R_{x,y,w,h}$ and has at least a pin not in $R_{x,y,w,h}$, the net must be routed through a bridge edge of $R_{x,y,w,h}$ to connect its pins and we regard this net as an outgoing net of $R_{x,y,w,h}$. Let $c(R_{x,y,w,h})$ denote the total capacity of the bridge edges of $R_{x,y,w,h}$, $S(R_{x,y,w,h})$ denote the set of outgoing nets of $R_{x,y,w,h}$, and $|S(R_{x,y,w,h})|$ denote the number of outgoing nets of $R_{x,y,w,h}$. If $|S(R_{x,y,w,h})|>c(R_{x,y,w,h})$, $R_{x,y,w,h}$ is defined to be an unroutable region

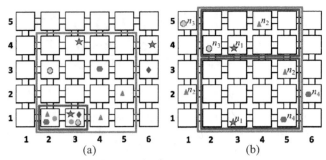

Fig. 1. (a) Example of judging whether a region is unroutable; (b) example of merging $S(R_{2,1,4,3})$ and $S(R_{2,4,4,2})$ to get $S(R_{2,1,4,5})$.

since $c(R_{x,y,w,h})$ is not enough to make every outgoing net of $R_{x,y,w,h}$ legally cross the boundaries of $R_{x,y,w,h}$ to connect their pins. As a result, overflow must happen on the bridge edges of $R_{x,y,w,h}$. For example, Fig. 1(a) shows a layout with 6 nets, where the capacity of each g-edge is one and different symbols denote the pins of different nets. Regions $R_{2,1,2,1}$ and $R_{2,1,4,4}$ are respectively in the blue and red windows. In this example, $c(R_{2,1,2,1})$, $c(R_{2,1,4,4})$, $|S(R_{2,1,2,1})|$, and $|S(R_{2,1,4,4})|$ are 4, 12, 5, and 2, respectively. Since $|S(R_{2,1,2,1})|> c(R_{2,1,2,1})$ and $|S(R_{2,1,4,4})|\leq c(R_{2,1,4,4})$, $R_{2,1,2,1}$ is unroutable but $R_{2,1,4,4}$ is not.

The proposed unroutable placement recognizer uses a sliding window to scan a layout and searches unroutable regions. If any unroutable region is discovered, we can claim that the placement is unroutable. In this work, *we present a layout scanning algorithm to explore every region whose dimensions are not larger than the sliding window*. Namely, let w_s and h_s respectively denote the width and height of the sliding window; every unroutable region whose width and height are respectively not greater than w_s and h_s *must be* examined by our layout scanning algorithm. The example in Fig. 1(a) explains why we need to explore every region whose dimensions are not larger than the sliding window, in which region $R_{2,1,4,4}$ is not unroutable but its sub-region $R_{2,1,2,1}$ is. By the proposed layout scanning algorithm, even if $w_s \times h_s$ is set to 4×4 or larger, the unroutable $R_{2,1,2,1}$ still can be discovered. Note that when w_s and h_s are set larger, the number of the regions explored by the layout scanning algorithm increases so that the number of found unroutable regions and the runtime both increase.

Section 3.1 presents a layout scanning algorithm that can efficiently explore every region whose dimensions are not larger than the sliding window. Section 3.2 details how to properly set the sliding window's dimensions to strike a good balance between the recognition rate and runtime. Section 3.3 details how to identify a LBTO for an unroutable layout.

3.1 Layout Scanning

Let w_s and h_s respectively denote the width and height of the sliding window. In the layout scanning algorithm, when the sliding window encloses a region and the bottom-left corner of the region is g-cell $g(x, y)$, we will explore every region $R_{x,y,w,h}$, $1 \leq w \leq w_s$ and $1 \leq h \leq h_s$, in the sliding window. However, to examine whether each $R_{x,y,w,h}$ is unroutable, we need to know the value of $|S(R_{x,y,w,h})|$ first. Constructing $S(R_{x,y,w,h})$ for each explored region from scratch is time-consuming, so the layout scanning algorithm uses a dynamic programming (DP) technique to construct $S(R_{x,y,w,h})$ efficiently based on the following property.

***Property* 1**. If $R_{x1,y1,w1,h1}$ and $R_{x2,y2,w2,h2}$ are the sub-regions of $R_{x,y,w,h}$, and all the equalities in either $\{x=x_1, x_2=x_1+w_1, w_1+w_2=w, h=h_1=h_2\}$ or $\{y=y_1, y_2=y_1+h_1, h_1+h_2=h, w=w_1=w_2\}$ hold, $S(R_{x,y,w,h})$ can be

Procedure Merge($S(R_{x1,y1,w1,h1})$, $S(R_{x2,y2,w2,h2})$)
Input: $S(R_{x1,y1,w1,h1})$ and $S(R_{x2,y2,w2,h2})$; **Output:** $S(R_{x,y,w,h})$
1. $S(R_{x,y,w,h}) = S(R_{x2,y2,w2,h2})$
2. **foreach** net n in $S(R_{x1,y1,w1,h1})$
3.   **if** n is not in $S(R_{x,y,w,h})$
4.   **insert** n into $S(R_{x,y,w,h})$
5. $P(n, R_{x,y,w,h}) = P(n, R_{x1,y1,w1,h1})$
6.   **else**
7. $P(n, R_{x,y,w,h}) = P(n, R_{x1,y1,w1,h1}) + P(n, R_{x,y,w,h})$
8.   **if** $P(n, R_{x,y,w,h}) = TP(n)$
9.   **remove** n from $S(R_{x,y,w,h})$
10.   **end if**
11.   **end if**
12. **end foreach**
13. **return** $S(R_{x,y,w,h})$

Fig. 2. Pseudo code of merging $S(R_{x1,y1,w1,h1})$ and $S(R_{x2,y2,w2,h2})$ to form $S(R_{x,y,w,h})$.

obtained by $S(R_{x1,y1,w1,h1}) \cup S(R_{x2,y2,w2,h2}) - I(R_{x,y,w,h})$, where $I(R_{x,y,w,h})$ denotes the set of nets whose pins are all in $R_{x,y,w,h}$.

Fig. 1(b) shows an example of merging $S(R_{2,1,4,3})$ and $S(R_{2,4,4,2})$ to obtain $S(R_{2,1,4,5})$, in which $R_{2,1,4,5}$ is in a red window, $R_{2,1,4,3}$ and $R_{2,4,4,2}$ are respectively in the bottom and top blue windows, and there are four nets n_1, n_2, n_3, and n_4. $S(R_{2,1,4,3})=\{n_1, n_2, n_4\}$, $S(R_{2,4,4,2})=\{n_1, n_2, n_3\}$ and $I(R_{2,1,4,5})=\{n_1\}$, so $S(R_{2,1,4,5})= S(R_{2,1,4,3}) \cup S(R_{2,4,4,2}) - I(R_{2,1,4,5})=\{n_2, n_4, n_3\}$.

Fig. 2 shows the pseudo code of merging $S(R_{x1,y1,w1,h1})$ and $S(R_{x2,y2,w2,h2})$ to form $S(R_{x,y,w,h})$ based on Property 1, in which $P(n, R)$ denotes the number of pins of net n in region R and the outgoing net set of each region is implemented by a hash structure. In Fig. 2, $S(R_{x,y,w,h})$ is initialized to be $S(R_{x2,y2,w2,h2})$ at line 1. Then, the loop from lines 2 to 12 checks whether each outgoing net n in $S(R_{x1,y1,w1,h1})$ is also in $S(R_{x,y,w,h})$. If n is in $S(R_{x1,y1,w1,h1})$ but not in $S(R_{x,y,w,h})$, line 4 inserts n into $S(R_{x,y,w,h})$ and line 5 initializes $P(n, R_{x,y,w,h})$ to be $P(n, R_{x1,y1,w1,h1})$; otherwise, we update the number of pins of n in $R_{x,y,w,h}$ at line 7. If the pin number of n in $R_{x,y,w,h}$ is equal to the total pin number of n denoted by $TP(n)$, net n will be removed from $S(R_{x,y,w,h})$ at line 9 because n is not an outgoing net of $R_{x,y,w,h}$. Finally, $S(R_{x,y,w,h})$ is returned at line 13.

By the merging procedure in Fig. 2, $S(R_{x,y,w,h})$ can be built efficiently if $S(R_{x1,y1,w1,h1})$ and $S(R_{x2,y2,w2,h2})$ are already obtained. Based on this idea, a layout scanning algorithm using a DP technique is presented in Fig. 3, in which $g(x,y)$ denotes a g-cell whose coordinate in $G(V, E)$ is (x,y) and $p(x,y)$ denotes a pin in $g(x,y)$. At first, lines 1-3 in Fig. 3 treat each g-cell as a region and insert each pin $p(x,y)$ to its corresponding g-cell to build the outgoing net set for every region whose dimensions are 1×1. Lines 4-15 use a sliding window to scan the layout, where $g(x,y)$ at line 4 is the g-cell located at the bottom-left corner of the sliding window. Next, the nested loops in lines 5-14 explore every region $R_{x,y,w,h}$, $1 \le w \le w_s$ and $1 \le h \le h_s$ in the sliding window. Notably, $gridX(G)$ and $gridY(G)$ respectively denote the x- and y-dimensions of the layout, and thus the conditions $min(h_s, gridY(G) - y+1)$ at line 5 and $min(w_s, gridX(G) - x+1)$ at line 6 can avoid the access out of the layout. For each region $R_{x,y,w,h}$, lines 7-10 build its outgoing net set by a DP technique, in which $R_{x,y+h-1,w-1,1}$, $R_{x+w-1,y+h-1,1,1}$, and $R_{x,y,w,h-1}$ are the sub-regions of $R_{x,y,w,h}$ and their outgoing sets are already obtained in the previous iterations of the nested loops in lines 5-14. Therefore, based on Property 1, line 8 can merge $S(R_{x,y+h-1,w-1,1})$ and $S(R_{x+w-1,y+h-1,1,1})$ to build $S(R_{x,y+h-1,w,1})$, and then $S(R_{x,y+h-1,w,1})$ and $S(R_{x,y,w,h-1})$ also can be merged to build $S(R_{x,y,w,h})$ at line 10. After that, lines 11-12 push $R_{x,y,w,h}$ into an unroutable region set UR if

Algorithm Layout Scanning
Input: Grid graph $G(V, E)$, nets N;
Output: Unroutable regions set UR
1. **foreach** net n in N
2.   Insert each pin $p(x,y) \in n$ to $S(R_{x,y,1,1})$
3. **end foreach**
4. **foreach** g-cell $g(x,y)$ in $G(V, E)$
5.   **for** $h=1$ to $min(h_s, gridY(G) - y+1)$
6.   **for** $w=1$ to $min(w_s, gridX(G) - x+1)$
7.   **if** $w > 1$
8. $S(R_{x,y+h-1,w,1}) \leftarrow$ Merge($S(R_{x+w-1,y+h-1,1,1}), S(R_{x,y+h-1,w-1,1})$)
9.   **if** $h > 1$
10. $S(R_{x,y,w,h}) \leftarrow$ Merge($S(R_{x,y+h-1,w,1}), S(R_{x,y,w,h-1})$)
11.   **if** $|S(R_{x,y,w,h})| > c(R_{x,y,w,h})$
12.   push $R_{x,y,w,h}$ into UR
13.   **end for**
14.   **end for**
15. **end foreach**
16. **return** UR

Fig. 3. Pseudo code of DP-based layout scanning algorithm

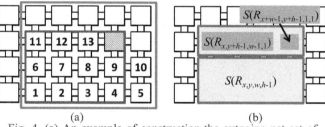

      (a)   (b)

Fig. 4. (a) An example of construction the outgoing net set of the region in the blue window; (b) the outgoing net sets that are already obtained.

$|S(R_{x,y,w,h})| > c(R_{x,y,w,h})$. Finally, all unroutable regions in UR are returned at line 16.

To better understand the behavior of the layout scanning algorithm, Fig. 4 illustrates an example. In Fig. 4(a), the red window represents a sliding window whose bottom-left corner is assumed to be g-cell $g(x,y)$, the g-cells with the numbers mean that the g-cells have been explored by the nested loops in lines 5-14 of Fig. 3, and the number denotes the exploring order. Note that exploring a g-cell $g(a,b)$ means that the outgoing net set of the region whose bottom-left corner is $g(x,y)$ and top-right corner is $g(a,b)$ is constructed. Assume the marked g-cell in Fig. 4(a) is $g(x+w,y+h)$ and is being explored, namely $S(R_{x,y,w,h})$ in the blue window is being constructed. Fig. 4(b) shows three outgoing net sets $S(R_{x+w-1,y+h-1,1,1})$, $S(R_{x,y+h-1,w-1,1})$, and $S(R_{x,y,w,h-1})$ that are already obtained before the nested loop explores the marked g-cell, so these outgoing net sets in Fig. 4(b) can be merged by lines 7-10 of Fig. 3 to form $S(R_{x,y,w,h})$ in Fig. 4(a).

Note that in this work, a lookup table is built to make the query of $c(R_{x,y,w,h})$ in a constant time. For example, let $E_R=\{e_1, e_2, e_3...\}$ denote the vertical g-edges in a row and the total capacity from e_1 to e_i is pre-computed and stored in $tc_R[i]$, where tc_R is an array and $tc_R[0]$ is zero. When e_i to e_j, $j>i$, are the bridge edges passing through a boundary of $R_{x,y,w,h}$, the total capacity from e_i to e_j can be obtained by $tc_R[j] - tc_R[i-1]$. Therefore, $c(R_{x,y,w,h})$ can be obtained in a constant time by querying the lookup table to get the total capacity of each boundary of $R_{x,y,w,h}$. Moreover, let $|V|$ denote the number of g-cells in the layout and M denote the maximum number of pins in a g-cell; the time complexity of the entire layout scanning algorithm is analyzed as follows.

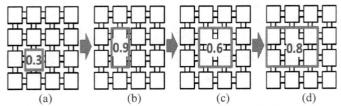

Fig. 5. The process of extending a seed window in (a) iteration 1; (b) iteration 2; (c) iteration 3; (d) the last iteration.

Fig. 6. The red box denotes a seed window, and the blue boxes denote the extension candidates of the seed window.

Lemma 1. The time complexity of the merging procedure in Fig. 2 is $O(|S(R_{x1,y1,w1,h1})|)$.

Proof: in Fig. 2, line 1 is implemented by passing reference, so it is constant time. Then, the loop from lines 2 to 12 runs $|S(R_{x1,y1,w1,h1})|$ iterations that dominate the time complexity of the merging procedure. In the loop, every operation such as *insert* and *remove* takes constant time because each outgoing net set is implemented by a hash structure. Therefore, the time complexity of the merging procedure is $O(|S(R_{x1,y1,w1,h1})|)$.

To make the merging procedure faster, when two regions are merged, we treat the smaller region as $R_{x1,y1,w1,h1}$.

Lemma 2. The size of $S(R_{x,y,w,h})$ is $O(whM)$.

Proof: $R_{x,y,w,h}$ contains $w \times h$ g-cells and each g-cell contains at most M pins, so the maximum number of pins in $R_{x,y,w,h}$ is $w \times h \times M$. In the worst case, every pin belongs to an outgoing net, so the size of $S(R_{x,y,w,h})$ is $O(whM)$.

Lemma 3. Given $S(R_{x,y+h-1,w-1,1})$, $S(R_{x+w-1,y+h-1,1,1})$, and $S(R_{x,y,w,h-1})$, the time complexity of building $S(R_{x,y,w,h})$ at lines 7-10 of Fig. 3 is $O(wM)$.

Proof: According to Lemma 2, the sizes of $S(R_{x,y+h-1,w-1,1})$ and $S(R_{x+w-1,y+h-1,1,1})$ are $O(wM)$ and $O(M)$, respectively. According to Lemma 1, the time complexity of merging $S(R_{x,y+h-1,w-1,1})$ and $S(R_{x+w-1,y+h-1,1,1})$ at line 8 to build $S(R_{x,y+h-1,w,1})$ is $O(M)$. Next, owing to the same reasons, the sizes of $S(R_{x,y+h-1,w,1})$ and $S(R_{x,y,w,h-1})$ are respectively $O(wM)$ and $O(whM)$, and the time complexity of merging $S(R_{x,y,w,h-1})$ and $S(R_{x,y+h-1,w,1})$ at line 10 to build $S(R_{x,y,w,h})$ is $O(wM)$. Therefore, the total time complexity of building $S(R_{x,y,w,h})$ is $O(M)+O(wM)=O(wM)$.

Lemma 4. The time complexity of the layout scanning algorithm is $O(|V|w_s^2 h_s M)$.

Proof: In Fig. 3, lines 1-3 insert every pin into its corresponding region and the total pin number in the layout must be not larger than $|V|M$, so the time complexity of lines 1-3 is $O(|V|M)$. Then, the outer loop from lines 4 to 15 runs $|V|$ iterations, and the time complexity of the nested loops in lines 5-14 is $\Sigma_{1 \leq w \leq w_s, 1 \leq h \leq h_s} O(wM) = O(w_s^2 h_s M)$ based on Lemma 3. Thus, the time complexity of lines 4-15 is $O(|V|w_s^2 h_s M)$ that dominates $O(|V|M)$, so the time complexity of the layout scanning algorithm is $O(|V|w_s^2 h_s M)$.

3.2 Window Dimension Determination

According to different purposes, users can set different areas for the sliding window to trade off the recognition rate and the runtime of the layout scanning algorithm. However, even with the same area, different widths and heights of a sliding window would affect the recognition rate. For example, when the area of the sliding window is set to 900, our experimental result shows that no unroutable region can be discovered when the sliding window's dimension is 20×45 for test case MPL_sb5, while 34 unroutable regions are discovered when the sliding window's dimension is 36×25. This implies how to decide the width and height for a sliding window is important.

Given a window area A_{max}, the problem here is to identify a width w_s and a height h_s for the sliding window such that $w_s \times h_s \leq A_{max}$, and the objective is to maximize the number of unroutable regions found by the layout scanning algorithm. We propose a two-stage method to decide w_s and h_s. At first, we sample a set of windows whose areas are not greater than A_{max} in the layout, and assign each sampling window a weight. If a sampling window encloses unroutable or hard-to-route regions, its weight is higher. In the second stage, the objective is to determine w_s and h_s for the sliding window to maximize the total weight of the sampling windows covered by the sliding window. Note that the sliding window is said to **cover** a sampling window if the width and height of the sliding window are both not smaller than the sampling window. If a sampling window encloses an unroutable region and the sliding window covers the sampling window, using this sliding window to scan the layout must find out the unroutable region. Therefore, if the sliding window covers more sampling windows with higher weights, using this sliding window to scan a layout has a higher chance to find out more unroutable regions.

In the sampling stage, if a window is the minimum box to enclose a rectangular region R, the weight of the window is the ratio of $|S(R)|$ to $c(R)$. A window with a high weight means the window encloses a hard-to-route or unroutable region, and the goal of this stage is to identify a set of sampling windows with higher weights. At the beginning of this stage, we create a set of windows whose dimensions are 1×1 to enclose each g-cell. Next, these windows are sorted in a nonincreasing order based on their weights, and then the first n windows in the sorted sequence are selected to be seed windows, where n is a user defined number and is set to 300 in this work. For each seed window, an extension process is adopted such that the process iteratively extends one of its boundaries to explore windows that have potential to be the sampling windows until any extension of the seed window would make its area exceed A_{max}. For example, assuming A_{max} is 7, Fig. 5 shows the windows explored by the extension process of a seed window, where the number in each explored window denotes its weight. In each iteration of the extension process, we tentatively extend different boundaries of the seed window outward by one g-cell to get four **extension candidates**, and then select the one with the highest weight to be an **explored window** and use it as the seed window at the next iteration. For example, Fig. 6 illustrates four extension candidates for the seed window in Fig. 5(c). At the end of the extension process of a seed window, three types of windows will become sampling windows and be inserted into a sampling window array *SWA*.

1. The seed window at the last iteration of the extension process (e.g., the seed window in Fig. 5(d)).
2. Any extension candidate whose weight is more than 1.
3. If the weights of all explored windows are not greater than 1, the explored window with the highest weight is inserted to *SWA*. In the example of Fig. 5, the explored window in Fig. 5(b) will be inserted into *SWA*.

After the extension process of each seed window finishes, *SWA* contains a set of sampling windows that enclose hard-to-route or

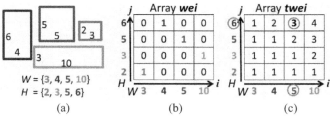

Fig. 7. (a) A set of sampling windows; (b) array *wei* and (c) array *twei* that corresponds to the sampling windows in (a)

Algorithm Determination of w_s and h_s
Input: 2D array *wei* with size of $m \times m$; **Output:** w_s and h_s

```
1.    int maxTwei=0;
2.    for j=1 to m
3.      int tmp=0
4.      for i=1 to m
5.        tmp = wei[i][j] + tmp;
6.        twei[i][j]= wei[i][j-1] + tmp;
7.        if twei[i][j] > maxTwei and wi×hj ≤Amax
8.          maxTwei = twei[i][j];
9.          ws = wi;   hs = hj;
10.     end if
11.    end for
12.  end for
13.  return ws and hs
```

Fig. 8. DP-based algorithm to determine w_s and h_s

unroutable regions. If the weight of a sampling window exceeds 1, we additionally add a large constant, say 10^5, to its weight to emphasize the fact that this sampling window encloses an unroutable region.

In the second stage, let m denote the number of sampling windows in *SWA*, and let $W=\{w_1, w_2,..., w_m\}$ and $H=\{h_1, h_2,..., h_m\}$ denote the sets of the widths and heights of sampling windows, respectively. This stage will select a width from W and a height from H to respectively be the sliding window's width w_s and height h_s such that $w_s \times h_s \leq A_{max}$ and the total weight of the sampling windows covered by the sliding window is maximized. Because there are at most m different widths in W and m different heights in H, there are at most m^2 pairs of width and height that can be the candidates for w_s and h_s. To select the best pair among these m^2 pairs, we evaluate each pair by the following efficient method.

At first, we sort W and H in a nondecreasing order and let w_i and h_j denote the i-th width and j-th height in the sorted W and H, respectively. Then, we build two $m \times m$ 2D arrays denoted by *wei* and *twei*, and initialize every element in *wei* to zero. Next, the weight of each sampling window whose width and height respectively are w_i and h_j is saved into *wei*[i][j]. For example, assume A_{max} is 30 and four windows obtained by the sampling stage are shown in Fig. 7(a). Fig. 7(b) shows array *wei* corresponding to Fig. 7(a) when the weight of each sampling window is assumed to be 1. Next, *twei*[i][j] denotes the total weight of the sampling windows whose width and height are respectively not greater than w_i and h_j, so *twei*[i][j] can be computed by the following equation.

$$twei[i][j] = \sum_{\forall p,q, 1\leq p \leq i \text{ and } 1 \leq q \leq j} wei[p][q]. \quad (1)$$

After the value of each entry in *twei* is computed, we select a width w_i from W and a height h_j from H to respectively be w_s and h_s such that $w_s \times h_s \leq A_{max}$ and *twei*[i][j] is maximized. To more efficiently compute the value of every entry in *twei*, Eq. (2) can be derived from Eq. (1) if *twei*[0][k] and *twei*[k][0], $1 \leq k \leq m$, are initialized to zero.

$$twei[i][j] = twei[i][j-1] + \sum_{\forall p, 1 \leq p \leq i} wei[p][j]. \quad (2)$$

According to Eq. (2), a DP-based algorithm in Fig. 8 can be used to efficiently compute the value of each entry in *twei* and select a pair of width and height to be w_s and h_s. Fig 7(c) shows array *twei* built by the algorithm in Fig. 8; for this case w_s and h_s are selected to be 5 and 6, respectively, such that $w_s \times h_s \leq 30$ and the sliding window can cover three sampling windows in Fig. 7(a).

The time complexities of the first and second stages are respectively $O(n|A_{max}M)$ and $O(|m|^2)$. Since these two stages are much faster than the layout scanning algorithm, the detailed analysis of its time complexity is skipped for saving space.

3.3 Lower-Bound Total Overflow Identification

Identifying the minimum total overflow for a layout is a hard problem and has never been studied. This work uses a heuristic method to identify a LBTO that must be not larger than the minimum total overflow but as close as possible. At first, the proposed layout scanning algorithm is used to identify a set of unroutable regions $UR=\{R_1, R_2,...\}$, where each R_i denotes an unroutable region, and $OF_i=|S(R_i)|-c(R_i)$ denotes that the amount of the intrinsic overflow of R_i. The intrinsic overflow of R_i is the overflow that must happen on the bridge edges of R_i. If no two regions in UR have common bride edges, we can add up the intrinsic overflow of every region to obtain a LBTO. However, if two regions R_i and R_j share bridge edges, adding up OF_i and OF_j may overestimate intrinsic overflow. For example, Fig 9(a) shows a set of unroutable regions identified by the layout scanning algorithm when the sliding window size is set to 3×3, in which the yellow g-edges are the bridge edges shared by more than one region. In Fig. 9(a), R_2 and R_4 share a bridge edge, and assume that $c(R_2)$ and $c(R_4)$ are both zero, $S(R_2)=S(R_4)=\{n_1\}$, and n_1 is a two-pin net. As a result, OF_2 and OF_4 are both one, so adding up OF_2 and OF_4 gets two. However, if n_1 routes through the bridge edge shared by R_2 and R_4 to connect its two pins, n_1 only induces a unit of overflow. This indicates that adding up OF_2 and OF_4 would overestimate the intrinsic overflow. To avoid overestimation, when two regions R_i and R_j share bridge edges, we only count one of OF_i and OF_j to compute the LBTO.

In this work, we reduce the LBTO identification problem to a maximum weight independent set (MWIS) problem. At first, we build a conflict graph, in which every node corresponds to an unroutable region in UR, the weight of each node denotes the intrinsic overflow of its corresponding region, and the conflict edge between two nodes denotes that the two regions share at least a bridge edge. If two nodes have a conflict edge to connect, we call them neighbors. Fig. 9(b) shows the conflict graph corresponding to the unroutable regions in Fig. 9(a), where each node v_i denotes the region R_i. Note that although some regions such as R_1 and R_3 overlap with each other in Fig. 9(a), their bridge edges are not shared. Thus, there is no conflict edge between them in Fig. 9(b). The MWIS problem is to select a set of nodes in the conflict graph and no conflict edge exists between any pair of selected nodes. The objective of the MWIS problem is to maximize the total weight of the selected nodes, and the total weight denotes the LBTO in the given layout. Since the MWIS problem is an NP hard problem [19], we adopt a greedy algorithm to solve it. We first sort every node, and then examine each node one-by-one based on the sorting order. At the beginning, the status of every node is unmarked. When an unmarked node is examined, we select the node and mark its neighbors. Later, if a marked node is examined, it would not be selected.

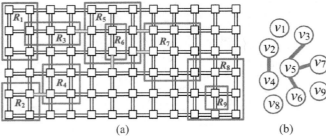

(a)   (b)

Fig. 9. (a) a set of unroutable regions; (b) the conflict graph corresponding to the unroutable regions in (a).

Obviously, the sorting order of nodes would impact the solution quality. Empirically, we sort each node based on the following scoring function in a nonincreasing order.

$$s(v_i) = w(v_i) - \alpha \sum_{\forall (v_i, v_j) \in CG} w(v_j), \qquad (3)$$

where $s(v_i)$ denotes the score of node v_i, $w(v_i)$ denotes the weight of v_i, (v_i, v_j) denotes an conflict edge connecting nodes v_j and v_j in the conflict graph CG, and α is a user defined constant. In this work, we set α to 0.1. The concept behind Eq. (3) is that the node with a higher weight would have a higher priority to be selected. Since the neighbors of a selected node cannot be selected, Eq. (3) decreases the priority of a node if the total weight of its neighbors is big.

Let $|UR|$ denote the number of unroutable regions. The time complexities of building the conflict graph and solving the MWIS problem by the greedy algorithm are respectively $O(|UR|^2)$ and $O(|UR|\log|UR|)$. However, the time complexity of building the conflict graph can be reduced to $O(|UR|\log|UR|)$ if the data structure R-tree is used for the region query, but we do not adopt it in the current implementation since the LBTO identification algorithm is already fast enough.

4   EXPERIMENTAL RESULTS

The proposed algorithms are implemented in C/C++/openMP and tested on a 2.4GHz Intel Xeon-based Linux server with 96GB memory. In this work, we select a set of hard-to-route placements from two benchmark suites to test the proposed algorithms. The first benchmark suite is from ISPD08 global routing contest [1]. Many global routing research works [2-10] adopt ISPD08 benchmark suite to test their routers, but so far no router can identify overflow-free results for 4 cases: newblue3, newblue4, newblue7 and bigblue4, which are considered as hard-to-route benchmarks. Note that the routers in [2-10] typically ignore the nets whose pins are more than 1000 in ISPD08 benchmarks to ease the routing effort, but this work does not ignore any net.

The second benchmark suite is the placement solutions released by ISPD11 placement contest [11], which are adopted to be the routing test cases in recent global routing research [12, 13]. ISPD11 contest has 8 placement benchmarks and each benchmark has four placement solutions respectively obtained by placers Ripple [14], simPLR [15], NTUplace4 [21] and mPL11 [22], so 32 placement solutions are released by the ISPD11 contest. Table 1 shows the total overflow (tof) and runtime in minute (cpu) of these 32 placement solutions routed by NCTU-GR 2.0 [9]. Note that NCTU-GR 2.0 is a leading and public academic global routing tool and it has been used to evaluate the routability of placements in papers of [16-18, 22]. Table 1 reveals that there are 19 placement solutions whose routing results have overflow, so we adopt these 19 placement solutions plus the 4 ISPD08 hard-to-route benchmarks to be our test cases. In our experiment, we would judge whether these 23 test cases are unroutable and identify the LBTOs for these test cases.

TABLE 1 ISPD11 PLACEMENTS ROUTED BY NCTU-GR 2.0

	NTUplace		mPL		Ripple		SimPLR	
	tof	cpu(m)	tof	cpu(m)	tof	cpu(m)	tof	cpu(m)
Sb1	0	1.0	0	0.6	0	0.5	0	0.8
Sb2	2890	35.4	6600	34.3	1648	7.0	97286	104.2
Sb4	84566	16.0	50	2.3	258	1.1	259346	11.0
Sb5	20952	21.9	15630	20.4	0	1.4	0	1.9
Sb10	0	5.2	9458	69.5	40806	77.0	33330	109.4
Sb12	2460706	111.7	1705820	102.5	0	9.6	0	3.6
Sb15	105256	57.1	0	1.0	0	1.3	51100	23.8
Sb18	22534	73.2	0	0.5	130046	29.4	0	0.6

4.1   Effectiveness of Unroutable Placement Recognizer

Table 2 shows the recognizing results obtained by the layout scanning algorithm with manually setting different sliding window sizes, in which $|UR|$ denotes the number of unroutable regions found by the layout scanning algorithm, T_f denotes the runtime of the layout scanning algorithm to find out the first unroutable region, and T_t denotes the runtime of the layout scanning algorithm to explore the entire layout. T_f and T_t are both measured in second. The entries of T_f for some test cases are shown as "—" in Table 2 because the layout scanning algorithm does not find any unroutable region for these test cases. Notably, $|UR|$ is an important factor to evaluate the capability of the proposed recognizer, because a placer could better improve the routability of a hard-to-route placement if the recognizer reports more unroutable regions to the placer.

Table 2 reveals that the total runtime and the recognition rate both increase as the sliding windows size increases. For instance, when the dimension of the sliding window is 15×15, the layout scanning algorithm can recognize 11 test cases that are unroutable out of 23 test cases and it only spends 90 seconds for each test case on average; moreover it can be even faster if the layout scanning algorithm terminates once any unroutable region is discovered, as indicated by the column "T_f". In contrast, when the sliding window size is increased to 100×100, there are 16 unroutable layouts recognized by the layout scanning algorithm. This implies that adjusting the window size can trade off the runtime and recognition rate to achieve different purposes. If we need to iteratively query whether a design is unroutable in the routability optimization flow, the window size should be set small. On the other hand, if we attempt to analyze the routability of a set of widely used benchmarks, we can make the layout scanning algorithm take longer runtime to get a higher recognition rate.

Table 2 reveals a benefit of using the proposed recognizer to evaluate the routability of a hard-to-route placement. When the sliding window size is set small, say 15×15, the layout scanning algorithm can be done in 1-4 minutes and $|UR|$ can be treated as an indicator to the routability. In contrast, using global routers to evaluate the routability of a hard-to-route case may spend more than 10 minutes (see non-overflow-free cases in Table 1).

Because the loop from lines 4 to 15 in Fig. 3 dominates the runtime of the layout scanning algorithm and it can be run by multiple threads independently, the layout scanning algorithm can be easily parallelized. The results shown in Table 2 are obtained by conducting experiments on 16 threads for time saving. To see the runtime difference when different numbers of threads are used, we set the window size to 30×30 and then run the layout scanning algorithm individually with 1, 2, 4, 8, and 16 threads. The experiments show that using 2, 4, 8, and 16 threads to run the layout scanning algorithm can achieve 1.7X, 2.6X, 3.5X, and 4.9X speedup compared to the single thread, respectively. Theoretically

TABLE 4 LBTO OF EACH TEST CASE

Test cases	LBTO	Test cases	LBTO	Test cases	LBTO
newblue3	26292	NTU_sb2	594	MPL_sb5	1802
newblue4	–	NTU_sb4	–	MPL_sb10	–
newblue7	58	NTU_sb5	1840	MPL_sb12	54638
bigblue4	–	NTU_sb12	199054	SimPLR_sb2	3206
Ripple_sb2	1540	NTU_sb15	5736	SimPLR_sb4	103696
Ripple_sb4	200	NTU_sb18	–	SimPLR_sb10	–
Ripple_sb10	–	MPL_sb2	1724	SimPLR_sb15	2082
Ripple_sb18	8456	MPL_sb4	42		

speaking, the speedup of the layout scanning algorithm should almost linearly increase as the number of threads increases. However, our machine has only four cores, so simultaneously running 16 threads is realized by using a superlinear technique to run 4 threads on each core. Due to the thread scheduling overhead and the cache memory shared by multiple threads, we cannot get the linear speedup.

4.2 Validation of Window Dimension Determination

To show that the sliding windows of the same area but with different widths and heights would affect the recognizing results, we manually set different w_s and h_s for the sliding window and make its area be always 900. The left major column in Table 3 shows the number of found unroutable regions when manually setting w_s and h_s. Table 3 reveals that test cases MPL_sb2 and MPL_sb5 can be confirmed to be unroutable when $w_s \times h_s = 30 \times 30$ but not when $w_s \times h_s = 50 \times 18$. Moreover, the amount of found unroutable regions for test cases newblue3 is the largest when $w_s \times h_s = 30 \times 30$, but the amount of found unroutable regions for test cases NTU_sb12 is the largest when $w_s \times h_s = 18 \times 50$. This implies that exploring different layouts should use different w_s and h_s to achieve a good recognition rate. The right major column in Table 3 shows the number of found unroutable regions ($|UR|$) as well as w_s and h_s ($w_s \times h_s$) for each test case when the method proposed in Section 3.2 is used to automatically decide w_s and h_s such that $w_s \times h_s \leq 900$. When w_s and h_s are automatically decided by the proposed method, there are 13 layouts that can be confirmed to be unroutable and the total number of found unroutable regions is more than manually setting $w_s \times h_s$. Note that the longest runtime of determining w_s and h_s for each test case is 15 seconds, which is much faster than the layout scanning algorithm.

4.3 Effectiveness of LBTO Identification

Table 4 shows the LBTO identified by the algorithm presented in Section 3.3 for each test case. In this experiment, the input of the LBTO identification algorithm is the unroutable region set UR found by the layout scanning algorithm when $w_s \times h_s = 100 \times 100$. The LBTOs for some test cases are shown as "–" in Table 4 because the layout scanning algorithm does not find any unroutable region for these test cases. Based on the LBTO results shown in Table 4, we can more precisely evaluate the capability of a routing tool. For instance, we can see that the total overflow of MPL_sb4 shown in Table 1 is very close to its LBTO shown in Table 4. This implies that NCTU-GR 2.0 may already work well on MPL_sb4. In contrast, as NCTU-GR 2.0 routes simPLR_sb15, we can see that its total overflow in Table 2 is much larger than its LBTO in Table 4. This implies that perhaps there are some improvements NCTU-GR 2.0 can further do for simPLR_sb15.

The LBTO represents the amount of overflow that cannot be solved by any routing means, which also can be treated as an indicator to the routability of a placement and may show a different aspect from the routability evaluation by the total overflow. For instance, Table 1 shows that Ripple_sb2 has lower total overflow than NTU_sb2.

Traditional routability evaluation method [1] would regard that Ripple_sb2 has better routability than NTU_sb2. However, Table 4 shows that Ripple_sb2 has the higher LBTO than NTU_sb2, and this tells a different story.

5 CONCLUSIONS AND FUTURE WORKS

The proposed unroutable placement recognizer can confirm that a placement is exactly unroutable when any unroutable region is discovered by the layout scanning algorithm. In addition, the recognizer can report a lower bound of total overflow for an unroutable placement. If the LBTO of a placement is known, the capability of a global router can be more accurately evaluated when the router is tested on the placement.

Using the proposed recognizer to cooperate with placers is our future direction. If the recognizer finds a set of unroutable regions in a placement, placers can improve the routability of the placement by moving some cells out of the unroutable regions. In addition, some cells enclosed by multiple unroutable regions should have a higher priority to be moved, because moving these cells can get a greater benefit to the routability improvement.

REFERENCES

[1] ISPD 2008 Global Routing Contest and Benchmark Suite. Available: http://archive.sigda.org/ispd2008/contests/ispd08rc.html

[2] M. D. Moffitt and C. N. Sze, "Wire synthesizable global routing for timing closure," in *Proc. ASP-DAC*, pp. 545-550, 2011.

[3] J. Hu *et al*, "Completing high-quality global routes," in *Proc. ICCAD*, pp. 35-41, 2010.

[4] H.-Y. Chen *et al*. "High-performance global routing with fast overflow reduction." in *Proc. ASP-DAC*, pp. 582-587, 2009.

[5] Y. Xu and C. Chu, "MGR: Multi-level global router," in *Proc. ICCAD*, pp. 250-255, 2011.

[6] Y.-J. Chang *et al*, "NTHU-Route 2.0: a fast and stable global router," in *Proc. ICCAD*, pp. 338-343, 2008.

[7] T.-H. Wu *et al.*, "GRIP: Scalable 3-D global routing using integer programming," in *Proc. DAC*, pp. 320-325, 2009.

[8] Y.-J. Chang *et al.*, "GLADE: A modern global router considering layer directives," in *Proc. ICCAD*, pp. 319-323, 2010.

[9] W.-H. Liu *et al.*, "NCTU-GR 2.0: multithreaded collision-aware global routing with bounded-length maze routing," *IEEE TCAD*, 32(5), pp. 709-722, 2013.

[10] K.-R. Dai *et al.*, "NCTU-GR: efficient simulated evolution-based rerouting and congestion-relaxed layer assignment on 3-D global routing," *IEEE TVLSI*, 20(3), pp. 459-472, 2012.

[11] N. Viswanathan et al., "The ISPD-2011 routability-driven placement contest and benchmark suite," in *Proc. ISPD*, pp. 141-146, 2011.

[12] H. Shojaei *et al.*, "Congestion analysis for global routing via integer programming," in *Proc. ICCAD*, pp. 256-262, 2011.

[13] W.-H. Liu *et al.*, "A fast maze-free routing congestion estimator with hybrid unilateral monotonic routing," in *Proc. ICCAD*, pp. 713-719, 2012.

[14] X. He *et al.*, "Ripple: an effective routability-driven placer by iterative cell movement", in *Proc. ICCAD*, pp. 74–79, 2011.

[15] M.-C. Kim *et al.*, "A SimPLR method for routability-driven placement," in *Proc. ICCAD*, pp. 80–84, 2011.

[16] J. Hu *et al.*, "Taming the complexity of coordinated place and route," in *Proc. DAC*, 2013.

[17] X. He *et al.*, "Ripple 2.0: High quality routability-driven placement via global router integration," in *Proc. DAC*, 2013.

[18] W.-H. Liu *et al.*, "Optimization of placement solutions for routability," in *Proc. DAC*, 2013.

[19] M. R. Garey and D. S. Johnson, "Computers and intractability: a guide to the theory of NP-Completeness," New York: W. H. Freeman, 1983.

[20] W.-H. Liu et al., "Routing congestion estimation with real design constraints," in *Proc. DAC*, 2013.

[21] M.-K. Hsu et al., "Routability-driven analytical placement for mixed-size circuit designs", in *Proc. ICCAD*, pp. 80–84, 2011.

[22] Jason Cong et al., "Optimizing routability in large-scale mixed-size placement," in *Proc. ASP-DAC*, pp.441-446, 2013.

TABLE 2   RECOGNIZING RESULTS OBTAINED BY THE LAYOUT SCANNING ALGORITHM WITH DIFFERENT SLIDING WINDOW SIZES.

$w_s \times h_s$ Test cases	5×5			15×15			30×30			100×100		
	$|UR|$	T_f (s)	T_t (s)	$|UR|$	T_f (s)	T_t (s)	$|UR|$	T_f (s)	T_t (s)	$|UR|$	T_f (s)	T_t (s)
newblue3	268	2	10	14443	25	93	162345	68	523	205252	25	2010
newblue4	0	—	5	0	—	77	0	—	522	0	—	2416
newblue7	0	—	13	3	185	220	3	1439	1626	3	6792	7271
bigblue4	0	—	7	0	—	142	0	—	925	0	—	4759
Ripple_sb2	0	—	6	206	57	99	2536	315	687	3713	1582	3278
Ripple_sb4	0	—	3	38	10	42	41	67	311	41	286	1401
Ripple_sb10	0	—	6	0	—	96	0	—	631	0	—	2955
Ripple_sb18	0	—	3	19	30	53	483	7	348	21441	23	1399
NTU_sb2	0	—	3	185	25	104	617	143	816	617	524	3875
NTU_sb4	0	—	5	0	—	41	0	—	299	0	—	1420
NTU_sb5	0	—	4	0	—	72	0	—	520	851	54	2486
NTU_sb12	917	<1	5	118974	2	93	601141	9	760	12528257	30	3842
NTU_sb15	0	—	6	0	—	85	0	—	584	12606	—	2654
NTU_sb18	0	—	3	0	—	47	0	—	307	0	—	1517
MPL_sb2	0	—	7	0	—	112	2253	716	870	3946	3485	4252
MPL_sb4	0	—	3	10	12	50	10	31	354	10	48	1646
MPL_sb5	0	—	5	0	—	74	3	322	553	34	62	2668
MPL_sb10	0	—	7	0	—	99	0	—	768	0	—	3805
MPL_sb12	727	<1	6	112747	2	121	418721	13	836	909560	71	3970
SimPLR_sb2	0	—	7	5	37	123	52	212	812	11629	630	4098
SimPLR_sb4	0	—	3	2	11	54	38	<1	352	12378	<1	1655
SimPLR_sb10	0	—	6	0	—	91	0	—	673	0	—	3303
SimPLR_sb15	0	—	7	0	—	93	0	—	609	1866	44	2655
Sum	0.2×10^4	2.49	129.31	2.5×10^4	396.35	2079.84	11.9×10^4	3342.29	14685.34	137.1×10^4	105186.3	583617
Uroutable cases	3			11			13			16		

TABLE 3   RECOGNIZING RESULTS COMPARISON BETWEEN MANUALLY AND AUTOMATICALLY SETTING $w_s \times h_s$.

Test cases	Manually setting $w_s \times h_s$									Automatically setting $w_s \times h_s$	
	15×60	18×50	20×45	25×36	30×30	36×25	45×20	50×18	60×15	$|UR|$	$w_s \times h_s$
newblue3	67268	90994	107031	142798	162345	156281	120075	102673	76085	122168	22×40
newblue4	0	0	0	0	0	0	0	0	0	0	23×39
newblue7	3	3	3	3	3	3	3	3	3	3	20×45
bigblue4	0	0	0	0	0	0	0	0	0	0	36×25
Ripple_sb2	206	503	776	1649	2536	3287	3704	3713	3427	3514	39×21
Ripple_sb4	41	41	41	41	41	41	41	41	38	41	16×56
Ripple_sb10	0	0	0	0	0	0	0	0	0	0	20×45
Ripple_sb18	130	130	130	131	483	685	433	208	35	574	33×27
NTU_sb2	185	360	459	596	617	617	617	617	617	617	32×28
NTU_sb4	0	0	0	0	0	0	0	0	0	0	14×64
NTU_sb5	0	0	0	0	0	0	0	0	0	0	25×36
NTU_sb12	856034	897768	880480	755053	601141	435448	273577	218846	148404	880480	20×45
NTU_sb15	0	0	0	0	0	0	0	0	0	0	23×39
NTU_sb18	0	0	0	0	0	0	0	0	0	0	23×39
MPL_sb2	0	16	340	2575	2253	205	0	0	0	682	21×42
MPL_sb4	10	10	10	10	10	10	10	10	10	10	18×50
MPL_sb5	0	0	0	0	3	34	9	0	0	34	34×26
MPL_sb10	0	0	0	0	0	0	0	0	0	0	23×38
MPL_sb12	372286	445563	470130	466812	418721	346542	248159	206435	143760	469585	21×42
SimPLR_sb2	5	22	36	52	52	52	52	52	52	42	21×42
SimPLR_sb4	2	8	11	41	38	22	13	13	13	4	16×56
SimPLR_sb10	0	0	0	0	0	0	0	0	0	0	39×23
SimPLR_sb15	0	0	0	0	0	0	0	0	0	0	3×226
Sum	13×10^4	14.4×10^4	14.6×10^4	13.7×10^4	11.9×10^4	9.4×10^4	6.5×10^4	5.3×10^4	3.7×10^4	$\mathbf{14.8 \times 10^4}$	
Unroutable cases	11	12	12	12	**13**	**13**	12	11	11	**13**	

Integrated Structured Placement Design Methodology in Place and Route Flow

Anand Arunachalam
Synopsys
700 E. Middlefield Road, Mountain View, California
94043
(001) 650 584 5170
anand@synopsys.com

ABSTRACT

Most of the high performance cores use some structured placement and routing as a means to achieve higher frequency, lower power, lower interconnect length, higher density and predictability. Structured placement techniques are typically used for compute intensive portions of data path but similar ideas are also applied for designing memories, register files and clock networks to reduce area, improve power and skew. Traditional processor designers typically use a custom built tool to place and route structured data path and memories. Though the required performance gains were usually achieved by this process, the cost involved was usually quite high and sometime results were sub optimal. Added to the effort, the tool design and capabilities vary among different design teams with no easy interface to general purpose commercial synthesis and place and route tools. Convergence for such designs were very time consuming as design closure involved two separate tools and back and forth cycles. Parameterizing or a template approach to reuse scripts to create similar structures for next generation designs is another difficulty designer faces while trying to meet tight design cycles. One way to directly work inside a general purpose place and route tool is to extract regularity from synthesized net lists and then place them. This is a problem that has been solved on and off for specific design styles and there is quite a bit of published work in this area but not consistently and successfully across different design styles, technology generations as the regularity is usually lost or hard to find by the time synthesis is complete. Extending structured placement ideas to clock networks was not easily achieved in a standalone custom tool as the clock network needed to be integrated with rest of the design. Another problem was the optimization of structured logic, often involved manual optimization and optimized without the context of the rest of design. After all these issues were overcome, other key problem designer's face in the traditional approach is finding appropriate locations in the floor plan for structured blocks. This is usually a trial and error approach and often time consuming as the combinations in presence of such blocks tend to be large.

One ideal approach is to find a way to integrate the designers IP and structured placement techniques transparently in to a general synthesis and place and route tool. The talk will detail such an approach.

ISPD'14, March 30–April 2, 2014, Petaluma, California, USA.
ACM 978-1-4503-2592-9/14/03.
http://dx.doi.org/10.1145/2560519.2565869

A new language and equivalent Graphical User Interface to capture designer intent easily in a scriptable environment integrated with a general purpose place and route tool will be discussed with examples and flows starting from synthesis through routing. This approach allows designers to specify and implement various design styles such as data paths, memories, clock networks, cross bars and any application where tight, ordered placement and routing is desired. This approach allows use of advanced placement and optimization algorithms implemented for general place and route tool seamlessly. Synthesis, mapping to target library can be controlled from hardware description language which supports structured placement constructs. Granularity of control can be as loose as standard cell random logic placement tightening all the way to almost a full custom design style. The blocks can be placed in a sea of gates with timing and placement of the internal cells visible to the rest of the design for global optimal placement and routing. The script based approach and easy interception of the design flow at various points and incremental placement and routing capabilities for structured designs provides ease of use and easy editing and modification capabilities. The language allows easy parameterization for different size blocks and reuse freeing the designer from tediousness of manually placing the cells legally and optimizing them every time when the design is changed.

This approach leads to quick convergence and achieves same or better results when compared to a solution of having specialized placement tool, saving huge amounts of time. This integrated methodology produces better quality of results when compared to unstructured placement when applied to designs suitable for structured placement. Additionally this approach makes structured placement ideas easily available for a larger pool of designs and designers, thus expanding the benefits of structured placement and routing for different and new applications enabling new functionalities for cores and end users.

Categories and Subject Descriptors

B 7.2 **[Design Aids]**: Layout, Placement and Routing

Keywords: Placement and Routing: Structured Placement: Data Path: Regularity Extraction: Clock Networks.

Short Bio:

Anand Arunachalam is currently a Principal Research and Development Engineer at Synopsys Inc. He received his M.S in Computer Science and Engineering from University of Michigan, Ann Arbor in 1994. He is leading the effort in developing technologies for structured placement and routing and Multi bit banking solutions in Synopsys Implementation tools.

Timing-Driven, Over-the-Block Rectilinear Steiner Tree Construction with Pre-Buffering and Slew Constraints

Yilin Zhang
ECE Department
University of Texas at Austin
Austin, TX 78712, USA
yzhang1@cerc.utexas.edu

David Z. Pan
ECE Department
University of Texas at Austin
Austin, TX 78712, USA
dpan@ece.utexas.edu

ABSTRACT

In this paper, we study a fundamental and crucial problem of building timing-driven over-the-block rectilinear Steiner tree (TOB-RST) with pre-buffering and slew constraints. We pre-characterize the tree topology and buffer distribution to provide accurate timing information for our final RST construction. In most previous work, the routing resources over the IP blocks were simply treated as routing blockages. Our TOB-RST could reclaim the "wasted" over-the-block routing resources while meeting user-specified timing (slack and slew) constraints. Before fixing topology, a topology-tuning is performed based on location of buffers to improve timing without increasing buffering cost. Experiments demonstrate that TOB-RST can significantly improve the worst negative slack (WNS) with even less buffering and wirelength compared with other slack-driven obstacle-avoiding rectilinear Steiner tree (SD-OARST) algorithms.

Categories and Subject Descriptors

B.7.2 [**Hardware,Integrated Circuit**]: Design Aids

General Terms

Algorithms, Design

Keywords

Over-the-block; Timing-driven RST; Slew Constraints

1. INTRODUCTION

As the semiconductor technology scales into deeper sub-micron domain, interconnection delay has become the dominant factor in determining circuit speed, contributing up to $50\% \sim 70\%$ of the clock cycle in high performance circuit [8]. Rectilinear Steiner tree (RST) is a fundamental tree structure to model the interconnection. Rectilinear Steiner minimum tree (RSMT) aims to minimize the wirelength. BOI [5], BI1S [10], RV-based RST [20] and FLUTE [7] are near-optimal RSMT heuristics while GeoSteiner [24] is optimal with reasonable runtime for small trees. Obstacle avoiding RSMT (OA-RSMT e.g. [2,12,17,18]) is one extension to RSMT, which avoids the pre-designed IP blocks and macros. More recently, [25] and [13] propose over-the-block RSMT (OB-RSMT) to properly use the routing resources over the pre-designed blocks in order to achieve better performance.

RSMT and related extensions produce good results regarding wirelength minimization, but they are not timing-optimal in deep sub-micron high-speed ICs. To help meet timing on critical paths, timing-driven RST is needed to optimize pin-to-pin delays on those paths. Approaches, such as [9,14,23], focus on the minimum delay routing tree (MDRT) problem which minimizes a linear combination of delays at sinks. Other approaches(e.g. [3,6,15]) are able to optimize the required arrival time at the driver as a more practical target. Besides, timing optimization and obstacle avoidance are simultaneously considered in [19], etc. However, most of the abovementioned timing-driven approaches have the following three problems:

1) In order to build an RST optimizing required arrival time at the driver, it is necessary to know the criticality at all sinks. The first problem is that most previous works (such as [3,19,21]) use simple estimation on arrival time and criticality for each sink, which is not accurate enough. For example in [3], an optimally buffered 2-pin direct connection from root to one node is used to estimate the potential delay; similarly in [21], the require arrival time is calculated based on distance from root to merging point, neglecting the coupling from other part of the tree. Estimation cannot fully capture interconnection delay, including delay on wires and buffers, decoupling effect by buffers and load capacitance from un-buffered branch, which would result in a sub-optimal timing-driven RST. One the other hand, a buffered tree with topology close enough to the final constructed tree could provide criticality at all sinks accurately. We propose a pre-buffering approach in place of estimation so as to provide more accurate timing information. During pre-buffering, a timing-driven RST is iteratively built and buffered to offer criticality information for the next generation of timing-driven RST until the tree topology converges.

As is shown in Fig.1, if only estimation is used, it would conclude that sink E is critical, resulting in the topology in Fig.1(a). However, if we insert buffers on the topology in Fig.1(a) and re-calculate criticality, we will find that sink D is as critical as E. Based on that finding, the new topology would re-clusters D with E with a direct connection to root S. Upon this new topology, a new buffer insertion is applied to re-calculate criticality at each sink. In this example, we find the set of critical sinks is not changed anymore and thus the topology converges to Fig.1(b) which has a better WNS since the slack on D is improved.

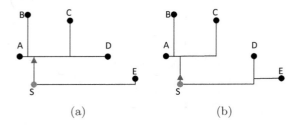

(a)　　　　　　　　(b)

Figure 1: (a) estimates only sink E is critical. (b) groups sink E and D as critical cluster.

2) From [25] and [13], it has been demonstrated that over-the-block RSMT (OB-RSMT) outperforms OA-RSMT in terms of wirelength. Over-the-block routing resources should be used in timing-driven RST construction as well to replace obstacle-avoiding detours with shorter over-the-block connection. In the meantime, certain slew constraints have to be satisfied for over-the-block routing to ensure the solution will not fail buffering. Fig. 2 compares obstacle-avoiding tree construction with over-the-block algorithm, in which the latter shifts part of the inside tree outside and keeps the remaining inside the block. As is shown in Fig.2(b), the algorithm reduces two buffers, some detouring wirelength and delay of paths in the tree.

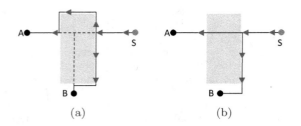

(a)　　　　　　　　(b)

Figure 2: (a) is an OA-RSMT with root S and two sinks A, B. (b) uses part of the over-the-block routing resources.

3) Following topology generation and buffering, it has never been discovered or discussed that a buffer-location-based tuning can achieve considerable timing improvement without consuming additional buffering cost and noticeable wirelength. During the buffering, in order to obtain a legal buffering solution, some buffers are placed at positions without fully using up their power. The proposed post-buffering tuning algorithm could tune the locations of Steiner points based on the buffering information to further improve slack. In Fig. 3(a), we observe that buffer $b2$ is clamped under the Steiner point D to shield part of the downstream capacitance of D. We can change the position of the Steiner point (Fig. 3(b)) which makes the sequential buffers $b1$ and $b2$ parallel. The delay of the path from root S to A is notably reduced since the path becomes a decoupled direct connection and delay on buffer b_1 is taken away. However in a traditional flow, it is hard to accurately predict these better buffer locations via only topology generation and buffering.

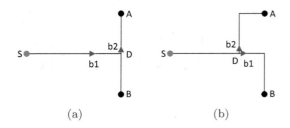

(a)　　　　　　　　(b)

Figure 3: (a) is a buffered RST with root S and two sinks A, B. (b) exhibits the tuned topology and new buffering.

Our work makes the following major contributions:

1. We first propose a timing-driven, over-the-block RST construction algorithm which utilizes over-the-block routing tracks to reduce delay to critical sinks and shorten wirelength to non-critical sinks.

2. Our constructed RST satisfies the slew constraints everywhere with buffers placed at empty space.

3. During the tree construction, we use pre-buffering scheme to provide more accurate timing information, which helps explore better topologies for timing-driven RST.

4. We analyze the final buffered tree and relocate certain Steiner points to further improve the delay on paths to critical sinks.

5. We conduct our algorithm and observe significant improvements in WS, wirelength and buffering cost compared with existing works.

The rest of paper is organized as follow. We first introduce basic concepts and our problem formulation in Section 2. Our timing-driven, over the-block RST construction algorithm will be presented in Section 3, which includes three subsections. Section 3.1 discusses how to use pre-buffering to guide the tree construction. Section 3.2 discusses how to use over-the-block routing resources to reduce delays on critical paths without violating slew constraints. modify BOB-RSMT to ensure slew for over-the-block part. Section 3.3 introduces the post-buffering topology tuning algorithm which achieves considerable timing improvement without consuming noticeable wirelength and buffering cost. Experimental results will be shown in Section 4, followed by conclusions in Section 5.

2. NOTATIONS AND PROBLEM FORMULATION

In a two-dimensional routing region, we are given a net $N = \{s_0, s_1, s_2, \ldots, s_n\}$ with $n + 1$ pins, where s_0 is the unique source and the rest are sinks. $L = \{b_1, b_2, \ldots, b_m\}$ is a set of non-overlapping rectilinear blocks in a two-dimensional space R. For $\forall~s_i \in N$, s_i is not inside the two-dimensional space occupied by L. Any area with high-density logic cells not allowed for buffering is also taken as buffering blockage into L.

Our algorithm constructs a timing-driven buffered tree $T(V, E)$ to connect all the pins in N, where V is the set of nodes and E is the set of horizontal and vertical edges.

T might intersect with blocks in L, which confines a set of trees $S = \{T_1, T_2, \ldots, T_l\}$ inside blocks. We call trees in S *inside trees*. The outside-the-block part of T is defined as T_0. The buffered tree $T_b(V_b, E_b)$ is generated from T after we insert a set of nodes V' which corresponds to the buffers chosen from buffer library B, and $V_b = V \cup V'$.

The Steiner tree has a unique path $P(s_0, s_i)$ from s_0 to each sink s_i. The presence of buffers along the path could separate the path into *stages*, each of which consists of a driver, a set of driven nodes as well as edges connecting the driver and the driven nodes. The total delay on a path is the summation of the delay on each stage along that path, which can be computed in many ways. As in this discussion, we adopt the Elmore model for wires and a switch-level linear model for gates. The models we adopt are simple and informative enough to guide our approach, yet our formulation is by no means restricted to these models. The delay of each stage in the path is expressed as:

$$t(d(u), u) = \sum_{e=(i,j) \in p(d(u), u)} r_e l_e (0.5 c_e l_e + C_u(j))$$
$$+ R_b C_d(d(u)) + D_b \quad (1)$$

Total delay of the path is the summation over all stages in the path:

$$d(s_0, s_i) = \sum_{u \in V' \cap p(s_0, s_i)} t(d(u), u) \quad (2)$$

The slack of sink s_i is defined as $slack(s_i) = RAT(s_i) - d(s_0, s_i)$. WS is defined as $WS(T) = min\{slack(s_i) | 1 \leq i \leq n\}$, and the worst negative slack is determined by $WNS(T) = min\{0, WS\}$. Notations amongst the formulation are as follows:

- l_e = length of edge e,
- r_e = unit length wire resistance on a chosen layer for edge e,
- c_e = unit length wire capacitance on a chosen layer for edge e,
- R_b = chosen buffer or source output resistance,
- C_b = chosen buffer or source input capacitance,
- D_b = internal buffer or source delay,
- $d(u)$ = the driver of node u,
- $t(u, v)$ = delay from node u to node v,
- $C_d(v)$ = total capacitance of the sub-tree rooted at node v down to the nearest downstream buffer or sinks, including the sink or buffer input capacitance,
- $C_u(v) = C_d(v)$ if v is not a buffer or source; C_b if v is a buffer or source node,

For slew calculation, we adopt the PERI model [16]:

$$S(v_j) = \sqrt{S(v_i)^2 + S_{step}(v_i, v_j)^2} \quad (3)$$

$S(v_j)$ is the slew at any node v_j, calculated as the root-mean square of the *step slew* from v_i to v_j and *output slew* at node v_i. The output slew at v_i is described by a 2-D lookup table of input slew and load capacitance. The experimental results in [16] show the error of PERI is within 1%, which is

indistinguishable from what is obtained using SPICE simulation. For simplicity, we use Bakoglu's metric [4] for step slew calculation:

$$S_{step}(v_i, v_j) = \alpha * Elmore(v_i, v_j), \alpha = ln9 \quad (4)$$

The combination of Bakoglu's metric and the PERI model is shown to have error within 4% [16], which is, in general, accurate enough for RST construction purpose.

Our algorithm will construct a buffered RST T to connect all sinks and root while ensuring the slew rate on every point in the tree is within constraints. We use *slew mode* buffering as our buffering scheme as it is more predominantly used ([11, 22]) and saves buffering cost. The slew mode buffering satisfies the slew constraints on every point of the buffered tree with minimum buffering cost. Our buffered tree will have edges over the blocks but no buffers are allowed over the blocks. The object is to minimize the WNS of the tree with the lowest buffering cost.

3. TIMING-DRIVEN OVER-THE-BLOCK RST

Our approach constructs a timing-driven, over-the-block RST with slew constraints. First, the approach uses coupled buffering and topology generation to provide AT and criticality at each sink. Then, a timing-driven RST is constructed based on pre-buffering. Second, the topologies of over-the-block trees are optimized to meet the slew constraints while maintaining the delay to critical sinks. Then, buffering is performed on the constructed tree structure. Finally, the constructed tree is tuned based on buffering information followed by buffering again. The overall algorithm of proposed approach is illustrated in Algorithm1.

Algorithm 1 *The overall algorithm*

Input: Set of pins N and blocks L
Output: Timing-driven over-the-block RST T
1: Construct timing-driven initial RST T with pre-buffering
2: Change the topology of T to meet the slew constraints
3: Perform buffering on T
4: Tune the topology of T based on buffering information
5: Perform buffering on T
6: **return** T

3.1 Initial Tree Generation with Pre-Buffering

Timing-driven RST requires the calculation of AT on each sink and might need RAT on internal nodes during the tree construction. Simple estimation of timing is inaccurate since there is no way to calculate the delay of un-constructed part of the tree or consider the final buffer distribution in the tree construction phase. Instead of using estimation, we apply pre-buffering to guide the tree construction.

Fig.4 depicts the proposed initial tree generation flow. We first generate a tree through any timing-driven RST algorithm. In this paper, we use state-of-the-art critical-trunk-based RST algorithm [19] to generate this initial tree (not considering blockages in this stage). Then pre-buffering part will buffer the RST and analyze timing. We save these topology and buffering if they are best-so-far. We calculate the real AT based on the buffered tree to substitute the pseudo time used in the tree topology generation algorithm as feedback information.

In the next iteration, all real critical sinks and critical trunks are re-determined because of the new timing information. In RST algorithm, we re-fix the critical trunks while

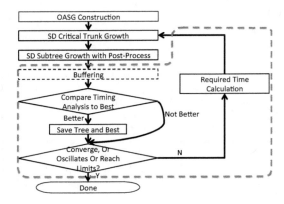

Figure 4: Flow of initial tree generation

the other two-pin nets are ripped up and re-routed by maze routing after the timing-driven critical trunk growth. Finally a post-process including rectilinearization and redirection is applied, which produces another RST. We will iterate

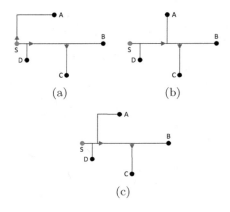

Figure 5: (a) is the initial critical trunk based tree with root S and sinks A,B,C,D. (b) reconstructs the tree according to the pre-buffering and timing information from (a). The tree topology converges in (c).

the whole procedure until the tree topology converges, or oscillates between several states, or the time limit is reached. Then we choose the best topology and WNS in our iterations as our initial tree. The new part of pre-buffering is indicated by dashed lines in Fig.4.

Example in Fig.5 shows that the topology and timing converge during the iterations. Initial structure in Fig.5(a) directly connects sink A to root as the RAT of A is small. In the next iteration, the topology generator decides to directly connect A to the trunk as in Fig.5(b), since according to Fig.5(a) the delay to A is small enough to meet the RAT, which in turn allows late branch. The late branch in Fig.5(b) leads to larger delay to sink A and eventually the topology converges to Fig.5(c) where the branch point of the path from root to A sits in the middle trunk leading to a star-like RSMT structure.

Table 1: Notation of variables in our formulation

X_{ij}	binary variable denoting the choice of PPS_{ij}^t, $X_{ij} = 1$ if it is chosen, otherwise $X_{ij} = 0$
E_{ij}	step slew reduction at EP_1^t if EP_i^t moves to PPS_{ij}
B_{ij}	output slew reduction on D^t if EP_i^t moves to PPS_{ij}
W_{ij}	estimated wirelength penalty of $\overline{EP_1^t}$ if EP_i^t moves to PPS_{ij}
C_i	estimated the timing criticality of EP_1^t

3.2 Buffering-Aware Over-the-Block Routing

We generate the initial tree without considering the blocks. The initial tree could cross over the blocks and break slew constraints even after buffer insertion. To prevent these violations, we change the topologies of over-the-block inside trees by approach similar to [25]. The objective in [25] is to minimize total wirelength only. Yet, in order to consider timing at the same time, we integrate criticality and slack into the objective function which minimize the wirelength of non-critical path as well as delay on critical path.

The initial tree confines a set of inside trees. For each inside tree, the ports, excluding the driver, on the boundaries of the block are called escaping points (EP). We use a mid-size hypothetical buffer at the driver and mid-size hypothetical buffers at each EP to determine if the tree has slew violation. Using mid-size hypothetical buffers instead of two extreme sizes will weaken the capability of utilizing more over-the-block routing resources, but the former turns out a more practical assumption and leads to less buffering cost as more solutions can propagate through this inside tree. If any inside tree violates the slew constraints, we apply three optimization primitives including parallel sliding, perpendicular sliding and EP merging [25] to fix the slew violations. Three optimization primitives are with different cost in our formulation since we consider timing as well.

For each inside tree t with slew violations, we first sort the illegal EPs per their slew violations. Next, in every iteration we choose the first illegal escaping point EP_1^t with the worst slew violation based on sorting. To improve slew for EP_1^t, each escaping point from $\{EP_1^t, EP_2^t, \ldots EP_{|EP^t|}^t\}$ may slide to a different position by taking a combination of primitives.

The combination of optimization primitives provides each escaping point a set of possible points. Each possible point in the set is a point on the boundary edge where escaping point may move to, which in turn improves the worst slew. Moving every escaping point to certain possible point guarantees $slew_1^t$ to meet slew requirement. In the extreme situation where maximum slew constraint is zero, EP_1^t can still become legal escaping point after we merge one escaping point to another until only the driver is left. For any non-fixed $EP_i^t \in \{EP^t\}$, the jth possible point associated with EP_i^t is denoted as PP_{ij}. PP_{ij} is stored in a 3-tuple format $\{E_{ij}, B_{ij}, W_{ij}\}$. E_{ij} and B_{ij} represent the step slew at EP_1^t and output slew reduction of the driver if EP_i moves to PP_{ij}. W_{ij} stands for the correspondingly estimated wirelength penalty. The possible point set associated with EP_i^t in the current iteration is denoted as PPS_i^t. $PPS_i^t = \{PP_{i1}^t, PP_{i2}^t, \ldots, PP_{ir}^t\}$, where r is the number of possible points inside.

In order to construct the inside tree under the slew constraint as well as meeting slack constraints, $\forall EP_i^t \in EP^t$ we need to decide which possible point to choose. The simultaneous point choice problem can be formulated in an optimization problem as follows (notation in Table 1):

$$\min. \sum_{i=1}^{|EP^t|} \sum_{j=1}^{|PPS_i^t|} X_{ij} W_{ij} (C_d(EP_i^t)C_i + \beta) \qquad (5)$$

$$\text{s.t.} (S_{step1}^t + \sum_{i=1}^{|EP^t|} \sum_{j=1}^{|PPS_i^t|} X_{ij} E_{ij}^t)^2 +$$

$$(S^t(D^t) + \sum_{i=1}^{|EP^t|} \sum_{j=1}^{|PPS_i^t|} X_{ij} B_{ij}^t)^2 <= {slew_{spec}^t}^2 \qquad (5a)$$

$$\sum_{j=1}^{|PPS_i^t|} X_{ij} = 1 \qquad \forall i \in \{1, 2, \ldots, |EP^t|\} \qquad (5b)$$

The objective function (5) is to minimize the increase in delay on the critical paths and wirelength on non-critical paths. $W_{ij}C_d(EP_i^t)$ is the multiplication of resistance and total downstream capacitance, which estimates the amount of increase in delay for every sink downstream from EP_i^t. $C_i = \sum_{s_k} |slack(s_k)|$ is the weight for critical paths below EP_i^t, summing all absolute values of negative slacks of sinks downstream from EP_i^t. The weight β in the objective function selects solution with less estimated wirelength penalty on non-critical paths. The value of β is set remarkably smaller than $C_d(EP_i^t)C_i$ to avoid affecting critical paths. This objective function prefers less change on the critical paths while [25] can choose to increase the wire on critical path and exacerbate the WNS. Through the change of formulation, our new formulation considers the delay on critical paths and wirelength of non-critical paths. One example is that Fig.6(c) is preferred to Fig.6(b) because the former reserves the timing for critical sink by moving escaping point on non-critical path to satisfy slew constraints. Constraint (5a) restricts that the total slew reduction on EP_i^t has to be able to pull $slew_1^t$ down below requirement. Constraint (5b) is used to limit only one position chosen for each escaping point.

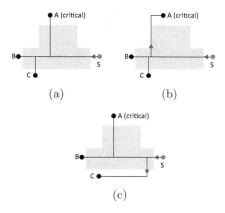

(a)

(b)

(c)

Figure 6: The root is S and three sinks are A, B, C. (a) is the initial timing-driven RST with slew violations. (b) fixes the slew violations with minimum wirelength penalty. (c) fixes the slew violations and considers the delay on critical path.

3.3 Timing-driven Buffer-location-based Tuning

We apply the slew mode buffering to the timing-driven, over-the-block RST, which satisfies slew constraints with minimum buffering cost. In the slew mode buffering, each buffer is desired to drive to its limit, implying that the worst slew rate among all receivers (buffers or sinks) should reach the slew limit. Similar to the concept of slack in timing calculation, we define *slew margin* which means the worst input slew rate among all receivers does not reach the slew limit. The existence of slew margin is because the driver or Steiner points in the tree topology may enforce the buffering solution to place one buffer to shield capacitance from one side.

3.3.1 Slew Margin

In a RST, a Steiner point is the joint point for at least two sub-branches to merge at. Before propagating buffer solutions through the Steiner point, each sub-branch will have an unbuffered segment connected to the Steiner point, such as OB, Ob_1 in Fig.7(a). These segments do not require buffers individually, but as a whole they may exceed the amount one large buffer can drive after propagating the Steiner point. The buffering tool has to place at least one buffer right below the Steiner point to shield one remaining segment to keep this solution legal. The buffering tool will place another buffer above the Steiner point to drive the unshielded parts along with the wire segment above the Steiner tree (this buffer can be saved if root is above the Steiner point with ability to drive). For instance, in fig.7(b), S is driver and O is a Steiner point. The segment OB is shielded by inserting a new buffer b_2. The shielding buffer b_2 will not drive to its limit as we already know that the length of driven segment is less than the optimal reach length. Therefore, the stage below b_2 ends up with slew margin. In Fig.7(a), the slew limit we adapt is 70ps, and the stage driven by b_2 exhibits slew margin with maximum slew 60ps at sink B. We also notice that the stage driven by driver S also has slew margin since the maximum slew is 65ps at the input of buffer b_1.

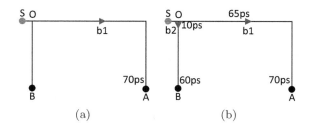

(a)

(b)

Figure 7: (a) bottom-up buffer solutions before merge at Steiner node O. (b) slew margin after propagation through Steiner node O

3.3.2 Buffer-location-based Tuning

Because the slew margin implies that the wire can be elongated to some extent without violating the slew constraints, the elongation of wires allows the change in topology without additional buffering cost. Per our approach, there exists a way of changing topology to improve timing on critical path by elongating the wire with slew margin. As the slew margin occurs below the Steiner point, we extracts the simplified pattern with one Steiner point and two buffers demonstrated in Fig.8(a). Buffer b_1 sits right below the Steiner point for shielding and buffer b_2 stays above the Steiner point as in Fig.8(a). We analyze this simplified pattern to generalize the way of changing topology used in our topology-tuning algorithm. We annotate the stage driven by b_1 as $stage_1$, that

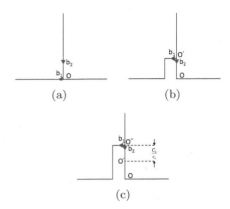

(a)   (b)

(c)

Figure 8: (a) depicts the pattern of slew margin. (b) shows buffer-location-based tuning if the input capacitance of buffers is negligible. (c) illustrates buffer-location-based tuning without neglecting the input capacitance of buffers.

driven by b_2 as $stage_2$ and that above b_2 as $stage_0$. Since $stage_1$ contains slew margin, we can calculate the elongation amount l to use up the slew margin. We denote the distance between b_2 and O as $l(b_2, O)$.

Observation I. If $l > l(b_2, O)$ and the input capacitance of buffers is negligible compared with wire capacitance, all slew constraints will be satisfied if we move the Steiner point to the location of b_2 and shift buffer b_1 up to the location right below the new location of the Steiner.

Fig.8(b) shows this buffer-location-based tuning. Under the assumption of negligible input capacitance of buffer, the load and slew of $stage_0$ are not changed. The slew of the $stage_1$ is still within constraints owing to $l > l(b_2, O)$.

Observation II. If $l > l(b_2, O) + C_b/c_e$ and the input capacitance of buffers is not neglected, we can keep all slew constraints satisfied by moving the Steiner point to C_b/c_e above b_2 and shifting buffer b_1 up to the location right below the new location of the Steiner node. (C_b is the input capacitance of buffer b_1 and c_e is the unit capacitance for the wire segment above b_2)

Fig.8(c) illustrates the topology and buffering after the relocation of Steiner point O to C_b/c_e above b_2 and buffer shifting. Because the wirelength above b_2 is curtailed by C_b/c_e, the downstream capacitance for $stage_0$ is reduced by $C_b/c_e * c_e$ accordingly. Buffer b_1 is attached to $stage_0$ during buffer-location-based tuning, including C_b into the downstream capacitance. Therefore the total downstream capacitance remains the same for $stage_0$. The amount of the downstream capacitance of $stage_2$ increases by $C_b/c_e * c_e$ as wire $O''O'$ is added below b_2. The input capacitance of

b_1 is removed from $stage_2$ where the downstream capacitance is reduced by C_b. Hence the total downstream capacitance below b_2 stays the same. Under the assumption $l > l(b_2, O) + C_b/c_e$, the slew of $stage_1$ is still under slew constraints.

Algorithm 2 *Buffer-location-based Tuning*

Input: Buffered tree T
Output: Timing improved buffered tree T
1: Sort sinks in ascending order of slack
2: **for** each sink s_i with negative slack **do**
3:   node $n = s_i$
4:   **while** $n! = s_0$ **do**
5:     **if** n is Steiner point **then**
6:       **if** find buffer buffers b_1 right below n and b_2 above n **then**
7:         Calculate l based on slew margin
8:         **if** $l > l(b_2, O) + C_b/c_e$ **then**
9:           $T_{copy} = T$
10:           Relocate n to C_b/c_e above b_2 and reconnect wires
11:           Shift buffer b_1 up to right below n
12:           **if** $WNS(T) <= WNS(T_{copy})$ **then**
13:             $T = T_{copy}$
14:           **end if**
15:         **end if**
16:       **end if**
17:     **end if**
18:     $n = Parent(n)$
19:   **end while**
20: **end for**
21: **return** T

3.3.3 Algorithms

Our proposed algorithm searches for the pattern which satisfies all the above assumptions. The algorithm scans the buffered topology in a bottom-up fashion. Once a pattern analyzed in Section3.3.2 is detected, we perform the abovementioned buffer-location-based tuning. The search starts from the worst negative slack sink among the set of sorted negative slack sinks. We evaluate the newly generated topology and commit the potential improvements. The algorithm is described in Algorithm2.

4. EXPERIMENTAL RESULTS

We have implemented our algorithm in the C++ programming language. The experiments are conducted on an Intel Core 3.0GHz Linux machine with 32GB memory. We choose Gurobi Optimizer 5.10 as our solver for the integer linear programming.

RC01-RC12 are benchmarks in our experiments, same as those in [19]. We use two sizes of buffers in our experiment. The output resistances for two buffers are 450 ohms and 850 ohms, and the input capacitance are 3.8 fF and 1.9 fF respectively. Environment settings for wire and slew are calculated based on ITRS [1]. We use different resistance and capacitance for both horizontal and vertical layers. Each Steiner tree is placed on pre-selected layers. The slew constraint is set as 70 ps. Since the benchmarks do not comprise any timing information, to test the effectiveness of the slack optimization in our approach, we set RAT such that about 15% of the sinks are with negative slack in a buffered minimum spanning tree interconnection.

We will evaluate pre-buffering, over-the-block routing and post-buffering tuning individually. We use the algorithm in [19] as baseline for our comparison since as far as we know it possesses state-of-the-art performance driven RST construction with buffering while others (such as [25] and [13])

Table 2: Comparisons between TOB-RST-1, TOB-RST-2 and TOB-RST

Bench -marks	Lin [19]			TOB-RST-1			TOB-RST-2			TOB-RST			
	WNS (ps)	Buff	WL (um)	WNS (ps)	Buff	WL (um)	WNS (ps)	Buff	WL (um)	WNS (ps)	Buff	WL (um)	CPU (s)
RC1	-86	32	30220	-86	32	30220	-34	31	29370	-34	31	29370	0.52
RC2	-206	58	55700	-157	54	50880	0	52	48750	0	52	48750	0.89
RC3	-160	77	75730	-141	71	64270	-92	63	59530	-92	63	59530	0.82
RC4	-347	80	76340	0	84	79720	0	76	72920	0	76	72920	0.85
RC5	-305	95	92650	-177	102	97570	-108	96	96570	-108	96	96570	1.03
RC6	-722	134	130055	-722	134	130055	-521	123	118342	-423	123	119545	1.26
RC7	-605	179	185064	-574	174	182188	-249	162	178504	-162	162	179051	3.08
RC8	-418	189	185320	-220	191	190775	0	175	176920	0	175	176920	4.51
RC9	-787	182	177603	-517	186	180089	-126	168	162815	0	168	167240	7.70
RC10	-455	203	210040	-272	206	211910	-23	198	205650	0	198	209908	6.85
RC11	-1268	259	282338	-1142	265	287312	-1027	262	284077	-965	262	285290	11.41
RC12	-1221	885	1107538	-1008	912	1144662	-687	881	1101521	-245	881	1108324	27.38
Average	-548	1	1	-418	1.02	1.02	-239	0.96	0.97	-169	0.96	0.98	5.525

are not timing-driven RST. We notate the timing-driven OA-RST constructed with pre-buffering as TOB-RST-1, the timing-driven RST with both pre-buffering, over-the-block routing as TOB-RST-2, and the final tree with pre-buffering, over-the-block routing and post-buffering tuning as TOB-RST.

4.1 Effectiveness of Pre-Buffering

First, to solely evaluate pre-buffering, we compare the performance of TOB-RST-1 with that of OA-RSMT generated by [19] in Table 2. Columns 5, 6, 7 in the table list the WNS, buffering cost and total wirelength of TOB-RST-1, while columns 2 to 4 present those for [19]. Since the required time of each sink is different in our experiments, the wirelength in column 2 is different from that of SD-OARST in [19]. As we can see, WNS is improved for most test cases, and the average improvement is 130 ps, while the change of buffering and wirelength is within 2%. The similarity of wirelength (buffering cost) demonstrates that the different set of critical sinks selected by pre-buffering benefits the slack with little impact on wirelength (buffering cost). In the experiments, the topologies of most benchmarks converge while only the topology of RC4 oscillates between two states and the better one of the two states is returned. Also, all of the benchmarks converge or oscillate remarkably fast within four iterations at most.

4.2 Over-the-Block RST

To evaluate the effectiveness of over-the-block routing in TOB-RST-2, we compare TOB-RST-2 with TOB-RST-1. Columns 5 to 7 in Table 2 illustrate the WNS, buffering cost and total wirelength of TOB-RST-1 while the columns 8 to 10 are for TOB-RST-2. As shown in the table, over-the-block routing can improve WNS for all benchmarks. The average WNS improved from over-the-block routing is 179 ps with buffering cost and wirelength reduced by 6% and 5% respectively.

4.3 Post-buffering Topology Tuning

We compare TOB-RST with TOB-RST-2 to evaluate the effectiveness of post-buffering topology tuning. We only apply buffer-location-based tuning on critical paths with negative slack. Columns 11 to 13 in Table 2 present the WNS, buffering cost and total wirelength of TOB-RST. TOB-RST acquires about 70 ps improvements in WNS on average with less than 1% more wirelength. The buffering cost is the same since the post-buffering topology tuning does not consume buffering resources. We include total CPU runtime for TOB-

RST algorithm in column 14 of Table 2, which contains total runtime of pre-buffering, over-the-block routing and post-buffering topology tuning. TOB-RST turns out to be fast since the maximum runtime is within one minute.

5. CONCLUSION

In this paper, we study a new class of RST problems, i.e., timing-driven over-the-block rectilinear Steiner minimum tree. We propose an effective and efficient algorithm which applies pre-buffering, over-the-block optimization and post-buffering tuning to optimize the slack on critical paths while saving wirelength on non-critical ones. Per our proposed approach, the generated topologies significantly improve WNS for all benchmarks along with 2% less wirelength and 4% less buffering cost than SD-OARST approach. Our proposed TOB-RST algorithm can be used in routing or post-routing stage to provide high-quality topologies to help close timing. This is the first work to solve timing-driven over-the-block RST problem crucial to high performance IC designs with multiple IP-blocks.

6. ACKNOWLEDGMENTS

This work is supported in part by Oracle. The authors would like to thank Dr. Salim Chowdhury and Dr. Akshay Sharma from Oracle for helpful discussions.

7. REFERENCES

[1] 2012 Overall Roadmap Technology Characteristics (ORTC) Tables. http://www.itrs.net/Links/2012ITRS/Home2012.htm.

[2] G. Ajwani, C. Chu, and W. Mak. FOARS: FLUTE Based Obstacle-Avoiding Rectilinear Steiner Tree Construction. In *Proc. ISPD*, pages 194–204, 2010.

[3] C. J. Alpert, M. Hrkic, J. Hu, A. B. Kahng, J. Lillis, B. Liu, S. T. Quay, S. S. Sapatnekar, A. J. Sullivan, and P. Villarrubia. Buffered Steiner Trees for Difficult Instances. In *Proc. ISPD*, pages 4–9, 2001.

[4] H. B. Bakoglu. Circuits, interconnections, and packaging for VLSI. Addison-Wesley, 1990.

[5] M. Borah, R. M. Owens, and M. J. Irwin. An edge-based heuristic for Steiner routing. *IEEE TCAD*, 13(12):1563–1568, 1994.

[6] Chung-Kuan Cheng, Ting-Ting Y. Lin, and Ching-Yen Ho. New performance driven routing techniques with explicit area/delay tradeoff and simultaneous wire sizing. In *Proc. DAC*, pages 395–400, 1996.

[7] C. Chu and Y. Wong. FLUTE: Fast Loopup Table Based Rectilinear Steiner Minimal Tree Algorithm for VLSI Design. *IEEE TCAD*, 27(1):70–83, 2008.

[8] J. Cong, L. He, K. Khoo, C. K., and D. Z. Pan. Interconnect Design for Deep Submicron ICs. In *Proc. ICCAD*, pages 478–485, 1997.

[9] J. Cong, K. Leung, and D. Zhou. Performance-Driven Interconnect Design Based on Distributed RC Delay Model. In *Proc. DAC*, pages 606–611, 1993.

[10] J. Griffith, G. Robins, J. S. Salowe, and T. Zhang. Closing the gap: Near-optimal Steiner trees in polynomial time. *IEEE TCAD*, 13(11):1351–1365, 1994.

[11] S. Hu, C.J. Alpert, J. Hu, S.K. Karandikar, Z. Li, W. Shi, and C.N. Sze. Fast algorithms for slew-constrained minimum cost buffering. *IEEE TCAD*, 26(11):2009–2022, 2007.

[12] T. Huang and E. F. Young. An Exact Algorithm for the construction of Rectilinear Steiner Minimum Trees among Complex Obstacles. In *Proc. DAC*, pages 164–169, 2011.

[13] T. Huang and E. F.Y. Young. Construction of rectilinear Steiner minimum trees with slew constraints over obstacles. In *Proc. ICCAD*, pages 144–151, 2012.

[14] k. D. Boese, A. B. Kahng, B. A. McCoy, and G. Robins. Rectilinear Steiner Trees with Minimum Elmore Delay. In *Proc. DAC*, pages 381–386, 1994.

[15] A. B. Kahng and B. Liu. Q-Tree: A New Iterative Improvement Approach for Buffered Interconnect Optimization. In *Proc. IEEE Annual Symp. on VLSI*, pages 183–188, 2003.

[16] C. V. Kashyap, C. J. Alpert, F. Liu, and A. Devgan. Closed Form Expressions for Extending Step Delay and Slew Metrics to Ramp Inputs. In *Proc. ISPD*, pages 24–31, 2003.

[17] L. Li, Z. Qian, and E. F. Young. Generation of Optimal Obstacle-avoiding Rectilinear Steiner Minimum Tree. In *Proc. ICCAD*, pages 21–25, 2009.

[18] L. Li and E. F. Young. Obstacle-avoiding Rectilinear Steiner Tree Construction. In *Proc. ICCAD*, pages 523–528, 2008.

[19] Y. Lin, S. Chang, and Y. Li. Critical-trunk-based obstacle-avoiding rectilinear Steiner tree routings and buffer insertion for delay and slack optimization. *IEEE TCAD*, 30(9):1335–1348, 2011.

[20] Ion I. Mandoiu, Vijay V. Vazirani, and Joseph L. Ganley. A new heuristic for rectilinear Steiner trees. *IEEE TCAD*, 19(10):1129–1139, 2000.

[21] T. Okamoto and J. Cong. Interconnect Layout Optimization by Simultaneous Steiner Tree Construction and Buffer Insertion. In *Proc. Asia and South Pacific Design Automation Conf.*, pages 44–49, 1996.

[22] P. J. Osler. placement driven synthesis case studies on two sets of two chips: hierarchical and flat. In *Proc. ISPD*, pages 190–197, 2004.

[23] M. Pan, C. Chu, and P. Patra. A Novel Performance-Driven Topology Design Algorithm. In *Proc. Asia and South Pacific Design Automation Conf.*, pages 244–249, 2007.

[24] D. M. Warme, P. Winter, and M. Zachariasen. Exact algorithms for plane steiner tree problems: a computational study, 2000.

[25] Y. Zhang, A. Chakraborty, S. Chowdhury, and D. Z. Pan. Reclaiming Over-the-IP-Block Routing Resources With Buffering-Aware Rectilinear Steiner Minimum Tree Construction. In *Proc. ICCAD*, pages 137–143, 2012.

A Fast Algorithm for Rectilinear Steiner Trees with Length Restrictions on Obstacles

Stephan Held and Sophie Theresa Spirkl
Research Institute for Discrete Mathematics
Lennéstr. 2
53113 Bonn, Germany
{held,spirkl}@or.uni-bonn.de

ABSTRACT

We study the minimum rectilinear Steiner tree problem in the presence of obstacles. Traversing obstacles is not strictly forbidden, but the total length of each connected component in the intersection of the tree with the interior of the blocked area is bounded by a constant.

This problem is motivated by the layout of repeater tree topologies, a central task in chip design. Large blockages might be crossed by wires on higher layers, but repeaters may not be placed within the blocked area. A too long unbuffered piece of interconnect would lead to timing violations.

We present a 2-approximation algorithm with a worst case running time of $\mathcal{O}((k \log k)^2)$, where k is the number of terminals plus the number of obstacle corner points. Under mild assumptions on the obstacle structure, as they are prevalent in chip design, the running time is $\mathcal{O}(k(\log k)^2)$. Compared to strictly obstacle-avoiding trees, the algorithm provides significantly shorter solutions. It solves real world instances with 783 352 terminals within 126 seconds, proving its practical applicability.

Categories and Subject Descriptors

B.7.2 [**Integrated Circuits:**]: Design Aids

Keywords

Steiner tree; obstacle-aware; interconnect planning; buffering

1. INTRODUCTION

The computation of Steiner topologies for buffering is a central task in VLSI design [2, 3, 8]. Buffering is often restricted by macro cells, where no repeaters can be placed. This holds particularly for top-level layout that is dominated by big macros leaving only small gaps for buffers.

The wires, on the other hand, may well reach over the macros on higher routing layers. However, if an unbuffered component of wire gets too long, it will lead to capacitances, slew, or delay violations. This motivates bounding the length of tree components on top of macros.

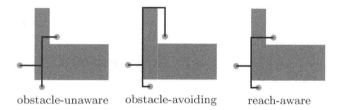

obstacle-unaware   obstacle-avoiding   reach-aware

Figure 1: Optimum solutions for different reach-lengths.

Given a finite set of rectilinear obstacles in the plane and a reach-length $L \geq 0$, a set of axis-parallel segments is called *reach-aware*, if the total length of every connected component of its intersection with the interior of the *blocked area* (the closed union of all obstacles) has length at most L. This definition of reach-awareness is motivated by the assumption that a repeater can be placed arbitrarily close to the boundary of the blocked area, but not in its interior. We call a point *blocked* if it is in the interior of the blocked area.

The *reach-aware Steiner tree problem* (RASTP) is also known as the *length restricted Steiner tree problem*, introduced by Müller-Hannemann and Peyer [16]. The input consists of a finite set $S \subset \mathbb{R}^2$ of terminals, a finite set O of rectangular obstacles such that no terminal is placed in the interior of the blocked area $(s \cap (\bigcup_{o \in O} o)^\circ = \emptyset$ for all $s \in S)$, and a parameter $L \in \mathbb{R}_{\geq 0}$. The goal is to find a shortest reach-aware rectilinear Steiner tree connecting these terminals.

For $L = \infty$ or $O = \emptyset$, the RASTP becomes the rectilinear Steiner tree problem, thus it is NP-hard. For $L = 0$, it is known as the *obstacle-avoiding rectilinear Steiner tree problem* [7]. Figure 1 shows examples of a minimum obstacle-unaware tree ($L = \infty$) with a large blocked component, a minimum obstacle-avoiding tree ($L = 0$) taking a long detour, and a minimum reach-aware tree, where only the thin vertical obstacle can be passed by the choice of L.

There is extensive literature on fast algorithms for the case $L = 0$, which typically provide an approximation guarantee of two, the Steiner-ratio in graphs, [6, 12, 13, 14]. Our algorithm is based on the early work of Clarkson et al. [5], which introduced the notion of a visibility graph containing shortest paths between all pairs of terminals and obstacle corner points (for $L = 0$). Its size is bounded by $\mathcal{O}(k \log k)$ and it can be constructed in $\mathcal{O}(k(\log k)^2)$ time, where $k = |S| + |O|$. The currently most efficient exact algorithms for $L = 0$ can be found in [10].

For arbitrary L, [16] developed approximation algorithms based on an augmented Hanan grid. The size of this grid, bounded by $\mathcal{O}(k^2)$, is denoted by l. Using a minimum spanning tree heuristic, they present an $\mathcal{O}(l \log l)$ algorithm with an approximation ratio of 2. Under the additional assumption that all blockages are disjoint rectangles, they refine their construction further, obtaining approximation guarantees of $\frac{5}{4}\alpha$ and $\frac{2s}{2s-1}\alpha$ for $s \geq 4$ with graph size $\mathcal{O}(l)$ and $\mathcal{O}(l^{s-2})$, respectively, where α is the performance guarantee of a Steiner tree algorithm in graphs. However, their results are predominantly of theoretical interest, since even their 2-approximation algorithm would be very slow in practice due to the quadratic size of the Hanan grid.

Our problem is related to [9], who consider slew constraints instead of a reach-length L and provide an exact algorithm for this problem. In the RASTP, the reach-length can be used to bound the slew degradation on wires, though not as precisely as in [9]. However, we believe that it enables simpler and faster algorithms that are more suitable for a quick processing of the majority of nets.

A similar problem was also considered by [17], who incrementally update a rectilinear Steiner minimum tree to satisfy slew constraints. However, they do not give any performance guarantee for the approximation quality or running time.

Our algorithm produces short trees, but does not balance source-sink path lengths within the tree. However, in combination with the shallow light Steiner arborescence algorithm in [8] it can easily be extended to provide not only short but also fast reach-aware Steiner trees.

Note that for our definition, the restriction due to obstacles depends only on the blocked area and is independent of its representation by a union of rectangles. It differs from the one used in many recent publications on obstacle-avoiding rectilinear Steiner trees even for $L = 0$. For example, [10, 9] consider line segments on which two (polygonal) obstacles touch as not blocked and specifically only consider rectangular blockages. This definition depends on the particular representation of the blockages by polygons or rectangles. As no buffers can be placed on a line between two obstacles, we consider our definition more appropriate for our application.

In Section 3, we will see that one of the standard benchmarks for obstacle-avoiding trees contains a terminal isolated by a ring of obstacles and becomes infeasible with our definition and $L = 0$ (see Figure 6), which was also noted by [17], whereas in [10, 9] this instance is reported as feasible due to their different definition of the blocked area. It should be noted that the approach in [10, 9] and many other publications would be adjustable to our definition (and $L = 0$).

In addition, our definition allows to compress or modify the representation of obstacles for the needs of the algorithm or its subroutines. In the following, we can assume that all obstacles are given as rectangles with pairwise disjoint interior and unblocked rectangle corners, e.g. by covering the blocked area with rectangles of maximal width.

Finally, we can naturally model rectilinear polygons with rectilinear holes, which are often left out of big macros to serve particularly as buffer positions.

The remainder of the paper is organized as follows. In Section 2 we will give a detailed description of our algorithm. The performance on standard benchmarks as well as on practical instances is demonstrated in Section 3, followed by a conclusion in Section 4.

2. ALGORITHM

Our algorithm has two main phases: First, we construct a shortest-path-preserving graph (*visibility graph*) for the set of *endpoints*, by which we denote the union of the terminals S and the corner points of obstacles. In this graph, we use a Dijkstra-Kruskal approach [13] to compute a Steiner tree for the terminal set S. Simple local search heuristics are used as a post-optimization step.

The approximation ratio of this algorithm is at most two, since the computed Steiner tree is as most as long as a minimum terminal spanning tree in the visibility graph.

2.1 Reach-Aware Visibility Graph

The concept of a visibility graph for dealing with paths among polygonal obstacles was first introduced by Clarkson et. al. [5] for the obstacle-avoiding case. It is based on the key idea that every shortest path can be modified (while preserving the length) in such a away that it consists of shortest paths from one endpoint (terminal or blockage corner point) to another and the interior of the bounding box of two consecutive endpoints intersects neither blockages nor terminals. We will prove similar results for the reach-aware case, and based on that, give a precise construction of our visibility graph in the next section.

The construction then ensures that between each pair of endpoints, there is a so called *median line*, a vertical line to which both endpoints are connected by a horizontal segment (if possible). If the bounding box is completely unblocked, this is always possible. Using the argument above, this construction is indeed shortest-path-preserving. Note that horizontal instead of vertical median lines could be used equivalently.

For the reach-aware case, there is a similar result about ℓ_1-shortest paths, i.e. paths whose length equals the ℓ_1-distance of their endpoints:

LEMMA 1. *Given a set of rectilinear obstacles, a set of terminals in the plane, and a parameter L, any shortest path between two points w.r.t. the ℓ_1-norm that is reach-aware can be modified so that the bounding box of two consecutive endpoints on the path does not contain another endpoint. This modification preserves length and reach-awareness.*

In the remainder of the paper, we will often use the notion of empty bounding boxes.

DEFINITION 2 (EMPTY BOUNDING BOX). *Given points $s, t \in \mathbb{R}^2$, their bounding box is called* empty *if it does not contain any endpoints except for (potentially) s or t.*

Note that empty bounding boxes may intersect blockages whose endpoints are located outside the box. The emptiness of a bounding box also depends on its boundary, thus it depends on the choice of its spanning corners s and t.

PROOF OF LEMMA 1. Let s and t be two points with non-empty bounding box and P an ℓ_1-shortest s-t-path that is reach-aware; without loss of generality let $s = (0,0)$ and $t = (x, y)$ with $x, y > 0$. Consider the set of endpoints in the bounding box of s and t. For these points, we define a staircase as the boundary of the (not necessarily closed) region of all $r \in \mathbb{R}^2_{\geq 0}$ such that the bounding box of s and r is empty (see Figure 2(a), staircase shown in purple). Let q be the first intersection point (starting from s) of P (black path) with this staircase as in Figure 2(b). Consider

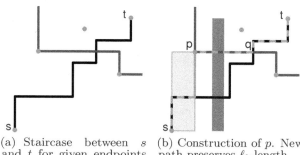

(a) Staircase between s and t for given endpoints (green); P is drawn schematically.

(b) Construction of p. New path preserves ℓ_1-length.

Figure 2: Subdivision of P for the proof of Lemma 1.

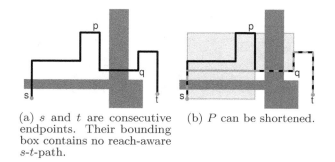

(a) s and t are consecutive endpoints. Their bounding box contains no reach-aware s-t-path.

(b) P can be shortened.

Figure 3: Configuration in the proof of Theorem 3.

Figure 4: Obstacle corner (green disk) and its mirror point (blue square).

the bounding box of q and s. By the choice of q, there is at least one endpoint on its boundary. Among these let p be the one closest to s. Modify P to pass through this point (light blue path) and note that the length remains the same. Furthermore, the bounding box of p and s is empty.

P remains reach-aware, because blockages intersecting the bounding box of s and q have a very simple structure; in fact, – because there can be no corner in its interior – all of them have to intersect the entire bounding box either in a vertical (as shown) or horizontal rectangle whose endpoints lie on the outside. Either way, the blockages must have intersected P before, and the intersected length of the new path with the blockage is minimal; since P was reach-aware, so is the new path. Inductive application of this modification to the rest of P between p and t transforms P into the desired form in at most $\mathcal{O}(|S| + |O|)$ steps. $\square$

This can be generalized to reach-aware shortest paths:

THEOREM 3. *Given a set of rectilinear obstacles, a set of terminals in the plane, and a parameter L, any path P between two endpoints that is reach-aware and shortest possible can be modified so that the bounding box of two consecutive endpoints on the path is empty, and P restricted to that bounding box is an ℓ_1-shortest path. This modification preserves length and reach-awareness.*

PROOF (SKETCH). We begin by applying Lemma 1 to all path segments of P that are ℓ_1-shortest paths. Now consider two consecutive endpoints s and t such that the path between them is not an ℓ_1-shortest path. We will show that P is not shortest possible. As a result, if we know that the path between two consecutive endpoints is always ℓ_1-shortest, the theorem follows from Lemma 1.

Let p be the last point on P from s to t such that the path from s to p is an ℓ_1-shortest path; let q be the last point or t (whichever comes first) from p to t on P such that pq is an ℓ_1-shortest path. Note that $p \neq t$ is not an endpoint, but $q = t$ is possible.

By our initial application of the previous lemma, we know that the bounding boxes of s and p and p and q are empty.

From the proof of Lemma 1, it is clear that between s and any point in the bounding box of s and p there is a reach-aware ℓ_1-shortest path, so q cannot be in that bounding box, because by choice of p and q, spq is not an ℓ_1-shortest path and replacing spq by sq would make P shorter and preserve reach-awareness, a contradiction.

If the bounding boxes of s and p and p and q intersect only in p, then sq is an ℓ_1-shortest path, which is a contradiction

to our choice of p. Hence, the bounding boxes must intersect in a line segment as in Figure 3.

As in the previous lemma, since we know that the gray shaded bounding boxes are empty, any blockage intersected by the modified path must be intersected by spq for at least as long a segment. The new path (shown in light blue) is therefore reach-aware, and an ℓ_1-shortest s-q-path; it is strictly shorter than spq. Therefore, P is not shortest possible, which concludes the proof. $\square$

With this theorem, a construction similar to Clarkson et al. [5] can produce a reach-aware visibility graph. However, further caution is required in this case, because we must guarantee that any Steiner tree extracted from the visibility graph is reach-aware. This entails more than ensuring that any edge is reach-aware, because several edges may belong to the same connected component when intersected with the interior of the blocked area.

A simple solution to this is forbidding blocked Steiner points, and making sure that every edge is reach-aware. Together with the condition that there is a shortest path (if it exists) between any two vertices with empty bounding box in the visibility graph, this implies the correctness of the second part of our algorithm.

In the obstacle-avoiding case as in [5], it is always possible to insert a median line and connecting segments if the bounding box of two endpoints is empty (and such a connection does not cross blocked area). Here, this does not hold and we have to develop a more elaborate construction.

First we extend the set of endpoints. As endpoints are connected to median lines via horizontal lines only, we provide vertical edges across blocked area in the following way.

If an obstacle corner is at the lower or upper boundary of the blocked area and the vertical connection across the blocked area to the next unblocked point has length bounded by L, we add that point and connect the two (see Figure 4). In the following we call such a connection point a *mirror point*, and add all mirror points to the (extended) set of endpoints

$$\mathcal{E} := \{ \text{ endpoints and mirror points } \}.$$

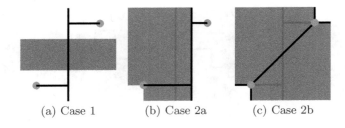

| (a) Case 1 | (b) Case 2a | (c) Case 2b |

Figure 5: Configurations in an empty bounding box.

Each obstacle corner has at most one mirror point, because if both vertical connections are in the interior of the blocked area, so is the obstacle corner, a contradiction.

Now, assume that there is an ℓ_1-shortest reach-aware path between two points in $\mathcal{E}$ with empty bounding box (w.r.t. $\mathcal{E}$), then the following three cases can occur:

1. If the median line is unblocked at the y-coordinate of one endpoint, it must be unblocked at the y-coordinate of the other endpoint (by the insertion of the mirror points). We simply connect the endpoints to the median (Figure 5(a)).

2. If the median is blocked at the y-coordinates of the endpoints, there are two possibilities.

   (a) We can connect at least one of them horizontally across and project the other to the boundary of the blocked area (Figure 5(b)),

   (b) No horizontal connections across the blocked area are possible. If the points can see each other, i.e. their ℓ_1-distance is less than L, we connect them (Figure 5(c)).

The black lines in Figure 5 show the new construction, the shaded black lines are the median and connecting lines that would be inserted without blockages.

Note that we call those points arising from vertical connections across blocked area mirror points and add them to $\mathcal{E}$. Horizontal connections will be added to the graph, but not to $\mathcal{E}$.

2.2 Visibility Graph Construction

Now we will show how to efficiently find a graph with the properties stated in the previous section. The main idea in [5] is to introduce the median lines recursively, i.e. to insert a median line at the median of all x-coordinates of the endpoints (and thus between every pair of endpoints such that one of them is to the left and one is to the right of the line), add a horizontal line from each endpoint to the median and introduce a Steiner point on the median line, if it is obstacle-avoiding, connect consecutive Steiner points on the median if possible, and then continue with the sets of endpoints left and right of the line separately. We will use a similar construction here.

In order to insert median lines efficiently, we need to know which endpoints can be connected to the median line by a horizontal segment, i.e. which endpoints can "see" the median. In the reach-aware case, there are further complications when the median is blocked by a (small) obstacle – even if an endpoint can see the median, the horizontal segment from

Function 1 Preprocessing

1: Compute connected components of blocked area.
2: Compute $\mathcal{E}$.
3: For every $p \in \mathcal{E}$, compute its visible interval.

the endpoint to the median line might intersect it in a blocked point, thus we cannot introduce a Steiner point there.

Much of the required information can be computed in preprocessing. We define the *visible interval* of an endpoint $p \in \mathcal{E}$ as the maximum horizontal read-aware line through p, which is well-defined as p is unblocked as an endpoint. This allows us to check if an endpoint can see a median line in constant time, independently of the size of the visible interval or the number of obstacles intersecting it.

Therefore, the steps in Function 1 are done as preprocessing using a sweepline algorithm:

In the obstacle-avoiding case, a horizontal sweepline that stores the obstacles in a binary search tree is sufficient. The reach-aware case is more complicated; here we have two binary search trees, one storing all blocked intervals and one only storing blocked intervals of width at least L. This allows insertion and deletion in $\mathcal{O}(\log |O|)$ time, as well as detecting visibility, and makes it possible to precompute visible intervals (horizontal sweepline) and mirror points (vertical sweepline) in $\mathcal{O}((|S| + |O|) \log |O|)$ time. This data structure, but with a vertical sweepline, is also used for determining visibility on the median later in the algorithm, i.e. in Function 2.

At the core of the algorithm is the INSERT_MEDIAN function (Function 2), which deals with the construction discussed in Section 2.1. The recursive insertion of median lines is implemented from left to right, so that our sweepline can keep track of the obstacles on the median. The set M in Function 2 represents the set of points on the current obstacle on the median that cannot see across horizontally, i.e. the points that are relevant for the case in Figure 5(c).

The overall construction of the visibility graph is given in Algorithm 3, where in a post-processing step vertices along a common obstacle boundary are connected, so that all the necessary connections for Figure 5(b) exist.

2.3 Steiner Tree Construction

Given a visibility graph $G = (V, E)$, we are now interested in extracting a Steiner tree. Since G is shortest-path-preserving, any minimum terminal spanning tree routine will provide an approximation guarantee of two. In our implementation, Steiner trees are found in $\mathcal{O}(|E| \log |E|)$ time using a Dijkstra-Kruskal approach from [13]. We also applied Mehlhorn's algorithm [15], with a faster running time of $\mathcal{O}(|E| + |V| \log |V|)$, but found it slower in practice.

This Steiner tree is a 2-approximation of an optimal reach-aware Steiner tree, because it is at most as long as a reach-aware minimum spanning tree. In fact, since Steiner points on obstacles are forbidden, is it a 2-approximation algorithm for a less restrictive version of the problem wherein the longest path across blocked area has length $\leq L$, since both problems coincide for minimum spanning trees and our solution is feasible for both.

2.4 Running Time

In the following, n will denote the number of terminals and m will denote the number of rectangles. For $L = 0$, this

Function 2 INSERT_MEDIAN($\mathcal{E}$)

1: Take the median x_m of the x-coordinates of $\mathcal{E}$.
2: INSERT_MEDIAN($\{(x,y) \in \mathcal{E} : x < x_m\}$)
3: Introduce a median line $L_m := \{(x_m, y) \ : \ y \in \mathbb{R}\}$.
4: $M = \emptyset$.
5: **for** every $p = (x,y) \in \mathcal{E}$ in non-incr. order of y **do**
6:    **if** (x_m, y) is not blocked and visible from p **then**
7:       Add new vertex (x_m, y) and edge $\{(x_m, y), p\}$.
8:       On the median line, connect (x_m, y) to the
        previous one $((x_m, y'))$ if existing and possible.
9:       $M = \emptyset$.
10:    **else**
11:       Let $[x_l, x_r] \ni x_m$ be the maximum interval s.t.
        the point (x', y) is blocked for all $x' \in [x_l, x_r]$.
12:       $r := \arg\max\{||p - p'||_1 \ : \ p' \in \{(x_l, y), (x_r, y)\}\}$.
13:       $q := \arg\min\{||p - p'||_1 \ : \ p' \in \{(x_l, y), (x_r, y)\}\}$.
14:       **if** p can see q **then**
15:          Add q and connect p with q.
16:       **end if**
17:       **if** p can (also) see r **then**
18:          Add r and connect q with r.
19:       **else if** $x = x_l$ or $x = x_r$ is corner **then**
20:          Connect p to all $p' \in M$ with $||p - p'||_1 \leq L$
21:          Add p to M
22:       **end if**
23:    **end if**
24: **end for**
25: INSERT_MEDIAN($\{(x,y) \in \mathcal{E} : x > x_m\}$)

Algorithm 3 Visibility graph construction

1: Preprocessing (Function 1).
2: Sort obstacles and initialize empty sweepline of obstacles
   on the median
3: INSERT_MEDIAN($\mathcal{E}$)
4: Connect points along obstacle boundaries

---

algorithm has a running time of $\mathcal{O}((n + m)(\log(m + n))^2)$ [5]. For $L > 0$, the running time can be bounded as follows: Let $k = n + m$. The preprocessing in Function 1 is done by our sweepline in $\mathcal{O}(k \log k)$.

The INSERT_MEDIAN function is called k times; each point is in the current set $\mathcal{E}$ for at most $\log_2 k$ medians. Thus, the for loop in lines 5–24 of this function is executed an amortized $\mathcal{O}(k \log k)$ times. Every step in the for loop takes at most $\mathcal{O}(\log k)$, except for line 20. This line takes $\mathcal{O}(n + m)$, which is an upper bound on the size of M. If M has size at most l, the running time of the visibility graph construction is bounded by $\mathcal{O}((k \log k)(l + \log k))$.

The number of vertices of the visibility graph is bounded by $\mathcal{O}(k \log k)$, because the number of mirror points is linear and the number of Steiner points is $\mathcal{O}(k \log k)$ – for each endpoint, a constant number of Steiner points is added every time it is in the set $\mathcal{E}$. The number of edges is bounded by $\mathcal{O}(kl \log k)$.

Constructing the Steiner tree from the visibility graph therefore takes $\mathcal{O}(kl \log k(\log k + \log l))$ time. In the worst case, with k the only upper bound on l, the algorithm has a running time of $\mathcal{O}(k^2(\log k)^2)$. However, this is rarely the case in practice (as is evident from the running times in the next section): If the complexity of each rectilinear polygon is bounded by a constant, the set M in INSERT_MEDIAN has

constant size, hence there are $\mathcal{O}(k \log k)$ edges and vertices in the visibility graph and the running time is $\mathcal{O}(k(\log k)^2)$ as in the obstacle-avoiding case.

2.5 Preprocessing of Obstacles

In practice, the running time of the algorithm can be decreased significantly, especially for large L, by preprocessing the obstacles and ignoring those that can never make our solution infeasible. If the diameter of an isolated rectangular obstacle is bounded by L, it could be ignored and a post-processing routine could replace non-reach-aware tree components on that obstacle by segments of its boundary.

We propose a different approach: If half the diameter of a rectangular obstacle is at most L, then a shortest path across this obstacle is always reach-aware. Therefore, we can ignore these obstacles during the construction of the visibility graph, and forbid Steiner points with a degree of more than three on obstacles during the MTST construction. This is slower in theory, but more efficient in practice, because the visibility graph construction takes up the majority of the running time.

The restriction that no Steiner points are allowed on obstacles does not affect the theoretical approximation guarantee and actually yields very useful solutions for applications in buffering: Buffers are often necessary at bifurcations to shield uncritical capacity, which is impossible if these occur on top of an obstacle.

Using these observations, many small rectangular obstacles can be ignored for the visibility graph construction. For sufficiently large L, constructing an ℓ_1-Steiner tree built by an obstacle-unaware heuristic initially and checking feasibility leads to better results and running times of our algorithm.

2.6 Post-Processing

Since the visibility graph only contains certain shortest paths, we found that a combination of simple local search heuristics can significantly improve the result for most instances.

Especially on practical instances, we often encountered large clusters of terminals in an unblocked area. For those, any (obstacle-unaware) Steiner tree algorithm could be used instead. Therefore, in post-processing, we collect maximal components of the constructed tree with unblocked bounding box and reconnect them using the exact FLUTE algorithm [4] for up to 9 terminals and a Prim heuristic in the Delaunay triangulation for larger terminal sets.

Furthermore, there some non-optimal local configurations, such as trunks with more branches on one side and L-shapes that can be mirrored to decrease the length, can be found and processed efficiently for the entire tree by changing the edge structure locally if the resulting tree is reach-aware.

This procedure can be iterated for better results; in our experience, a good trade-off of running time and solution quality is achieved by one iteration for chip instances and three iterations for benchmark instances.

2.7 Multiple Nets

In chip design, there is usually a persistent set of obstacles, but thousands or millions of nets. Many nets consist of only two or three terminals and it would be too time-consuming to compute the visibility graph from scratch for each net. Therefore, we proceed as follows when processing all nets of a chip: Some preprocessing steps are independent of the terminal set and can be precomputed for all nets. Using this information, we construct an obstacle visibility graph, i.e. a visibility graph for an empty set of terminals. This obstacle graph can be extended to a visibility graph for a given set of terminals by inserting a new median line through every terminal and connecting all obstacle endpoints and other terminals to this line (if possible). This preserves the visibility graph invariant of having a median line between each pair of endpoints with empty bounding box containing an ℓ_1-shortest path between them.

This construction is most useful if a net has few terminals and L is small. In our experience, the number of terminals for which this construction is applied should be less than logarithmic in the number of obstacles and linear (with a very small slope) in L.

3. EXPERIMENTAL RESULTS

We carried out experiments on standard benchmarks from the literature for the obstacle-avoiding Steiner tree problem, as well as some very big industrial instances. Furthermore, for three industrial chips we computed Steiner trees for all existing nets. All tests were carried out on an Intel® Xeon® CPU X5690 @ 3.47GHz, 192 GB RAM with 12 cores.

3.1 Standard Benchmarks

The standard benchmarks are composed as follows. RC01-RC12 are randomly generated instances by Feng et. al. [6], IND1-IND5 are industrial test cases by Synopsys, RT01-RT05 have a fixed ratio of terminals to obstacles of 5, 10 and 50 and were introduced by Lin et. al. [12], and RL01-RL05 are large random instances by Long et. al. [14].

Table 3 shows the lengths of reach-aware Steiner trees found by our algorithm for different values of L, relative to the length of the longer side of the bounding box of the instance including obstacle corners. In most of these benchmarks, no obstacle has both width and height exceeding 10% of the size of the bounding box.

For these instances, the obstacles are given as a set of rectangles whose union represents the blocked area. Here, Opt* denotes the optimum solution (if known) for the obstacle-avoiding Steiner tree problem according to Huang and Young [10]. We added them as a reference value, but recall that they have a slightly different definition of obstacle-avoiding. Edges between two rectangles that share a boundary may be used, whereas with our definition, they would pass through the interior of the blocked area and not be obstacle-avoiding.

Thus, their Steiner trees can be strictly shorter than the optimum according to our definition for any $L < \infty$. For some of the larger instances (marked by $\leq$), the optimum solution is actually unknown; here we present the best value from literature [1, 11]. For two instances, we improve on the best known value from literature for $L = 0$ despite our stricter definition.

With our definition, IND5 becomes infeasible for small L ($\leq 1\%$ of bounding box), as seen in Figure 6 – there is a vertex isolated by a ring of obstacles in the upper right corner. The picture shows our solution for $L = 10\%$ of the instance width, i.e. the difference of the maximum and minimum x-coordinates in the input.

Except for the RL instances, one can see that the tree length gradually decreases with increasing value of L. The RL instances have many terminals that are spread uniformly across the unblocked area. For such instances, the obstacles

Figure 6: Our solution for IND5 with $L = 10\%$ instance width.

do not affect the length of a minimum Steiner tree significantly and the length variation is dominated by the Steiner tree approximation. For $L = 0$, our results on three of the RL instances are better than the best previous upper bounds.

The reported running times are generally fast. For some instances, the running time first increases and then decreases with growing L. The reason is that we first add more and more edges reaching over obstacles, thereby increasing the size of the visibility graph. Later, increasingly many obstacles can be pruned according to Section 2.5 and the running time decreases. This effect will become even more evident when routing all nets on a chip in Section 3.3.

3.2 Big Chip Instances

Eight industrial test instances arise from a cooperation with IBM. They have between 109 and 783 352 terminals. The bigger ones represent reset trees with low performance requirements, where short length is a major focus. These instances are published as the "BONN" instances as part of the 11th DIMACS benchmark suite on Steiner trees:

http://dimacs11.cs.princeton.edu/instances.

Table 1 shows results for eight real-world instances. The first three columns show the number of terminals, the number of rectangular obstacles, and the reach-length $L^\star$, which depends on the technology and the metal stack of the underlying chip. We then report the lengths for obstacle-avoiding trees ($L = 0$), for the given reach-length $L^\star$ and for ignoring all obstacles ($L = \infty$). Again, one can observe that the lengths gradually decrease with growing L, even though large parts of the length are incurred by unblocked clusters of terminals.

The running times (given for $L = L^\star$) demonstrate that our algorithm is capable of handling even largest instances efficiently.

Figure 7 shows a plot of BIG5 for $L = L^\star$. The reach-length does not allow to pass over the biggest obstacles, but some wires cross smaller obstacles in the center of the chip.

3.3 Computations for Entire Chips

The benefit of allowing components to reach over obstacles becomes very evident when computing reach-aware Steiner trees for all nets on a chip. We tested our algorithm on three chips in $65\,nm$ technology, also provided by IBM.

Table 2 shows the total net lengths for $L = 0$, $L = 0.5\,mm$, $L = 1\,mm$, $L = 2.5\,mm$ and $L = \infty$. For small L, some nets are infeasible. For those nets, the solution consists of a reach-aware forest with minimum number of components

Instance	$|S|$	$|O|$	$L^\star$	Length			RT
				$L = 0$	$L = L^\star$	$L = \infty$	sec.
BIG1	109	101	90	31695	31566	28485	<1
BIG2	23292	54	2400000	364338561	363004401	361726146	1
BIG3	35574	158	1500000	746523861	746495841	735059181	2
BIG4	46269	127	1500000	1071883920	1071827520	1068448860	4
BIG5	108500	141	4200000	1973406390	1964154690	1957120800	10
BIG6	129399	210	1500000	infeasible	2608227090	2616871950	14
BIG7	639639	382	4200000	3060914728	3028456768	3013106038	99
BIG8	783352	175	1200000	1948056132	1944546732	1931964162	126

Table 1: Results for the BIG instances.

(a) AndreTop, 3 899 379 nets

L	Length	#inf.	CPU	Wall
0	562 032	0	11:23	05:45
0.5	535 453	0	21:47	07:21
1	469 175	0	15:22	06:21
2.5	440 680	0	10:17	05:54
∞	440 537	0	08:18	05:12

(b) AlexTop, 2 674 754 nets

L	Length	#inf.	CPU	Wall
0	580 318*	1 955	21:58	06:10
0.5	536 358*	1	24:52	06:29
1	532 307	0	21:46	06:06
2.5	530 284	0	17:58	05:55
∞	529 301	0	07:07	04:38

(c) LeonardTop, 525 498 nets

L	Length	#inf.	CPU	Wall
0	201 127*	6 669	13:33	02:42
0.5	249 067*	40	16:54	03:11
1	246 862	0	17:41	03:24
2.5	203 378	0	11:31	02:32
∞	199 216	0	01:52	01:24

Choices of L and total net lengths are reported in mm, running times in mm:ss using 8 threads. Total lengths marked by $\star$ include infeasible nets with (large) opens!

Table 2: Results on entire chips.

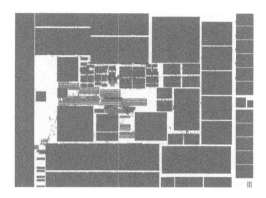

Figure 7: Industrial instance with 108500 terminals.

to existing 2-approximation algorithms [16], fast enough for practical computations.

The computational results, in particular on entire chips, demonstrate the big length reductions compared to obstacle-avoiding Steiner trees for the purpose of computing short and reach-aware buffer tree topologies.

5. REFERENCES

[1] G. Ajwani, C. Chu and W.-K. Mak. *FOARS: FLUTE Based Obstacle-Avoiding Rectilinear Steiner Tree Construction*, IEEE Transactions on Computer-Aided Design of Integrated Circuits and Systems 30 (2011), 194–204.

[2] C. J. Alpert, A. B. Kahng, C. N. Sze and Q. Wang. *Timing-driven Steiner trees are (practically) free*, Proceedings of the Design Automation Conference (2006), 389–392.

[3] C. Bartoschek, S. Held, J. Maßberg, D. Rautenbach and J. Vygen. *The repeater tree construction problem*, Information Processing Letters 110 (2010), 1079–1083.

[4] C. Chu and Y.-C. Wong. *FLUTE: Fast Lookup Table Based Rectilinear Steiner Minimal Tree Algorithm for VLSI Design*, IEEE Transactions on Computer-Aided Design of Integrated Circuits and Systems 27 (2008), 70–83.

[5] K. Clarkson, S. Kapoor and P. Vaidya. *Rectilinear shortest paths through polygonal obstacles in $\mathcal{O}(n(\log n)^2)$ time*, Proceedings of the Symposium on Computational Geometry (1987), 251–257.

[6] Z. Feng, Y. Hu, T. Jing, X. Hong, X. Hu and G. Yan. *An $\mathcal{O}(n \log n)$ algorithm for obstacle-avoiding routing tree construction in the λ-geometry plane*, Proceedings of the International Symposium on Physical Design (2006), 48–55.

and only the length of this forest is included in the total length. Therefore, on LeonardTop the total net length for $L = 0$ is lower than for larger reach-lengths, where all nets become feasible. The number of infeasible nets is listed in the "#inf."-columns.

Compared to obstacle-avoiding trees, the reduction in total net length is substantial, e.g. 2.5%, 14.8%, 19.8% and 20% on AndreTop or 8.7%, 9.5%, 9.8% and 10% on AlexTop, here even in presence of infeasible nets for $L = 0$.

LeonardTop contains 26 macros with width and height above $2\,mm$. Thus, a significant length reduction only occurs when raising L to $2.5\,mm$.

Again, the running times first rise with growing L, because the size of the visibility graph increases, and then fall due to the pruning of obstacles. The wall times were obtained using 8 threads.

4. CONCLUSION

We have proposed a new algorithm for computing reach-aware Steiner trees that is fast in theory and on real-world instances from chip design. It provides a 2-approximation for minimum reach-aware Steiner trees and is, in contrast

Name	$|S|$	$|O|$	Opt*	Lengths					Running times in seconds				
				$L=0$	1%	5%	10%	∞	$L=0$	1%	5%	10%	∞
RL01	5000	5000	≤ 481813	493372	486836	490658	491565	472780	0.65	1.02	0.26	0.28	0.13
RL02	9999	500	≤ 637753	638206	638151	638276	638612	634187	0.66	0.68	0.66	0.65	0.25
RL03	9999	100	≤ 640902	639495	639314	639195	638851	636566	0.72	0.73	0.73	0.72	0.25
RL04	10000	10	≤ 697125	694654	694654	691612	691612	691660	0.76	0.76	0.27	0.27	0.24
RL05	10000	0	≤ 728438	723102	723102	723102	723102	723102	0.27	0.26	0.26	0.26	0.24
RC01	10	10	25980	27360	27360	25290	25290	25290	0.00	0.00	0.00	0.01	0.00
RC02	30	10	41350	43010	43010	42540	41460	41330	0.00	0.00	0.00	0.01	0.00
RC03	50	10	54160	55080	55080	54650	55660	52470	0.01	0.00	0.00	0.00	0.00
RC04	70	10	59070	60300	60300	57410	56120	55330	0.00	0.01	0.00	0.00	0.00
RC05	100	10	74070	75060	75060	73330	73460	71610	0.01	0.00	0.00	0.01	0.00
RC06	100	500	79714	85133	84200	81983	82145	77472	0.03	0.03	0.01	0.01	0.01
RC07	200	500	108740	114225	112168	111249	110343	107190	0.03	0.03	0.03	0.01	0.00
RC08	200	800	112564	120394	116649	113778	115090	109589	0.05	0.05	0.03	0.02	0.00
RC09	200	1000	111005	118116	115169	112665	113571	107561	0.07	0.06	0.02	0.03	0.01
RC10	500	100	164150	168350	168350	166910	166330	164600	0.03	0.02	0.03	0.02	0.00
RC11	1000	100	230873	235424	234930	234827	235407	230620	0.06	0.06	0.06	0.05	0.01
RC12	1000	10000	≤ 756998	792417	785857	785857	785857	754414	0.82	0.11	0.11	0.11	0.08
RT01	10	500	2146	2283	2012	1817	1817	1817	0.01	0.03	0.00	0.01	0.01
RT02	50	500	45852	49500	46762	45772	45772	45747	0.02	0.03	0.00	0.01	0.00
RT03	100	500	7964	8380	8034	8092	8046	7697	0.03	0.03	0.01	0.01	0.01
RT04	100	1000	9693	10616	8160	7788	7788	7788	0.05	0.07	0.01	0.02	0.02
RT05	200	2000	51313	55507	45479	45581	46101	43099	0.12	0.15	0.06	0.04	0.02
IND1	10	32	604	629	629	609	609	609	0.01	0.00	0.00	0.00	0.00
IND2	10	43	9500	10600	10600	9100	9100	9100	0.00	0.00	0.01	0.00	0.00
IND3	10	50	600	678	678	600	587	587	0.00	0.00	0.00	0.00	0.00
IND4	25	79	1086	1160	1160	1137	1121	1092	0.01	0.00	0.00	0.00	0.01
IND5	33	71	1341	infeas.	infeas.	1364	1343	1312	0.00	0.00	0.00	0.01	0.00
Sum									3.62	4.13	2.56	2.56	1.29

Opt* denotes the optimum solution for $L=0$ from [10] w.r.t. a slightly more relaxed interpretation of obstacles. Running times of 0.00 were positive but less than 0.01 seconds.

Table 3: Solution length and running times for different choices of L.

[7] J. L. Ganley and J. P. Cohoon. *Routing a multi-terminal critical net: Steiner tree construction in the presence of obstacles*, Proceedings of the IEEE International Symposium on Circuits and Systems vol.1 (1994), 113–116.

[8] S. Held and D. Rotter. *Shallow Light Steiner Arborescences with Vertex Delays*, Proceedings of the International Conference on Integer Programming and Combinatorial Optimization (2013), 229–241.

[9] T. Huang and E. F. Y. Young. *Construction of rectilinear Steiner minimum trees with slew constraints over obstacles*, Proceedings of the International Conference on Computer-Aided Design (2012), 144–151.

[10] T. Huang and E. F. Y. Young. *ObSteiner: An Exact Algorithm for the Construction of Rectilinear Steiner Minimum Trees in the Presence of Complex Rectilinear Obstacles*, IEEE Transactions on Computer-Aided Design of Integrated Circuits and Systems 32 (2013), 882–893.

[11] L. Li and E. F. Y. Young. *Obstacle-avoiding Rectilinear Steiner Tree Construction*, Proceedings of the International Conference on Computer-Aided Design (2008), 523–528.

[12] C.-W. Lin, S. Y. Chen, C.-F. Li, Y.-W. Chang and C.-L. Yang. *Obstacle-Avoiding Rectilinear Steiner Tree Construction Based on Spanning Graphs*, IEEE Transactions on Computer-Aided Design of Integrated Circuits and Systems 27 (2008), 643–653.

[13] C.-H. Liu, S.-Y. Yuan, S.-Y. Kuo and S.-C. Wang. *High-performance obstacle-avoiding rectilinear Steiner tree construction* ACM Transactions on Design Automation of Electronic Systems 14 (2009), article 45.

[14] J. Long, H. Zhou and S. O. Memik. *An $\mathcal{O}(n \log n)$ edge-based algorithm for obstacle-avoiding rectilinear Steiner tree construction*, Proceedings of the International Symposium on Physical Design (2008), 126–133.

[15] K. Mehlhorn. *A faster approximation algorithm for the Steiner problem in graphs*, Information Processing Letters 27 (1988), 125–128.

[16] M. Müller-Hannemann and S. Peyer. *Approximation of Rectilinear Steiner Trees with Length Restrictions on Obstacles*, Proceedings of the Workshop on Algorithms and Data Structures (2003), LNCS 2748, 207–218.

[17] Y. Zhang, A. Chakraborty, S. Chowdhury and D. Z. Pan. *Reclaiming over-the-IP-block routing resources with buffering-aware rectilinear Steiner minimum tree construction*. Computer-Aided Design (ICCAD), 2012 IEEE/ACM International Conference on, pp. 137-143. IEEE, 2012.

FPGA Place & Route Challenges

Rajat Aggarwal
Xilinx, Inc
2100 Logic Dr
San Jose, CA 95124
rajat.aggarwal@xilinx.com

ABSTRACT

In this paper, we describe the challenges that Place and Route tools face to implement the user designs on modern FPGAs while meeting the timing and power constraints.

Categories and Subject Descriptors

B.7.2 [Hardware, Integrated Circuits]: Design Aids—Placement and routing

General Terms

Algorithms, Performance

Keywords

Physical Design; FPGA; Placement; Routing

1. INTRODUCTION

FPGAs (Field Programmable Gate Arrays) are pre-fabricated and programmable ICs that are experiencing big growth in many areas including wired and wireless communications, industrial, aerospace and defense, and consumer electronics. In order to meet the needs of these areas, FPGAs are evolving rapidly and over time becoming bigger, faster and starting to look more like SoCs. The complexity and size of the current generation FPGAs pose many challenges to the implementation tools. Synthesis and Place-and-Route for the modern day FPGAs not only have to deploy ASIC-CAD like algorithms for handling millions of objects, but they also have to address unique FPGA specific challenges, because of the constraints imposed by the pre-fabricated device.

The sizes of FPGAs keep growing as they are typically at the fore-front of adopting lower geometry processes. The growth got a boost recently with the introduction of Stacked Silicon Interconnect (SSI) [1][7], or 3D ICs by Xilinx. As a result, Xilinx FPGA sizes have been increasing at a rate higher than that predicted by Moore's law [2]. 3D FPGAs connect several dice on a single silicon interposer, allowing FPGAs chips to pack very large number of logic cells. Xilinx Virtex®-7 family can implement designs up to 2M logic cells, 4-input LUT-equivalent, corresponding to 20M ASIC gates [3]. This number is set to increase to 4.4M logic cells (50M ASIC gates) in the UltraScale™ family [5].

ISPD'14, Mar 30 - Apr 02 2014, Petaluma, CA, USA
ACM 978-1-4503-2592-9/14/03.
http://dx.doi.org/10.1145/2560519.2568050

The number and types of hard IPs (like embedded memory or Block RAMs, DSPs, PCIEs) used in an FPGA have increased many folds as well. While there have been previous generations of FPGAs that have embedded processors, Xilinx Zynq™ device [4] has created an unprecedented level of integration with the processing subsystems. High speed serial IOs have enabled tremendous bandwidth to go in and out of an FPGA. Table 1 lists the components of some UltraScale™ FPGAs [5][6] and illustrates how current generation FPGAs are becoming more like SoCs with many hard blocks in each device such as Block RAMs, DSP blocks, PCIE and Interlaken cores, gigabit transceivers, etc

Table 1. Components of some UltraScale™ FPGAs [5]

	XCVU145	XCVU160	XCVU440
Logic Cells	1,435,000	1,621,200	4,407,480
BlockRAM (Mb)	98	115.2	88.6
DSP Slices	1,365	1,560	2,880
PCI Express® Blocks	4	4	6
Interlaken	9	9	0
100G Ethernet	7	7	3
GTH 16 Gb/s Transceivers	52	52	48
GTY 32.75 Gb/s Transceivers	52	52	0
I/O Pins	1,040	1,040	1,456

The simplest way to think of current generation FPGAs is a large set of configurable hard IPs in a sea of programmable fabric. Increased FPGA sizes, high speed serial IOs, configurable IPs located at discrete locations and constraints imposed by pre-fabricated silicon pose significant challenges to the Place and Route tools.

2. PLACEMENT AND ROUTING CHALLENGES

FPGA Placement problem is essentially assigning synthesized netlist components on to the physical locations in the FPGA array. The resulting solution needs to be a routable placement which meets timing and power constraints.

Each FPGA die has placement sites that consist of large number of LUTs, LUT RAMs and Flops with I/O interfaces and configurable IPs, such as Block RAMs, DSPs and PCIEs, located at discrete locations. Clock nets use special resources in a low skew network that tiles the device. These dice are stacked together to form the 3D FPGA. Each aspect of FPGA offers a different challenge during placement and routing of the designs.

Analytical or quadratic placers favor locality by reducing wire length, but in FPGAs wire length can be a poor metric of timing.

- FPGA architectures have fast long lines which can connect two distant cells with better performance than if they were placed close to one another
- The delay of a path of a given distance can vary significantly with path's location depending on the presence of inter-die crossing, IO columns or configurable IPs on the path

The presence of limited number of clocks and control networks in FPGAs limits the number of control signals that can be accommodated in a given region. This restriction leads to inconsistency between the area calculation of global and detail placement steps. This, in turn, can lead to large errors during the detail placement step, resulting in worse congestion and timing.

Limited number of clocks in any given region of FPGA also requires Placement tool to define clock regions. These clock regions are provided to global and detailed placement steps as region constraints. This step needs to be performed before the rest of the logic is placed and before accurate timing information is available, which presents a challenge.

Discrete locations of configurable IPs, such as Block RAMs, DSPs present restrictions during the global and detail placement steps. These blocks in the design tend to have a large number of critical connections to the rest of the fabric. Suboptimal placement of these blocks with respect to the rest of the fabric can cause timing closure issues. The discrete locations of these hard IPs preclude easy post-placement fixes to the placement of these blocks. Small variations in the placement of these blocks from run to run can also result in solution stability issues, when the designer is making small changes to the netlist.

Routing network in FPGAs is made of discrete pre-defined routing segments or hops. Hops can span 2 tiles, 4 tiles or up to 50 tiles. Traditional FPGA routing theory uses variations around the PathFinder algorithm [8]. However, the size of current generation FPGAs mandate adoption of more scalable approaches similar to those used in the ASIC world, with unique FPGA specific variations.

Timing closure in router needs to consider both setup and hold violations while coming up with a legal routing solution. Less number of wires used during routing can help in reducing the power consumption. Timing closure also requires closing timing across multiple process corners. This compounds the problems of setup and hold during the routing phases.

Traditionally, timing closure problems in ASIC placement and routing tools have been resolved through physical synthesis algorithms such as buffer insertion and gate sizing. FPGA tools cannot use these techniques and require distinct solutions in placement, routing and physical synthesis steps to solve for both setup and hold.

3. RUNTIME AND MEMORY

With the increased device sizes, both the runtime and memory need to be optimized without sacrificing other metrics like timing, routability and power. Multi-threading has become default in most FPGA implementation tools to help in runtime but scalability of solutions with increased number of threads is always a challenge. Adding to the complexity, place and route solutions need to be deterministic as well, independent of the number of threads used. One of the aspects which hurts scalability is cache misses which requires algorithms to be written such that threads use more and more local data.

Runtime is even a bigger concern for prototyping, emulation and reconfigurable-computing designs. These designs require an order of magnitude improvement in runtimes over default solutions.

Place and Route tools need to provide these different solutions in the same algorithmic framework.

4. CONCLUSION

FPGAs have come a long way to become the de-facto platforms for building entire SOCs in several markets. Tremendously large device sizes with 3D technology and large number of discretely positioned configurable IPs pose significant challenges to the Place and Route tools.

A lot of innovation has gone into the current implementation tools to create viable solutions for these huge and complex devices, but still a lot more is needed to keep up with the increase in size and complexity of the devices. The need to achieve timing and power closure for the designs on larger and more complex devices while consuming less and less runtime and memory will always remain a challenge.

5. REFERENCES

[1] Xilinx, "Stacked Silicon Interconnect - Enabling All Programmable 3D ICs", http://www.xilinx.com/products/technology/stacked-silicon-interconnect/index.htm

[2] Xilinx, "All Programmable 3D ICs", http://www.xilinx.com/products/silicon-devices/3dic/index.htm

[3] Xilinx. "Virtex-7 FPGA Overview", http://www.xilinx.com/support/documentation/data_sheets/ds180_7Series_Overview.pdf

[4] Xilinx, "All Programmable SoC", http://www.xilinx.com/products/silicon-devices/soc/

[5] Xilinx, "UltraScale Architecture", http://www.xilinx.com/products/technology/ultrascale.html

[6] Xilinx, "Virtx UltraScale FPGAs", http://www.xilinx.com/publications/prod_mktg/ultrascale-virtex-product-table.pdf

[7] Liam Madden, "Heterogeneous 3-d stacking, can we have the best of both (technology) worlds?", ISPD 2013, pp. 1-2

[8] Larry McMurchie, Carl Ebeling, "PathFinder: A Negotiation-based Performance-driven Router for FPGAs", FPGA 1995, pp. 111-117

Placement-Driven Partitioning for Congestion Mitigation in Monolithic 3D IC Designs

Shreepad Panth[†], Kambiz Samadi[§], Yang Du[§], and Sung Kyu Lim[†]
[†]School of ECE, Georgia Institute of Technology, Atlanta, GA
[§]Qualcomm Research, San Diego, CA
{spanth,limsk}@ece.gatech.edu

ABSTRACT

Monolithic 3D is an emerging technology that enables integration density which is orders of magnitude higher than that offered by through-silicon-vias (TSV). In this paper we demonstrate that a modified 2D placement technique, coupled with a post-placement partitioning step, is sufficient to produce high quality monolithic 3D placement solutions. We also present a commercial router based monolithic inter-tier via (MIV) insertion methodology that dramatically improves the routability of monolithic 3D-ICs. We develop a routing demand model for monolithic 3D-ICs, and use it to develop an $O(N)$ min-overflow partitioner that enhances routability by off-loading demand from one tier to another. This technique reduces the routed wirelength and the power delay product (PDP) by up to 4% and 4.33% respectively, under the same half-perimeter wirelength. This allows a two-tier monolithic 3D-IC to achieve, on average, 19.2% and 12.1% improvement in routed wirelength and PDP over 2D, even with reduced metal layer usage.

Categories and Subject Descriptors

B.7.2 [**Integrated Circuits**]: Design Aids—*Placement and routing*

General Terms

Algorithms, Design

Keywords

Monolithic 3D; Partitioning; Routing Congestion

1. INTRODUCTION

Three dimensional integrated circuits (3D-ICs) have emerged as a promising solution to extend the 2D scaling trajectory predicted by Moore's Law. Current 3D-ICs are through-silicon-via (TSV) based, but the integration density is limited by the pitch of TSVs. Monolithic 3D IC is an emerging technology that enables orders of magnitude higher integration density than TSV based 3D, due to the extremely small size of the *monolithic inter-tier vias* (MIVs). In

This work is supported by Qualcomm Research.

monolithic 3D integration technology, two or more tiers of devices are fabricated sequentially, instead of bonding two pre-fabricated dies. This eliminates the need for die alignment, enabling smaller via sizes. Each MIV has essentially the same size as an intra-tier via ($< 100nm$ diameter) [1].

Early works on monolithic 3D focussed on fabrication techniques [1, 8]. Several design works exist on transistor-level monolithic 3D-ICs, where the PMOS and NMOS of each logic gate is split onto different tiers [2, 10]. Block-level design studies have also been carried out [11]. However, in terms of gate-level solutions, where each logic gate is confined to a given tier, prior work is limited.

The monolithic 3D gate-level placement problem is similar to the TSV-based problem, except that we do not need to minimize the via count. The first approach to TSV-based 3D placement is folding-based [6]. This takes an existing 2D placement and transforms it to 3D by several folding operations. This has been demonstrated to be inferior to other placement approaches [5]. The next method is partitioning based analytical placement [9], where the netlist is first partitioned, and all tiers are placed simultaneously using an analytical engine. This approach suffers from the fact that we need to decide on a partition beforehand, and no good guidelines exist. Lastly, true 3D placement approaches exist [5], where the half-perimeter wirelength (HPWL) is minimized in the x,y and z dimensions. All of these engines are geared towards TSV-based 3D, and try to minimize the via count. In this paper, we demonstrate the fact that since monolithic vias are so small, modified 2D placement suffices, and separate 3D placement engines are not required.

In this work, we focus on two-tier monolithic 3D-ICs only, and assume that each tier supports as many metal layers as required. The contributions of this work are as follows: (1) We empirically demonstrate that modified 2D placement coupled with a post placement partitioning step is sufficient to produce a high-quality monolithic 3D-IC placement. (2) This is the first work to study routability issues in gate-level monolithic 3D-ICs. Routability improvements are reported as a reduction in detail-routed wirelength using a commercial router. (3) We present a probabilistic monolithic 3D routing demand model, and use it to develop an $O(N)$ min-overflow partitioner. This yields upto 4% and 4.33% in the routed wirelength and power-delay product, respectively. (4) We present a router-based MIV insertion algorithm that dramatically improves the routed wirelength by up to 16.6%. (5) We demonstrate that the above techniques enable us to reduce the metal layer count in a two-tier monolithic 3D and still on average improve the routed wirelength and power-delay product by 19.2% and 12.1% over 2D, respectively.

The remainder of the paper is organized as follows: Section 2 presents our modified 2D placement methodology and our routability-

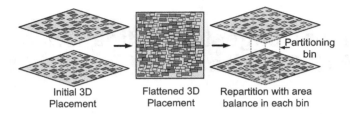

Initial 3D Placement   Flattened 3D Placement   Repartition with area balance in each bin

Figure 1: Placement-aware partitioning. The initial monolithic 3D placement is flattened into 2D, and then repartitioned with area balance in each partitioning bin.

driven partitioning algorithm. Next, Section 3 presents our router-based MIV insertion heuristic. Section 4 presents our experimental results and Section 5 concludes this paper.

2. PLACEMENT-AWARE PARTITIONING

2.1 Problem Formulation

We define the "flattened HPWL" as the HPWL of a monolithic 3D-IC if all the gates are projected onto a single placement layer. We also define the total routing overflow as the sum of routing demand minus routing supply on all global routing bins that are congested. The problem that we are trying to solve can then be stated as: *Given an initial monolithic 3D placement, repartition the gates without changing the flattened HPWL, such that the total routing overflow is minimized.*

The HPWL constraint is possible because changing only the z location of a cell does not change its flattened HPWL. The negligible z height in monolithic 3D-ICs guarantees that there will be minimal impact on the total 3D half-perimeter bounding-box. Several routability-driven placement engines exist, but none of them are readily available for 3D. Therefore, we choose to apply our placement-driven partitioning on top of a purely HPWL-driven placement. However, our partitioning method is equally valid applied on top of *any* initial placement, routability-driven or otherwise.

2.2 Overall Methodology

An overview of our proposed methodology is shown in Figure 1. We first start with a monolithic 3D global placement, and then project it to 2D to obtain a *Flattened 3D Placement*. Partitioning bins are defined, and this flattened placement is repartitioned to 3D, while maintaining local area balance within each partitioning bin.

Strictly speaking, the flattening step is not necessary, as repartitioning can directly be applied on top of the initial 3D placement. However, we present a method to leverage existing 2D placers to mimic generating a flattened monolithic 3D placement, without actually running any 3D placement. This method has the advantage of requiring minimal modifications to any existing 2D placer and therefore can be quickly deployed as and when superior placement engines are developed.

All 2D placement engines have the concept of *chip capacity* (or target density), which is the maximum number of std. cells that can be placed in a given area. A two-tier monolithic 3D chip has half the footprint area of a 2D chip, and since we want to fit all the gates into half the area, we simply double the capacity of the chip. Any existing 2D placer can be modified to perform flattened placement, and we choose to implement our own version of KraftWerk2 [12].

Note that while this may appear similar to the local stacking transformation (LST) presented in [6], it is superior in one major aspect – the handling of pre-placed macros. The LST method scales the (x,y) locations of all the cells from a *legal* 2D placement, and

therefore has no way to handle pre-placed macros. Handling them in our method is straightforward: First, project all of the macros on to a single 2D plane. Those regions that have macros from both tiers overlapping cannot contain any cells, and regions that contain only one pre-placed macro can still contain cells, but the capacity is not doubled in those regions. This approach can also be extended to arbitrarily many tiers. For example, if we want three tiers, we need to divide the area by three, and multiply the capacity by three.

Once we have the 3D flattened placement (either from an initial 3D placement or modified 2D placement), we need to split this into two tiers, minimizing the change to the placement solution. We first present a min-cut partitioning heuristic that is used as an initial solution, a routing demand model for monolithic 3D-ICs, and finally a min-overflow partitioning heuristic that uses the routing demand model to minimize the routing overflow.

2.3 Min-Cut Partitioning

Modifying the traditional Fiduccia-Mattheyses [7] (FM) min-cut partitioner is straightforward, and an overview of the modified heuristic is given below.

Initially, a random area-balanced (within each partition-bin) solution is created. The gain of a cell is defined as the reduction in the cutsize if the cell's tier is changed. A cell is termed as legal if moving it does not violate the area-balance constraints within its partition bin. Initially, all the cell gains are computed and stored in a bucket structure, and all the cells are marked as unlocked. The first legal cell with the highest gain is picked, moved to the other tier, and locked. Once a cell is moved, only the gains of its neighbours (connected by a net) needs to be updated. This process is continued until all the cells are locked. This is termed a *pass*. Several passes are performed until no more cutsize gains are achieved. Due to the nature of the incremental gain update, this algorithm runs in $O(C)$ time, where C is the number of cells. Once we settle on a partitioning solution, each tier is legalized separately.

However, MIVs are extremely small, so there is no real need to perform a min-cut on the netlist. Additional MIVs can be tolerated, if there is good reason to use them. We now derive a routing demand model for monolithic 3D-ICs, and use it to present a routability-driven partitioning heuristic that minimizes the total overflow instead of the cutsize.

2.4 Monolithic 3D-IC Routing Demand Model

We maintain a 3D routing graph for the entire chip, and the demands of each net are added into it. The supply on each edge is computed from the technology LEF files depending on the number of metal layers. This section is divided into two parts: The first part discusses the decomposition of multi-pin nets into two-pin nets by constructing 3D Rectilinear Steiner Tress (RST), and the second part discusses adding the demands of each two-pin net into the routing graph.

2.4.1 Decomposing Multi-Pin Nets into Two-Pin Nets

In this section, we present our method of decomposing multi-pin nets into two-pin nets by constructing 3D RSTs. Currently, no tool exists to efficiently compute a 3D RST, so we project the net to 2D, construct a 2D RSMT, and then expand it back to 3D.

Consider the points to be routed as shown in Figure 2(a). We first project the points to a 2D plane and construct a 2D RMST using FLUTE [4] (Figure 2(b)). Now, while expanding this 2D RSMT to a 3D RST, the tiers of all the fixed points are already known, and the tier of each steiner point is determined by a majority vote of the tier of its neighbors. Ties are broken in any arbitrary, deterministic manner. The resulting 3D RST is shown in Figure 2(c).

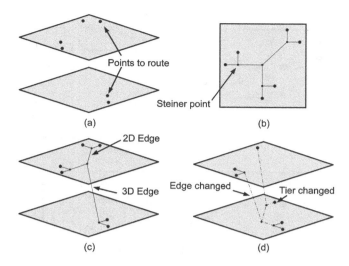

Figure 2: Construction of a 3D RST. (a) The points to be routed. (b) Project to 2D and construct a 2D RSMT. (c) Expand the 2D RSMT to a 3D RST. (d) If a cell changes tier, the 2D RSMT can be re-used.

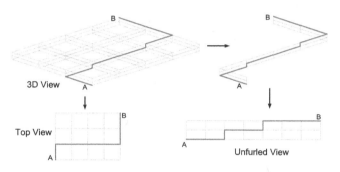

Figure 3: A legal route from A to B in a $4 \times 3 \times 2$ grid. The top-view is limited to two bends, while the unfurled view can have unlimited bends.

Since we wish to perform move-based partitioning, we need to be able to quickly evaluate the change in the topology if the tier of a particular cell is changed. Since such a change does not change the x & y co-ordinate of the cell, the same 2D RSMT can be reused. Only the quick majority vote operation needs to be redone on the steiner points. We change the tier of one cell and show the resulting 3D RST in Figure 2(d). As seen from this figure, a lot of the routing demand on the top tier is offloaded to the bottom tier, with an unchanged 3D bounding-box. In summary, to evaluate the change in demand if the tier of a given cell is changed, we need to: (1) Redo the majority vote operation for all nets connected to that cell, (2) Delete the old topology (rip-up) of the changed two-pin nets from the demand estimate, and (3) Add the new topology (re-route) of the changed two-pin nets into the demand estimate. Handling each two-pin net is described next.

2.4.2   3D Demand Model for Two-Pin Nets

As mentioned earlier, we maintain a 3D routing graph for the entire chip. This section assumes that we are looking only at that sub-graph that a given two-pin net spans. We choose a probabilistic demand model because: (1) It is very fast, and (2) The predicted demand numbers are independent of net-ordering. The second property is essential for a partitioner, as each re-compute of the demand

of the same two-pin net must yield the same result. Note that our model is general and applicable to any number of tiers, even though this paper uses only the two-tier version.

Assume that the net (A-B) spans a $l \times m \times n$ routing sub-graph. We wish to compute the probabilistic routing demand contributed by this two-pin net on each edge within this sub-graph. An example $4 \times 3 \times 2$ three-tier grid is shown in Figure 3, along with one sample route from point A to B. We make two key observations that help us to derive the demand model: (1) Each bend in the top view represents the usage of a local via. Therefore, we are limited two bends in this view [3]. (2) We define the unfurled view as a view such that movement along the x and y directions look the same (see Figure 3). Unlike in the top view, an additional bend in this view does not imply an additional MIV. The total number of MIVs is always $n - 1$. Therefore, there are no limits to the number of bends in the unfurled view.

Assuming the above constraints, the total number of routes from A to B is $(l + m) \times^{(l+m+n)} C_n$. First, given the top-view constraint, the sum of all the probabilities along all the edges that look identical in the top-view is given by:

$$\sum_{i=1}^{n} P_{(x,x+1),y,i} = \frac{1}{l+m} \times \begin{cases} (l - x), & \text{if } y = 0 \\ (x + 1), & \text{if } y = m \\ 1, & \text{otherwise} \end{cases} \quad (1)$$

A similar expression can also be written for all the y edges. Next, in the unfurled view, all edges with the same $(x + y)$ look the same. Therefore, let i represent $(x + y)$. Since there is no limit to the number of bends, the routing probability on any horizontal edge is given by a uniform probability distribution:

$$P_{(i,i+1),z} = \frac{{}^{(i+z)} C_i \times {}^{(l+m+n-i-z-1)} C_{(l+m-i-1)}}{{}^{(l+m+n)} C_n} \quad (2)$$

Equations (1) & (2) can be combined to give the routing probability on any x edge in the 3D graph:

$$K_{3D} = \frac{{}^{(x+y+z)} C_z \times {}^{(l+m+n-x-y-z-1)} C_{(l+m-x-y-1)}}{(l + m) \times {}^{(l+m+n)} C_n}$$

$$P_{(x,x+1),y,z} = K_{3D} \times \begin{cases} (l - x), & \text{if } y = 0 \\ (x + 1), & \text{if } y = m \\ 1, & \text{otherwise} \end{cases} \quad (3)$$

A similar expression can also be computed for all the y edges. Once the probabilities of the x & y edges have been computed, the probability on each z edge can be computed by visiting them in turn, and setting the probability to be the sum of the probability on all incoming edges (towards A) minus the sum of the probability on all the outgoing edges (towards B).

2.5   Routability-Driven Partitioning

Given our 3D demand model, we can now perform routability-driven (min-overflow) partitioning. We first perform a min-cut as described in Subsection 2.3. We then perform min-overflow partitioning on top of this solution. The overflow-gain of a cell is computed by the procedure outlined in Subsection 2.4.1.

Let C be the set of all cells and N be the set of all the nets in the design. In the min-cut partitioner, once a cell is moved, only the gains of its neighbours needs to be updated. However, the overflow depends on *all* nets that use a particular routing edge. Therefore, if a cell is moved, any cell that has a net using a common routing edge will need to have its gain updated. All it takes is a few nets with reasonably large bounding-boxes to give us a $O(C^2)$ complexity on

Algorithm 1: Our Min-Overflow Partitioning Heuristic

```
1 Function MinOverflow()
2 |   demandEstimate →Clear();
3 |   Stage(build);
4 |   Stage(refine);
5 end

6 Function Stage(type)
7 |   if (type == build) then ∀n ∈ N : n →valid = false;
8 |   Sort N in descending order of bounding-box;
9 |   foreach n ∈ N do
10 |      if (type == build) then
11 |         demandEstimate →AddRST(n →rst);
12 |         n →valid = true;
13 |      end
14 |      FM( n → cₙ );
15 |   end
16 end
```

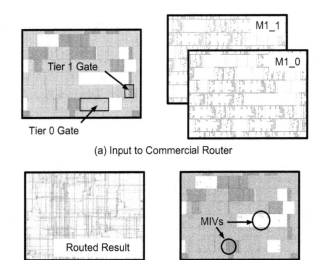

(a) Input to Commercial Router

Routed Result

MIVs

(b) Output from Commercial Router

Figure 5: Screenshots of router-based MIV insertion (a) All the gates are placed in the same placement layer, but no overlap exists in the routing layers. (b) The result after routing. The MIV locations are highlighted in red.

Table 1: The various benchmarks considered in this paper

Circuit	Clock Period (ns)	#Cells	#Nets	Cell Area (mm^2)	#ML
mul_64	1.2	21,671	22,399	0.078188	4
rca_16	0.4	67,086	75,786	0.262669	4
aes_128	0.5	133,944	138,861	0.348812	5
jpeg	1.5	193,988	238,496	0.739017	4
fft_256	1.0	488,508	492,499	1.833195	5

the default FM algorithm. We now present a heuristic that reduces the time complexity significantly.

Our heuristic is shown in Algorithm 1, with the top-level function being $MinOverflow()$. Initially, the demand estimate is cleared i.e, all nets are removed, and the utilization on each routing edge is set to 0. Next, there are two stages, build and refine, both of which are similar, and handled by the $Stage()$ function. In the build phase, all the nets are initially set to invalid. In both stages, the nets are then sorted by bounding-box. This is because nets with a larger bounding box have a greater impact on the routing graph, and will be processed first. During the build phase, the 3D-RST of the net currently being processed is added into the demand estimate, and the net is set to valid. Next, irrespective of stage, the $FM()$ function (to be described later) is performed on the cells of the current net. Note that in the build phase, the demand estimate does not have all the nets included, only the ones that have been processed so far. This is to avoid any noise introduced by a bad initial random partitioning of the unprocessed nets.

The $FM()$ function is similar to the basic algorithm described in Subsection 2.3, with a few differences: (1) We use a heap instead of a bucket, as the gains are not integer values, (2) We only look at a subset of cells that belong to a given net, (3) When a cell is moved to another tier, we update the gains of all cells within the current subset, and (4) The gain function is the global max-overflow gain, considering all "valid" nets in the design.

The above heuristic adds one net at a time into the demand estimate, maintaining a local optima of the global total overflow after each net is added. Once all the nets are added, we go over each net again to further reduce the overflow. This approach leads to a time complexity of $O(N.(rms_{N_d})^2)$, where rms_{N_d} is the root-mean-square of the net degrees. This value does not scale much with circuit size, and therefore, our heuristic is more or less linear.

3. ROUTER-BASED MIV INSERTION

To continue with the P&R flow, we need to perform routing, and then parasitic extraction. However, current routers can only handle 2D-ICs, and the usual approach is to to split the 3D design into separate designs for each tier, each of which can be routed independently. This requires the locations of the MIVs to be known, so that they can be represented as I/O pins within each tier.

Once the partition of all cells are finalized, current TSV-based placers perform a TSV and cell co-placement step [9, 5] to determine the via locations. However, MIVs are so small that they can actually be handled by the router (although they occupy silicon space). The only hurdle is the lack of an existing 3D commercial router. In this paper, we present a method to trick existing 2D commercial routers into performing MIV insertion.

An illustration of our approach is shown in Figure 4. First, all the metal layers in the technology LEF are duplicated to yield a new 3D LEF with twice the number of metal layers. Next, for each std. cell in the LEF file, we define two flavours – one for each tier. The only difference between the two flavours is that their pins are mapped onto different metal layers depending on its tier. Next, each cell in the 3D space is mapped to its appropriate flavour, and forced onto the same placement layer. Note that this will lead to cell overlap in the placement layer, but there will be no overlap in the routing layers (Figure 5). We also place routing blockages in the via layer between the two tiers, to prevent MIVs being placed over cells. This entire structure is then fed into an existing commercial router (Cadence Encounter). Once routed, we trace the routing topology to extract the MIV locations, and generate separate verilog/DEF files for each tier.

4. EXPERIMENTAL RESULTS

We choose five benchmarks from the OpenCores benchmark suite that vary in size from a few tens of thousands of gates to half a million gates. They are synthesized with a 28nm cell library, and their

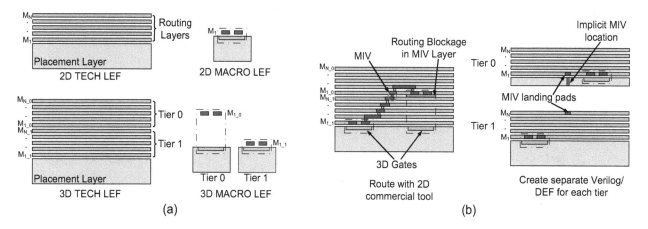

Figure 4: An overview of our router-based MIV insertion methodology. (a) The technology and macro LEF are modified to represent a two-tier monolithic 3D-IC. (b) The structure that is fed into the commercial router, which is then routed. The MIV locations are extracted and separate verilog/DEF files are created for each tier.

statistics are tabulated in Table 1. In addition to the clock period, number of cells, and number of nets, we also tabulate the minimum number of metal layers with which our 2D placement is routable. This is used as the number of metal layers for both 2D and monolithic 3D versions of each design.

The diameter of each MIV is assumed to be $100nm$, with a resistance of 2Ω and a capacitance of $0.1fF$ [10]. All monolithic 3D designs are implemented such that they have exactly 0% area overhead compared to its corresponding 2D version, i.e, exactly 50% footprint area, *irrespective of MIV count*. All routed WL results presented have been both global and detail routed using Cadence Encounter. After routing is complete, we dump parasitics for each tier separately. We then feed the tier netlists and parasitics, as well as the top-level parasitics (for MIVs) into Synopsys Primetime, which stitches everything together. We can then obtain the 3D timing and power, from which we obtain power delay product (PDP) numbers. We now conduct several experiments that demonstrate the benefits and scalability of our approach.

4.1 Comparison with Existing 3D Placement

Since no congestion-driven 3D placement exists, we run our placer in purely HPWL mode. We use the modified 2D placement scheme, followed by a placement-aware partitioning step that performs mincut alone. We compare our placer against two existing techniques for 3D placement. We first compare our work with 3D-Craft [5] which performs true 3D placement, and next we compare with the partition-then-place approach [9].

4.1.1 Comparison with 3D-Craft [5]

Only the binary version of this tool is available, and it does not a support target density driven mode. The cells are preset to always be placed with a target density of 1, or *without any whitespace in between them*. Such placements are inherently *not routable*, so we only compare the 3D half-perimeter wirelength (HPWL)in this section.

We first run both our placer and 3D-Craft with the number of dies set to one, which gives a 2D placement. Next, we run both placers with the number of dies set to two, which gives us a 3D placement. We compare only the improvement in HPWL when going to 3D. Our placer is run with a target density of 1, and the via weight parameter in 3D-Craft is set to 0 so that it is purely HPWL driven.

Table 2: Comparison between 3D-Craft and Our Placer

Circuit	Ours				3D-Craft			
	HPWL (m)			#MIV	HPWL (m)			#MIV
	2D	3D	3D/2D	$\times 10^3$	2D	3D	3D/2D	$\times 10^3$
mul_64	0.39	0.29	0.75	4.74	0.34	0.27	0.79	14.67
rca_16	1.15	0.91	0.79	14.94	1.22	0.97	0.80	49.07
aes_128	2.61	1.91	0.73	37.54	2.52	1.87	0.74	87.82
jpeg	4.96	3.65	0.73	54.00	5.09	3.78	0.74	147.34
fft_256	18.95	13.07	0.69	81.95	19.57	13.31	0.68	312.55
geo-mean	2.56	1.89	0.74	25.95	2.54	1.90	0.75	78.13
Norm.	1.00	1.00	1.00	1.00	0.99	1.00	1.01	3.01

We tabulate the results in Table 2. In this table, the number of MIVs is simply the number of 3D nets.

From this table, we observe that both placement approaches produce comparable wirelength improvements when going to 3D. The 1% difference could be due to minor differences in setting various parameters. We also note that our placer uses $3\times$ less 3D connections to provide more or less the same 3D HPWL. Although adding a single MIV incurs only a minor penalty w.r.t. the routed WL (as we can insert them only in whitespace), the penalty for $3\times$ the number of MIVs will be quite significant.

This shows that modified 2D placement is indeed sufficient to generate good 3D solutions for monolithic 3D, and development of new 3D specific placers is not really necessary. From a theoretical perspective, a true 3D placer solves force equations in the x,y, and z dimensions independently. Since each axis is independent, a modified 2D placer will solve identical equations in the x and y axis. In monolithic 3D, the entire z dimension is so small (a few μm), that solving for this axis is not really necessary. Any advancement in 2D placement techniques can thus be quickly deployed to get monolithic 3D placements. All of our routability enhancements that follow are equally valid on any starting placement.

4.1.2 Comparison with Partition-then-Place [9]

This technique of 3D placement first performs partitioning, and then 3D placement. During placement, it looks at all gates in the 3D space, but does not move gates between tiers. Therefore, the initial partition solution is very important, as it greatly affects solution quality. The advantage of this method is that it requires minimal modification to existing 2D placers. The only change required is to allow overlap between cells marked to be in different tiers. In com-

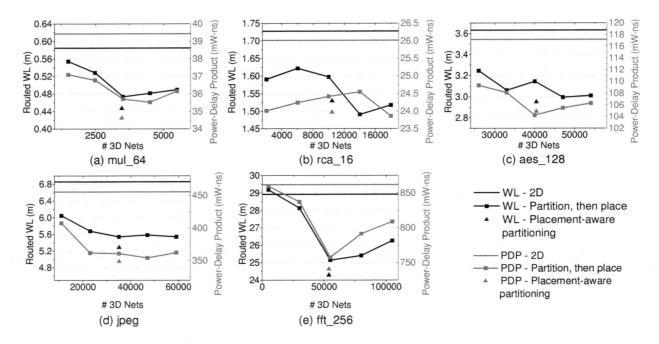

Figure 6: Comparison of 2D, partition-then-place, and placement-aware partitioning methods.

parison, our placement-aware partitioning approach requires even less modification to existing placers, as the partitioning is done as a post-process.

We use our own engine to perform both types of placement, so they have identical 2D numbers. In addition, the utilization of each circuit is set to 70%. Both placement solutions are taken through router-based MIV insertion. To generate initial partitions for the partition-then-place approach, we modify an existing multi-level partitioner to give us any target cutsize between min-cut and max-cut. First, we run the placement-aware partitioning approach and compute the number of 3D nets it uses. Next, we generate partitions starting from this cutsize, in increments of ±5% of the number of nets. The wirelength and PDP for 2D, partition-then-place and placement aware partitioning are plotted in Figure 6.

From these graphs, we first observe that choosing an appropriate cutsize is very important to the solution quality. In every case, reducing the number of 3D connections from that predicted by placement-aware partitioning worsens the routed WL. In some cases, it actually leads to solutions with worse quality than 2D (fft_256). Next, we observe that our placer offers upto 5.7% better routed WL than the partition-then-place approach, and the WL is lower in all benchmarks except rca_16. Even in the case of this benchmark, we get much lower WL for the same number of 3D connections.

Since the placer is not timing-driven, we expect, but cannot guarantee that the PDP is the best, and we observe that it is the minimum achieved in most cases, or very close. Lastly, we observe that even for the partition-then-place approach, the best solution quality is achieved for cutsizes close to that predicted by placement-aware partitioning.

4.2 Reducing Metal Layers in Monolithic-3D

Cost is one of the primary concerns that needs to be addressed before monolithic 3D can be widely adopted. If each tier uses the same number of metal layers as 2D, the additional cost over 2D is the bonding of the empty silicon wafer. One method to offset the increased cost is to reduce the metal layer count in 3D.

To that end, we now explore reducing the number metal layers in monolithic 3D. Note that this section incorporates all the routability enhancement techniques which will be described in detail in Subsection 4.3. The default case is when both tiers have the same number of metal layers as 2D (Table 1) . We term reducing one metal layer from the top-tier alone as "Tm1", and reducing one metal layer from each of the top and bottom tiers as "Tm1_Bm1". For each of these cases, we go through P&R and plot the wirelength and PDP for both the min-cut and min-overflow partitioners in Figure 7. We also plot the curves for 2D as comparison.

The first thing we observe is that all designs are able to be routed with zero violations even with reduced metal layers. These designs were not routable with fewer metal layers in 2D, so the fact that they are now routable indicates that monolithic 3D reduces the routing demand significantly. The next thing to note is that, as expected, reducing the metal layer count increases the wirelength and PDP. The magnitude of this increase depends on how congested the initial design is to begin with. We also note that our min-overflow partitioner helps both wirelength and PDP significantly. In many cases, the "Tm1" min-overflow result is better than the min-cut with all metal layers. Finally, we note that the difference between the min-cut and min-overflow partitioners is most pronounced in the "Tm1" case. This is because the tiers have unequal number of metal layers, and the min-overflow partitioner shifts the routing load to the tier that can handle it. Since reducing one metal layer is usually enough to offset increased cost, the subsequent sections focus on "Tm1" alone and detail the benefits of our routability-enhancement techniques.

4.3 Routability Enhancement Techniques

We assume that one metal layer is reduced from the top tier ("Tm1") and we discuss two techniques that make monolithic 3D-ICs more routable: (1) Router-based MIV insertion, and (2) Min-overflow partitioning. A summary of results is listed in Table 3, and we go over these subsequently.

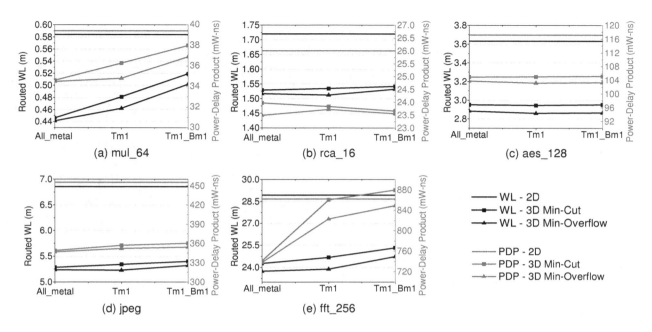

(a) mul_64   (b) rca_16   (c) aes_128

(d) jpeg   (e) fft_256

WL - 2D
WL - 3D Min-Cut
WL - 3D Min-Overflow

PDP - 2D
PDP - 3D Min-Cut
PDP - 3D Min-Overflow

Figure 7: The impact of reducing the metal layer count. "Tm1" means one metal layer is removed from the top tier.

Table 3: Comparison between 2D and different 3D placement techniques. "-" indicates that that version is unroutable.

Circuit	2D			Monolithic 3D									
				Flattened	Placement-driven			Router-driven (min-cut)			Router-driven (min-overflow)		
	HPWL	WL	PDP	HPWL	#MIV	WL	PDP	#MIV	WL	PDP	#MIV	WL	PDP
	(m)	(m)	(mW-ns)	(m)	($\times 10^3$)	(m)	(mW-ns)	($\times 10^3$)	(m)	(mW-ns)	($\times 10^3$)	(m)	(mW-ns)
mul_64	0.470	0.584	39.432	0.331	-	-	-	5.248	0.482	36.342	6.838	0.462	34.834
rca_16	1.250	1.727	26.010	0.973	10.515	1.600	23.803	17.762	1.534	23.835	23.623	1.513	23.723
aes_128	2.864	3.632	117.148	2.116	40.567	3.102	108.160	62.725	2.945	105.000	69.732	2.861	103.160
jpeg	5.630	6.857	455.220	4.040	35.128	6.273	378.831	52.592	5.342	357.014	62.909	5.230	351.788
fft_256	20.475	28.922	861.750	15.025	-	-	-	138.580	24.682	859.886	176.797	23.870	822.625
geo-mean	2.868	3.735	136.353	2.105	-	-	-	33.567	3.101	122.797	41.646	3.016	119.793
Norm.	1.000	1.000	1.000	0.734	-	-	-	1.000	0.830	0.901	1.241	0.808	0.879

4.3.1 Impact of Router-Based MIV Insertion

The conventional method for via insertion is to perform a post-place cell & via co-placement [9, 5]. We perform this and tabulate the results in Table 3 under the "Placement-driven" sub-heading. In addition, we also perform router-based MIV insertion and tabulate it under the "Router-driven (min-cut)" sub-heading.

As observed from this table, the placement-driven MIV insertion often produces results that are un-routable. In those cases that are routable, our router-based MIV insertion improves the routed WL by up to 16.6% and the PDP by up to 6.1%. This clearly shows the superiority of router-based MIV insertion. The reason behind this is shown in Figure 8. The placement-based method tends to cluster vias together, leading to large clumps of vias, and large areas without any vias. The vias are so small that it becomes difficult to route to them, causing huge issues during the track assignment stage (no problems are reported during trial-route). The router-based method, although it has more MIVs, spreads them out, dramatically increasing the routability.

4.3.2 Impact of Routability-Driven Partitioning

We now demonstrate the benefit of our min-overflow partitioner. We take the best min-cut solution from the previous step, and run our min-overflow partitioning heuristic on top of it. The results are shown in Table 3. Note that both the min-cut and min-overflow re-

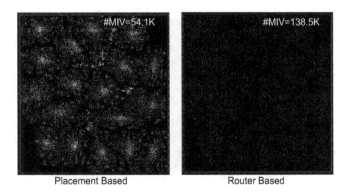

Placement Based   Router Based

Figure 8: Comparison of MIV insertion techniques for fft_256. Although router-based insertion has more MIVs, it spreads them out, dramatically improving the routability.

sults have the *same flattened HPWL*. Therefore, any gains in routed wirelength are purely from intelligent partitioning.

When compared with the min-cut solution, we see that we can reduce the routed WL by up to 4% (mul_64) and the PDP by up tp 4.33% (fft_256). On average, the min-overflow partitioner beats the min-cut w.r.t. wirelenth and PDP by 2.73% and 2.44% respec-

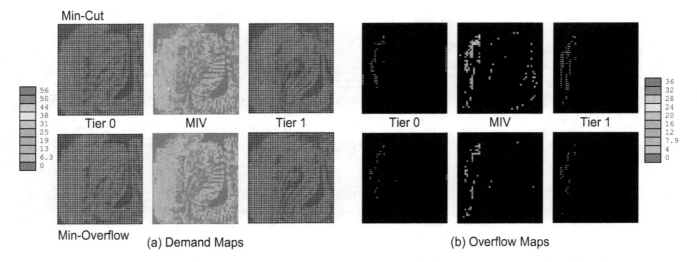

Min-Cut

Tier 0   MIV   Tier 1   Tier 0   MIV   Tier 1

Min-Overflow   (a) Demand Maps   (b) Overflow Maps

Figure 9: Demand and overflow maps of the mul_64 benchmark for the min-cut and min-overflow partitioners. Additional MIVs are used to reduce the overflow.

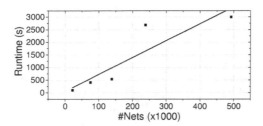

Figure 10: #Nets vs. runtime for our min-overflow partitioner.

tively. These gains are significant, especially given by the fact that we do not change the target density, and the flattened HPWL remains the same. The MIV count increases by 24.1%, so in essence, we utilize the fine-grained nature of MIVs to improve routability. We also show demand and overflow maps for both our min-cut and min-overflow partitioners in Figure 9.

To demonstrate the scalability of our partitioner, we also plot the runtime vs. the number of nets in Figure 10. As seen from this figure, our partitioner is more or less linear in runtime, and can scale well to larger benchmarks.

5. CONCLUSION

In this work, we have demonstrated that modified 2D placement coupled with a placement-aware partitioning step is sufficient to produce high quality monolithic 3D-IC placement results. We have presented a router-based MIV insertion algorithm that makes previously unroutable designs routable. We developed a monolithic 3D demand model, and used it to build a fast $O(N)$ min-overflow partitioning heuristic. Under the same flattened HPWL, this algorithm helps reduce the routed wirelength by up to 4% and the power delay product by up to 4.33%. This algorithm enables us to reduce the metal layer count of monolithic 3D without sacrificing quality. Finally, when compared to 2D, monolithic 3D with reduced metal layers is observed to be improve the routed WL and PDP by 19.2% and 12.1% respectively.

6. REFERENCES

[1] P. Batude et al. Advances in 3D CMOS Sequential Integration. In *Proc. IEEE Int. Electron Devices Meeting*, 2009.

[2] S. Bobba et al. CELONCEL: Effective design technique for 3-D monolithic integration targeting high performance integrated circuits. In *Proc. Asia and South Pacific Design Automation Conf.*, 2011.

[3] U. Brenner and A. Rohe. An Effective Congestion Driven Placement Framework. *IEEE Trans. on Computer-Aided Design of Integrated Circuits and Systems*, 2003.

[4] C. Chu and Y.-C. Wong. FLUTE: Fast Lookup Table Based Rectilinear Steiner Minimal Tree Algorithm for VLSI Design. *IEEE Trans. on Computer-Aided Design of Integrated Circuits and Systems*, 2008.

[5] J. Cong and G. Luo. A Multilevel Analytical Placement for 3D ICs. In *Proc. Asia and South Pacific Design Automation Conf.*, 2009.

[6] J. Cong, G. Luo, J. Wei, and Y. Zhang. Thermal-Aware 3D IC Placement Via Transformation. In *Proc. Asia and South Pacific Design Automation Conf.*, 2007.

[7] C. M. Fiduccia and R. M. Mattheyses. A linear-time heuristic for improving network partitions. In *Proc. ACM Design Automation Conf.*, 1982.

[8] S.-M. Jung et al. 500-MHz DDR High-Performance 72-Mb 3-D SRAM Fabricated With Laser-Induced Epitaxial c-Si Growth Technology. In *IEEE Trans. on Electron Devices*, 2010.

[9] D. Kim, K. Athikulwongse, and S. Lim. A study of Through-Silicon-Via Impact on the 3D Stacked IC Layout. In *Proc. IEEE Int. Conf. on Computer-Aided Design*, pages 674–680, 2009.

[10] Y.-J. Lee, D. Limbrick, and S. K. Lim. Power Benefit Study for Ultra-High Density Transistor-Level Monolithic 3D ICs. In *Proc. ACM Design Automation Conf.*, 2013.

[11] S. Panth, K. Samadi, Y. Du, and S. K. Lim. High-Density Integration of Functional Modules Using Monolithic 3D-IC Technology. In *Proc. Asia and South Pacific Design Automation Conf.*, 2013.

[12] P. Spindler, U. Schlichtmann, and F. M. Johannes. Kraftwerk2 - A Fast Force-Directed Quadratic Placement Approach Using an Accurate Net Model. *IEEE Trans. on Computer-Aided Design of Integrated Circuits and Systems*, 2008.

Coupling-Aware Force Driven Placement of TSVs and Shields in 3D-IC Layouts

Caleb Serafy and Ankur Srivastava
University of Maryland, College Park, MD, USA
{cserafy1, ankurs}@umd.edu

ABSTRACT

In 3D ICs, TSV cross coupling can seriously degrade circuit performance if it is not sufficiently considered in a design. Cross coupling is heavily dependent on how TSVs are placed, and should be considered during the floorplanning of the chip. In this work we propose a coupling-aware TSV placement algorithm that attempts to reduce both wirelength and TSV cross coupling. TSV shielding is another method for coupling mitigation, and the proposed algorithm combines coupling-aware TSV placement with shield insertion to yield better results than either technique alone. With regard to the most heavily coupled TSV pair in a design, our results show that applying both techniques simultaneously produces a 12.3% improvement in maximum S-parameter compared to traditional TSV placement which optimizes wirelength only. Using coupling-aware TSV placement or shield insertion alone produces a 4.2% and 4.8% improvement respectively. The improvement offered by using both techniques simultaneously is actually more than the sum of the improvement offered by using each technique on its own. This implies that the two techniques are not independent of one another, and that when used simultaneously each technique increases the effectiveness of the other, giving strong motivation for using them both simultaneously. Furthermore, the percent increase in wirelength due to using these two techniques is an order of magnitude less than the percent improvement to coupling, justifying the tradeoff made by our algorithm.

Categories and Subject Descriptors

B.7.2 [**Integrated Circuits**]: Design Aids—*Placement and routing*

Keywords

3D-IC; TSV placement; TSV sheilding; Coupling Awareness

1. INTRODUCTION AND MOTIVATION

Recently, vertical stacking of ICs (3D ICs) has become a viable technology, and is currently being heavily researched to facilitate large-scale commercial use in the near future.

3D integration can offer many advantages, such as decreasing the length of global interconnects and facilitating chip level integration of circuits manufactured in disparate technologies. Vertical integration can drastically decrease wire delays and increase bandwidth between circuits. 3D ICs requires vertical interconnects between layers, and the most common such interconnect is the through silicon via (TSV). Vertical integration brings new challenges, such as removal of heat, maintaining sufficient manufacturing yield, and deciding where to place TSVs.

Most TSV placement algorithms seek to place TSVs such that the total wirelength of a circuit is minimized, but another important goal is to maintain the signal integrity of the circuit by keeping the cross coupling between TSVs below a given threshold. The physical characteristics of TSVs give them fundamentally different cross coupling behavior than that of traditional planar (2D) wires, so new coupling models are needed. Using TSV coupling models, the effect of TSV cross coupling must be considered in the TSV placement stage of a design.

In this paper an algorithm is presented for determining the placement of TSVs in a layout. It is assumed that transistor placement is done prior to TSV placement using standard analytical placement algorithms configured to leave enough empty whitespace in the layout to accommodate TSVs. After transistor placement, TSVs are placed using our proposed force driven placement algorithm, which is inspired by analytical transistor placement tools. Our proposed algorithm has standard TSV placement forces which reduce wirelength and overlap, as well as an additional force to reduce TSV cross coupling, thus making our algorithm coupling-aware. Beyond the coupling mitigation provided by coupling-aware TSV placement, the algorithm also performs shield insertion, leading to better results than could be produced using either method on its own. Shielding is achieved by adding undriven TSVs to the layout [7], but requires reserving additional whitespace during the transistor placement stage. The models used for estimating TSV coupling and the algorithm used for shield insertion were developed in previous work [7].

Specifically, this work makes the following contributions:

- To the best of our knowledge, this is the first paper to present a TSV placement algorithm that performs coupling-aware placement and shield insertion simultaneously.

- Our proposed algorithm offers a 12.3% improvement to the S-parameter of the most heavily coupled TSV pair as compared to layouts produced by traditional TSV placement that optimizes wirelength only.

- Our results show that the improvement offered by using both techniques together is greater than the sum of the improvement offered by each technique alone, implying that each technique improves the effectiveness of the other, and giving strong motivation for using both techniques simultaneously.

- Our results show that the percent increase in wire-length caused by these techniques is an order of magnitude less than the percent improvement to the coupling profile, justifying the tradeoffs made by our algorithm.

The rest of this paper is laid out as follows: Section 2 gives some background information concerning TSV-TSV coupling, TSV shielding, and force driven placement. Section 3 presents our TSV placement algorithm which includes a shield insertion algorithm from [7]. Experimental setups and results from our analysis are presented in Section 4, where we compare TSV placement with and without coupling-awareness, and with and without shield insertion. Finally, the paper concludes in Section 5.

2. BACKGROUND

3D ICs are formed by stacking multiple layers of traditional (2D) ICs one atop the other. Some nets in the 3D circuit span multiple layers, and are connected with vertical interconnects called through silicon vias (TSVs). TSVs are vertical columns of metal that pass through the silicon substrate and connect the horizontal metal wires in adjacent IC layers, as shown in Figure 1. Because a TSV passes through the substrate, transistors and TSVs cannot coexist at that same location in the same layer. TSVs pass through the electrically charged and conductive silicon substrate, and so they must be surrounded by a layer of insulating material to decouple them from the substrate. This layer of insulation is called the liner, and is typically made of silicon dioxide (SiO2). In current manufacturing technologies, TSV aspect ratios are constrained, making TSVs much thicker than traditional planar wires. There exists a minimum spacing between TSVs and other features such as transistors and other TSVs, which must be enforced in order to guarantee proper functionality of the chip. This minimum spacing is called the keep out zone (KOZ) and is determined by the precision of the manufacturing process and TSV effects such as thermal stress around a TSV due to the mismatch in thermal expansion of the silicon, the liner, and the TSV [8].

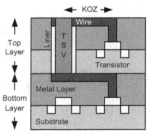

Figure 1: 3D IC cross section

2.1 TSV-TSV Coupling

Although the liner completely decouples a TSV from the substrate for DC components of a signal, high frequency AC components can capacitively couple from the TSV into the substrate, and then through the substrate into other TSVs. This coupling path is shown in Figure 2. To reduce coupling between TSVs one can reduce the liner capacitance, reduce the substrate capacitance or increase the substrate

resistance. Reducing the liner capacitance would require using thicker liners or a liner material with a lower dielectric constant, both of which would require changing the manufacturing process and potentially decreasing manufacturing yield or increasing cost. Likewise, increasing/decreasing the substrate resistance/capacitance would require using a different substrate material, or increasing the separation between TSVs. Changing the substrate material can potentially be quite costly, and moreover a more resistive substrate will degrade the performance of the circuit. Increasing the separation between TSVs can reduce coupling, but might require TSVs to be so far spread apart that the circuit area and net wirelengths becomes unreasonable large [5].

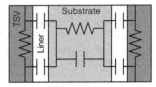

Figure 2: Electrical model of TSV coupling

2.2 Shielding

In addition to changing the electrical parameters of the coupling path as discussed in Section 2.1, another way to reduce coupling between TSVs is to insert shields between them [7, 5]. A shield can be any piece of conductive material which blocks the propagation of EM fields in a circuit. Coupling between TSVs occurs throughout the thickness of the substrate due to the vertical nature of the TSV structure, which makes traditional shielding techniques such as guard rings ineffective [2]. We propose using TSVs as shields, as they can provide shielding throughout the thickness of the substrate. Shield TSVs are not electrically connected to the circuit and solely exist to improve the signal integrity of the 3D nets. To differentiate the two types of TSVs, electrically connected TSVs are referred to as signal TSVs. The drawback to shield insertion is that adding shield TSVs to a layout inherently takes up more chip area than a layout without shield TSVs. Increasing the spacing between TSVs and insertion of shield TSVs are two orthogonal approaches to coupling mitigation, and each has its own advantages and disadvantages. In this work we will show that using both techniques together can improve signal integrity much more than using either technique alone, and that the two techniques actually increase each other's effectiveness. Previous work has developed a geometric model of TSV coupling which considers the effects of shields [7], and we use this model to estimate coupling parameters in this work.

2.3 Force Driven Placement

In this work, we attempt to use a force driven placement algorithm to determine where to place TSVs in a layout, assuming transistors have already been placed. The idea of force driven placement has been used in many analytical placement algorithms in the past, such as Kraftwerk2 [9] and Fastplace [10]. The general idea of force driven placement is that there are multiple opposing forces acting on each placeable body (usually standard cells and/or TSV cells [4]) and the algorithm finds the placement which results in zero net force on each body (i.e. the equilibrium point). As the bodies move, the forces exerted on one body by another changes, so force driven placement algorithms are solved iteratively by evaluating the forces due to the current position, finding the equilibrium point, and then reevaluating the forces caused by the new placement. This process iterates until the entire system converges. Common forces used in force driven placement are wirelength force which pushes bodies towards the position which minimizes their associated wirelength, and overlap force which pushes overlapping bodies away from each other. In this work we introduce a new force: the coupling force, which pushes TSVs away from the TSV to which it is most strongly coupled.

2.4 Previous Work

In [7], an algorithm was developed for inserting shields into a layout, but it assumed that the position of signal TSVs was already fixed, so coupling-aware TSV placement was not considered. In [6] the force driven placement algorithm from Kraftwerk2 [9] is modified to include a coupling force, but shield insertion is not considered. [3] performs transistor placement while reserving whitespace, and then places TSVs in the reserved whitespace, but that work does not consider reserving whitespace for both signal and shield TSVs, so shielding is not considered. Moreover, the TSV placement in [3] is not coupling aware. In the work presented here, we assume whitespace for both signal and shield TSVs has been reserved during transistor placement. We present a force driven placement algorithm to place signal TSVs while simultaneously performing shield insertion.

3. TSV PLACEMENT ALGORITHM

Our proposed algorithm places TSVs by performing a coupling-aware force driven placement in two steps, with shield insertion performed in between the two steps. The objective of our TSV placement algorithm is to place TSVs such that wirelength is minimized while keeping the coupling profile of each TSV above some threshold. Our algorithm starts with a transistor layout containing inserted whitespace [3]. Enough whitespace must be inserted to the transistor layout to accommodate all signal TSVs plus a sufficient number of shield TSVs . The initial transistor layout is discretized to a grid of arbitrary granularity such that each grid point is considered either a whitespace or blackspace point (i.e. a grid point where transistors are placed). Each vertical net is assumed to have two pins: one on the top layer and one on the bottom. These pins define a netbox which is the smallest rectangle that encloses both pins, as illustrated in Figure 7(b). Although this work only considers a two-layer 3D IC with two-pin nets, the algorithm could easily be extended to work with an arbitrary number of layers and multi-pin nets.

Once the transistor layout has been discretized to a grid, TSVs must be assigned an initial placement. The routine for initially placing TSVs is presented in Section 3.1. After assigning each TSV an initial placement, the first iterative stage of our algorithm begins. On each iteration, placement forces are evaluated for each signal TSV, and the TSVs are moved along their net force vector. This process repeats until the signal TSVs reach an equilibrium state where the net force on each TSV is zero. Once the layout (which until this point contains only signal TSVs) reaches equilibrium, shield TSVs are inserted into the layout using the shield insertion algorithm from [7], described in section 3.3. Shield insertion causes the TSV forces to no longer be at equilibrium, and a second iterative stage occurs, changing the positions of both signal and shield TSVs. Once all TSVs reach equilibrium in the second iterative stage, the algorithm terminates and

returns a final TSV placement which includes both shield and signal TSVs. The algorithm is illustrated in Figure 3

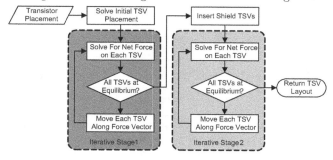

Figure 3: Our Proposed TSV Placement Algorithm

There are four placement forces used in the two iterative phases of our algorithm: (1) KOZ force, (2) Wirelength force, (3) Coupling force and (4) Shielding force. Each force is explained in detail in Sections 3.2 and 3.4, but a brief description of each is given here. The KOZ force is a repulsive force that is exerted on TSVs by other TSVs, and by blackspace grid points. This force keeps TSVs from getting too close to each other or the transistors, which could result in improper circuit functionality. The wirelength force is a force that attracts TSVs towards their netbox in order to reduce wirelength. The coupling force is a repulsive force similar to the KOZ force, but it affects signal TSVs only, and its magnitude is proportional to the degree of coupling between two TSVs. The shielding force is similar to the wirelength force, and only applies to shield TSVs. Each shield TSV is assigned a set of signal TSVs which it is to provide shielding to. The shielding force attracts each shield to its assigned signal TSVs in order to optimize shield placement. The net (total) force exerted on a signal and shield TSV is defined in Table 1. The coefficients λ_1 and λ_2 are weighting factors, and changing the ratio between them can cause the algorithm to put more emphasis on wirelength or coupling.

Signal TSV	Shield TSV
$\sum F_{KOZ} + \lambda_1 F_{WL} + \lambda_2 \max(F_C)$	$\sum F_{KOZ} + F_{Shielding}$

Table 1: Net force definitions

3.1 Initial TSV Placement

Given a 3D transistor placement, each grid point on each layer is defined as either a whitespace or a blackspace grid point. Unconnected whitespace regions are identified by constructing a graph where each grid point represents a node. If two whitespace nodes are adjacent on the grid, an edge exists between them. A graph traversal is performed to identify unconnected subgraphs, and the members of each such subgraph define a whitespace region, as illustrated in Figure 4.

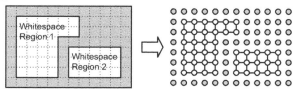

Figure 4: Two unconnected whitespace regions

The initial signal TSV placement is determined by solving a min cost flow (MCF) formulation that assigns each 3D net to a whitespace region. The MCF formulation is shown in Figure 5. Each 3D net corresponds to a net node, and each whitespace region corresponds to a region node. There is also a source and sink node, such that N units of flow are inserted into the source node and N units of flow are extracted from the sink node, where N is the number of 3D nets. An edge exists from the source node to each net node, which has zero cost and unit capacity. In this way, one unit of flow passes through each net node. An edge connects from each net node to each region node, such that one unit of flow passes from each net node to some region node. The region node that carries flow from a given net node defines which whitespace region will contain the TSV for that 3D net. The cost associated with an edge between a net node and a region node corresponds to the increase in wirelength that would occur if that 3D net places its TSV in the center of that whitespace region. An edge connects from each region node to the sink node with a capacity equal to the number of TSVs that can fit inside each whitespace region. In this way, no region is assigned more TSVs than it can physically accommodate. By solving this MCF formulation, each 3D net assigns a TSV to a region such that the total wirelength is minimized.

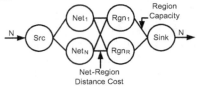

Figure 5: MCF formulation for assigning nets to regions

Once the TSV associated with each 3D net is assigned to a whitespace region, each TSV must be assigned to a unique grid point in its assigned region such that the initial placement is a valid placement, and wirelength is close to minimized. TSVs are assigned positions one by one, starting with the TSV with the largest cost between its associated net node and chosen region node (i.e. largest net-region weight). After each TSV is assigned a position, the KOZ (KOZ radius is 2.5 um in this work) around that position is no longer available to other TSVs, so by placing TSVs in order of decreasing net-region weight, we give the most optimized positions to those TSVs associated with the 3D nets with the longest wirelengths. After the initial placement is made, the two iterative stages of the algorithm improve the signal integrity at the expense of slightly increasing wirelength. The initial placement algorithm is enumerated here as follows:

1. Identify each unconnected whitespace region

2. Remove the KOZ around the edge of each region

3. Assign each region a capacity: $\lceil area/(2 \times KOZ)^2 \rceil$

4. Assign each net-region pair a weight: distance between region center and netbox

5. Solve MCF problem to assign nets to regions (Figure 5)

6. Assign TSVs to chosen region in descending order of net-region weight such that KOZ is not violated

3.2 TSV Placement Forces: First Iterative Phase

Once all signal TSVs have been assigned an initial position on the layout grid, the first iterative step of the algorithm begins. During this step the net force on each signal TSV is calculated as a sum of the three signal TSV placement forces (see Table 1) which are defined in this section, and TSVs are moved along their force vectors. This process repeats iteratively until the TSV placement converges and the net force on each TSV is zero.

KOZ Force: The keep out zone (KOZ) is the minimum spacing between two TSVs or a between a TSV and a transistor. In this work the KOZ radius is 2.5 um. The KOZ force repels TSVs from one another and from blackspace grid points. Ideally the KOZ force would be a discontinuous step function, such that when an object is inside the TSV's KOZ, the TSV is repelled from that object, and if the object is outside the TSV's KOZ, then no force exists. In this work we use a continuous and differentiable approximation of the step function to calculate the magnitude of the KOZ force. The magnitude of the KOZ force is defined in Equation (1) and plotted in Figure 6, where d is the distance between the two TSVs, or a TSV and a blackspace grid point. The parameter p in Equation 1 is the smoothing factor. As p approaches infinity, the KOZ force approaches the ideal step function, but a reasonably small p must be chosen to avoid numerical overflow. In this work $p = 10$ is chosen. To solve for the net force on a TSV, the force vectors created by each TSV and blackspace grid point is added together (see Table 1).

$$F_{KOZ}(d) = \exp\left[-(d/KOZ)^p\right] \qquad (1)$$

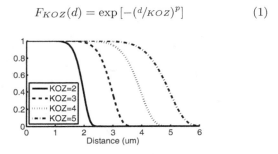

Figure 6: KOZ Force as a function of distance ($p = 10$)

Wirelength Force:

In two-layer 3D ICs with two-pin nets, which are considered in this work, the wirelength (WL) of a net is defined as the sum of the half perimeter (i.e. width plus height) of the bounding box on each layer that contains the TSV and the pin. This is illustrated in Figure 7(a), where $WL = x_1 + y_1 + x_2 + y_2$. If a TSV exists anywhere within the bounding box containing both pins (i.e. the netbox), the total WL is equal to the half perimeter of the netbox. An illustration of a netbox is show in Figure 7(b). The half parameter of its netbox is the minimum wirelength possible for a net. As a TSV moves outside of the netbox, the wirelength increases at a constant rate. F_{WL} is a force that pushes a TSV towards the netbox, with magnitude linearly proportional to how far a TSV is outside the netbox.

Since the WL calculation consists of x and y components that are independent of each other, the x and y components of F_{WL} can be solved independently. Ideally, the wirelength force is proportional to how far outside the netbox a TSV is. Let d_x be the difference between the x components of the center of the netbox and the TSV position, and let w

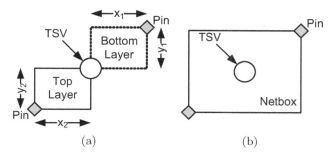

Figure 7: (a) Wirelength calculation (b) Netbox illustration

be the width of the netbox. Equation (4) shows the ideal formulation for the x component of the wirelength force. We smooth this undifferentiable function using the identity $\min(a, b) = -\max(-a, -b)$ and the log-sum-exponent relaxation in [1], which is shown in Equation (5). The x component of the smoothed wirelength force is defined in Equations (6) and (7), and is plotted in Figure 8. Analogous equations are used for solving $F_{y,WL}$, using height h instead of width w. In this work we use $k = 10$ as a reasonable smoothing factor which avoids numerical overflow.

$$L_x = d_x + 0.5w \quad (2) \qquad R_x = d_x - 0.5w \quad (3)$$

$$F_{x,WL}^{Ideal}(d_x, w) = \max(-L_x, \min(0, -R_x)) \quad (4)$$

$$\max(a, b) = \lim_{k \to \infty} k^{-1} \log[\exp(ka) + \exp(kb)] \quad (5)$$

$$m_x = -k^{-1} \log[\exp(-k \times 0) + \exp(-k \times -R_x)] \quad (6)$$

$$F_{x,WL}(d_x, w) = k^{-1} \log[\exp(k \times -L_x) + \exp(k \times m_x)] \quad (7)$$

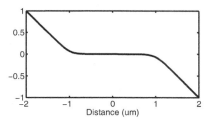

Figure 8: Wirelength Force as a function of distance ($w = 2, k = 10$)

Coupling Force: Cross coupling between TSVs is quantified by the S-parameter between two TSVs, which is the ratio between the voltage swing on one TSV (i.e. the aggressor TSV) and the coupled noise swing on the other TSV (i.e. the victim TSV) [7]. We model the S-parameter between two TSVs as a function of their geometric placement (as well as the placement of shield TSVs) using the geometric model of coupling defined in [7]. During the first iterative step of our algorithm, there are only signal TSVs, and the S-parameter is approximated using the equation for unshielded S-parameter is shown in Equation (8), where d represents the distance between two TSVs. The coupling force is a repellent force that pushes signal TSVs away from each other, and is proportional to the S-parameter between the two TSVs. The geometric model of coupling [7] estimates S parameters in units of decibels, so when calculating coupling force we

convert the values back to magnitudes using Equation (9). The subtraction $S(d) - S(0)$ normalizes the coupling force to unity when two TSVs are completely overlapping. Unshielded coupling force F_C is plotted in Figure 9.

$$S(d) = 8.79 \times 1.04^{-d} - 0.0126 \times d - 33.2 \quad (8)$$

$$F_C(d) = 10^{\frac{S(d) - S(0)}{20}} \quad (9)$$

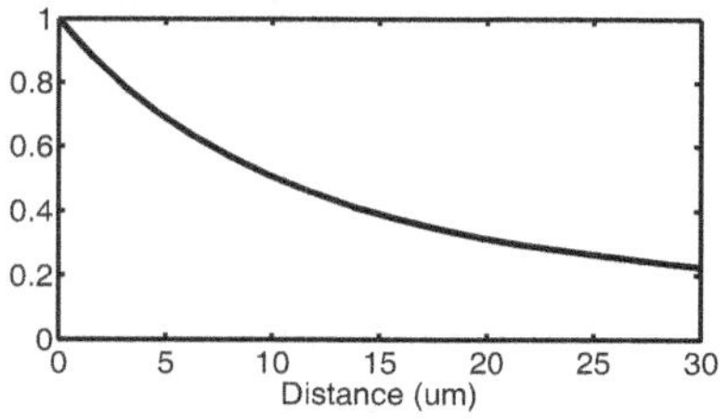

Figure 9: Unshielded Coupling Force as a function of distance

A coupling force can be evaluated between each pair of signal TSVs. Because the objective of coupling-aware placement is to minimize the *worst case* coupling across all pairs, each signal TSV only applies the force from the TSV to which it is coupled most heavily (i.e. $\max(F_C)$, see Table 1). In this way many TSVs with a small coupling force cannot overpower one TSV with a large coupling force. In other words our algorithm will not reduce the average coupling between all pairs at the expense of increasing the coupling between the worst case pair.

3.3 Shield Insertion

Once the force driven placement algorithm has finished iterating (i.e. all TSV forces come to equilibrium), we insert shields into the layout to further improve signal integrity. Pairs of signal TSVs that have S-parameters below a certain threshold T are identified, and shields are assigned to those pairs. Each shield can be assigned to one or more pairs (because the same shield TSV can shield multiple pairs of signal TSVs [7]), and each pair can have multiple shields assigned to it. The method used for shield insertion used in this work is a slightly modified version of the shield insertion algorithm developed in [7]. The shield insertion algorithm is explained in detail in that paper, and a brief overview is given in the following paragraphs. After shield insertion is completed, a second iteration phase begins, allowing the forces to once again come to equilibrium. The addition of shields causes the coupling forces to change, resulting in the signal TSVs no longer being at equilibrium. Also, the shields may not be at equilibrium in their initial positions. Thus, both shield and signal TSVs may change position in the second iteration phase.

Shield Assignment: Shield TSVs are assigned to pairs of signal TSVs by solving a min cost flow (MCF) formulation. The formulation is solved iteratively, and the cost coefficients are augmented on each iteration based on the results of the previous iteration. The costs are augmented in such a way as to entice multiple TSV pairs to share the same shield, thus minimizing the number of inserted shields. Iteration stops when the difference between two sequential formulations is below some threshold. The MCF formulation contains the following nodes: a source node, a sink node, one pair node for each signal TSV pair requiring shielding, and a point node for each point in the layout grid that can accommodate a shield TSV. Points that are too close to transistors or signal TSVs are excluded from the set of considered points, thus ensuring that all shield placements adhere to the KOZ constraint.

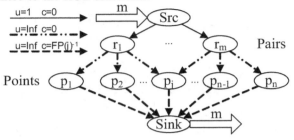

Figure 10: MCF formulation for shield insertion

The described MCF formulation is shown in Figure 10, where m is the number of TSV pairs that require shielding and n is the number of points on the layout grid which can accommodate a shield TSV. The variables u and c represent the capacity and cost of each edge. There exists an edge from the source node to all pair nodes ($r_1 \ldots r_m$), and there exists an edge from each point node ($p_1 \ldots p_n$) to the sink node. There is an edge from each pair node to each point node which can shield it sufficiently, as determined by the geometric model of coupling. To solve the MCF formulation, one unit of flow moves from the source node to each pair node. From each pair node, a unit of flow passes through some point node and into the sink node. The unit of flow at each pair node represents that pair's need for shielding, and the point node through which that flow passes represents the best position for a shield to satisfy that pair's need.

For each TSV pair and for each point, the amount of shielding (change in S-parameter) offered to that pair by placing a shield at that point is calculated. The amount of shielding offered to TSV pair i due to placing a shield at point j is defined as $S_s(d_i, y_{ij})$, which is formally explained in the following paragraph. If a point provides a sufficient level of shielding (i.e. $S_s(d_i, y_{ij})$ is greater than some threshold T_s), then an edge exists from pair node i to point node j. If $S_s(d_i, y_{ij}) < T_s \; \forall j$, then pair i cannot feasibly be shielded because no edges exist to carry the flow out of pair node i. If this occurs, pair node i is removed from the formulation.

The definition of $S_s(d, y)$ was published in [7], and is repeated here in Equations (10) through (12). The value d_i is the length of pair line i, which is the line segment connecting the center of the two TSVs constituting TSV pair i. The value y_{ij} is the length of the line segment which has the following three properties: (1) it is perpendicular to pair line i, (2) one endpoint exists on pair line i, and (3) the other endpoint is point j. If no such line exists, then y_{ij} is defined to be infinity. These variables are illustrated in Figure 11.

$$a(d) = 2.81 \times 1.24^{-d} + 0.545 \tag{10}$$

$$b(d) = 0.616 \times 1.32^{-d} + 1.02 \tag{11}$$

$$S_s(d, y) = -a(d) \times b(d)^{-|y^{1.5}|} \tag{12}$$

The cost $FP(j)$ is associated with each point, and it is a function of the total amount of shielding offered to all the pairs by placing a shield at point j. The exact method of solving for $FP(j)$ can be found in [7]. Once the MCF

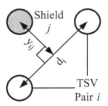

Figure 11: Shielding model variable definitions

formulation is solved, the identified shields are inserted into the layout.

3.4 TSV Placement Forces: Second Iterative Phase

Once shield TSVs have been inserted into the layout grid, the second iterative step of the algorithm begins. During this step the net force on each signal TSV is calculated just as it was in the first iterative stage, although the addition of shields changes the S-parameters between TSVs, and thus changes the magnitude of the coupling forces. The net force on shield TSVs is calculated by evaluating a KOZ force, just like signal TSVs, and a shielding force, which is defined in this section.

Coupling Force: During the second iterative stage of the algorithm, the addition of shields to layout changes the S-parameters between signal TSVs, and requires a more complicated S-parameter model. The full shielded geometric model is explained in [7]. The coupling force is not applied to shield TSVs because they are not electrically connected, and so they do not cause electrical coupling.

Shielding Force: The shielding force is a force that only applies to shield TSVs. When shields are inserted (see Section 3.3), each shield is associated with a set of signal TSVs that it is intended to shield. The shielding force pushes a shield towards its assigned signal TSVs. The shielding force can be defined using the wirelength force formulation by considering each assigned signal TSV as a netbox of width/height zero, centered at the location of the signal TSV. The shielding force $F_{shielding}$ is defined in Equation (13), where A represents the set of signal TSVs assigned to a given shield. In this way, each shield TSV is forced towards the signal TSVs it is assigned to provide shielding to, ensuring that as signal TSV's move during the second iterative stage, the shields follow along and continue to provide shielding.

$$F_{Shielding} = \sum_{a \in A} F_{,WL}(d_a, 0) \tag{13}$$

4. EXPERIMENTAL RESULTS

In order to evaluate the effectiveness of the proposed TSV placement algorithm, we generate some example cell layouts and run the algorithm. By default $\lambda_1 = \lambda2 = 1$, which means the algorithm is coupling aware and gives equal weight to coupling and wirelength forces. The algorithm can be configured to do traditional TSV placement (i.e. wirelength optimization only) by setting $\lambda_2 = 0$, and can be configured to forgo shield insertion by terminating the algorithm after the first iterative stage. We compare the different results produced by the following four cases:

1. Traditional TSV Placement: wirelength optimization only, no shield TSV insertion

2. CA: coupling-aware TSV placement, no shield TSV insertion

3. SI: wirelength optimization only with shield TSV insertion

4. CA+SI: coupling-aware TSV placement with shield TSV insertion

When comparing these results, we consider the maximum degree of coupling (S-parameter) between two TSVs, as well as the total wirelength. S-parameters are estimated using the geometric model of coupling introduced in [7], and the wirelength measurement is discussed in Section 3.2. The benchmarks used to run our algorithm are created by randomly inserting whitespace into a 150 um by 150 um layout. An example layout is shown in Figure 12 where the black areas contain transistors and the white areas are the whitespace available for TSV insertion. The final results are tabulated and discussed in Section 4.1, where results are reported in terms of the percent increase or decrease in each metric when comparing CA, SI and CA+SI to traditional TSV placement. The physical dimensions of TSVs are given in Table 2.

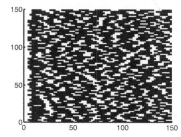

Figure 12: Example cell placement

TSV Radius	1 um
TSV Liner Thickness	0.2 um
Substrate Thickness	50 um

Table 2: TSV physical parameters

4.1 Results

Table 3 reports the percent increase or decrease as compared to traditional TSV placement in each of the metrics. Results are reported for case CA (coupling-aware TSV placement), SI (shield insertion) and CA+SI (coupling-aware TSV placement with shield insertion). The table also shows the number of signal TSVs (i.e. 3D nets) in each benchmark, and the number of shield TSVs inserted using each method. An example TSV placement result using each of the four methods is shown in Figure 13. It can be seen that in the cases where coupling-aware TSV placement is used, TSVs end up spread farther apart. This spreading of the TSVs not only decreases their coupling, but also provides more room to insert shields, which can be observed when comparing shield insertion with and without coupling-aware TSV placement. This implies that there exists an interaction between coupling-aware TSV placement and shield insertion where coupling-aware TSV placement actually improves the effectiveness of shield insertion. Our results verify that this is indeed true.

An important metric relating to the overall performance of the chip is the maximum S-parameter across all signal TSV

pairs. In all benchmarks, CA+SI gives the best results w.r.t. lowering the maximum S-parameter. In some benchmarks, such as B6, coupling-aware TSV placement alone (CA) can come close to matching the improvement offered by CA+SI, and in others, such as B3, shield insertion alone (SI) can do the same. However, in most benchmarks the level of improvement offered by CA+SI is much higher than that which is offered by either technique alone. Moreover, the improvement offered by CA+SI is often higher than even the sum of the improvement offered by CA and SI, implying that the use of one technique improves the effectiveness of the other. This gives a strong motivation for using both techniques simultaneously. On average, CA offers 4.2% improvement, SI offers 4.8% improvement, and CA+SI offers 12.3% improvement, which is significantly more than the sum of either technique alone (i.e. $12.3 > 4.2 + 4.8 = 9$). The main interaction between these two techniques that explains this phenomenon is that the coupling-aware placement spreads TSVs farther apart during the first iteration phase, which not only decreases the coupling between TSVs, but also allows more space to insert shields directly in between pairs during the shield insertion phase, making shield insertion more effective.

The tradeoff posed by coupling-aware TSV placement is to reduce the amount of coupling between TSVs, but at the expense of spreading the TSVs farther apart and increasing the wirelength of many nets. Considering the wirelength results we see that shield insertion does not effect the wirelength, but that coupling-aware TSV placement increases the total wirelength by about 0.4%. Since CA+SI can offer more than a 10% improvement to the worst case coupling in a circuit, paying less than 1% in increased wirelength seems to be a good tradeoff to make.

5. CONCLUSION

In this paper we have considered mitigating cross coupling between TSVs in a 3D IC layout. Our results show that coupling-aware TSV placement and shield TSV insertion are both good techniques for solving this problem, and that the use of both techniques simultaneously can make each one more effective. We also show that the percent increase in wirelength due to these techniques is an order of magnitude less than the percent decrease in worst case TSV coupling, which makes the tradeoff offered by our techniques well worth making.

6. REFERENCES

[1] T.-C. Chen, Z.-W. Jiang, T.-C. Hsu, H.-C. Chen, and Y.-W. Chang. Ntuplace3: An analytical placer for large-scale mixed-size designs with preplaced blocks and density constraints. *Computer-Aided Design of Integrated Circuits and Systems, IEEE Transactions on*, 27(7):1228–1240, 2008.

[2] J. Cho, J. Kim, T. Song, J. S. Pak, J. Kim, H. Lee, J. Lee, and K. Park. Through silicon via (tsv) shielding structures. In *Electrical Performance of Electronic Packaging and Systems (EPEPS), 2010 IEEE 19th Conference on*, pages 269–272. IEEE, 2010.

[3] M.-K. Hsu, Y.-W. Chang, and V. Balabanov. Tsv-aware analytical placement for 3d ic designs. In *Proceedings of the 48th Design Automation Conference*, DAC '11, pages 664–669, New York, NY, USA, 2011. ACM.

Benchmark	Signal TSVs	# Shield TSVs Inserted			% Decrease Max S			% Increase Total WL		
		CA	SI	CA+SI	CA	SI	CA+SI	CA	SI	CA+SI
B1	134	-	25	13	2.1	−0.1	12.6	0.3	0.0	0.3
B2	136	-	21	13	3.2	7.2	14.7	0.4	0.0	0.4
B3	136	-	25	14	1.4	10.5	11.5	0.4	0.0	0.4
B4	122	-	24	21	5.7	0.7	14.9	0.2	0.1	0.3
B5	137	-	20	14	2.4	9.9	13.0	0.5	0.0	0.6
B6	139	-	22	10	10.2	7.1	11.5	0.5	0.0	0.5
B7	138	-	21	22	8.0	3.1	15.5	0.4	0.0	0.4
B8	134	-	22	10	0.7	−0.2	5.1	0.5	0.0	0.5
Average	134.5	-	22.5	14.6	4.2	4.8	12.3	0.4	0.0	0.4

Table 3: Results compared to traditional TSV placement [i.e. without coupling awareness (CA) or shield insertion (SI)]

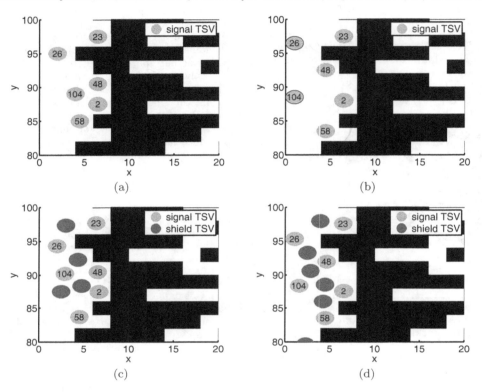

Figure 13: Layout Results: (a) Traditional Placement (b) CA (c) SI (d) CA+SI

[4] D. H. Kim, K. Athikulwongse, and S.-K. Lim. A study of through-silicon-via impact on the 3d stacked ic layout. In *Computer-Aided Design - Digest of Technical Papers, 2009. ICCAD 2009. IEEE/ACM International Conference on*, pages 674–680, 2009.

[5] C. Liu, T. Song, J. Cho, J. Kim, J. Kim, and S.-K. Lim. Full-chip tsv-to-tsv coupling analysis and optimization in 3d ic. In *Design Automation Conference (DAC), 2011 48th ACM/EDAC/IEEE*, pages 783–788, 2011.

[6] C. Liu, T. Song, and S.-K. Lim. Signal integrity analysis and optimization for 3d ics. In *Quality Electronic Design (ISQED), 2011 12th International Symposium on*, pages 1–8, 2011.

[7] C. Serafy, B. Shi, and A. Srivastava. Geometric approach to chip-scale tsv shield placement for the reduction of tsv coupling in 3d-ics. In *Proceedings of the 23rd ACM international conference on Great lakes symposium on VLSI*, GLSVLSI '13, pages 275–280, New York, NY, USA, 2013. ACM.

[8] B. Shi and A. Srivastava. Thermal stress aware 3d-ic statistical static timing analysis. In *Proceedings of the 23rd ACM international conference on Great lakes symposium on VLSI*, GLSVLSI '13, pages 281–286, New York, NY, USA, 2013. ACM.

[9] P. Spindler, U. Schlichtmann, and F. Johannes. Kraftwerk2—a fast force-directed quadratic placement approach using an accurate net model. *Computer-Aided Design of Integrated Circuits and Systems, IEEE Transactions on*, 27(8):1398–1411, 2008.

[10] N. Viswanathan, M. Pan, and C. Chu. Fastplace 3.0: A fast multilevel quadratic placement algorithm with placement congestion control. In *Design Automation Conference, 2007. ASP-DAC '07. Asia and South Pacific*, pages 135–140, 2007.

3DIC System Design Impact, Challenge and Solutions

William Wu Shen
Taiwan Semiconductor Manufacturing Company, Ltd.
8, Li-Hsin Rd, 6, Hainchu, Taiwan, 300-78, R.O.C.
+886 3-5636688 Ext. 712-6393
wushen@tsmc.com

ABSTRACT

In last few decades, the semiconductor industry has advanced as Moore's law predicted. With the introduction of 3D IC, it has extended the Moore's law into another dimension.

The 3DIC vast interconnecting capabilities and ultra-short die to die distance can be fully explored for high bandwidth, low power applications. These 3D IC's are capable of enhancing overall chip performance and achieving high density heterogeneous system integration by utilizing through-silicon-vias (TSV), multiple die can be 3D stacked and/or stitching through Interposer into 3DIC platform. With the 3DIC memory family become standard last year, this also made a full computer system within 3DIC.

Here we shall introduce one of test vehicles using TSMC CoWoS(tm) platform and using one of the JEDEC standard WideIO DRAM. We shall use it as example to explore 3DIC system advantages, design for test challenges and proposed solutions. Also we shall share a brief lesson learned from this Test Vehicle as well as some suggestions for future considerations.

Categories and Subject Descriptors

C.5.4 [**VLSI Systems**]

Keywords

3DIC design

ISPD'14, March 30–April 2, 2014, Petaluma, CA, USA.
ACM 978-1-4503-2592-9/14/03.
http://dx.doi.org/10.1145/2560519.2565870.

Physical Design and FinFETs

Robert Aitken[1], Greg Yeric[2], Brian Cline[2], Saurabh Sinha[2],
Lucian Shifren[1], Imran Iqbal[1], Vikas Chandra[1]

ARM Inc.
1=San Jose, CA
2=Austin, TX
first.last@arm.com

ABSTRACT

FinFETs have recently overtaken bulk CMOS transistors as the device of choice for systems-on-chip. This paper provides some background on FinFETs together with their associated manufacturing processes and shows how they influence physical design of standard cells as well as place & route and timing closure for larger blocks.

Categories and Subject Descriptors

B.7.1 [**Hardware**]: Integrated Circuits – *Types and Design Styles, Advanced Technologies;* B.7.2 [**Hardware**]: Integrated Circuits – *Design Aids: Placement and Routing*; B.8.2 [**Hardware**]: Performance and Reliability – *Performance Analysis and Design Aids*

General Terms

Measurement, Performance, Design, Verification.

Keywords

FinFET, standard cell, placement, routing, double patterning.

1. INTRODUCTION

Moore's law and Dennard scaling continued for over 30 years with CMOS logic and bulk transistors as the dominant implementation. However, bulk devices have hit the end of the roadmap at the 20nm node, due primarily to short channel effects. For the next node, variously labeled as 16nm and 14nm, CMOS FinFETs have taken over. To a first approximation, the effects of switching to FinFETs are confined to designers of physical IP such as standard cells and memories. However, there are subtle changes that logic designers and chip implementation teams will need to be aware of. This paper details some of these, including changes in Vt and other library options, changes in voltage operating points, parasitic resistances and capacitance, and so on. For physical IP designers, additional complexity in device sizing, layout, pin placement, and local parasitics will also be important. Other challenges, such as double and triple patterning, will also become more pronounced in the FinFET era, but these are due more to lithography scaling than to FinFETs themselves.

2. BACKGROUND

Standard cell library design involves making tradeoffs among a variety of parameters in order to produce a set of cells that enable chip designers to achieve their area, power and performance goals. A typical commercial library contains on the order of 1000 cells, usually split about 70%-30% in terms of combinational and sequential cells. The combinational cells range from basic logic functions (INV, AND, NOR, etc.) to more complex cells (AND-OR-INVERT, MUX, XOR) to adders and other regularly used functions. The sequential cells are variants on standard themes (D flip-flops with and without scan, presets and clears, both synchronous and asynchronous, gated or inverted clocks, inputs, outputs and so on). For each class of cell, multiple drive strengths and device beta ratios are often provided. In addition, for a given process, additional cell sets will be provided for various device threshold voltage (Vt) options, gate length options, power control options and more.

Beyond 28nm, the required lithography dimensions forced the use of multiple patterning [1]. While a line/space grating can achieve the peak density offered by double patterning lithography (DPL), the average density in implemented standard cells ranges from this peak value toward the single-mask density. Figure 1 shows example layout of a cell with a high pin density and the set of shapes requiring resolution of a two-color conflict (where the two masks in double patterning are referred to as being different "colors"). In many cases such as this, there is no solution except to increase cell size, and the full entitlement of the pitch scaling is not achievable [2].

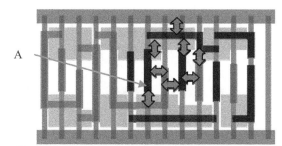

Figure 1: Example of complex DPL coloring conflict in standard cell.

The conventional approach to finding coloring conflicts is cycle identification [3]. Cycles can be as simple as a three body problem (e.g. location "A" in Figure 1) or a more complex problem (e.g. the set of all red arrows in Figure 1).

Conventional bulk CMOS processes have not scaled below the 20nm node, primarily due to degraded short channel effects (e.g. increased leakage) and variability challenges. FinFETs have been introduced to address these concerns. A simplified FinFET is shown in Figure 2. The fin provides a fully depleted channel surrounded on 3 sides by gate material and features improved short channel control (and hence reduced leakage) and lower doping (and hence reduced dopant fluctuation and random variation). Larger transistors are built by grouping fins together. Since fins are quantized, the opportunities for device sizing are bounded, and when "tapered" devices are needed, significant complexity can arise, as shown in Figure 3. Additional discussion on this point can be found in Yeric et al [4].

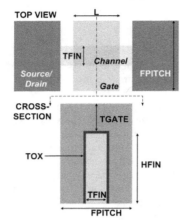

Figure 2: Top view and idealized cross section of a FinFET device [6]

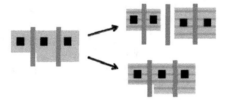

Figure 3: Device taper in older planar technology on the left, and choices for FinFET on the right [4].

A final point to consider with FinFET-based design is the limitation on device variants. Manufacturing issues limit the options available in gate lengths. For example, TSMC's 16nm process allows for 3 discrete gate lengths: 30nm, 34nm, and 50nm [5]. In addition, the amount of doping feasible in a fin is also limited, which restricts the number of available device Vt options (e.g. to 3 in TSMC 16nm [5]).

3. STANDARD CELL DESIGN

There are many complex issues relating to the design of standard cell libraries in FinFET processes, but we will concentrate on two of the most important for physical design: track height and pin access. Double patterning and cell placement is also very important, but not strictly a FinFET related issue. See Liebmann et al [2] for more information.

3.1 Track Height

In previous technologies with relatively un-quantized device widths, a standard cell designer could receive M2 pitch and device characterization from a PDK and then independently determine which cell height (in number of M2 tracks) represented the optimal end result for a given standard cell library. For example, a high density library might be 7 tracks tall, a high

performance library might be 12 tracks tall, and a power-optimized library might be 9 tracks tall. The additional constraint of fitting a fixed number of fins within a cell complicates this.

The existing paradigm can easily remain if the fin pitch equals the M2 pitch. However, fin and metal pitches have different scaling pressures, so they have not tended to line up. For example, at 14nm GlobalFoundries has stated that it uses a fin pitch of 48nm and a metal pitch of 64nm [7]. The same values are used in TSMC's 16nm process [5]. In addition, not all fin tracks are available for active transistors. Power rail connections at the top and bottom of the cell typically force the removal of 1 fin each, and typically 2 additional fin tracks must be removed in the center of the cell to accommodate gate input connections, which (as of today) are not allowed over the active diffusion regions.

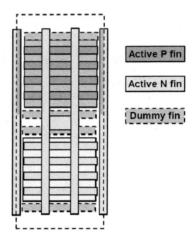

Figure 4: Example allocation of 12 fins in a cell

The following discussion uses the previously noted TSMC and GlobalFoundries numbers as a reference, but similar considerations apply to any combination of M2 and fin pitch. In this 14/16nm example, a 9 track standard cell would be 9x64=576nm tall. This height will accommodate 576/48=12 fins. Excluding 2 for power and 2 for pin connection leaves 8 active fins. Similarly, a 12 track height includes 16 fins, of which 12 will be active. To a first approximation, then, a 12 track FinFET library will have 50% more current drive per cell than a 9 track library.

Note that only certain integral combinations of fin and M2 pitch are possible: 6, 9, 12, etc. A 6 track cell height is unlikely to be viable for two reasons. First, it will contain at most 4 active fins (2N and 2P), and second there is unlikely to be enough room to route internal signals for complex cells such as flip-flops. A library containing 6 active fins (3N and 3P) would be 10 fins tall. This equates to 10x48=480nm, which is equivalent to 7.5 M2 tracks. This is likely to be the smallest feasible library in this type of technology, and comes with the obvious issues relating to non-integral track heights for physical design (power routing etc.)

3.2 Pin Placement

Routers prefer that standard cell pins be placed on a fixed grid. In a library with an integral number of M2 tracks, the grid is reasonably well defined (on pitch at the cell border, or at the half-pitch at the cell border). With non-integral track heights and FinFET libraries, grid placement becomes important. Some possible options are shown in Figure 4 for a 10.5 track (5N and 5P) library. The "standard" option uses 9 metal routing tracks and two wide power buses. The "flexible" option uses narrower power rails but allows routing track 6 to have tabs or jogs. The "colorable" library allows the power rails to be colored independently of the routing tracks. Several other similar variations can be constructed.

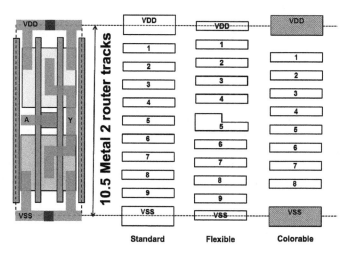

Figure 4: Possible M2 track allocations for 10.5T library

Once grid points have been defined, it is necessary to design standard cells in a way that maximizes the flexibility for a router to contact pins. The pin design challenge is more severe for FinFET processes due to restrictions on pin placement in the cell, multiple patterning rules, and the lack of scaling in minimum metal area. The last two issues are not strictly FinFET issues, but reflect the lithography and metal deposition challenges resulting from process scaling.

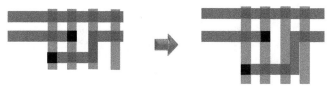

Figure 5: Double patterning forces >1 track jogs

Multiple patterning extends beyond double patterning to include triple and even quad patterning. Double patterning is a deterministic problem, but triple patterning is NP-complete (equivalent to deciding if a planar graph is 3-colorable). This means that post-coloring of standard cells (that is to say, color decomposition conducted post placement independent of the standard cell library's internal decomposition) is not likely to be a viable library design option (see Figure 6 for a cell-level challenge). In addition to challenges with decomposition etc., coloring also needs to meet density solutions (each color mask must have reasonably consistent density across the chip). One such approach is two-coloring of intra-cell wiring on M1 and using the third color for power rails and fixing small local cycle problems (e.g. the center pin in Figure 7).

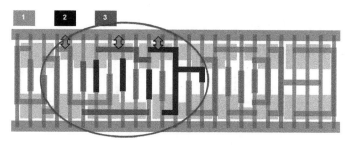

Figure 6: Triple Patterning Color Conflict

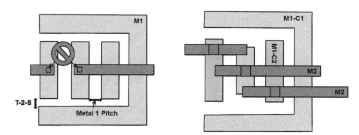

Figure 7: Pin Placement Issues with Double Patterning

Figure 7 shows an example of pin connection challenges. Connections such as those shown on the left are illegal due to via spacing, tip-to-tip and other rules. Instead, something like the connections on the right are needed. Double patterning restricts the length of the center pin (same color tip-to-side) to one on-grid or two off-grid hit points to connect to metal 2. The presence of the other two pins limits this to a single option, and tip-to-tip spacing on metal 2 leads to essentially two connection options – the one shown in the figure or a mirrored version along the middle M2 line. Rules vary from process to process, but this type of situation is not uncommon.

4. PLACE AND ROUTE
4.1 Double Patterning
Double patterning presents significant levels of complexity in cell design, but also in placement and routing. Placement issues have been covered well by Liebmann et al [2], and mostly relate to cell boundary decisions. Standard cells may have color independent boundaries, or varying levels of color restriction. For example, if all cell left edges are color 1 and all right edges are color 2, cells cannot be flipped left-right. The example in Figure 8 shows some example issues and solutions.

Routing is also made more challenging by double patterning, especially when stitching (using multiple colors on the same object) is not permitted. In most cases, it makes sense to alternate colors on routing layers (see Figure 4). As a result, when lines jog, they need to jog by multiples of two tracks in order to retain the same color. The specifics of routing rules depend on the type of double patterning used. The most restrictive case is self-aligned double patterning (SADP), where line end positions on nearby lines are also restricted, increasing the need for a holistic solution that considers multiple wires on multiple layers [9].

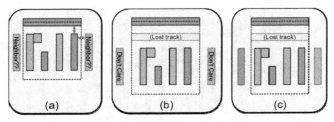

Figure 8: Standard cell DPL color conflict (a) and potential fixes. Fix (b) sacrifices area at left/right cell edges to make placement of abutting cells color-insensitive. Fix (c) does not increase cell size horizontally but requires restrictions on cell abutment combinations.[4]

4.2 Timing Closure

FinFETs have more drive current per unit area than planar devices, because the channel of the fin is effectively equal to 2xHfin+Tfin (see Figure 1), and this channel exists in an area bounded by fin pitch. For a fin pitch of 48nm and a fin thickness of (for example) 8nm, any fin height greater than 20nm will have a larger effective device width than a conventional flat channel (as a reference point, Intel's 22nm FinFETs have 8nm fin thickness and 34nm fin height [8]). The ratio of the effective device width to linear channel width is sometimes referred to as the "3D factor" [6].

The added performance capability of FinFETs can be used to achieve higher top end frequency numbers (at a fixed power budget) or significantly lower power (at a fixed performance budget). In the latter case, power reduction comes from a combination of reduced area (due to reduced need for high-drive standard cells to meet timing), reduced leakage, and possibly reduced nominal operating voltage. The effect can be seen in Figure 9, which shows relative power/performance points for implementations of a CPU in a FinFET process and a bulk process with similar back-end design rules. At the high end, a 20% performance improvement is seen along with a 20% power reduction. Other tradeoffs are also possible, as seen by the various points on the curves (e.g. 30% power saving at iso-performance).

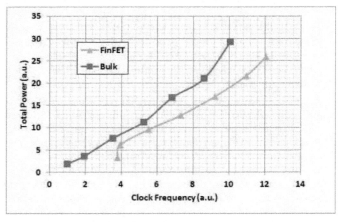

Figure 9: CPU Performance/Power implementations with FinFET, bulk processes

In most cases, the added performance makes design easier. The exception is hold time violations, where high speed logic paths need to be slowed down to accommodate clock uncertainty. With logic gate delays well under 20ps, many levels of logic can be required to reach a 100ps safety margin. Using lock-up latches on scan paths [10] can help reduce the number of added delay buffers in DFT logic, which often contains a majority of hold violations.

5. CONCLUSIONS

The introduction of FinFETs into the foundry ecosystem creates some challenges for physical design, but these are manageable and well worth the power, performance and area benefits of scaling to advanced nodes.

6. REFERENCES

[1] Chen, J., Staud W., and Arnold, B., DFM challenges for 32nm node with double dipole lithography (DDL) and double patterning technology (DPT), IEEE Symp. Semiconductor Manufacturing (ISSM), Sept. 2006, pp. 479-482.

[2] Liebmann, L. Pietromonaco, D., and Graf, M., Decomposition aware standard cell design flows to enable double-patterning technology, Proc. SPIE 7974, Design for Manufacturability through Design-Process Integration V, 2011

[3] Kahng, A.B., Park, C.-H., Xu, X., and Yao, H., "Layout decomposition for double patterning lithography," in Proc. Int. Conf. Comput. Aided Design, Nov. 2008, pp. 465–472.

[4] Yeric, G., Cline, B., Sinha, S., Pietromonaco, D., Chandra, V., Aitken, R. The Past, Present, and Future of Design-Technology Co-Optimization, Proc Custom Integrated Circuits Conf (CICC) 2013.

[5] Wu, S-Y et al, A 16nm FinFET CMOS Technology for Mobile SoC and Computing Applications, Proc Inter. Electron Devices Meeting (IEDM) 2013.

[6] Sinha, S., Yeric, G., Chandra, V., Cline, B., Cao, Y, Exploring sub-20nm FinFET design with predictive technology models, Proc Design Automation Conf., 2012, pp. 283-288

[7] Collins, L., FinFET processes demand delicate tradeoffs for mobile SoCs – GlobalFoundries process architect, Tech Design Forum, June 2013
http://www.techdesignforums.com/blog/2013/06/05/finfet-processes-optimsation/

[8] Bohr, M. Silicon technology leadership for the mobility era, Intel Developer's Forum, 2012.
http://www.intel.com/content/dam/www/public/us/en/documents/presentation/silicon-technology-leadership-presentation.pdf

[9] Gao, J-R, Pan, D.Z., Flexible self-aligned double pattern aware detailed routing with prescribed layout planning, Proc. Int. Symp. on Physical Design (ISPD), 2012, pp. 25-32

[10] Wagner, K., Robust scan-based logic test in VDSM technology, IEEE Computer, Vol. 32, No. 11, November 1999, pp. 66-74.

Clock Tree Resynthesis for Multi-corner Multi-mode Timing Closure

Subhendu Roy[‡], Pavlos M. Mattheakis[†], Laurent Masse-Navette[†], David Z. Pan[‡]

[‡]Department of Electrical and Computer Engineering, University of Texas at Austin, USA

[†]Mentor Graphics, Grenoble, France

subhendu@utexas.edu, {pavlos_matthaiakis,Laurent_Masse-Navette}@mentor.com,
dpan@ece.utexas.edu

ABSTRACT

With aggressive technology scaling and complex design scenarios, timing closure has become a challenging and tedious job for the designers. Timing violations persist for multi-corner, multi-mode designs in the deep-routing stage although careful optimization has been applied at every step after synthesis. Useful clock skew optimization has been suggested as an effective way to achieve design convergence and timing closure. Existing approaches on useful skew optimization (i) calculate clock skew at sequential elements before the actual tree is synthesized, and (ii) do not account for the implementability of the calculated schedules at the later stages of design cycle. Our approach is based on a skew scheduling engine which works on an already built clock tree. The output of the engine is a set of positive and negative offsets which translate to the delay and accelerations respectively in clock arrival at the clock tree pins. A novel algorithm is presented to accurately realize these offsets in the clock tree. Experimental results on large-scale industrial designs demonstrate that our approach achieves respectively 57%, 12% and 42% average improvement in total negative slack (TNS), worst negative slack (WNS) and failure-end-point (FEP) with an average overhead of 26% in clock tree area.

Categories and Subject Descriptors

B.7.2 [**Hardware, Integrated Circuits**]: Design Aids;

Keywords

Useful skew, clock skew scheduling, ECO, MCMM, CTS

1. INTRODUCTION

Clock skew is the difference in clock arrival times at different sequential elements in the clock-distribution network. A lot of work has been done in the past to minimize clock-skew [1][2][3]. Targeting global zero skew not only costs in area and power, but also limits the achievable operating frequency to the maximum data path delay in the circuit. This has led to a paradigm shift from skew minimization to useful skew optimization as the latter has the potential to significantly improve design performance [4][5][6][7][8][9].

As technology scales aggressively in the nanometer regime, interconnects play a determining role in timing and uncertainty due to process variations [10][11] and the multi-corner analysis becomes more and more tedious. [12] has proposed an algorithm for chip-level clock tree synthesis (CTS) to tackle clock divergence issue in different corners. However, it does not take into account the timing information on data path for CTS. Also, a chip has to operate in several modes to reduce power dissipation. For instance, a design can be in active and sleep modes when performance and power are the main concerns respectively. Consequently, timing closure has posed a challenging job for designers to meet stringent silicon delivery targets [13], especially with multi-corner, multi-mode (MCMM) designs. In [14][15] clock tree aware placements are performed with the objective of reducing total wire-length and/or switching power, but they do not account for any timing improvements. Several works have focused on timing optimization during placement and routing as well [16][17][18]. But in spite of all these efforts, timing violations still exist after detail routing in MCMM designs. So the designers have to intervene manually to analyze and fix the timing violations considering every mode and process variation altogether in an iterative and non-convergent way, where as the verification engineers need to run timing analysis for each scenario[1].

Engineering change order (ECO) is always used after detail routing in order to fix existing timing violations by incremental adjustment of pertaining cells and nets [19][20]. These ECO adjustments, focused mainly on data path optimization, are not sufficient to handle all timing violations. So data path aware clock scheduling becomes an important step for timing closure, as it allows modifications in the clock tree which is towards timing closure. Several works study the clock scheduling problem. In [7] clock skew scheduling is formulated as a constrained quadratic problem, minimizing the least square error between the computed clock schedule, consistent to the interconnection between the registers, and the target clock schedule. [21] presents a fast primal-dual based approach for minimal clock period, improving over Burn's algorithm [22] in run-time complexity. [9] even tackles the clock scheduling problem in presence of process variations by ILP formulation. But the issues with these approaches are (i) actual implementation of that clock schedul-

---

[1]any mode/corner combination

ing is difficult to achieve in real designs, especially at later design stages (ii) they are unaware of MCMM scenarios.

[23] formulates an LP problem to optimize clock period in the post-CTS stage by bounded delay buffering at the leaves of the clock tree. But since this work only considers inserting delay but not speeding up clock arrival at the leaves, the scope of the optimization is limited and buffering at the leaf level introduces a high area overhead in clock tree. Furthermore, [23] does not tackle MCMM scenarios. A recent work [24] focuses on the realization of the useful skew on industrial-scale designs at post-routing stage. It also performs local transformations at the leaf-level by inserting/removing buffers to minimize negative D-slack/Q-slack[2] violations. For instance, if $Dslack < 0$, it means the data arrives too late or clock arrives too early. Fig. 1 shows an example to mitigate D-slack violation by delaying the clock arrival. But it might cause Q-slack violation if there is no enough positive Q-slack available. The main issues of this work are (i) it does not have the global view of the clock tree, instead performs timing optimization greedily. So this approach can not handle negative slacks at both sides (D and Q) or negative slack at one side with very less available positive slack at the other side, which is a common situation in today's high-performance time-constrained real designs, (ii) area-overhead in clock tree is high as it works only at leaf-level, (iii) Speeding up clock arrival to fix Q-slack violations by only removing buffer is hardly realizable in practice to be discussed in Section 2.3 (Fig. 5).

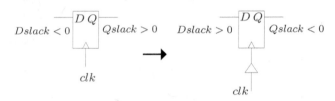

Figure 1: Buffer insertion to mitigate D-slack violation can cause Q-slack violation

To tackle these issues, a novel clock tree resynthesis methodology is presented in this paper. Instead of estimating clock schedule at the leaf level registers, our approach considers offsets in clock arrival at the clock tree driver pins of any placed design with already synthesized and routed clock tree. To consider MCMM scenarios, we develop an LP solver based on [25], for calculating these offsets. We illustrate in Section 2.2 that it is easier to realize the positive offsets by inserting buffer chains, but at the cost of clock tree area. On the other hand, the negative offset realization is disruptive and can have catastrophic effects on the timing profile of the design unless handled properly. As a result, realization of an arbitrarily large negative offset is not feasible. We run experiments with the LP solver for industrial designs and come to the conclusion that a significant gain in timing metrics is possible by realizing positive offsets and bounded negative offsets. We develop a slack manager infrastructure which keeps track of the available slacks for clock arrival at the clock pins of the clock tree network. By utilizing the positive slack at the fan-out cone of the clock tree elements

---

[2]The slack at the input/output pin of a register is defined as D-slack/Q-slack

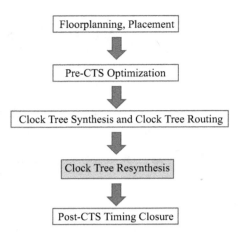

Figure 2: Our methodology in a conventional back-end flow

as a safe margin, our algorithm realizes the negative offsets incrementally through clock tree restructuring or sizing.

Fig. 2 illustrates the steps of a conventional back-end flow and where our methodology for clock tree resynthesis fits into this. The benefits of our methodology are two fold. Firstly, it helps to lead to the timing closure. Secondly, post-CTS timing closure involves ECO adjustments, such as data path optimization etc., which generally cost a significant area/power penalty. So more we advance towards the timing closure by clock tree resynthesis, better is the savings in terms of area/power. The key contributions of our paper are as follows.

- To the best of our knowledge, this is the first work to consider offsets at output pins of clock tree cells for improving timing metrics in a placed design with already routed clock tree instead of estimating clock schedule at the leaf level registers. Moreover, the offset calculation is tightly coupled with feasibility in realizing those offsets.

- A novel algorithm which is non-intrusive and area-efficient is presented that realizes negative offsets.

- A methodology for clock tree resynthesis is presented which has significantly improved timing metrics of large scale industrial designs (after placement and clock tree routing) under MCMM scenarios.

The rest of the paper is organized as follows. Section 2 illustrates the concept of feasibility aware clock scheduling in presence of MCMM scenarios using an LP solver. Section 3 presents our novel algorithm to realize the negative offsets predicted by the LP solver and the overall methodology for clock tree resynthesis. Section 4 presents the experimental results of our approach for industry-strength designs. Section 5 discusses about the applicability of our methodology and future work with a conclusion in Section 6.

2. FEASIBILITY AWARE CLOCK SCHEDULING

In this section we first present an LP solver based on [25] to calculate the offsets in clock arrival at the clock driver pins under MCMM scenarios. Although this LP solver is not our main contribution in this work, it is imperative to address concisely how the LP solver tackles various modes and corners in the design. Then we illustrate the approach for positive offset realization and the issues in realizing negative offsets. Finally, the notion of feasibility aware clock scheduling is introduced.

2.1 LP Solver

In [25] an LP engine is presented, which estimates the clock-scheduling for a design under MCMM scenarios targeting the minimization of timing metrics, such as the total negative slack (TNS) and total hold slack (THS)[3]. To include the various corners in the design, scaling factors (c_i) for each corner i are calculated having as reference the constraint corner i.e., $c_i = 1$ for the constraint corner and $c_i < 1$ for any other corner. These scaling factors are used in the set-up/hold time analysis for different corners. With respect to multiple mode handling, the functional timing paths across all active modes are analyzed. Additionally, on-chip-variation (OCV) derates [26] calculated on the already built tree are introduced in the LP solver as means to reduce the variability effects on the resultant timing profile.

We develop an LP solver based on [25], to calculate the positive and negative offsets at the output pins of the leaf-level gates/buffers (driving sequential leaf cells) in terms of clock tree level which corresponds to intrinsic buffer delay (minimum buffer delay in the design), denoted by D_{min}^{buf}. Positive (negative) offset of d_{off} at any pin signifies that the clock-arrival at that pin is to be delayed (fastened) by d_{off}. Any offset d_{off} in the constraint corner is equivalent to an offset of $c_i \times d_{off}$ in the ith corner. We can specify the range of these offsets by constraining minimum level (L_{min}^{off}) and maximum level (L_{max}^{off}). For instance, suppose the D_{min}^{buf} of a design is 60 pico seconds (ps) and we specify $L_{min}^{off} = -2$ and $L_{max}^{off} = 3$, then the LP solver will estimate the offsets of values $-120ps$, $-60ps$, $60ps$, $120ps$, $180ps$ along with a prediction of timing improvement. The calculation and realization of the offsets are tightly coupled in this work. Additionally, the realization maintains the timing profile of the parts of the design which should not be affected.

2.2 Positive Offset Realization

Positive offset realization is accomplished by inserting route aware delay elements. Fig. 3 illustrates the realization of a positive offset at the output pin of repeater B_1. Initially, the LP solver predicts that a positive offset (d_{off}) should be realized at the output pin (op) of the buffer B_1, i.e. the clock arrival of the buffers/leaf-cells driven by B_1 should be delayed by d_{off}. We can implement this positive offset by incorporating a delay element D (merely a buffer chain) of d_{off} at op. While doing this, we consider various corners and insert/size/place the delay block accordingly to realize this positive offset as accurate as possible across all corners. Additionally it should be guaranteed that the offset realization does not degrade the quality of the clock tree e.g. design rule check (DRC) violations are not increased. It should be stressed that the positive offset realization is not intrusive as the parts of the clock tree which are irrelevant to the inserted offset are not affected. For instance in the example shown in Fig. 3 there is no impact of D on B_2 and B_3, the siblings of B_1, as B_1 effectively acts as a shield buffer.

---

[3]Here THS signifies total negative hold slack

Consequently, there is no side-effect on the clock tree.

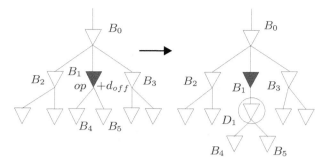

Figure 3: Positive offset realization

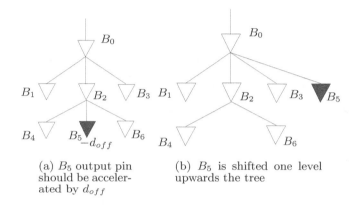

(a) B_5 output pin should be accelerated by d_{off}

(b) B_5 is shifted one level upwards the tree

Figure 4: Negative offset realization

2.3 Issues in Negative Offset Realization

The negative offset realization poses more challenges. A representative example is the following. Let us assume that the LP engine predicts a negative offset (d_{off}) for the output pin of buffer B_5 as shown in Fig. 4. This offset can be realized by placing, sizing, or changing the clock tree structure. Each one of the aforementioned approaches has its own drawbacks. For instance, placing B_5 at another location will force its parent (B_2) to drive a different amount of load than before, altering thus the arrival time of all clock tree nodes at B_2's transitive fanout (TFO). Sizing has similar effects on B_5's siblings as B_2 will again have to drive a different amount of load defined by the gate sizing result. Another option is to restructure the clock tree, moving upwards cell B_5. In this case, the arrival time to FFs at the TFO of B_5 is reduced but multiple side effects alter the arrival times to the old and the new siblings of B_5. This is due to the load decrease and increase at the nets driven by B_2 and B_0 respectively and that affect all the FFs at the TFO of B_0. [24] has illustrated that clock arrivals could be accelerated by removing the corresponding buffer B_1 (Fig. 5). But this can be useful only when it does not have any sibling, which is not common in practice. Furthermore, this technique might not be effective in that case as well as (i) B_0 is now driving 3 buffers instead of 1, viz. B_2, B_3 and B_4, (ii) B_0 has to drive more wire-load. When B_1 is far away from B_0, then the wire-load increase is even more. As a result the clock arrival is delayed at the TFO cone of B_0.

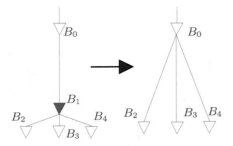

Figure 5: Buffer removal might not be effective in realizing negative offset

From the above it can be concluded that realizing negative offsets in the clock tree imposes side effects which may significantly change the timing profile of the design and possibly cancel the expected timing gains. Additionally, it should be noted that the more the negative an offset is, the more the pin should be moved upwards the tree. As a consequence, more FFs downwards the tree will be affected increasing the probability of degrading the timing instead of optimizing it.

2.4 Offset Bounds

Any positive offset can be realized by injecting a delay element with delay equal/close to the offset. Negative offsets, on the other side, can not always be realized. For instance, if a pin has a negative offset with delay greater than the arrival time from the clock root to this pin, then it can be deduced that this offset is infeasible for this pin. Hence, the pins which can carry offsets should be bounded to guarantee that the calculated negative offset can be realized. A per-pin negative offset bound would be cumbersome as the side effects of each negative offset realization should be modeled into the LP solver, thus a global bound was selected for all pins. An experiment was performed to calculate a negative bound which should deliver as much timing gain as possible and at the same time be as less disruptive as possible, *i.e.*, closer to zero.

Three LP runs were performed with real industry-strength benchmarks. The first run corresponds to LP solutions with only positive offsets, whereas the second and the third allow for one and three levels of negative offset respectively. For all three runs the positive offset bound was set to three. The results are shown in Fig. 6, where TNS predicted by the solver for each one of the three aforementioned experiments are normalized w.r.t. the original TNS of each design, which is the TNS after placement, clock tree synthesis and routing by an industrial tool. We observe that there is a significant improvement from original TNS to the TNS predicted in first run and from predicted TNS in first run to the second run, but the same trend does not continue as the bound further decreases. From the above it can be concluded that most of the potential TNS gain can be acquired by pairing a single level of negative offset with many levels of positive offset. This finding will be used throughout this work as the solver will be bounded to produce solutions with a single level of negative offset.

3. CLOCK TREE RESYNTHESIS

Section 2.4 showed that significant TNS gains can be enjoyed if pins which can carry offsets are bounded to -1 level ($L_{min}^{off} = -1$). In this section we present a methodology for clock tree resynthesis to improve timing in a routed clock

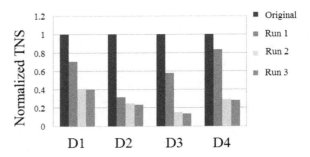

Figure 6: Normalized TNS prediction by LP solver for industrial designs

tree. A novel algorithm is presented which realizes accurately one level of negative offset, so that the predicted TNS gain is maintained after offset realization. The two basic operations used are sizing and restructuring. It should be stressed that the restructuring is always performed within the scope of a hyper-net to guarantee that the clock gating function will be preserved by the clock tree restructuring. A hyper-net is a set of logically equivalent or opposite polarity nets separated by buffers/inverters in the same physical partition as the root driver of the top net, and thus this set is necessarily connected in a tree topology. The root of this tree (hyper-root) is either the driver pin of a clock gate or a clock root. The elements of any hyper-net are comprised of all the nets traversed until another hyper-root is visited. Fig. 7 demonstrates a clock tree comprised of 3 hyper-nets. The datapath logic and the enable signals at the clock tree clock gates are omitted in the figure.

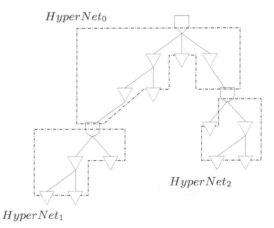

Figure 7: Clock tree decomposition to hyper-nets

The key to accurately realizing negative offsets is the utilization of the positive slack. If a clock tree driver pin has only sequential cells with positive slack (more specifically Q-slack) at its transitive fanout it is annotated as a potential acceptor of pins with negative offset. In this way, negative offsets are realized accurately without degrading the total negative slack. We develop an engine, called slack manager, which helps to extract the potential acceptors for pins with negative offset.

3.1 Slack Manager

The slack manager is an engine, that keeps track of certain parameters at any pin corresponding to the D-slack and Q-slack of the leaf-cells in the TFO cone of that pin $(leafCells_{fo(pin)})$. We define the following parameters.

- $Qslack_{sum}(pin)/Dslack_{sum}(pin) =$ sum of the negative Q/D-slacks at $leafCells_{fo(pin)}$

- $Qslack_{cnt}(pin)/Dslack_{cnt}(pin) =$ count of $leafCells_{fo(pin)}$ having negative Q/D-slack

We store these parameters per scenario, *i.e.* corner and mode combination. These parameters are calculated recursively in a bottom-up fashion. Algorithm 1 presents the procedure 'BUSlackParamCalculate(*pin*, *mode*)', which stores the slack-parameters in any pin for all the scenarios active in that *mode*. Lines 3-7 first initialize the parameter values at each scenario. Then at Line 8 it is checked whether the pin is a leaf, and in this case it gets the Q-slack value from the timer (Line 5). If the Q-slack is less than a threshold, then (Lines 13-14) we set $Qslack_{cnt}$ to be 1 and $Qslack_{sum}$ to be the Q-slack value. In the other case, *i.e.*, for non-leaf pins, Line 22 calls the procedure recursively for all of its children pins (Note children of a pin depends on *mode*) and then it accumulates the values of its children (Lines 23-24). In our implementation, we have set this threshold to be 0, and thus these parameters respectively estimates the count of $leafCells_{fo(pin)}$ with negative Q-slack and sum of negative Q-slacks of $leafCells_{fo(pin)}$.

Algorithm 1 Procedure to calculate slack parameters

1: **Procedure** BUSlackParamCalculate(*pin*, *mode*);
2: $activeCorners \leftarrow$ corners active in *mode*;
3: **for all** $cor \in activeCorners$ **do**
4:    $scn \leftarrow$ combination(*mode*, *cor*);
5:    $Qslack_{sum}(pin, scn) \leftarrow 0$;
6:    $Qslack_{cnt}(pin, scn) \leftarrow 0$;
7: **end for**
8: **if** isLeaf(*pin*) **then**
9:    **for all** $cor \in activeCorners$ **do**
10:      $scn \leftarrow$ combination(*mode*, *cor*);
11:      $Qslack \leftarrow getQslack(pin, scn)$;
12:      **if** $Qslack < slackThreshold$ **then**
13:        $Qslack_{cnt}(pin, scn) \leftarrow 1$;
14:        $Qslack_{sum}(pin, scn) \leftarrow Qslack$;
15:        **return**
16:      **end if**
17:    **end for**
18: **end if**
19: **for all** $childPin \in childList(pin, mode)$ **do**
20:    **for all** $cor \in activeCorners$ **do**
21:      $scn \leftarrow$ combination(*mode*, *cor*);
22:      BUSlackParamCalculate(*childPin*, *scn*);
23:      $Qslack_{cnt}(pin, scn) \leftarrow Qslack_{cnt}(pin, scn) + Qslack_{cnt}(childPin, scn)$;
24:      $Qslack_{sum}(pin, scn) \leftarrow Qslack_{sum}(pin, scn) + Qslack_{sum}(childPin, scn)$;
25:    **end for**
26: **end for**
27: **return**
28: **end Procedure**

The execution of the algorithm is demonstrated with a representative example in Fig. 8. Cells B_2 and B_3's output pins have $Qslack_{cnt}$ equal to 1 due to cells $ff3$ and $ff5$ respectively. B_1's output pin has $Qslack_{cnt}$ equal to 2 which

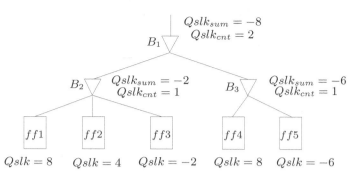

Figure 8: Q-slack parameter calculation

results from the addition of its children's corresponding values. The $Qslack_{sum}$ values are calculated accordingly.

Similar calculation is done for D-slack parameters and it has not been shown in Algorithm 1 or Fig. 8 for brevity.

3.2 Negative Offset Realization Algorithm

The slack manager exposes the space that is available for negative offset realization in terms of slack. The Negative Offset Realization Algorithm (NORA) utilizes this space to (i) accurately realize all negative offsets and (ii) gain the improvement in total negative slack calculated by the LP solver.

Algorithm 2 captures the functionality of NORA for a single pin, p (output pin of a cell c), with negative offset. Initially, a reference (constraint) scenario is chosen along with p's parent, p_{par}. Then, (Line 5) it is decided whether the negative offset will be realized by restructuring the clock tree or by sizing. This decision is made after the slack parameters calculated by the slack manager for p_{par} are modified to compensate for the case when p is detached from p_{par}. These new values are named $Qslack_{sum}^{eff}$ and $Qslack_{cnt}^{eff}$ and they are calculated according to the following formulas:

$$Qslack_{sum}^{eff}(p_{par}, scn) = Qslack_{sum}(p_{par}, scn) - Qslack_{sum}(p, scn) \quad (1)$$

$$Qslack_{cnt}^{eff}(p_{par}, scn) = Qslack_{cnt}(p_{par}, scn) - Qslack_{cnt}(p, scn) \quad (2)$$

The effective *Dslack* values are calculated accordingly. If $Qslack_{count}^{eff}$ is greater than $Dslack_{count}^{eff}$ for p_{par}, then it is preferable to reduce the load at p_{par} fanout as in this way the clock will arrive faster to the sequential cells and the negative slack at the Q side will be reduced. Thus, it is chosen to detach p from p_{par} and connect it to another node higher in the tree, as in this way not only the negative offset will be realized, but also the negative slack at the Q-side of the sequential cells at p_{par}'s TFO will be reduced. The above will have a negative impact on the D-side of the sequential cells at p_{par}'s TFO, but it is better to optimize in favor of the Q-side, as the latter affects multiple endpoints with negative slack.

In order to realize the negative offset at p, a driver pin is found higher in the clock tree, so that if p is connected to it, the difference in Arrival Time (AT) will effectively realize the offset. However, these driver pins, called from now on acceptors, should reside at the same scope of hyper-net as p to guarantee the same functionality as mentioned earlier. In addition, the polarity is also matched to take care of

Algorithm 2 Procedure to realize a negative offset

1: **Procedure** NORA($p, offset$);
2: $scn \leftarrow getConstratintSchenario$;
3: $p_{par} \leftarrow parent(p)$;
4: bestSol $\leftarrow$ currentSol;
5: **if** $Qslack_{cnt}^{eff}(p_{par}, scn) \geq Dslack_{cnt}^{eff}(p_{par}, scn)$ **then**
6:    $a_{cand} \leftarrow$ driver pins in $p's$ hyper-root;
7:    prune a_{cand} based on level;
8:    remove a_{cand} elements if their AT is $\geq$ AT(p)$-2*$ $offset$;
9:    **for all** $a \in a_{cand}$ **do**
10:       **if** $Qslack_{cnt}(inPin(a), scn) > 0$ **then**
11:          remove a from a_{cand};
12:       **end if**
13:    **end for**
14:    sort a_{cand} according to geometric distance from p;
15:    **for all** $a \in a_{cand}$ **do**
16:       connect p with a;
17:       buffer(p);
18:       **if** cost(currentSol) $<$ cost(bestSol) **then**
19:          bestSol $\leftarrow$ currentSol;
20:       **end if**
21:    **end for**
22: **else**
23:    size(p);
24:    **if** cost(currentSol) $<$ cost(bestSol) **then**
25:       bestSol $\leftarrow$ currentSol;
26:    **end if**
27: **end if**
28: **return** bestSol;

inverters in the clock tree.

We use the level of any clock-element within the scope of the hyper-net as a coarse knob to identify these acceptor pins a_{cand} (Line 7), *i.e.*, any driver pin which is at higher level than p in the hyper-net would be considered for a potential candidate acceptor. Out of all the candidate driver pins, a finer tuning is done on the basis of AT. The candidates which have AT greater than AT(p) - 2 $\times$ $offset$ are disregarded (Line 8) as connecting p to them would not result to the desired arrival time AT(p) - $offset$, considering a best case delay of $offset$ (which is also equal to the intrinsic buffer delay in the design) from the input pin to the output pin p of the corresponding cell c. Finally we prune a_{cand} on the basis of available slack in the TFO of the acceptor pin a (Line 9-13). If there is no available slack, then we remove the element from a_{cand}. This is to ensure that although a would drive more load in case c is connected to a and might worsen Qslack at TFO of a, the available slack is sufficient to account for that (not shown in Algorithm 2).

Then the candidate acceptor pins are sorted according to their proximity to the pin p as it is assumed that the acceptors which are closer will be directly connected realizing the desired offset without incurring extra buffering which would increase the total area (Line 14).

Afterwards, the sorted candidate acceptor pins are examined. Initially, p is connected to the candidate acceptor pin a and buffering is applied on the net between them. Then the cost of the current solution is estimated. The solution with the minimum cost is committed by backtracking mechanism. This cost estimation depends on the accuracy of realizing the offset. The closer the AT difference seen at

p approaches the desired negative offset value, lesser is the cost. In addition, if it introduces any new DRC violation, then the cost is set to infinity making the solution infeasible. If there are lot of candidate acceptors, the first 10 acceptors are explored. This reduces run time, and at the same time helps to achieve area-efficient restructuring due to the proximity of the acceptors to the pin p. If there is no potential acceptor with available slack, the acceptor with maximum $Qslack_{sum}$ across all scenarios is chosen.

In the case where buffering was chosen instead of clock tree restructuring (Line 5), p is sized and the solution is committed. Interestingly, sizing can approximately realize the offset as the amount of negative offset is only 1 level of intrinsic buffer delay or D_{min}^{buf}.

The execution of the above algorithm is illustrated with a representative example shown in Fig. 9(a). In this example, pin p of clock tree buffer B_1 is annotated with a negative offset which is equal to one clock tree level. Assuming that restructuring is selected instead of sizing, the candidate acceptors are initially extracted and suppose B_6 driver pin is the best acceptor for p that can realize the offset most accurately. Then, the restructuring is applied by detaching B_1 from B_0's fanout and connecting it at B_6. The resultant clock tree is shown in Fig. 9(b).

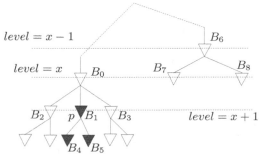

(a) Clock tree hyper-net where p has negative offset of 1 clock tree level.

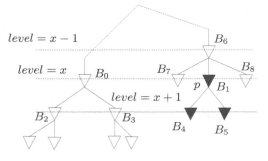

(b) Resultant clock tree hyper-net where the negative offset at p is realized by restructuring.

Figure 9: Negative offset realization example

3.3 Our Methodology

Algorithm 3 shows the steps of our methodology for clock tree resynthesis. Initially, the LP solver calculates the offsets in the clock tree. In the case that the offset at a pin is positive, a buffer chain is inserted according to the methodology presented in section 2.2 (Line 5). Otherwise, if the offset is negative, the slack manager is updated (Line 7) and then 'NORA' is used to realize the offset (Line 8).

Algorithm 3 Clock Tree Resynthesis

1: Calculate clock tree offsets, S_{offset} by LP solver;
2: Execute 'BUSlackParamCalculate' for all clock tree roots and operating modes;
3: **for all** $(p, offset) \in S_{offset}$ **do**
4:    **if** $offset > 0$ **then**
5:       Insert route-aware buffer(s) at p;
6:    **else**
7:       Update slack manager;
8:       NORA$(p, offset)$;
9:    **end if**
10: **end for**
---

4. EXPERIMENTAL RESULTS

We have implemented the algorithms presented in this work in C++ and ran it on a Linux machine with 16-Core 3GHz CPU and 256GB RAM. Table 1 presents the characteristics of 7 industrial designs using cutting-edge technology nodes (20-32nm), in terms of total number of cells (Column 2), number of scenarios (Column 3) and initial timing metrics after placement, clock tree synthesis and routing by an industrial tool. Columns 4, 5 and 6 respectively specify the TNS, worst negative slack (WNS) and failure-end-point (FEP) across all scenarios.

Table 1: Design Specification

Design	Cells (M)	Scenarios	TNS (ps)	WNS (ps)	FEP
A	0.35	5	-789723	-4433	1907
B	0.62	8	-1586320	-414	12850
C	0.62	8	-82529	-218	1262
D	0.7	8	-1129784	-6433	2408
E	0.85	1	-8032671	-1483	17491
F	1.17	5	-8968128	-6394	43938
G	2.03	6	-4289746	-15418	31946

Table 2 presents the results of our approach. Columns 2-6 exhibit that if the LP solver is constrained to use only one level of negative offset and none of positive ones, then an average improvement of 15.85%, 1.05% and 11.64% is achieved in TNS, WNS and FEP respectively with average clock tree area overhead less than 2%. If three positive offset levels are allowed as well (Columns 7-11), then an average improvement of 56.68%, 12.04% and 41.82% in TNS, WNS and FEP respectively is achieved with an average clock tree area overhead of 26.17%.

Results show that negative offset realization does not increase the clock tree area significantly, as it is only gate upsizing which introduces area in this case and this reinforces our claim of area-efficient negative offset implementation. If positive offsets are allowed as well, the area overhead increases on average to 26.17% as positive offsets are typically realized by introducing delay chains comprised of multiple buffers. *The aforementioned percentage in area increase is in terms of buffers/inverters/combinational elements in clock tree network only and this does not include sequential leaf cells and data path combinational logic, which dominate the total area of the design.* So if we consider the total design area or even include the registers, the percentage increase would be negligible. For instance, for design 'E', the percentage increase in area in clock tree is maximum (55%), but *if we consider the total area of the design, the percentage area increase is less than 1%.*

With respect to the timing optimization, using only negative offsets suffices to reduce TNS for designs D and G by more than 30%. On the contrary, TNS improvement for designs E and F is below 10%. WNS is almost not reduced, as the realized offsets correspond to a single clock tree level which is a relatively small portion of WNS. FEP reduction follows the corresponding reduction of TNS for all the designs but A and B, for which FEP reduction is significantly smaller than the one of TNS.

In the case that three levels of positive offset are allowed as well, TNS reduction reaches 56.68% on overage, with most of the designs exhibiting TNS reduction by more than 62%. WNS is improved more when compared to only using a single level of negative offset as offset values now span from -1 to 3 levels. FEP reduction again follows the TNS reduction, with designs A and D exhibiting significantly less FEP optimization compared to TNS.

It should be stressed that for designs 'B' and 'D', besides TNS, THS is optimized as well, by 88% and 15% respectively with positive and negative offset realization and by 14.5% and 13% respectively with only negative offset realization (not mentioned in Table 2). For rest of the designs, hold corner analysis is not enabled. For design 'D', compared to the case of realizing only negative offsets, TNS/FEP improvement decreases while realizing both positive and negative offsets, but WNS and THS improvement is more.

The biggest design in this benchmark suite contains more than 2M cells and it has 6 scenarios. Our approach achieves 62% improvement in TNS with 11% overhead in clock tree area. Runtime for this benchmark is less than 7 hours, which is quite reasonable. However, it is counter-intuitive that run time is high in few designs ('C' and 'G') for realizing only negative offsets than for realizing both positive and negative offsets. This is due to the behavior of the LP engine, as for those designs the total number of negative offsets to be realized in the case where only negative offsets are allowed is more than the total number of offsets when both positive and negative ones are allowed.

5. DISCUSSION AND FUTURE WORK

In Fig. 2, we place the block of our methodology just before the post-CTS timing closure. Nevertheless it is worth mentioning that this is not the limitation and we can perform the clock tree resynthesis after the post-CTS data-path optimizations as well. But then the post-CTS data path optimizations would cost a significant area/power penalty and the potential of our approach to recover timing with minor area overhead in the design would not have been fully exploited. Furthermore, our approach can be suitably used for reducing design frequency as well by targeting aggressive clock cycle period. It should also be noted that although the realization of bounded negative offsets is feasible for deep clock-trees, the scope to introduce any negative offset might be limited for short-depth trees. In that case, our approach can tackle this situation by only realizing the positive offsets (by running the LP solver accordingly), but that would introduce larger area overhead in the clock tree.

We plan to extend this framework to improve on the area overhead in the clock tree. We can see that the area over-

Design	Only Negative Offset Realization					Positive and Negative Offset Realization				
	% TNS Imprv.	% WNS Imprv.	% FEP Imprv.	% Clock Tree Overhead	Run time (min)	% TNS Imprv.	% WNS Imprv.	% FEP Imprv.	% Clock Tree Overhead	Run Time (min)
A	10.70	-0.13	5.61	2.56	43	77.65	1.20	39.54	20.10	46
B	11.67	0.24	3.61	7.33	175	56.25	0.97	47.32	47.09	189
C	13.35	0.92	9.75	1.05	178	76.62	49.08	57.84	8.63	140
D	32.80	2.64	25.46	1.11	125	31.58	18.51	17.57	11.51	129
E	2.24	2.83	2.20	1.36	98	69.79	10.05	44.43	54.98	306
F	5.91	0.75	7.31	0.17	161	22.80	0.72	35.69	29.78	250
G	34.30	0.08	27.54	0.04	410	62.09	3.80	50.33	11.12	368
Average	15.85	1.05	11.64	1.95	-	56.68	12.04	41.82	26.17	-

head in the clock tree is mainly due to the positive offset realization. It should be noted that restructuring might not be helpful in realizing positive offset at any pin as the place-holders for offsets are typically leaf-level gates/buffers and so it is difficult to find an acceptor in the clock tree which can match the desired arrival time of the pin on restructuring. But we can consider the partial realization of the positive offsets, while realizing the negative offsets so that the size of the buffer to be inserted for realizing positive offsets decreases and area overhead improves. For instance, when we choose potential acceptor for realizing negative offset, a priority can be given (by modifying the cost function in Algorithm 2) to the acceptors which have place-holders (driver pins) for positive offsets in its TFO cone as the restructuring would result some delay in clock arrival for those pins, thereby realizing the positive offsets partially. It will be also interesting to study the impact of OCV derates on our result. Incorporating buffers (to realize positive offsets) might have adverse OCV impact, and on the other hand as restructuring (to realize negative offsets) involves moving clock elements upward (as discussed in Section 3.2), the chance of common paths between launch flop and capture flop might increase, leading to improve OCV due to common-path-pessimism-removal (CPPR) [26].

6. CONCLUSION

This work introduces algorithms which significantly improve timing metrics in large-scale industrial designs under MCMM scenarios. To our best knowledge this is the first work to implement a feasibility aware clock scheduling, realized by solving a constrained LP problem globally, and using the clock tree elements as place holders for the resultant offsets. Our approach has achieved an average TNS improvement of 57% in industrial designs with an average overhead of 26% in clock tree area. We have proposed to extend our current framework to improve in clock tree area overhead. In the future we plan to study the impact of OCV derates on our approach and examine the space between solutions with only negative offsets and that with both negative and positive offsets by using area and power bounds.

7. REFERENCES

[1] R. Tsay, "Exact zero skew clock routing algorithm," *Computer Aided Design of Integrated Circuits and Systems*, pp. 242–249, 1993.

[2] K. D. Boese and A. B. Kahng, "Zero skew clock-routing trees with minimum wirelength," *ASIC Conference and Exhibit*, pp. 17–21, 1992.

[3] J. L. Tsai, T. H. Chen, and C. C. Chen, "Zero skew clock-tree optimization with buffer insertion/sizing and wire sizing,"

Computer Aided Design of Integrated Circuits and Systems, pp. 565–572, 2004.

[4] J. P. Fishburn, "Clock skew optimization," *IEEE Trans. on Computers*, pp. 945–51, 1990.

[5] R. Deokar and S. Sapatnekar, "A graph-theoretic approach to clock skew optimization," *ISCAS*, pp. 407–10, 1994.

[6] L. F. Chao and H. M. Sha, "Retiming and clock skew for synchronous systems," *ISCAS*, pp. 283–86, 1994.

[7] I. S. Kourtev and E. G. Friedman, "Clock skew scheduling for improved reliability via quadratic programming," *ICCAD*, pp. 239–43, 1999.

[8] X. Liu, M. C. Papaefthymiou, and E. G. Friedman, "Maximizing performance by retiming and clock skew scheduling," *DAC*, pp. 231–36, 1999.

[9] V. Nawale and T. W. Chen, "Optimal useful clock skew scheduling in the presence of variations using robust ILP formulations," *ICCAD*, pp. 27–32, 2006.

[10] Y. Taur and D. Buchanan, "CMOS scaling in nanometer regime," *Proc. IEEE*, pp. 486–503, 1997.

[11] V. Mehrotra and D. Boning, "Technology scaling impact of variation on clock skew and interconnect delay," *Interconnect Tech. Conference*, pp. 4–6, 2001.

[12] A. Rajaram and D. Z. Pan, "Robust chip-level clock tree synthesis for SOC designs," *DAC*, pp. 720–723, 2008.

[13] S. Jilla, "Multi-corner multi-mode signal integrity optimization," *EDA Tech Forum*, 2008.

[14] D. Lee and I. L. Markov, "Obstacle-aware clock-tree shaping during placement," *ISPD*, pp. 123–130, 2011.

[15] Y. Wang, Q. Zhou, X. Hong, and Y. Cai, "Clock-tree aware placement based on dynamic clock-tree building," *ISCAS*, pp. 2040–43, 2007.

[16] K. Rajagopal, T. Shaked, Y. Parasuram, T. Cao, A. Chowdhury, and B. Halpin, "Timing driven force directed placement with physical net constraints," *ISPD*, pp. 60–66, 2003.

[17] Y. Liu, R. S. Shelar, and J. Hu, "Delay-optimal simultaneous technology mapping and placement with applications to timing optimization," *ICCAD*, pp. 101–106, 2008.

[18] S. W. Hur, A. Jagannathan, and J. Lillis, "Timing driven maze routing," *TCAD*, pp. 234–241, 2000.

[19] K. Sato, H. E. M. Kawarabayashi, and N. Maeda, "Post-layout optimization for deep sub-micron design," *DAC*, pp. 740–745, 1996.

[20] Y. P. Chen, J. W. Fang, and Y. W. Chang, "ECO timing optimization using spare cells," *ICCAD*, pp. 530–535, 2007.

[21] M. Ni and S. O. Memik, "A revisit to the primal-dual based clock skew scheduling algorithm," *ISQED*, pp. 755–764, 2010.

[22] S. M. Burns, *Performance Analysis and Optimization of Asynchronous Circuits*. PhD thesis, California Institute of Technology, 1991.

[23] J. Lu and B. Taskin, "Post-CTS clock skew scheduling with limited delay buffering," *International Midwest Symposium on Circuits and Systems*, pp. 224–227, 2009.

[24] W. Shen, Y. Cai, W. Chen, Y. Lu, Q. Zhou, and J. Hu, "Useful clock skew optimization under a multi-corner multi-mode design framework," *ISQED*, pp. 62–68, 2010.

[25] V. Ramachandran, "Functional skew aware clock tree synthesis," *ISPD*, 2012.

[26] J. Bhaskar and R. Chadha, *Static Timing Analysis for Nanometer Designs: A Practical Approach*. Springer, 2009.

Power Optimization for Clock Network with Clock Gate Cloning and Flip-Flop Merging

Shih-Chuan Lo, Chih-Cheng Hsu, and Mark Po-Hung Lin
Department of Electrical Engineering
National Chung Cheng University
168 University Rd., Minhsiung, Chiayi 621, Taiwan
tony770627@gmail.com, twf1400@gmail.com, marklin@ccu.edu.tw

ABSTRACT

Applying clock gates (CGs) and multi-bit flip-flops (MBFFs) are two of the most effective techniques for low power clock network design. Some previous works had proposed to optimize clock network with either CGs or MBFFs, but none of them simultaneously considers both CGs and MBFFs during clock network optimization. Although CGs and MBFFs can be optimized separately, the resulting dynamic power may not be optimal. This paper presents the *first* problem formulation in the literature for gated clock network optimization with simultaneous CG cloning and FF merging. To effectively solve the problem, a novel optimization flow consisting of MBFF-aware CG cloning, CG-based FF merging, and MBFF and CG placement optimization is introduced. Experimental results show that the proposed flow results in better dynamic power and clock wirelength compared with other flows which optimize gated clock network with CGs and MBFFs separately.

Categories and Subject Descriptors

B.7.2 [**Integrated Circuits**]: Design Aids - Layout, Placement and Routing

General Terms

Algorithms, Design

Keywords

clock network, clock gating, multi-bit flip-flop, power optimization

1. INTRODUCTION

Minimizing power consumption of clock network plays an important role in modern digital integrated circuit (IC) design. According to [1], up to 50% of the dynamic power, or the dominant power source, is dissipated by clock network because the clock net has the highest switching rate and the largest capacitive load. Consequently, it is essential to minimize the power consumption of clock network. Recent studies have shown that applying either clock-gating cells [2, 3, 4, 5, 6] or multi-bit flip-flops (MBFFs) [7,

8, 9, 10, 11, 12, 13, 14] to the clock network is very effective in reducing clock power.

A clock-gating cell, or clock gate (CG) can turn off the clocks at flip-flop (FF) inputs when they are not required. Fig. 1 shows two example circuits without and with a CG. For the circuit in Fig. 1(a), the data input "D_{in}" of the FFs is controlled by the enable logic with a synchronous load-enable multiplexer. The FFs will load new data at their input pins "D" only when the enable signal "EN" is active. For the other circuit in Fig. 1(b), "D_{in}" is controlled by the gated clock signal "$gclk$". The CG can shut off "$gclk$" to the FFs when "D_{in}" is not changed. Although the functions of both circuits in Fig. 1 are exactly the same, the circuit in Fig. 1(b) has less clock network power consumption and smaller chip area [2].

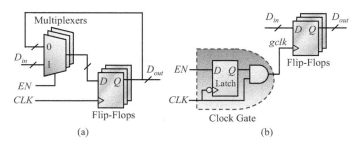

Figure 1: (a) A circuit with synchronous load-enable multiplexers at the FF data input. (b) A modified circuit of (a) after replacing the multiplexers with a CG consisting of a latch and an AND gate.

When a CG drives a very large number of FFs, as shown in Fig. 2(a), a large number of serially connected clock buffers need to be inserted into the gated clock network between the CG and FFs for sufficient driving capability. Such clock buffer chain may result in longer delay, degrade the circuit performance, and induce more power consumption. To minimize the power consumption of the gated clock network with satisfied circuit performance, we shall replicate sufficient CGs and connect each CG to a smaller number of FFs, as shown in Fig. 2(b). After CG cloning, the number of required clock buffers is reduced, and hence the power consumption and path delay of the gated clock network can be minimized.

In addition to CG cloning, the FFs connected to the same CG and replicated CGs, as seen in Figs. 2(a) and (b), can further be merged into MBFFs, as seen in Fig. 2(c). According to [12], replacing 1-bit FFs with MBFFs can reach up to 30% total clock power reduction. An MBFF contains several 1-bit FFs which share common inverters generating opposite phase clock signals in the MBFF cell [9]. As the process technology advances to 65 nm and beyond, even a minimum-sized inverter/buffer can still drive multiple FFs. Re-

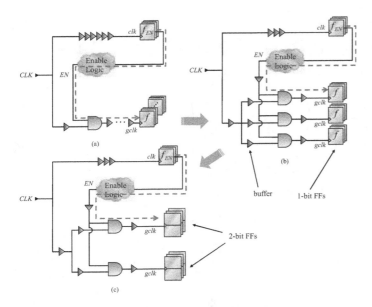

Figure 2: (a) A gated clock network without CG cloning and FF merging. (b) A gated clock network with CG cloning resulting in fewer clock buffers on the enable logic path, lower power consumption, and shorter path delay. (c) A gated clock network with both CG cloning and FF merging resulting in even lower power consumption due to fewer CGs and/or clock buffers.

placing several 1-bit FFs with an MBFF will significantly reduce the number of inverters in FF cells, and the numbers of clock sinks, clock drivers, and CGs in the clock network. Consequently, the total power, area, and delay of the clock network are reduced.

1.1 Previous Work

The previous works only optimize the clock network with either CG cloning or FF merging. For CG cloning, Teng and Soin [5] introduced cutting-based algorithm to split a CG and redistribute the CG fanout according to the cut line. The CG splitting algorithm is iteratively performed until the timing violation of each CG's enable signal is eliminated. Vishweshwara et al. [6], on the other hand, proposed a clustering-based algorithm to recursively replicate a CG when the CG has a large number of fanout, or when the spreading area of its fanout is larger than a limit.

For FF merging, the idea was first proposed in [7], which merges 1-bit FFs into MBFFs before floorplanning and placement based on the bread-first-search algorithm. Kretchmer [8] and Chen et al. [9] introduced a design methodology for logic optimization with MBFFs. Such methodology creates the models of multi-bit registers in a cell library which can be inferred by existing logic synthesis tools. Based on the multi-bit register inference, it is possible to map an RTL design directly to a gate-level design with multi-bit register cells during logic synthesis. Most recently, it is suggested to optimize a design with MBFFs in physical design [10, 11, 12, 13, 14], for more accurate timing budgets.

Although the problems of CG cloning and FF merging can be solved separately based on the previous works, the resulting clock network after CG cloning and FF merging may not be optimal. For example, if CG cloning is performed before FF merging, the 1-bit FFs, which are better to be merged into the same MBFF, may be separated into different fanout sets of the replicated CGs. On the contrary, if FF merging is performed before CG cloning, the 1-bit

FFs, which are better to be driven by the same CG may be merged into different MBFFs.

1.2 Our Contributions

In this paper, we tackle even more challenging problem for clock network optimization, as illustrated in Fig. 2. Instead of solving the problem of CG cloning and FF merging separately based on different problem formulations in the previous works, we propose to optimize clock network with simultaneous CG cloning and FF merging. Our contributions can be summarized as follows:

- We present the *first* problem formulation in the literature for gated clock network optimization with simultaneous CG cloning and FF merging.

- We introduce a novel optimization flow consisting of MBFF-aware CG cloning, CG-based FF merging, and MBFF and CG placement optimization to solve the presented problem.

- We formulate the MBFF-aware CG cloning optimization problem as a partitioning problem. Different from the classical partitioning problem which minimizes the cut size among different partitions subject to balanced partitions with bounded size constraints, our formulation is to maximize skew slack corresponding to different CGs subject to bounded slack constraints.

- Our experimental results show that the proposed approach leads to better dynamic power and clock wirelength compared with those approaches which optimize gated clock network with CGs and MBFFs separately.

The remainder of this paper is organized as follows. Section 2 formulates the problem of clock network optimization with both CGs and MBFFs. Section 3 presents novel ideas and algorithms to solve the problem. Section 4 reports the experimental results, and finally Section 5 concludes this paper.

2. PRELIMINARIES

Before proposing our algorithms for gated clock network optimization with simultaneous CG cloning and FF merging, we shall introduce the power model of the gated clock network, inter-CG clock skew due to CG cloning, control-path timing constraint for CGs, data-path timing constraint for MBFFs, placement density constraint for newly generated CGs and MBFFs, and finally our problem formulation.

2.1 Power Model of Gated Clock Network

According to [4], the power dissipated by the clock net, gated clock tree, and enable signal net in the gated clock network can be modelled by Fig. 3 and Equation (1), where the notations we use throughout this paper are listed in Table 1.

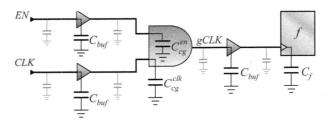

Figure 3: Power modelling for a gated clock network [4].

$$P_d = \left[\alpha_{clk} \cdot \left(c_0 l_{clk} + C_{buf} + C_{cg}^{clk} \right) + \alpha_{gclk} \cdot \left(c_0 l_{gclk} + C_{buf} + C_f \right) + 0.5 \cdot \alpha_{en} \cdot \left(c_0 l_{en} + C_{buf} + C_{cg}^{en} \right) \right] \cdot V_{dd}^2 \cdot \frac{1}{T_{period}}. \quad (1)$$

Table 1: The notations in this paper.

c_0	unit wire capacitance
C_{buf}	input capacitance of the buffer
C_{cg}^{en}	input capacitance at the enable pin of the CG
C_{cg}^{clk}	input capacitance at the clock pin of the CG
C_f	input capacitance of the gated FF
f_{EN}	the FF connected to the enable logic
$f\ (f_i)$	the (i^{th}) gated FF
g_i	the ith CG
l_{clk}	wirelength of the clock net
l_{gclk}	wirelength of the gated clock net
l_{en}	wirelength of the enable signal net
P_d	dynamic power consumption of the clock network
P_f	total power consumption of the gated FFs
T_{period}	clock period
T_{skew}	inter-CG clock skew among gated FFs
T_i^{clk}	interconnection delay from the clock root to g_i
T_i^{en}	interconnection delay from the enable logic to g_i
T_i^{gclk}	interconnection delay from g_i to the farthest gated FF
T^{CG}	CG delay
T^{EL}	enable logic delay
V_{dd}	supply voltage
α_{clk}	switching activity of the clock net
α_{gclk}	switching activity of the gated clock tree
α_{en}	switching activity of the enable signal net

As V_{dd}, T_{period}, and the switching activities in Equation (1) cannot be changed during gated clock network optimization, to minimize P_d, it is essential to reduce both wirelength and capacitive loads which correspond to the numbers of clock buffers, CGs, and MBFF cells.

2.2 Inter-CG Clock Skew due to CG Cloning

When a CG is replicated in the gated clock network, as shown in Fig. 4, the inter-CG clock skew, T_{skew}, between a gated FF, f_i, connected to the original CG, g_i, and another gated FF, f_j, connected to the replicated CG, g_j, can be calculated by Equation (2).

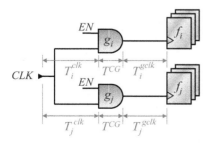

Figure 4: Inter-CG clock skew among gated FFs after CG cloning.

$$T_{skew} = |(T_i^{clk} + T_i^{gclk}) - (T_j^{clk} + T_j^{gclk})|. \quad (2)$$

In Equation (2), T_i^{clk} (T_j^{clk}) depends on the wirelength from the clock root to g_i (g_j), while T_i^{gclk} (T_j^{gclk}) depends on the wirelength from g_i (g_j) to all its fanout flip-flops and the number of total fanout flip-flops. Therefore, to minimize T_{skew}, we shall balance the wirelength and flip-flop fanout numbers among all clock paths passing through different CGs.

2.3 Control-Path Timing Constraint for Gated Clock Network

In addition to inter-CG clock skew, the control-path timing constraint should also be considered during CG cloning. Fig. 5 shows the control-path timing of the gated clock network. The propagation delay from f_{EN} to a gated flip-flop, f, which is the summation of T^{EL}, T_i^{en}, T^{CG}, and T_i^{gclk}, must be less than or equal to T_{period}. When performing CG cloning, T^{EL} and T^{CG} cannot be changed due to fixed f_{EN} and enable logic locations, and gate delay. Consequently, the control-path timing constraint can be derived, as seen in Equation (3), where T_i^{en} is determined by the wirelength from the enable logic to g_i, and T_i^{gclk} is determined by the wirelength from g_i to all its fanout flip-flops and the number of total fanout flip-flops.

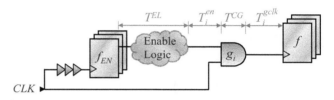

Figure 5: Control-path timing of the gated clock network.

$$T_i^{en} + T_i^{gclk} \leq T_{period} - T^{EL} - T^{CG}. \quad (3)$$

2.4 Data-Path Timing Constraint for FF Merging

Similar to the timing constraint defined in [10, 11, 12], to satisfy the data-path timing constraint when replacing several 1-bit FFs with one MBFF, only the FFs which have common intersection of their timing-feasible regions, as seen in Fig. 6, can be merged. The timing-feasible region of a flip-flop can be obtained from the available timing slack on the corresponding data paths.

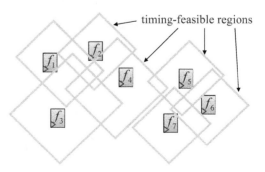

Figure 6: Timing-feasible regions for all FFs.

2.5 Placement Density Constraint for CGs and MBFFs

The newly generated CGs and MBFFs during gated clock network optimization should satisfy the placement density constraint in order to avoid routing congestion. According to [10, 11, 12], we divide the chip area into a number of bins with equal size. A CG or an MBFF can only be placed in a bin whose density is less than the maximum placement density.

2.6 Problem Formulation

Based on the aforementioned power model of gated clock network, inter-CG clock skew due to CG cloning, and all the design constraints, we propose the new problem formulation for gated clock network optimization.

DEFINITION 1. *A clock gating domain contains a set of FFs which are controlled by the gated clock signals whose switching activities are the same.*

PROBLEM 1. *Given a clock-gating domain containing a set of placed FFs, and a cell library containing both CG and MBFF cells, the problem of* Clock Network Optimization with CG Cloning and FF Merging *is to minimize* P_d *and* T_{skew} *of the clock-gating domain subject to the control-path timing constraint, data-path timing constraint, and placement density constraint.*

In Problem 1, P_d is the primary objective, while T_{skew} is the secondary one because T_{skew} can be further minimized after clock tree routing. We use the Synopsys Liberty Library [15] for timing modelling, where the wire loading is estimated by the product of half-perimeter wirelength (HPWL) and c_0.

In Fig. 2(a), the FFs which are controlled by the gated clock signal "$gclk$" belong to the same clock gating domain.

3. THE PROPOSED ALGORITHMS

Based on the problem formulation, we propose novel ideas and algorithms to optimize the gated clock network with simultaneous CG cloning and FF merging. The flow of our algorithms consists of three major steps: (1) MBFF-aware CG cloning, (2) CG-based FF merging, and (3) MBFF and CG placement optimization.

3.1 MBFF-aware CG Cloning

When a control path violates the timing constraint, as illustrated in Section 2.3, or when a CG drives too many FFs leading to larger clock power consumption, the CG on the control path must be replicated, and the FFs driven by the CG must be divided into groups for shorter delay and lower power consumption.

We propose a novel MBFF-aware CG cloning algorithm which simultaneously considers inter-CG clock skew and FF merging during CG cloning. When optimizing the gated clock network of a clock gating domain, the fanout FFs are recursively bisected and a new CG is simultaneously replicated until the clock-path timing constraint is satisfied, and P_d cannot be further reduced. During each bisecting iteration, we present novel *cut-line determination with inter-CG skew budgeting* and *MBFF-aware FF swapping* techniques to improve inter-CG clock skew and inner-CG FF merging quality.

3.1.1 Cut-line Determination with Inter-CG Skew Budgeting

When separating a set of placed FFs in the same clocking gating domain into two sets with a physical cut line, the cut direction is determined by the physical dimension of the FF bounding box [5]. A

vertical (horizontal) cut is applied if the dimension in x-direction is larger (smaller) than that in y-direction. Fig. 7(a) shows the bounding box of a set of placed FFs in a clock gating domain and a physical cut line which bisects the FFs. The resulting bounding box of each set of FFs after the bisection is shown in Fig. 7(b).

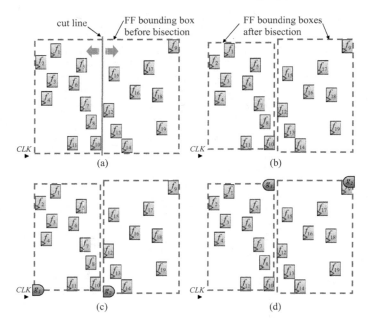

Figure 7: (a) A cut line which separates a set of placed FFs in a clock gating domain. (b) The FF bounding boxes after bisecting the fanout FFs. (c) The original CG, g_1, and the replicated CG, g_2, are placed closest to the clock root within the respective FF bounding boxes. (d) g_1 and g_2 are placed farthest from the clock root within the respective FF bounding boxes.

To find out a good physical cut line position with inter-CG skew budgeting, we shall minimize and balance the clock signal delay, $T^{clk}+T^{CG}+T^{gclk}$, from the clock root to the FFs passing through different CGs, as illustrated in Fig. 4. Given the clock root position and the bisected FF bounding boxes, as seen in Fig. 7(b), the clock signal delay is determined by the original and replicated CG positions. Due to the large number of CG fanout, T^{gclk} may dominate the clock signal delay among the three terms. Therefore, a CG should be placed within the bounding box of its fanout FFs for shorter T^{gclk}.

Figs. 7(c) and (d) demonstrate two extreme cases of the CG positions inside the corresponding FF bounding boxes. In Fig. 7(c) (Fig. 7(d)), the CGs are placed at the positions closest to (farthest from) the clock root within the respective FF bounding boxes, resulting in the shortest (longest) clock signal delay, $(T^{clk}+T^{CG}+T^{gclk})_{min}$ $((T^{clk}+T^{CG}+T^{gclk})_{max})$ from the clock root to the FFs. To better and more easily balance the delay passing through different CGs for clock skew minimization, we would like to find out a physical cut line which maximizes the skew slack among the clock signal paths passing through different CGs. The skew slack, T_{skew_slack} can be calculated by finding the difference between the minimum longest clock signal delay and the maximum shortest one passing through different CGs, as seen in Equation (4).

We sweep the physical cut line to search for the maximum skew slack, $T_{skew\_slack}^{max}$, as demonstrated in Fig. 7(a). At the beginning, the FFs are sorted in the ascending order with respect to the x-coordinates (y-coordinates) when a vertical (horizontal) cut is ap-

$$T_{skew\_slack} = \min\{(T_i^{clk} + T_i^{gclk})_{max}, (T_j^{clk} + T_j^{gclk})_{max}\} - \max\{(T_i^{clk} + T_i^{gclk})_{min}, (T_j^{clk} + T_j^{gclk})_{min}\} \qquad (4)$$

plied. An initial physical cut line is first located at the position which evenly separates the numbers of FFs. The cut line is then swept to the left (bottom) and to the right (top) until $T_{skew\_slack}^{max}$, is obtained. The sweeping steps can be dynamically adjusted according to the physical density of the FFs in the sorted array to speed up the search process.

3.1.2 MBFF-aware FF Swapping

Once the physical cut line with $T_{skew\_slack}^{max}$ is found, the FFs near the physical cut line are further swapped between two separated FF sets for better succeeding FF merging and MBFF replacement in each FF set. Before swapping the FFs, we first construct the hypergraph, $H(V, E)$, according to the timing-feasible region of each FF, as seen in Fig. 6. Each vertex, v_i, in $H(V, E)$ represents the timing-feasible region of a gated FF, f_i, and each hyper edge, e_i, in $H(V, E)$ corresponds to the intersection among the timing-feasible regions of different FFs. The edge weight, $w(e_i)$, indicates the number of vertices connected by e_i, or the number of the corresponding intersected timing-feasible regions. Fig. 8 shows the hypergraph corresponding to the intersected timing-feasible regions in Fig. 6, where the edge weights, $w(e_1)$, $w(e_2)$, and $w(e_3)$, are 4, 2, and 3, respectively.

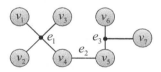

Figure 8: The hypergraph corresponds to the intersected timing-feasible regions of different FFs in Fig. 6.

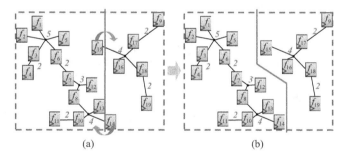

Figure 9: (a) The hypergraph for the design in Fig. 7, and the physical cut line with $T_{skew\_slack}^{max}$, where the cut size is equal to 8. (b) Minimized cut size after swapping f_{14} and f_{15} based on the FM algorithm [16].

After constructing $H(V, E)$, we then perform the FM algorithm [16] on $H(V, E)$ to move FFs between different FF sets such that the cut size (i.e. sum of edge weights on the cut line) is minimized. We set a balance condition that the skew slack after moving an FF to the other FF set must not less than $\gamma \times T_{skew\_slack}^{max}$, where $0 < \gamma < 1$, and γ is a balance factor. Fig. 9(a) shows the hypergraph corresponding to the design in Fig. 7, as well as the physical cut line which maximizes T_{skew_slack} based on the proposed cut line determination with inter-CG skew budgeting technique. The number at each hyperedge in the hypergraph indicates the corresponding

edge weight. Fig. 9(b) shows the result after performing the FM algorithm [16] on the hypergraph. The cut size reduces from eight to zero after swapping two gated FFs, f_{14} and f_{15}, between the FF sets on different sides.

3.2 CG-based FF Merging

For each set of FFs controlled by a CG, we merge 1-bit FFs into MBFFs starting from the four boundaries of the FF bounding box to the center area, as illustrated in Fig. 10(a), based on INTEGRA [12] and the spiral clustering technique [17]. The reason is because INTEGRA can achieve the best merging quality in terms of FF power reduction compared with all the other previous works, and the spiral clustering technique can merge the FFs near the boundaries of the FF bounding box first, which may have fewer choices to be merged with other FFs inside the FF bounding box. Fig. 10(b) shows the merging result of the FF set in Fig. 10(a), which are controlled by the same replicated CG.

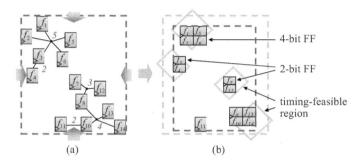

Figure 10: Inner-CG FF merging. (a) Merging the FFs controlled by a CG starting from the four boundaries of the FF bounding box. (b) The FF merging result based on 2-bit and 4-bit FF cells in the cell library.

3.3 MBFF and CG Placement Optimization

After replicating CGs and merging 1-bit FFs into MBFFs, we shall further perform MBFF and CG placement optimization to minimize inter-CG clock skew, wirelength, and required clock buffers while satisfying control/data-path timing, and placement density constraints. We first optimize MBFF placements to minimize the wirelength of each gated clock signal from a CG to all its fanout FFs. After that, we then adjust the CG positions to minimize the inter-CG clock skew, required clock buffers, and wirelength from the clock root and enable logic to each CG.

When placing the MBFFs controlled by the same CG, we search for the placement bins, which satisfy placement density constraint, in the timing-feasible region corresponding to each MBFF such that the FF bounding box of the CG fanouts is minimized, as seen in Fig. 10(b). The smaller FF bounding box in Fig. 10(b) can result in shorter gated clock signal wirelength, and hence smaller T^{gclk} and P_d.

The CGs are initially placed inside their feasible positions which satisfy the control-path timing constraints, as described in Section 2.3. According to Fig. 5 and Equation (3) with the timing modelling based on the Synopsys Liberty Library [15], the feasible region of a CG is roughly an ellipse whose the two foci are at the positions of the enable logic and one of the CG fanout FFs. We perform an iterative optimization algorithm to move CGs around their feasible regions until the inter-CG clock skew cannot be further minimized. During the iterative optimization, we may gradually add clock buffers to either clock path from the clock root to a CG for delay balance, or insert buffers to either enable signal path from the enable logic to a CG for a larger feasible region of the CG. Consequently, the buffer numbers are also minimized.

4. EXPERIMENTAL RESULTS

We implemented our algorithms in the C++ programming language, and performed the experiment on a 2.26GHz Intel Xeon machine under the Linux operating system. We adopted the benchmark circuits in [12] by additionally adding other logical, physical, and timing information for CGs, clock root, and enable logic such that the power and skew can be estimated according to the corresponding models. We referred to the Nangate $45nm$ Open Cell Library [18] to set the input capacitance of all cells in each circuit. To simplify the experimental setup, we assumed that all FFs in each circuit belong to the same clock gating domain, and they are initially connected to the same CG. As some of the circuits in [12] are too large, which is unreasonable to be considered as a single clock gating domain, we only chose the circuits containing less than 6,000 FFs with reasonable FF bounding boxes. Table 2 lists the name of each benchmark circuit we adopted, the numbers of 1-bit and 2-bit FFs ("# of FFs"), and the bit numbers of available MBFF cells in the cell library ("Bit # of available MBFF Cells") for each circuit.

Table 2: The benchmark circuits obtained from [12].

Circuit	# of FFs		Bit # of available
	1-bit	2-bit	MBFF Cells
S1	120	0	1, 2, 4
S2	120	0	1, 2, 4
T3	953	0	1, 2, 4, 8
C1	76	22	1, 2, 4
C2	366	57	1, 2, 4

Since this is the first work in the literature that optimizes clock network with simultaneous CG cloning and FF merging, we compared the proposed flow with two reference flows which optimize clock network with CG cloning and FF merging separately, as demonstrated in Fig. 11, to show the effectiveness of the presented simultaneous optimization. The first flow ("Reference Flow 1") applies CG cloning first followed by FF merging, while the second flow ("Reference Flow 2") applies FF merging first followed by CG cloning. The CG cloning technique in both reference flows is based on the proposed MBFF-aware CG cloning without applying MBFF-aware FF swapping, while the FF merging technique in both reference flows is exactly the same as the presented CG-based FF merging.

We compared the numbers of MBFFs and CGs, dynamic power consumption of gated clock network, clock/signal net wirelength, and runtime for two reference flows and the proposed flow. Table 3 lists the names of the benchmark circuits ("Circuit"), numbers of MBFFs with different bit numbers ("# of FFs"), CG numbers ("# of CGs") for the three different flows, and Table 4 lists the names of the benchmark circuits ("Circuit"), dynamic power consumption of gated clock network ("P_d"), clock net wirelength ("Clk WL"), signal net wirelength ("Sig. WL"), and runtime ("Time") for the three different flows, where P_d was calculated according to Equation (1), and both clock and signal net wirelength were obtained by constructing rectilinear steiner trees based on the algorithms in [19].

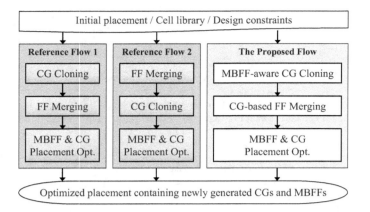

Figure 11: Three different flows for gated clock network power optimization with CG cloning and FF merging.

We normalized the P_d value of each benchmark circuit resulting from both reference flows with respect to that resulting from the proposed flow.

When comparing with "Reference Flow 1", the proposed flow results in much more MBFFs with similar clock gate numbers. The dynamic power and clock wirelength resulting from the proposed flow is 15% and 22% less than that resulting from "Reference Flow 1", respectively, while the signal net wirelength resulting from the proposed flow is almost the same as that resulting from "Reference Flow 1". When comparing with "Reference Flow 2", the proposed flow results in much slightly more CGs and slightly fewer MBFFs. The dynamic power and clock wirelength resulting from the proposed flow is 10% and 18% less than that resulting from "Reference Flow 2", respectively, while the signal net wirelength resulting from both flows are still quite similar. Consequently, the proposed gated clock network power optimization with simultaneous CG cloning and FF merging is very effective in reducing both dynamic power and wirelength of the gated clock network.

5. CONCLUSIONS

We have presented a new problem formulation for clock network optimization with both CGs and MBFFs. Based on the problem formulation, we have also introduced novel techniques to optimize gated clock network with CG cloning and FF merging simultaneously. The experimental results have shown that the proposed approach results in better dynamic power and clock wirelength compared with those which optimize gated clock network with CGs and MBFFs separately.

6. ACKNOWLEDGMENTS

This work was partially supported by National Science Council of Taiwan, under Grant No's. NSC 100-2220-E-194-007-, NSC 101-2220-E-194-006-, and NSC 102-2220-E-194-006-.

7. REFERENCES

[1] D. Liu and C. Svensson, "Power consumption estimation in cmos vlsi chips," *IEEE J. Solid-State Circuits*, vol. 29, no. 6, pp. 663–670, Jun. 1994.

[2] M. Keating, D. Flynn, R. Aitken, A. Gibbons, and K. Shi, *Low Power Methodology for System-on-Chip Design*. Springer, 2007.

[3] Q. Wu, M. Pedram, and X. Wu, "Clock-gating and its application to low power design of sequential circuits," *IEEE*

Table 3: Comparisons of the numbers of MBFFs and CGs and clock skew for Reference Flow 1, Reference Flow 2, and the proposed flow.

Circuit	Reference Flow 1 (CG Cloning → FF Merging)		Reference Flow 2 (FF Merging → CG Cloning)		The Proposed Flow (Simultaneous CG Cloning & FF Merging)	
	# of FFs 1-, 2-, 4-, 6-, 8-, 13-bit	# of CGs	# of FFs 1-, 2-, 4-, 6-, 8-, 13-bit	# of CGs	# of FFs 1-, 2-, 4-, 6-, 8-, 13-bit	# of CGs
S1	0, 6, 27, –, –, –	4	0, 4, 28, –, –, –	4	2, 5, 27, –, –, –	4
S2	8, 12, 22, –, –, –	13	0, 2, 29, –, –, –	9	2, 3, 28, –, –, –	13
T3	5, 8, 11, –, 111, –	6	1, 0, 4, –, 117, –	6	5, 4, 5, –, 115, –	7
C1	0, 6, 27, –, –, –	4	0, 4, 28, –, –, –	4	2, 7, 26, –, –, –	4
C2	10, 37, 99, –, –, –	23	0, 6, 117, –, –, –	19	10, 27, 104, –, –, –	23

Table 4: Comparisons of dynamic power consumption of gated clock network, clock/signal net wirelength, and runtime for Reference Flow 1, Reference Flow 2, and the proposed flow.

Circuit	Reference Flow 1 (CG Cloning → FF Merging)				Reference Flow 2 (FF Merging → CG Cloning)				The Proposed Flow (Simultaneous CG Cloning & FF Merging)			
	P_d (%)	Clk WL (μm)	Sig. WL (μm)	Time (s)	P_d (%)	Clk WL (μm)	Sig. WL (μm)	Time (s)	P_d (%)	Clk WL (μm)	Sig. WL (μm)	Time (s)
S1	1.11	24,068	86,309	0.03	1.11	24,360	86,037	0.05	1.00	20,683	84,075	0.03
S2	1.24	29,945	78,300	0.04	1.13	27,461	84,038	0.06	1.00	21,262	82,254	0.05
T3	1.14	88,064	624,698	0.17	1.10	86,310	623,404	0.03	1.00	75,892	576,754	1.83
C1	1.10	24,068	86,309	0.03	1.10	24,414	86,065	0.02	1.00	20,900	90,613	0.02
C2	1.15	107,175	340,018	0.03	1.07	100,398	354,950	0.01	1.00	89,135	354,666	0.02
Comp.	1.15	1.22	1.00	0.98	1.10	1.18	1.02	0.88	1.00	1.00	1.00	1.00

Trans. Circuits Syst. I, vol. 47, no. 3, pp. 415–420, Mar. 2000.

[4] W. Shen, Y. Cai, X. Hong, and J. Hu, "An effective gated clock tree design based on activity and register aware placement," *IEEE Trans. VLSI Syst.*, vol. 18, no. 12, pp. 1639–1648, Dec. 2010.

[5] S. K. Teng and N. Soin, "Regional clock gate splitting algorithm for clock tree synthesis," in *Proceedings of IEEE International Conference on Semiconductor Electronics*, Jun. 2010, pp. 131–134.

[6] R. Vishweshwara, N. Mahita, and R. Venkatraman, "Placement aware clock gate cloning and redistribution methodology," in *Proceedings of IEEE/ACM International Symposium on Quality of Electronic Design*, Mar. 2012, pp. 432–436.

[7] R. Pokala, R. Feretich, and R. McGuffin, "Physical synthesis for performance optimization," in *Proceedings of IEEE International ASIC Conference and Exhibit*, Sep. 1992, pp. 34–37.

[8] Y. Kretchmer, "Using multibit register inference to save area and power," *EE Times Asia*, May 2001.

[9] L. Chen, A. Hung, H.-M. Chen, E. Tsai, S.-H. Chen, M.-H. Ku, and C.-C. Chen, "Using multi-bit flip-flop for clock power saving by DesignCompiler," in *Proceedings of Synopsys Users Group*, 2010.

[10] M. P.-H. Lin, C.-C. Hsu, and Y.-T. Chang, "Post-placement power optimization with multi-bit flip-flops," *IEEE Trans. Computer-Aided Design*, vol. 30, no. 12, pp. 1870–1882, Dec. 2011.

[11] S.-H. Wang, Y.-Y. Liang, T.-Y. Kuo, and W.-K. Mak, "Power-driven flip-flop merging and relocation," *IEEE Trans. Computer-Aided Design*, vol. 31, no. 2, pp. 180–191, Feb. 2012.

[12] I. Jiang, C.-L. Chang, and Y.-M. Yang, "Integra: Fast multi-bit flip-flop clustering for clock power saving," *IEEE Trans. Computer-Aided Design*, vol. 31, no. 2, pp. 192–204, Dec. 2012.

[13] Y.-T. Shyu, J.-M. Lin, C.-P. Huang, C.-W. Lin, Y.-Z. Lin, and S.-J. Chang, "Effective and efficient approach for power reduction by using multi-bit flip-flops," *IEEE Trans. VLSI Syst.*, vol. 21, no. 4, pp. 624–635, Apr. 2013.

[14] C.-C. Tsai, Y. Shi, G. Luo, and I. H.-R. Jiang, "FF-Bond: Multi-bit flip-flop bonding at placement," in *Proceedings of ACM International Symposium on Physical Design*, 2013, pp. 147–153.

[15] Synopsys, Inc., *Library Compiler User Guide: Modeling Timing and Power Technology Libraries*, 2003.

[16] C. M. Fiduccia and R. M. Mattheyses, "A linear-time heuristic for improving network partitions," in *Proceedings of ACM/IEEE Design Automation Conference*, Jun. 1982, pp. 175–181.

[17] C.-L. Chang, I. H.-R. Jiang, Y.-M. Yang, E. Y.-W. Tsai, and A. S.-H. Chen, "Novel pulsed-latch replacement based on time borrowing and spiral clustering," in *Proceedings of ACM International Symposium on Physical Design*, 2012, pp. 121–128.

[18] Nangate 45nm Open Cell Library. [Online]. Available: http://www.nangate.com/

[19] A. Kahng, I. Mandoiu, and A. Zelikovsky, "Highly scalable algorithms for rectilinear and octilinear steiner trees," in *Proceedings of IEEE/ACM Asia South Pacific Design Automation Conference*, Jan. 2003, pp. 827–833.

Current Density Aware Power Switch Placement Algorithm for Power Gating Designs *

Jai-Ming Lin, Che-Chun Lin,
Zong-Wei Syu
Dept. of Electrical Engineering,
National Cheng Kung University
Tainan 70101, Taiwan
jmlin@ee.ncku.edu.tw,
n26011364@mail.ncku.edu.tw,
n26021555@mail.ncku.edu.tw

Chih-Chung Tsai, Kevin Huang
Himax Technologies, Inc.
Tainan 74148, Taiwan
cctsai@himax.com.tw,
kevin_huang@himaxms.com

ABSTRACT

Due to advances in manufacture technology, leakage current increases dramatically in modern ICs. Power gating technique is an efficient and effective method to resolve this problem. In order to turn off supply voltage in a low-power domain, it has to insert power switches into designs. However, chip area and IR-drop of circuits are impacted by the number and locations of inserted power switches. Unlike previous works using greedy algorithm to handle this problem, this paper proposes a simple model to approximate the equivalent resistance of power switches in a low-power domain, and uses the binary search method to get the precise value. Based on this value, power switches are allocated by a partition-based approach. Experimental results demonstrate that our approach can insert less number of power switches and still satisfy the IR-drop constraint than other approaches. Moreover, this method is very efficient.

Categories and Subject Descriptors

B.7.2 [**Integrated Circuits**]: Design Aids

General Terms

Algorithms, Design

Keywords

Power Gating Designs, Power Switch, IR Drop

1. INTRODUCTION

Power-saving is a hot issue in VLSI designs. Due to stringent demands in mobile electronic equipment such as GPS,

*This work was partially supported by the National Science Council of Taiwan ROC under Grant No. NSC-101-2220-E-006-006-.

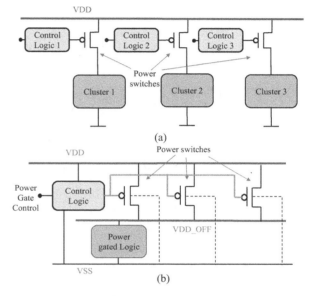

Figure 1: Two types of power gating structures. (a) The fine-grain structure. (b) The coarse-grain structure.

PDA and cell phones, increasing power lasting capabilities has become great concern in IC designs. As the advance in process technology, threshold voltage of a device is reduced, and thinner gate-oxide thickness causes leakage power to increase exponentially. According to the study by Sery *et al.* [12], leakage power contributes to more than 50% of total power in 65 nm design. Thus, leakage power becomes a serious problem in modern design.

Multi-Threshold CMOS, MTCMOS, is an effective method to reduce power consumption. To keep chip performance, it uses low threshold voltage devices to implement original circuits in a low-power domain. However, low threshold voltage devices usually lead to significant leakage current. It has to insert power switches, which are implemented by high threshold voltage (V_{th}) devices, to cut off power supply in the domain. This method is widely applied in industry, and it is also called the power gating technique.

Kao *et al.* [6] and Mutoh *et al.* [10] first use a single power switch to turn off the power supply of idle modules for reduc-

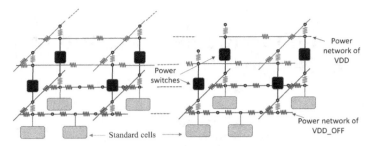

Figure 2: Power networks in the coarse-grain structure.

ing power consumption, which is called the module-based design. According to the maximum current consumed by the modules, the proper size of the power switch can be determined easily. As design complexity increases, circuits consume significantly large current, which causes it to insert an unacceptably large size power switch. Therefore, Anis *et al.* [1] and Wang *et al.* [16] propose the fine-grain structure to handle this problem. Circuits in a low-power domain are divided into several clusters, and one power switch is inserted into each cluster to control power-on and power-off of the cluster. Although the total width of power switches is smaller than that in the module-based design, the design complexity increases a lot since it needs to divide the circuits into several clusters based on their geometrical locations, and add respective control logic into each cluster. Moreover, the fine-grain structure is not supported by current commercial tools. Fig. 1 (a) shows a fine-grain structure. The whole circuit is divided into three clusters and each cluster has its own power switch and control logic to control power-on and power-off of the cluster.

Due to the problems of the fine-grain structure, Long and He [9] propose a distributed sleep transistor network (**DSTN**) in power gating designs, which is also considered as the coarse-grain structure. This structure contains two kinds of power networks, which are a global power network and a local power network. A set of power switches are parallel connected between the global power network and the local power network, and the local power network provides the supply voltage for the circuits in a low-power domain. By turning off power switches, the power supply of the circuits in the low-power domain is cut off. Fig. 1 (b) shows the coarse-grain structure. The global power network is denoted by VDD and the local power network is denoted by VDD_OFF. The block labeled with power gated logic denotes the circuits in a low-power domain, and its power is provided by VDD_OFF. All power switches are connected between VDD and VDD_OFF. Because the coarse-grain structure has superior properties than the fine-grain structure, this paper focuses on the coarse-grain structure. Fig. 2 shows the power networks of the coarse-grain structure in three-dimension view.

There exists a trade-off between IR-drop and chip area in inserting power switches in power gating designs. Because more and more transistors are integrated into a chip, IR-drop problem becomes more serious. It is even worse while modern ICs prefer to use lower supply voltage for reducing dynamic power, which makes tolerable drop margin of circuits further decline. Since power supply provided for a low-power domain must go through a global power network,

power switches and a local power network before it reaches cells, more serious IR-drop may be induced if these cells are located far away from power pads or they have larger power consumption. Because a local power network is connected to a global power network through power switches, standard cells in a low-power domain can obtain stronger power supply while more power switches are inserted into the power networks. However, this inevitably wastes more chip area.

1.1 Previous Works

Previous works [1], [2], [3], [5], [7], [14], [15], [17] can be divided into two classes based on their structures. Some papers [1], [2], [5] discuss the fine-grain structure, and others [3], [7], [14], [15], [17] focus on the coarse-grain structure. Because the papers [1], [2], [5] handle the fine-grain structure, the details of methods are not described here.

There exist different operation modes in power gating designs, which include the power-off mode, the power-on mode, and the ramp-up mode. To reduce power consumption, circuits are shut down in the power-off mode. At the moment that power switches are turned on, there may exist huge transient current flowing into a low-power domain if power switches are turned on too fast. This is considered as the ramp-up mode. To reduced rush current, Chen *et al.* [3] and Chang *et al.* [2] discuss how to arrange power-up sequence of power switches. The details of these papers are not described because they are not in the scope of this paper. Circuits work normally in the power-on mode. Due to insertion of power switches into power networks, their functions and timings may be affected by the IR-drop effect. The methods to insert proper number of power switches at suitable locations are discussed by [7], [14], [17].

Shi *et al.* [14] consider each legal location for placing a power switch as a through-silicon via (TSV). They apply a mathematical methodology to determine resistances of the TSVs under consideration of chip area and IR-drop constraint. However, there may exist no power switch corresponding to the computed equivalent resistance, which makes the approach impractical. Kozhaya and Bakir [7] first place a lot of power switches at legal locations. According to the results of static IR-drop analysis, the power switches which are located at the locations with lower current sources are removed. On the contrary, the power switches are added to the locations with higher current sources and the IR-drop constraint is violated. Similar to the approach [7], Yong and Ung [17] place power switches at all legal locations. They assume that every power switch has a certain effect region. The number of power switches is reduced by removing those power switches whose effect regions are overlapped by others.

1.2 Our Contribution

Insertion of power switches is very important for power gating designs. However, current commercial tools do not support this function well. To avoid inducing IR-drop problem, engineers usually insert a large amount of power switches and regularly place them inside a placement region. This may waste unnecessary chip area. To handle this problem, previous works [7], [14], [17] all apply greedy algorithms to place power switches. Since quality of these greedy algorithms is not good enough, this paper proposes an efficient and effective approach to handle this problem. Unlike previous works, our method is able to insert proper number of

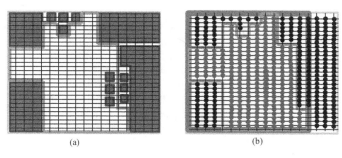

Figure 3: (a) A low-power domain in a chip. (b) The bounding box of a low-power domain.

power switches and place them at suitable locations because of the following reasons:

- **Model of Power Switches in the Coarse-Grain Structure:** with the proposed model, the equivalent resistance of power switches in the coarse-grain structure can be approximated.

- **Binary Search Method:** since the equivalent resistance of power switches has a great impact on the area of inserted power switches and IR-drop of a design, the binary search method is applied to find correct value.

- **Partition-based Approach:** according to correct equivalent resistance of power switches, a recursively partition-based approach is used to allocate power switches to suitable locations based on the current density in each region.

Experimental results show that the Yong and Ung [17]'s algorithm consumes 13.9% larger power switch area than our approach and induces serious IR-drop than our results.

The remaining of the paper is organized as follows: Section 2 introduces the basic of power switches and gives the problem formulation. Section 3 proposes a model to approximate the equivalent resistance of power switches in power gating designs. Section 4 illustrates a partition based placement algorithm to place power switches. Then our methodology is shown in Section 5, and Section 6 shows experimental results on real designs. Finally, Section 7 gives conclusion.

2. PRELIMINARIES AND PROBLEM FORMULATION

Due to placement of blocks in other power domains, the shape of a low-power domain is usually not rectangular. Fig. 3 (a) shows a chip with two power domains, which are always-on and low-power domains, respectively. The yellow frame denotes the boundary of a chip outline. After blocks (denoted by the blue squares) in the always-on domain are placed, the shape of the lower-power domain, which is surrounded by green lines, becomes irregular. Let D denote a low-power domain. For simplicity, the region of a low-power domain is represented by a minimum bounding box B which encloses the whole low-power domain. As shown in Fig. 3(b), the region of the low-power domain is represented by the bounding box B with red border.

In order to reduce routing area, power switches have better to be placed at certain locations in a low-power do-

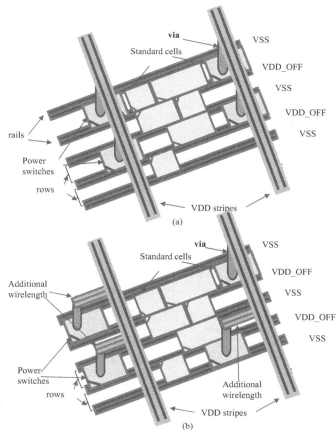

Figure 4: (a) Legal locations of power switches. Power switches are placed at cross locations of global power stripes and rows. Power switches are marked by red squares. (b) Illegal locations of power switches. Additional wirelength is required for connecting power switches to global power stripes.

main. Each power switch has three pins, which are VDD, VDD_OFF, and VSS, respectively. Since the rails of a row respectively supply VDD_OFF and VSS, a power switch is connected to VDD_OFF and VSS after it is placed into a row. If its location is also under a global power stripe VDD, the power switch can be connected to VDD through vias without using additional metal wires. The cross location between a row and a global VDD stripe is defined as a **legal location** for placing a power switch. Once powerplanning is completed, legal locations are determined. Let M denote total number of legal locations in a low-power domain.

Fig. 4 (a) shows four rows for placement of standard cells. Each row has two rails passing through it, which are VDD_OFF and VSS, respectively. Global power stripes VDD are routed at top metal layer. Since the four power switches are all placed under VDD stripes, they can directly connect to VDD through vias. However, additional wirelength is required to connect to VDD because there exist three power switches which are not placed under VDD stripes as shown in Fig. 4 (b).

Given a set L of power switches with different types, where s_i denotes one type of power switch, $s_i \in L, 1 \leq i \leq p$. Let a_i and r_i denote the area and the equivalent resistance

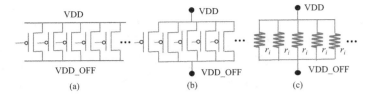

Figure 5: (a) Power switches connected between two power networks in parallel. (b) Power switches connected between two nodes in parallel. (c) Model of power switches inserted in the coarse-grain structure.

of s_i, respectively. After placement and powerplanning are completed, we have to select power switches from L, and place them at suitable locations. The target is to minimize the total area of inserted power switches under a given IR-drop constraint. Let VDD_t denote tolerable voltage drop value, which can be computed as follow:

$$VDD_t = (VDD * \alpha\%) \qquad (1)$$

where VDD is the ideal power supply voltage value and α is a user specified parameter.

3. MODEL FOR POWER GATING DESIGNS

In order to insert less number of power switches and still satisfy the IR-drop constraint, we first try to find the equivalent resistance of power switches in a low-power domain. If this value is obtained, suitable number of power switches can be determined based on the value (the method will be introduced in the next section). Since the power network of a power gating design is quite complex, it is not easy to analyze the resistance of the whole network. Thus, a simple model is proposed to approximate the value.

Originally, all power switches are connected between a global power network (VDD) and a local power network (VDD_OFF) in parallel as shown in Fig. 5 (a). Because of mass parallel-connection of power wires with low resistances, the equivalent resistances of two power networks are extremely small comparing to that of power switches. Thus, each power network is considered as one single node. Then the power switches are connected to the two nodes in parallel as shown in Fig. 5 (b). Because there exists small voltage variation in the power-on mode, voltage-current relation of a power switch is considered as linear based on the small-signal analysis. By replacing each power switch s_i with a resistance r_i, the course-grain structure can be described by the model shown in Fig. 5 (c). Then the equivalent resistance of power switches in a low-power domain can be computed easily with the model.

4. PARTITION BASED ALGORITHM

Let R_t denote the equivalent resistance of power switches in a low-power domain based on our model. The methodology to get accurate R_t will be introduced in Section 5. Once R_t is obtained, this section proposes a recursively partition-based approach to allocate power switches into a design based on the value and the current density in each region.

4.1 Partition a Region

This subsection first shows a cost function to cut a region into two subregions, and determines the resistance in each subregion.

Given a region B and the associated equivalent resistance R_B, the region B is cut into two parts, which are denoted by B_0 and B_1, respectively. The cutting direction is determined by the aspect ratio (i.e., height of B /width of B) of B. A power switch can be considered as a voltage source for the devices close to it. In order to provide stable voltage, power switches have better to be placed evenly inside a placement region. However, distribution of legal locations is not uniform. If the aspect ratio of B_0 (or B_1) is too large (or small), legal locations inside the region may become less. Thus, a vertical cutting is applied if the width of B is larger than its height; otherwise, a horizontal cutting is applied.

After cutting direction is determined, the location of a cutline has to be determined. Let C_0 and C_1 (N_0 and N_1) respectively represent the summation of current (the number of legal locations) in B_0 and B_1. In order to reduce IR-drop, a region should be inserted more power switches if it consumes larger current. Making C_0 equal to C_1 is a straightforward approach to divide a region. However, larger C_0 (C_1) does not mean that B_0 (B_1) has larger N_0 (N_1). Thus, cutting a region according to its current may cause it to have insufficient locations for placing power switches. To resolve the problem, the following cost function is used to determine the location of cutline in B:

$$\beta|\frac{C_0}{N_0} - \frac{C_1}{N_1}| + (1 - \beta)|C_0 - C_1| \qquad (2)$$

where β is a user specified parameter. To ensure B_0 (or B_1) has enough legal locations for placing power switches, the first term tries to make the ratio of $\frac{C_0}{N_0}$ close to $\frac{C_1}{N_1}$. Moreover, the second term minimizes the difference between C_0 and C_1 to reduce the iterations of partitioning procedure.

After the dimension of B_0 (and B_1) is determined, the resistance R_B of B is then allocated to B_0 and B_1. Note that the resistance of a region implies the number of power switches required to be inserted into it. Based on the model proposed in Section 3, the resistance R_0 (R_1) is inversely proportional to the current in B_0 (B_1) (i.e., R_0 (R_1) is small while C_0 (C_1) is larger). Thus, R_0 and R_1 are computed by the following equations (i.e., $R_B = R_0 || R_1$.):

$$\begin{array}{l} R_0 = R_B * \frac{C_0 + C_1}{C_0}, \\ R_1 = R_B * \frac{C_0 + C_1}{C_1} \end{array} \qquad (3)$$

4.2 Placement of Power Switches

After the partition procedure stops, this subsection shows the method to allocate power switches into a subregion. The procedure includes selecting different types of power switches from L and placing them at suitable locations such that the equivalent resistance of these power switches is equal to the assigned resistance of the subregion based on the model proposed in Section 3. Moreover, the total area of these power switches is minimized.

Let L contain p types of power switches, where the area of i-th power switch is a_i and the equivalent resistance is r_i. For each type of power switches in L, we first compute the product of resistance and area (i.e., $r_i \times a_i$), and the power switches in L are sorted by the value from small to large (i.e., s_1 denotes the type of power switch with the

```
Algorithm Recursive_Partition_Placement (R_t, D)
//R_t denotes the total equivalent resistance of a low-power
domain D.
1.  B = Construction_of_Minimum_Bounding_Box(D)
2.  R_B = R_t
3.  Q.enqueue(B)
4.  While !Q.empty() Do
5.      B = Q.dequeue( )
6.      (R_0, R_1) = CuttingPowerDomain(B, R_B)
7.      If ( ( (r_1/R_0 > N_0||r_1/R_1 > N_1)||(r_1/R_0 < 1||r_1/R_1 < 1)

        ||(N_0 == 0||N_1 == 0))

8.          PlacePowerSwitch(B, R_B, L)
9.      Else
10.         Q.equeue(B_0)
11.         Q.enqueue(B_1)
12. Endwhile
```

Figure 6: The recursively partition algorithm.

smallest product of resistance and area). In the beginning, we first pick up s_1 from L and set R_1 as R_B. Then, $num_1 = \lfloor r_1/R_1 \rfloor$ power switches with type s_1 are inserted if num_1 is larger than one. The equivalent resistance r_1' of these power switches equals to r_1/num_1. To satisfy the equation $R_1 = r_1'||R_1'$, it still requires to insert power switches whose equivalent resistance equal to $R_1' = \frac{r_1' R_1}{r_1' - R_1}$ after insertion. Then, power switches with type s_2 are inserted. Similarly, it inserts $num_2 = \lfloor r_2/R_1' \rfloor$ power switches if $num_2 > 1$, where the equivalent resistance r_2' of the inserted power switches with type s_2 is r_2/num_2. Similarly, power switches with resistance $R_2' = \frac{r_2' R_1'}{r_2' - R_1'}$ are required after insertion. The procedure repeats until $num_i < 1$ while a power switch s_i is selected.

After the number and types of power switches are determined, they have to be placed into legal locations inside the subregion. To consider IR-drop effect, the legal locations are sorted according to the currents associated with them. Then the selected power switches are placed into locations in serial according to the order.

4.3 Our Algorithm

Our partition based method used to allocate power switches into a low-power domain is illustrated in this subsection.

The pseudo code of our algorithm is shown in Fig. 6. First, the bounding box B of a low-power domain D is found (line 1), and R_B is set as R_t, where R_t denotes the total equivalent resistance of a low-power domain D. Then, B is pushed into a Queue, which is denoted by Q (lines 2-3). The algorithm will repeat until Q is empty (lines 4-12). In each iteration, a region B is pop from Q and is cut into two subregions B_0 and B_1. The equivalent resistances R_0 and R_1 of B_0 and B_1 are determined according to the procedure in Section 4.1 (lines 5-6). The recursive procedure stops if any of the following conditions is satisfied (line 7):

- $\frac{r_1}{R_0} > N_0$ (or $\frac{r_1}{R_1} > N_1$): there exist not enough legal locations in B_0 (B_1) for placing desired number of power switches.

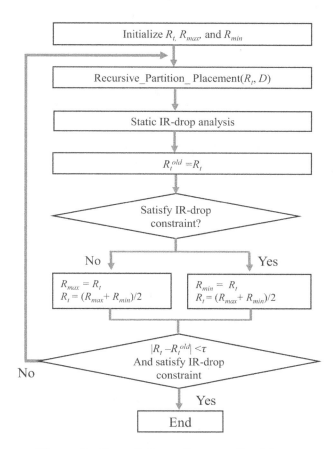

Figure 7: Overall flow of our methodology.

- $\frac{r_1}{R_0} < 1$ (or $\frac{r_1}{R_1} < 1$): it needs less than one power switch inside B_0 (B_1).

- $N_0 == 0$ (or $N_1 == 0$): B_0 (B_1) contains no legal location.

Note that r_1 denotes the equivalent resistance of the power switch with type s_1. The power switches in L are sorted, and s_1 is the type of power switch who has the smallest resistance area production (i.e., $r_1 \times a_1$). If any of the above conditions happens, the partition procedure stops and it starts to place power switches into B according to the procedure in Section 4.2 (line 8). Otherwise, the partition procedure continues and B_0 and B_1 are pushed into Q (lines 10-11).

5. OUR METHODOLOGY

This section shows the methodology to allocate power switches for the power gating designs.

5.1 Our Flow

First, the equivalent resistance R_t of a low-power domain D is initialized. Since the precise value of R_t cannot be obtained in the beginning, it is bounded by R_{max} and R_{min}, where R_{max} and R_{min} respectively denote the maximum and the minimum values of the equivalent resistance in the domain. R_t is computed by the following formula:

$$R_t = (VDD_t)/C \qquad (4)$$

where VDD_t is the tolerable voltage drop value computed by Equation 1. Let C denote the summation of current in D. Moreover, R_{max} is set as the largest resistance value of the power switch in L, and R_{min} is set as zero.

Once an equivalent resistance value R_t of D is determined, power switches are allocated and placed into it by the partition algorithm illustrated in Section 4.3. To verify if the current placement of power switches satisfies IR-drop constraint, a static IR-drop analyzer was implemented by us. It is based on the matrix equation $GV = I$ [8] [13], where G denotes the conductance matrix for the resistors in a 3D power network and V (I) denotes the vector of voltages (current loads) for the nodes in the power network. If IR-drop constraint is not satisfied in the current placement, the value R_t is adjusted by the binary search method [11].

After the IR-drop result of the current placement is obtained, a more accurate R_t is found. New R_t is determined by the following steps: first, the original R_t is recorded into R_t^{old}. If the current placement satisfies the voltage drop constraint, the minimum bound is replaced by R_t (i.e., $R_{min} = R_t$). Otherwise, the maximum bound is replaced by R_t (i.e., $R_{max} = R_t$). Then, R_t is adjusted according to the medium value of R_{max} and R_{min} (i.e., $R_t = (R_{max} + R_{min})/2$). If the absolute difference between R_t and R_t^{old} is larger than a given threshold τ, the procedure continues; otherwise, it stops. The overall flow of our methodology is shown in Fig. 7.

5.2 Modification of Allocation of Equivalent Resistance

In Section 4.1, the equivalent resistance of a region is only determined by the current density in the region (see Equation 3). However, IR-drop of a region is affected by several factors such as distribution of power pads or density of a power mesh. If a region has serious IR-drop because its location is far away from a power pad, it still needs to insert more power switches to the region even though it has small current density. This is ignored by Equation 3.

To resolve the above problem, the allocation of equivalent resistance also has to consider the voltage drop value in a region. Since our methodology is an iterative procedure (see Fig. 7), the voltage drop value of a region can be obtained by the analysis results in the previous stages. Let D_0 (D_1) denote the average voltage drop value in B_0 (B_1) obtained in previous stages. After the values R_0 and R_1 are computed by Equation 3, they are further adjusted by the following equations:

$$R_0 = \begin{cases} R_0(1 + \gamma \frac{D_1}{D_0}), & \text{if } \frac{D_1}{D_0} \geq 1 \\ R_0(1 - \gamma \frac{D_1}{D_0}), & \text{otherwise} \end{cases} \quad (5)$$

where γ is a user specified parameter. Since $\frac{D_1}{D_0}$ is close to 1, γ is set a very small value. Then, R_1 is computed as follows:

$$R_1 = \frac{R_B R_0}{R_0 - R_B} \quad (6)$$

6. EXPERIMENTAL RESULTS

Our algorithm was implemented by C++ programming language and compiled under g++4.6.2. It was run under quad core CPU Intel Xeon(R) E5520 2.27GHz and Cent OS 5.1 workstation with 62GB memory. We verify our methodology based on real circuits designed by Himax Technolo-gies Inc. using physical libraries of GLOBAL FOUNDRIES 55nm [20].

TABLE 1 displays the information of the circuits used in the experiment. Columns 1 shows the names of the circuits, and the number of standard cells in each circuit is shown in Column 2. Column 3 shows power consumptions of the circuits and the values are dumped from real layouts in IC compiler [19]. Columns 4 and 5 give the actual voltage values of VDD and the tolerable IR-drop values (assume $\alpha = 3\%$ in Equation 1), respectively. TABLE 2 shows two types of power switches provided by GLOBAL FOUNDRIES 55nm physical libraries. Column 1 shows the names of power switches in different types, and their equivalent resistances are shown in column 2. The height, width, and area of each power switch are shown in columns 3, 4, 5, respectively.

To demonstrate the effectiveness of our algorithm, we compare our algorithm with the uniform placement approach and Yong and Ung's algorithm [17], which were both implemented by us. The uniform placement approach tries to imitate engineers' work, which evenly inserts power switches at legal locations inside a placement region. Yong and Ung's algorithm has been introduced in Section 1.1. In the results of the uniform placement approach and Yong and Ung's algorithm, only PS2 is used because PS2 is more efficient than PS1 in area.

The comparison results are shown in TABLE 3. The first column shows the names of the circuits. Columns 2-5 show the results of the uniform placement approach, columns 6-10 show the results of Yong and Ung's algorithm [17] while columns 11-16 show our results. Columns 2 and 6 respectively show the number of inserted power switches for the uniform placement approach and Yong and Ung's algorithm in PS2 type. The numbers of power switches in PS1 and PS2 types for our algorithm are shown in columns 11 and 12, respectively. Different from other approaches, our algorithm chooses different types of power switches for obtaining smaller area (see the procedure in Section 4.2). The total area of the power switches are shown in column 3, 7, and 13, respectively, while the maximum and minimum voltage drop values are shown in columns 4-5, 8-9, and 14-15, respectively. The IR-drop analyzer was implemented by us. The running times of Yong and Ung's algorithm and our approach are shown in columns 10 and 16, respectively. Because the uniform placement approach is very straightforward, its running time is not listed here. The uniform placement approach and Yong and Ung's Algorithm respectively require 21.9% and 13.9% power switch area larger than our results in average. Even though the uniform placement approach inserts 1/5 larger power switch area than our approach, its results still

Table 1: INFORMATION OF CIRCUITS.

Circuit	# of std. cells	Total power (mw)	Global VDD (V)	IR-drop constraint(V)
Cir.1	1595662	260.421	1.08	0.0342
Cir.2	2540941	1597.52	1.32	0.0396

Table 2: INFORMATION OF POWER SWITCHES.

Circuit	R (Ω)	Height (μm)	Width(μm)	Area(μm^2)
PS1	720.0	1.8	3.2	5.76
PS2	280.5	1.8	6.4	11.52

Table 3: COMPARISON OF OUR ALGORITHM WITH THE UNIFORM PLACEMENT APPROACH AND YONG AND UNG [17]'s ALGORITHM.

Cir. Name	Uniform placement				Yong and Ung's algorithm [17]					Our algorithm					
	Num.	Area (μm^2)	IR-drop (V)		Num.	Area (μm^2)	IR-drop (V)		Time (S)	Num.		Area (μm^2)	IR-drop (V)		Time (S)
	PS2		Max	Min	PS2		Max	Min		PS1	PS2		Max	Min	
Cir.1	4982	57393	0.0420	0.0296	4724	54420	0.0248	0.0212	332	641	3602	45187	0.0149	0.0106	313
Cir.2	11777	135671	0.0748	0.0293	10940	126028	0.0378	0.0162	625	1783	8934	113189	0.0347	0.0104	453
-		1.219	-	-	-	1.139	-	-	1.25	-	-	1	-	-	1

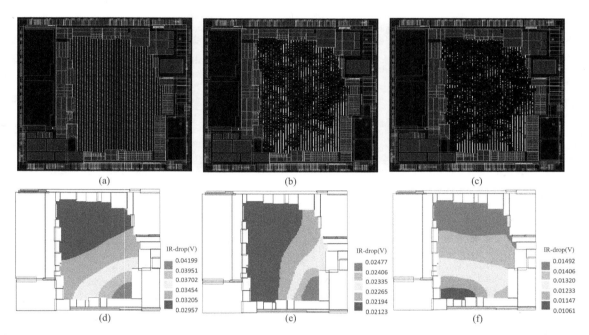

Figure 8: Placements of power switches and the associated IR-drop maps on Cir.1. (a) and (d) The uniform placement approach. (b) and (e) Yong and Ung's algorithm [17]. (c) and (f) Our algorithm.

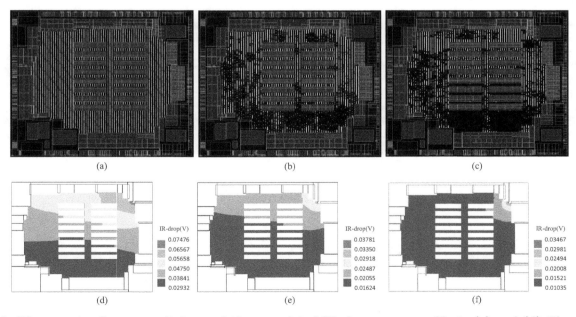

Figure 9: Placements of power switches and the associated IR-drop maps on Cir.2. (a) and (d) The uniform placement approach. (b) and (e) Yong and Ung's algorithm [17]. (c) and (f) Our algorithm.

cannot satisfy IR-drop constraint. This demonstrates that power switch placement locations have great impacts on the resulting IR-drop.

Fig. 8 shows the power switch placement results of Cir.1 in IC compiler and the associated IR-drop maps. Fig. 8 (a), (b), and (c) show the placement results of the uniform placement approach, Yong and Ung's algorithm, and our algorithm while the associated IR-drop maps are shown in Fig. 8 (d), (e), and (f), respectively. The yellow points in the placements show the distribution of power switches. The figures reveal that the uniform placement approach has the worse IR-drop result even though it inserts more number of power switches than other approaches. On the contrary, our approach insert less number of power switches than other approaches; however, our IR-drop result is much better than other approaches. Even the serious IR-drop value in our approach is slight than the worse value of other approaches. Fig. 9 shows the placements of power switches and the associated IR-drop maps on Cir.2. Fig. 9 (a), (b), (c) show the results of the uniform placement approach, Yong and Ung's algorithm [17], and our algorithm while Fig. 9 (d), (e), and (f) show the IR-drop maps.

7. CONCLUSION

This paper has proposed an effective methodology to allocate power switches into the power gating designs. Instead of applying greedy algorithms to handle this problem, our approach first proposes a simple model to approximate the equivalent resistance of power switches in a low-power domain, and then solves the problem by the binary search algorithm and partition based approach. The experimental results have demonstrated that this method can satisfy the IR-drop constraint using less number of power switches.

8. REFERENCES

[1] M. Anis, S. Areibi, M. Mahmoud and M. Elmasry, "Dynamic and leakage lower reduction in MTCMOS circuits using an automated efficient gate clustering," *Proc. DAC*, pp. 480-485, 2002.

[2] T. W. Chang, T. T. Hwang, and S. Y. Hsu, "Functionality directed clustering for low power MTCMOS design," *Proc. ASP-DAC*, pp. 862-867, 2005.

[3] S. H. Chen, Y. L. Lin, M. and C. -T. Chao, "Power-up sequence control for MTCMOS designs," *IEEE Transactions on VLSI*, vol. 21, no. 3, pp. 413-423, 2013.

[4] H. Jiang, M. M. Sadowska, and S. Nassif, "Benefits and cost of power-gating technique," *Proc. ICCD*, pp. 559-566, 2005.

[5] V. Khandelwal, and A. Srivastava, "Leakage control through fine-grained placement and sizing of sleep transistors," *Proc. ICCAD*, pp. 533-536, 2004.

[6] J. Kao, S. Narendra, and A. Chandrakasan, "MTCMOS hierarchical sizing based on mutual exclusive discharge patterns," *Proc. DAC*, pp. 495-500, 1988.

[7] J. N. Kozhaya, and L. A. Bakir, "An electrically robust method for placing power gating switches in voltage islands," *Proc. CICC*, pp. 321-324, 2004.

[8] Z. Li, Y. Ma, Q. Zhou, Y. Cai, Y. Wang, T. Huang, and Y. Xie, "Thermal-aware power network design for IR drop reduction in 3D ICs," *Proc. ASP-DAC*, pp.47-52, 2012.

[9] C. Long and L. He, "Distributed sleep transistor network for power reducing," *IEEE VLSI*, vol. 12, no. 9, pp. 937-946, 2004.

[10] S. Mutoh, S. Shigematsu, Y. Matsuya, H. Fukuda, T. Kaneko, and J. Yamada, "A 1-V multi threshold-volage CMOS digital signal processor for mobile phone application," *J. Solid-State Circuits*, vol. 31, no. 11, pp. 1795-1802, 1996.

[11] S. Sartaj, Data structures, Algorithms, and Applications in C++. McGraw2-Hill. 1998. ISBN 978-0072362268.

[12] G. Sery, S. Borkar, and V. De, "Life is CMOS: Why hase the life after," *Proc. DAC*, pp. 78-83, 2002.

[13] K. Shi, Z. Lin, and Y. M. Jiang, "A power network synthesis method for industrial power gating designs," *Proc. ISQED*, pp. 362-367, 2007.

[14] K. Shi, Z. Lin, Y. M. Jian, and L. Yuan, "Simultaneous sleep transistor insertion and power network synthesis for industrial power gating designs," *Journal of Computer*, vol.3, no.3, pp. 6-13, 2008.

[15] T. M. Tseng, M. C.-T. Chao, C. P. Lu, and C. H. Lo, "Power-switch routing for coarse-grain MTCMOS technologies," *Proc. ICCAD*, pp. 39-46, 2009.

[16] W. Wang, M. Anis, and S. Areibii, "Fast techniques for standby leakage reduction in MTCMOS circuits," *Proc. SOCCC*, pp. 21-24, 2004.

[17] L. K. Yong and C. K. Ung, "Power density aware power gate placement optimization scheme," *Proc. ASQED*, pp. 38-42, 2010.

[18] http://www.nspark.org.tw/webfiles/Power_Analysis.pdf

[19] http://www.synopsys.com/home.aspx

[20] http://www.globalfoundries.com

Incremental Transient Simulation of Power Grid

Chia-Tung Ho
CAD Service Dept.
Macronix Intl. Co., Ltd.
Hsinchu, Taiwan
chiatungho@mxic.com.tw

Yu-Min Lee
Shu-Han Wei
ECE Dept., NCTU
Hsinchu, Taiwan
yumin@nctu.edu.tw,
littlelittle821@gmail.com

Liang-Chia Cheng
ITRI
Hsinchu, Taiwan
aga@itri.org.tw

ABSTRACT

The power grid needs to be frequently analyzed during the design process of power distribution network. Hence, an effective method being able to capture its transient behavior is desired for designers.

This work utilizes macro modeling techniques, sparse recovery mechanisms, a proposed pseudo-node value estimation method, and an adaptive error control procedure to develop an efficient and reliable incremental power grid transient simulator. This incremental simulator not only can deal with adjusted values of the circuit elements but also can handle modified topologies of the design.

Categories and Subject Descriptors

B.7.2 [**Integrated Circuits**]: Design Aids – Simulation, Verification

Keywords

Power distribution network; Incremental analysis

1. INTRODUCTION

With the advent of technology, low-power, ultra-low-voltage, and three-dimensional stacked integrated circuit designs are becoming vital design methodologies. However, they are vulnerable to power supply noises such as IR drop and Ldi/dt noise. Hence, the power grid design and analysis are much more important than in the past.

Typically, given the supply voltage, wire sizing and topology modification techniques can be utilized to design the power grid. Wire sizing adjusts its element values, and topology modification adds/deletes its nodes and elements. Power grid analysis is a challenging task since there are numerous amounts of power grid nodes on a chip. Therefore, lots of approaches such as hierarchical methods [1], krylov-subspace methods [2, 3], multi-grid techniques [4, 5], random walk algorithms [6], and vectorless verified methods [7] have been developed . Though they perform pretty well on power grid analysis, they may reanalyze the modified design as a brand new one even though the power grid is only locally changed. As a result, incremental power grid simulation or verification methods that utilize the information of original design to simulate or

verify the updated design were proposed [8–10]. To deal with adjusted values of elements, Sun et al. used the sparse approximation (orthogonal matching pursuit (OMP)) to extract the approximated basis set of system for performing the incremental steady-state simulation [8]. To enhance [8], Lee et al. integrated the macro modeling technique, OMP, and a modified topology consideration procedure to develop another incremental steady-state simulator, MA-OMP^r [9]. However, only the resistance effect was considered for the modified topology in [9], and both methods [8,9] are not suitable for the incremental transient simulation due to the inconsistent basis issue that will be addressed in Section 3. Due to the lack of current waveforms drawn by devices, Abhishej and Najm used the macro modeling technique and vectorless method to perform the early incremental verification of RC power grid network [10].

From all the points of view, an efficient incremental transient simulation or verification method is highly needed during the design process. This work focuses on the incremental transient simulation. In this work, the macro modeling technique, the sparse recovery mechanism, a proposed pseudo-node value estimation method, and an innovated adaptive error control procedure are utilized to build an effective incremental transient simulator for the power grid. The developed incremental simulator not only can deal with the adjusted values of elements but also can handle the modified topologies under the dynamic status. Its major features are

1. To manipulate the modified topology, a pseudo-node value estimation method is proposed to build *artificial* original electrical values of the added nodes by simultaneously considering the effects of capacitances, inductances, and resistances.

2. To improve the accuracy and ease the inconsistent basis issue while performing the sparse recovery technique during the incremental transient simulation, a basis-set adjustment criterion is proposed. To enhance the efficiency of simulation, an adaptive error control procedure is established to choose suitable time points for adjusting the basis set and avoiding the wasteful use of computational power.

The remainder of this article is organized as follows. Several related techniques are reviewed in Section 2. After that, the inconsistent basis issue of incremental circuit simulation is discussed in Section 3. Then, the proposed incremental transient simulator is detailed in Section 4. Finally, the experimental results and conclusion are given in Sections 5 and 6, respectively.

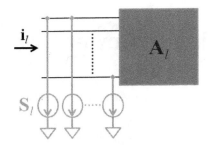

Figure 1: Macromodel.

2. RELATED TECHNIQUES

2.1 Hierarchical Analysis of Power Grid

The divide-and-conquer strategy is used to analyze the power grid by partitioning it into several blocks [1]. There are internal (local) grids in each block and external (global) grids between blocks. Branches between blocks are called global links. Each block l is modeled as a multi-port element and is considered as a macro model that is illustrated in Figure 1. The currents passing through the interface between block l and other blocks can be written as

$$\mathbf{i}_l = \mathbf{A}_l \mathbf{V}_l + \mathbf{S}_l; \ \mathbf{i}_l \in \mathbb{R}^m, \ \mathbf{A}_l \in \mathbb{R}^{m \times m}, \ \mathbf{V}_l \in \mathbb{R}^m, \ \mathbf{S}_l \in \mathbb{R}^m. \quad (1)$$

Here, $\mathbf{A}_l$ is the admittance matrix of ports, $\mathbf{V}_l$ is the vector of port voltages, and $\mathbf{S}_l$ is the current source vector.

With (1) and the trapezoidal technique, the AC global matrix equation can be integrated by all $\mathbf{A}_l$'s, $\mathbf{S}_l$'s, and global links as

$$\left(\mathbf{G}_g + \frac{2}{h} \mathbf{C}_g \right) \mathbf{x}_g^j = \left(-\mathbf{G}_g + \frac{2}{h} \mathbf{C}_g \right) \mathbf{x}_g^{j-1} - \mathbf{S}^j + \mathbf{u}_g^{j-1} + \mathbf{u}_g^j. \quad (2)$$

Here, $\mathbf{G}_g$ is a global conductance matrix, $\mathbf{C}_g$ is a global capacitance and inductance matrix, and $\mathbf{S}^j = \left[\mathbf{S}_1^{jT} \cdots \mathbf{S}_l^{jT} \cdots \mathbf{S}_k^{jT} \ \mathbf{0}^T \right]^T$. $\mathbf{S}_l^j$ is the equivalent current source vector between the ports of l-th partition and the ground node at the j-th sampling time, k is the number of macros, and h is the time step. $\mathbf{x}_g^{j-1}/\mathbf{x}_g^j$ and $\mathbf{u}_g^{j-1}/\mathbf{u}_g^j$ are the electrical variable vector and the global independent source vector at the $(j-1)$-th/j-th sampling time, respectively.

After solving (2), the port values are substituted into each partition to obtain its internal node voltages and branch currents. Then, the currents flowing through the interfaces of partitions are updated. The preceding procedure is executed repeatedly.

2.2 Incremental Steady-State Simulation

2.2.1 OMP [8]

The DC system equation of a power grid network can be built as

$$\mathbf{G}\mathbf{x} = \mathbf{b}. \quad (3)$$

Here, $\mathbf{G}$ is an $m \times m$ conductance matrix, $\mathbf{x}$ is an $m \times 1$ vector consisting of electrical variables, and $\mathbf{b}$ is an $m \times 1$ independent source vector.

After redesigning several element values locally (without modifying the topology), its system equation becomes

$$\overline{\mathbf{G}}\overline{\mathbf{x}} = \overline{\mathbf{b}}, \quad (4)$$

where $\overline{\mathbf{G}}$, $\overline{\mathbf{b}}$, and $\overline{\mathbf{x}}$ are modified $\mathbf{G}$, $\mathbf{b}$, and $\mathbf{x}$, respectively.

Rewriting $\overline{\mathbf{x}}$ as $\mathbf{x} + \Delta\mathbf{x}$ and substituting it back into (4), we have

$$\overline{\mathbf{G}}\Delta\mathbf{x} = \widetilde{\mathbf{b}}, \quad (5)$$

where $\Delta\mathbf{x}$ is the incremental vector of $\mathbf{x}$, and $\widetilde{\mathbf{b}} \triangleq \overline{\mathbf{b}} - \overline{\mathbf{G}}\mathbf{x}$.

Because of the locality characteristic of power grids, there are lots of zeros in $\Delta\mathbf{x}$, and (5) can be solved by the OMP algorithm [11]. The main idea of OMP algorithm is to representing $\widetilde{\mathbf{b}}$ by few important columns of $\overline{\mathbf{G}}$, and the chosen criterion can be

$$c_i = \left| \frac{\langle \overline{\mathbf{G}}_i, \widetilde{\mathbf{b}} \rangle}{\langle \overline{\mathbf{G}}_i, \overline{\mathbf{G}}_i \rangle} \right|, \ (i = 1, 2, \cdots, m), \quad (6)$$

where $\langle \cdot, \cdot \rangle$ is an inner product operator, and $\overline{\mathbf{G}}_i$ is the i-th column vector of $\overline{\mathbf{G}}$.

If c_i exceeds a given threshold, $\overline{\mathbf{G}}_i$ is chosen as an important column vector. After searching all column vectors of $\overline{\mathbf{G}}$, an initial column vector set is obtained and viewed as an approximated basis set. Then, this over-determined system is solved by the least squares fitting. Here, a preconditioner is used to decrease the condition number, and the normal equation is utilized to obtain the approximated values $\Delta\mathbf{x}$. As the residual $\mathbf{r} = \widetilde{\mathbf{b}} - \overline{\mathbf{G}}\Delta\mathbf{x}$ is not small enough, $\widetilde{\mathbf{b}}$ is replaced by $\mathbf{r}$, a smaller threshold value is chosen, and (6) is repeatedly executed to pick up more column vectors until the residual is less than a user-defined value.

2.2.2 MA-OMP^t [9]

MA-OMP^t utilizes the macro modeling technique [1] and extends the OMP method [8] to perform the incremental steady-state simulation. Because solving the global matrix equation takes the most computational cost while doing the macro model simulation, hence, the OMP technique is extended to solve it with an initialization procedure for dealing with the topology modification.

It updates $(\mathbf{A}_l, \mathbf{S}_l)$'s of the modified blocks and uses an initialization procedure to construct the original node-voltage vector as

$$\mathbf{v}' = \widehat{\mathbf{v}} + \Delta\mathbf{v}. \quad (7)$$

Here, $\widehat{\mathbf{v}}$ consists of the original port voltages and zeros for the added nodes. $\Delta\mathbf{v}$ consists of the artificial node voltages of added nodes and zeros for the original ports.

According to Ohm's law, the unknown artificial voltage of an added node is assumed to be proportional to the conductances between this node and its adjoint nodes. As shown in Figure 2, the node voltage v of an added red node is estimated by its adjoint existed nodes as

$$v = \frac{g_1}{g_{total}} v_1 + \frac{g_2}{g_{total}} v_2 + \frac{g_3}{g_{total}} v_3. \quad (8)$$

Here, $g_{total} = g_1 + g_2 + g_3$. g_1, g_2, and g_3 are the conductances of elements. v_1, v_2, and v_3 are the known original node voltages.

Sometimes, its adjoint nodes might also be added nodes. MA-OMP^t searches the nearest existed nodes to estimate v. After establishing $\mathbf{v}'$, MA-OMP^t computes $\mathbf{r}$ and utilizes the similar procedure shown in Section 2.2.1 to incrementally solve the global system. Finally, the internal node voltages and branch currents of each block are updated by those solved global electrical values.

3. INCONSISTENT BASIS ISSUE OF INCREMENTAL CIRCUIT SIMULATION

Transient behavior of power grids is continuous, and its behavior at the current sampling time is related to the previous states. Heuristically applying the incremental steady-state simulation methods [8,9] to perform the incremental transient simulation by choosing bases repeatedly at different sampling times can cause the inconsistent problem of bases and lead to severe errors.

The system equation of a power grid network can be written as

$$\mathbf{G}\mathbf{x} + \mathbf{C}\frac{d\mathbf{x}}{dt} = \mathbf{b}. \quad (9)$$

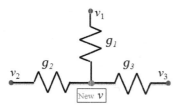

Figure 2: The initial voltage assignment of an added node in MA-OMP^t.

Here, $\mathbf{C}$ is an $m \times m$ capacitance and inductance matrix. Utilizing the trapezoidal method, (9) becomes

$$(\mathbf{G} + \frac{2}{h}\mathbf{C})\mathbf{x}^j = (-\mathbf{G} + \frac{2}{h}\mathbf{C})\mathbf{x}^{j-1} + \mathbf{b}^{j-1} + \mathbf{b}^j. \tag{10}$$

Here, $\mathbf{x}^{j-1}/\mathbf{x}^j$ and $\mathbf{b}^{j-1}/\mathbf{b}^j$ are the electrical variable vector and the independent source vector at the $(j\text{-}1)$-th/j-th sampling time, respectively. h is the time step.

After redesigning several element values, its electrical variable vector can be obtained by solving

$$(\overline{\mathbf{G}} + \frac{2}{h}\overline{\mathbf{C}})(\mathbf{x}^j + \Delta\mathbf{x}^j) = (-\overline{\mathbf{G}} + \frac{2}{h}\overline{\mathbf{C}})(\mathbf{x}^{j-1} + \Delta\mathbf{x}^{j-1}) + \overline{\mathbf{b}}^{j-1} + \overline{\mathbf{b}}^j. \tag{11}$$

Here, $\overline{\mathbf{G}}$ and $\overline{\mathbf{C}}$ are the modified $\mathbf{G}$ and $\mathbf{C}$, respectively. $\overline{\mathbf{b}}^{j-1}/\overline{\mathbf{b}}^j$ and $\Delta\mathbf{x}^{j-1}/\Delta\mathbf{x}^j$ are the modified $\mathbf{b}$ and the incremental electrical variable vector at the $(j\text{-}1)$-th/j-th sampling time, respectively.

Moving the known terms of (11) to its right hand side, we have

$$\overline{\mathbf{M}}\Delta\mathbf{x}^j - \overline{\mathbf{N}}\Delta\mathbf{x}^{j-1} = \widetilde{\mathbf{b}}^j, \tag{12}$$

where $\overline{\mathbf{M}} = \overline{\mathbf{G}} + \frac{2}{h}\overline{\mathbf{C}}$, $\overline{\mathbf{N}} = -\overline{\mathbf{G}} + \frac{2}{h}\overline{\mathbf{C}}$, and $\widetilde{\mathbf{b}}^j = -\overline{\mathbf{M}}\mathbf{x}^j + \overline{\mathbf{N}}\mathbf{x}^{j-1} + \overline{\mathbf{b}}^j + \overline{\mathbf{b}}^{j-1}$.

After $\Delta\mathbf{x}^{j-1}$ being estimated at the $(j\text{-}1)$-th sampling time, (12) can be rewritten as

$$\sum_{i=1}^{m} \overline{\mathbf{M}}_i \Delta x_i^j = \widetilde{\mathbf{b}}^j + \sum_{i=1}^{m} \overline{\mathbf{N}}_i \Delta x_i^{j-1}. \tag{13}$$

Here, $\Delta x_i^{j-1}/\Delta x_i^j$ is the i-th entry of $\Delta\mathbf{x}^{j-1}/\Delta\mathbf{x}^j$. $\overline{\mathbf{M}}_i$ and $\overline{\mathbf{N}}_i$ are the i-th column of $\overline{\mathbf{M}}$ and $\overline{\mathbf{N}}$, respectively.

Because the locality characteristic of power grids, $\Delta\mathbf{x}^{j-1}$ and $\Delta\mathbf{x}^j$ are sparse vectors. Hence, they can be recovered by the the OMP technique [11].

Assume that two basis sets $\mathcal{T} = \left\{ \overline{\mathbf{M}}_{s_1}, \cdots, \overline{\mathbf{M}}_{s_i}, \cdots, \overline{\mathbf{M}}_{s_l} \right\}$ and $\mathcal{S} = \left\{ \overline{\mathbf{M}}_{s_1}, \cdots, \overline{\mathbf{M}}_{s_i}, \cdots, \overline{\mathbf{M}}_{s_k} \right\}$ consist of l and k column vectors picked from $\overline{\mathbf{M}}$, respectively. Here, $l < k < m$, $\overline{\mathbf{M}}_{s_i}$ is the s_i-th column of $\overline{\mathbf{M}}$, and $\mathcal{T} \subset \mathcal{S}$. $\Delta\mathbf{x}^{j-1}$ is estimated by using $\mathcal{T}$, and only l corresponding values in $\Delta\mathbf{x}^{j-1}$ ($\Delta x_{s_1}^{j-1}, \cdots, \Delta x_{s_l}^{j-1}$) are non-zeros. Later, the basis set is changed to $\mathcal{S}$ at the j-th sampling time, and (13) is approximated as

$$\sum_{i=1}^{k} \overline{\mathbf{M}}_{s_i} \Delta x_{s_i}^j = \widetilde{\mathbf{b}}^j + \sum_{i=1}^{l} \overline{\mathbf{N}}_{s_i} \Delta x_{s_i}^{j-1}. \tag{14}$$

On the other hand, let us consider that $\mathcal{S}$ is utilized to estimate the incremental electrical variable vector all the time as

$$\sum_{i=1}^{k} \overline{\mathbf{M}}_{s_i} \Delta \overline{x}_{s_i}^j = \widetilde{\mathbf{b}}^j + \sum_{i=1}^{k} \overline{\mathbf{N}}_{s_i} \Delta \overline{x}_{s_i}^{j-1}, \tag{15}$$

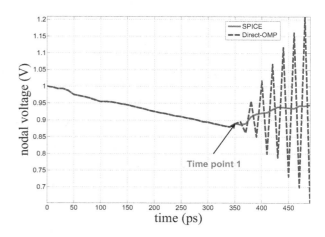

Figure 3: The effect of inconsistent bases in incremental transient analysis.

where $\Delta\overline{x}_{s_i}^{j-1}/\Delta\overline{x}_{s_i}^j$ is the estimated incremental value of the s_i-th electrical variable at the $(j\text{-}1)$-th/j-th sampling time.

Obviously, the estimated incremental electrical variables between (14) and (15) are different. By subtracting (14) from (15), the error gap between them can be obtained as

$$\sum_{i=1}^{k} \overline{\mathbf{M}}_{s_i} e_{s_i}^j = \sum_{i=1}^{l} \overline{\mathbf{N}}_{s_i} e_{s_i}^{j-1} + \sum_{i=l+1}^{k} \overline{\mathbf{N}}_{s_i} \Delta\overline{x}_{s_i}^{j-1}, \tag{16}$$

where $e_{s_i}^{j-1} = \Delta\overline{x}_{s_i}^{j-1} - \Delta x_{s_i}^{j-1}$, and $e_{s_i}^j = \Delta\overline{x}_{s_i}^j - \Delta x_{s_i}^j$.

From (16), the error gap will influence the estimated results of succeeding sampling times due to the continuous characteristic of transient behavior. Though we assume $\mathcal{T} \subset \mathcal{S}$, the situation could be worse in the reality. These picked bases might be partially different or even totally different. Hence, heuristically extending the incremental steady-state simulation methods [8,9] to incrementally estimate the transient behavior can cause severe error because bases might be inconsistent at every sampling time, and lead the estimated values to be unrecoverable.

To illustrate the error gap phenomenon, a test circuit with 40,000 nodes is generated by using the industrial parameters. After changing several element values, the incremental steady-state simulation method is directly extended to perform the incremental transient simulation, and the number of bases is changed from 16 to 53 at the time point 1. The voltage waveform at a node is shown in Figure 3. It can be observed that the voltage at that node starts to move up and down after the time point 1.

4. INCREMENTAL TRANSIENT SIMULATOR

Given an RLC power grid network, in the beginning, its circuit graph is built and partitioned by METIS [12]. Then, its transient analysis is performed by using the macro modeling technique [1]. After that, its element values might be modified, or its topology might be changed by designers.

To reanalyze this modified design, first, its graph information needs to be reconstructed and will be described in Section 4.1. Then, the developed incremental transient simulation procedure presented in Algorithm 1 is executed in three phases as follows.

Phase I: Establishment of Required Information

$(\mathbf{A}_l, \mathbf{S}_l)$'s for the steady states of modified blocks are updated. If there are added nodes, their artificial original electrical variable values will be estimated by using a pseudo-node value estimation method described in Section 4.2. After that, the global conductance matrix $\overline{\mathbf{G}}_g$, the global capacitance and inductance matrix $\overline{\mathbf{C}}_g$, and the AC global matrix $\overline{\mathbf{M}}_g = \overline{\mathbf{G}}_g + \frac{2}{h}\overline{\mathbf{C}}_g$ of the modified network are constructed. Since the topology of power grids might be changed, the dimension of $\overline{\mathbf{G}}_g$, $\overline{\mathbf{C}}_g$, and $\overline{\mathbf{M}}_g$ might be different with that of the original global matrices.

Phase II: Estimation of Incremental Steady-State Values

The updated steady-state $\mathbf{S}_l$'s and global independent sources are utilized to construct $\overline{\mathbf{b}}$, and the incremental global steady-state equation is written as

$$\overline{\mathbf{G}}_g \Delta \overline{\mathbf{x}} = \widetilde{\mathbf{b}}_g. \tag{17}$$

Here, $\widetilde{\mathbf{b}}_g = \overline{\mathbf{b}} - \overline{\mathbf{G}}_g \mathbf{x}$. $\mathbf{x}$ and $\Delta \overline{\mathbf{x}}$ are $p \times 1$ original and incremental steady-state electrical variable vectors, respectively.

MA-OMP^t [9] is used to extract a basis set $\mathcal{I}$ and estimate the incremental global steady-state electrical variable values. Here, $\mathcal{I} = \left\{ \overline{\mathbf{G}}_{g,s_1}, \cdots, \overline{\mathbf{G}}_{g,s_i}, \cdots, \overline{\mathbf{G}}_{g,s_k} \right\}$, and each $\overline{\mathbf{G}}_{g,s_i}$ is the s_i-th column of $\overline{\mathbf{G}}_g$. Then, the solution of (17) is substituted back into each partition to obtain the internal steady-state electrical variable values.

Phase III: Estimation of Incremental Transient Values

The local $\mathbf{S}^j$ and global independent source vector $\mathbf{u}_g^j$ are updated at the beginning of each sampling time, and the incremental AC global equation is written as

$$\overline{\mathbf{M}}_g \Delta \overline{\mathbf{x}}^j = \widetilde{\mathbf{b}}_g^j + \overline{\mathbf{N}}_g \Delta \overline{\mathbf{x}}^{j-1}. \tag{18}$$

Here, $\Delta \overline{\mathbf{x}}^{j-1}/\Delta \overline{\mathbf{x}}^j$ is a $p \times 1$ incremental electrical variable vector of ports at the $(j\text{-}1)$-th/j-th sampling time, $\overline{\mathbf{N}}_g = -\overline{\mathbf{G}}_g + \frac{2}{h}\overline{\mathbf{C}}_g$, and $\widetilde{\mathbf{b}}_g^j = -\overline{\mathbf{M}}_g \mathbf{x}^j + \overline{\mathbf{N}}_g \mathbf{x}^{j-1} - \mathbf{S}^j + \mathbf{u}_g^{j-1} + \mathbf{u}_g^j$.

Given the estimated $\widetilde{\mathbf{b}}_g^j$ and $\Delta \overline{\mathbf{x}}^{j-1}$, the goal is to estimate $\Delta \overline{\mathbf{x}}^j$. According to $\mathcal{I}$, the AC initial basis set is constructed as $\mathcal{D} = \left\{ \overline{\mathbf{M}}_{g,s_1}, \cdots, \overline{\mathbf{M}}_{g,s_i}, \cdots, \overline{\mathbf{M}}_{g,s_k} \right\}$, and each $\overline{\mathbf{M}}_{g,s_i}$ is the s_i-th column of $\overline{\mathbf{M}}_g$. Hence, (18) can be approximated as

$$\sum_{i=1}^{k} \overline{\mathbf{M}}_{g,s_i} \Delta \overline{x}_{s_i}^j = \widetilde{\mathbf{b}}_g^j + \overline{\mathbf{N}}_g \Delta \overline{\mathbf{x}}^{j-1}. \tag{19}$$

With a preconditioner and the normal equation, (19) is solved by the least squares fitting, and the residual is calculated as $\mathbf{r}^j = \widetilde{\mathbf{b}}_g^j + \overline{\mathbf{N}}_g \Delta \overline{\mathbf{x}}^{j-1} - \overline{\mathbf{M}}_g \Delta \overline{\mathbf{x}}^j$. Here, a developed adaptive error control procedure is used to control the fitting error. It can automatically adjust the basis set $\mathcal{D}$ for simultaneously satisfying the accuracy requirement and easing the inconsistent problem mentioned in Section 3.

Then, the incremental global transient solution is substituted back into each partition to obtain the internal electrical variable values.

The preceding procedure is repeatedly used to solve (18) for each sampling time. The criterion of basis set adjustment and the developed error control procedure will be detailed in Sections 4.3 and 4.4, respectively.

4.1 Graph Information Reconstruction

Two different change types, Change *without* adding nodes and Change *with* adding nodes, are treated in the graph information reconstruction task.

Algorithm 1 Incremental Transient Simulation

Require: Information of the modified power grid network;
1: Do graph information reconstruction;
2: Update $(\mathbf{A}_l, \mathbf{S}_l)$'s for changed blocks;
3: **if** there are added nodes **then**
4:     Do original information estimation of added nodes;
5: **end if**
6: Extract DC initial basis set $\mathcal{I}$;
7: Do OMP and modify $\mathcal{I}$ until residual $\mathbf{r}$ is sufficiently small;
8: Resolve electrical variables of internal nodes for chosen blocks;
9: Construct AC initial basis set $\mathcal{D}$;
10: Generate the approximated AC incremental global equation with $\mathcal{D}$;
11: **for** $j = start\_time \rightarrow end\_time$ **do**
12:     Update $\mathbf{S}^j$ and $\mathbf{u}_g^j$;
13:     Do least squares fitting and calculate residual $\mathbf{r}^j$;
14:     **if** basis adjustment metric changes significantly **then**
15:         Memorize j as the potential resetting point.
16:     **end if**
17:     **if** γ^j exceeds a threshold **then**
18:         Add more column vectors to $\mathcal{D}$ and $\mathcal{I}$;
19:         Track *potential basis resetting points*;
20:         **if** no *basis resetting point* **then**
21:             Go back to Step 7;
22:         **else**
23:             Generate the approximated AC incremental global equation with $\mathcal{D}$;
24:             Set $j = basis\ resetting\ point$ and go back to Step 12;
25:         **end if**
26:     **end if**
27:     Resolve electrical variables of internal nodes for chosen blocks;
28: **end for**

4.1.1 Change without adding nodes

Three different situations, value modification of existing element, element insertion between nodes, and node deletion, are considered. As an element value is modified, we only need to find its corresponding link in the original graph and change its value. After inserting an element between two nodes, we just need to add a new link between them. To delete a node, we need to find its adjoint nodes, eliminate all links connected to this deleted node, and remove the information of this deleted node.

4.1.2 Change with adding nodes

To add nodes into the design, we not only need to insert extra nodes and links to the original graph, but also need to determine which partitions these extra nodes belong to. To have less number of global links, we should take the cut set of modified graph into consideration. Therefore, an inserted node is assigned to the partition which most of its adjoint nodes belong to. However, the adjoint nodes of an inserted node might also be inserted nodes. The preceding assigned rule is utilized to these adjoint nodes first, and this procedure is repeatedly performed until all inserted nodes have been assigned. After the partition of each inserted node being determined, the macro modeling information will be constructed.

4.2 Pseudo-Node Value Estimation for Added Nodes

To build the *artificial* original electrical variable values of added nodes at each sampling time, let's consider the companion model of a capacitance or an inductance as shown in Figure 4(a). It consists of a resistance and a current source in parallel.

Capacitance: The voltage across the capacitance at the j-th sampling time is equal to

$$u_C^j - \frac{I_{Ceq}}{g_{Ceq}} = \frac{i_C^j}{g_{Ceq}}. \tag{20}$$

Here, $I_{Ceq} = i_C^{j-1} + g_{Ceq} u_C^{j-1}$. u_C^{j-1}/u_C^j and i_C^{j-1}/i_C^j are the voltage across the capacitance and the current flowing through the capacitance at

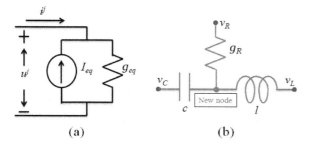

(a)   (b)

Figure 4: (a) Companion model. (b) An example of added node with capacitance and inductance.

(j-1)-th/j-th sampling time, respectively. $g_{Ceq} = \frac{2c}{h}$, $i_C^j = g_{Ceq}u^j - I_{Ceq}$, and c is the capacitance value.

Inductance: The voltage across the inductance at the j-th sampling time is equal to

$$u_L^j - \frac{I_{Leq}}{g_{Leq}} = \frac{i_L^j}{g_{Leq}} \qquad (21)$$

Here, $I_{Leq} = -i_L^{j-1} - g_{Leq}u_L^{j-1}$. u_L^{j-1}/u_L^j and i_L^{j-1}/i_L^j are the voltage across the inductance and the current flowing through the inductance at (j-1)-th/j-th sampling time, respectively. $g_{Leq} = \frac{h}{2l}$, $i_L^j = g_{Leq}u_L^j - I_{Leq}$, and l is the inductance value.

(20) and (21) are similar to Ohm's law. Hence, the same idea in Section 2.2.2 can be used to build the artificial original electrical variable value of an added node except that the term $\frac{I_{Ceq}}{g_{Ceq}}/\frac{I_{Leq}}{g_{Leq}}$ needs to be included. For example, as shown in Figure 4(b), the red node is an added node after modifying the power grid, and blue nodes are its adjoint nodes with known original electrical variable values. The artificial original voltage of this added node is built as

$$v_{new} = \frac{g_R}{g_{total}}v_R + \frac{g_{Ceq}}{g_{total}}(v_C + \frac{I_{Ceq}}{g_{Ceq}}) + \frac{g_{Leq}}{g_{total}}(v_L + \frac{I_{Leq}}{g_{Leq}}). \qquad (22)$$

Here, g_{Ceq} and I_{Ceq} are the parameters of capacitance's companion model. g_{Leq} and I_{Leq} are the parameters of inductance's companion model, and $g_{total} = g_R + g_{Ceq} + g_{Leq}$.

The adjoint nodes of an added node might also be added nodes. The preceding estimation method is applied to these adjoint nodes first, and this procedure is repeatedly performed until the artificial original electrical variable values of all added nodes are calculated.

4.3 Basis Set Adjustment Criterion

To simultaneously maintain the accuracy requirement and ease the inconsistent problem while changing the basis set, the error gap between different basis sets must be small enough. To judge the error gap at the j-th sampling time, first, the incremental values are estimated separately by the current basis set $\mathcal{T}$ and a new basis set $\mathcal{S}$. After that, both estimated incremental values corresponding to each column vector of $\mathcal{T}$ are compared. If each difference satisfies the following criterion, the basis set adjustment is allowed.

$$\begin{cases} |\Delta\bar{v}_\mathcal{T} - \Delta\bar{v}_\mathcal{S}| \leq 10^{-3} & \& \quad \left|\frac{\Delta\bar{v}_\mathcal{T} - \Delta\bar{v}_\mathcal{S}}{\Delta\bar{v}_\mathcal{T}}\right| \leq 10^{-4}, \\ |\Delta\bar{i}_\mathcal{T} - \Delta\bar{i}_\mathcal{S}| \leq 10^{-6} & \& \quad \left|\frac{\Delta\bar{i}_\mathcal{T} - \Delta\bar{i}_\mathcal{S}}{\Delta\bar{i}_\mathcal{T}}\right| \leq 10^{-4}, \end{cases} \qquad (23)$$

where $\Delta\bar{v}_\mathcal{T}/\Delta\bar{i}_\mathcal{T}$ and $\Delta\bar{v}_\mathcal{S}/\Delta\bar{i}_\mathcal{S}$ are the incremental voltage/current values estimated by $\mathcal{T}$ and $\mathcal{S}$, respectively.

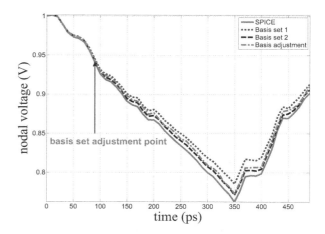

Figure 5: An example of basis set adjustment.

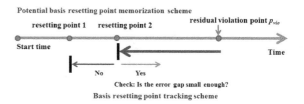

Figure 6: An example of adaptive error control.

For example, given a modified power grid network that is solved by the macro modeling technique [1] and incrementally estimated by two different basis sets, the voltage waveform of a node is shown in Figure 5. The point that we are seeking is the "basis set adjustment point" presented in Figure 5. It shows that the estimated values by *Basis set 1* and *Basis set 2* are almost the same at this sampling time, and the accuracy is improved after this sampling time if the basis set is switched to *Basis set 2* at this sampling time. Therefore, we can combine *Basis set 1* and *Basis set 2* to perform the simulation as shown in the red line of Figure 5(b).

To find basis set adjustment points by checking all previous sampling times is time consuming. An effective searching procedure will be introduced and described in the next section.

4.4 Adaptive Error Control Procedure

The adaptive error control procedure consists of two schemes– Potential basis resetting point memorization scheme and Basis resetting point tracking scheme, and is illustrated in Figure 6. The memorization scheme checks and stores several sampling times as the potential basis resetting points such as the resetting points 1 and 2 while performing the incremental transient simulation. As the residual exceeds the threshold at the sampling time p_{vio}, the tracking scheme goes back to the nearest potential resetting point 2. If the error gap at this sampling time is small enough, the incremental simulator will keep analyzing the circuit for succeeding sampling times from this basis resetting point. Otherwise, the tracking scheme goes back further to check another potential basis resetting point. These two schemes are detailed in the following subsections.

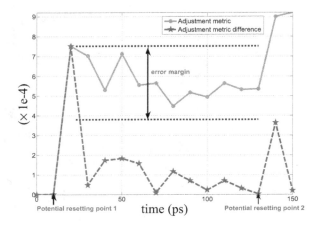

Figure 7: Relation between basis adjustment metric and basis adjustment metric difference.

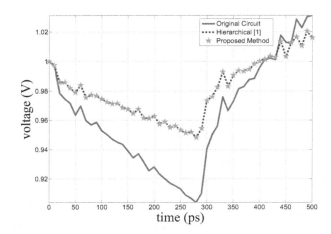

Figure 8: The voltage waveform at a node of the 1.05M **test case.**

4.4.1 *Potential Basis Resetting Point Memorization Scheme*

The basis sets can be switched only when the error gap between them is small enough. However, it wastes too much time and resource for checking the error gap node by node at each sampling time. Hence, instead of using the basis set adjustment criterion (23), the potential basis resetting point memorization scheme utilizes the residual to search *potential* (possible) resetting sampling times.

The basis adjustment metric at the j-th sampling time, γ^j, is defined as the root mean square value of non-zero parts in the residual at the j-th sampling time, and its difference is defined as $\delta^j = |\gamma^j - \gamma^{j-1}|$. Given a suitable basis set, generally, its basis adjustment metrics are within an error margin as shown in Figure 7. When the basis adjustment metric difference changes significantly, it means that the basis set currently used is not suitable for estimating the incremental values at the current sampling time and needs to be reset. Hence, as the basis adjustment metric difference changes significantly at the j-th sampling time, the (j-1)-th sampling time is memorized as a potential basis resetting point.

With this scheme, as the residual exceeds the threshold, only these memorized points need to be checked. As shown in Figure 7, the sampling time before the residual intending to drastically grow is saved as a potential point for resetting the basis set.

4.4.2 *Basis Resetting Point Tracking Scheme*

The main function of this scheme is choosing a suitable sampling time to reset the basis set for continuously finishing the incremental transient simulation. If the residual at the current sampling time exceeds a given threshold, it will track back, pick the nearest potential reseting point, and check whether the basis set adjustment criterion (23) is satisfied. If the error gap is sufficiently small, the developed simulator will go back to this potential resetting point, reset the basis set, and continuously perform the incremental transient analysis. Otherwise, it will go back further and perform the above procedure until a suitable resetting point is reached.

By the preceding schemes, only very few sampling times need to be checked, and the incremental transient simulation procedure can be more efficient and smooth.

5. EXPERIMENTAL RESULTS

The developed incremental transient simulator is implemented by C++ language and tested on Linux with Intel Xeon 2.4GHz CPU and 96G RAM. The test circuits are randomly generated RLC power grid networks by using industrial parameters with 1 volt supply voltage. The results are compared with a hierarchical method [1], an iterative solver GMRES [13], and a heuristic OMP-like incremental solver[1]. The time step is 10 ps.

To show the ability of the proposed method for dealing with the change of multiple-element values, several element values and the values of current drawn in different blocks are changed, and the results are shown in Table 1. There are four test circuits, and the percentage of modified blocks is around 3.75% for each circuit. Here, e_{max} and e_{avg} of GMRES [13], the OMP-like incremental solver, and the proposed method represent the maximum and average absolute errors compared with the hierarchical method [1], respectively. It can be observed that the proposed method not only achieves orders of magnitude speedup and 10× speedup over the hierarchical method [1] and GMRES [13], respectively, but also maintains the accuracy. The maximum absolute error is less than 1 mV for each circuit, and the average absolute error is very small. Compared with the OMP-like incremental solver, the speedup ratio is over 2.3 for each circuit. The voltage waveform at a node is shown in Figure 8. The pink line is its original waveform. The blue dash line and the green star line are its modified waveform calculated by the hierarchical method and the proposed method, respectively. The distribution of incremental voltages at 420 ps for the 1.05M test case is shown in Figure 9. Figures 9(a) and (b) are obtained by the hierarchical method [1] and the proposed method, respectively. It can be observed that the results of proposed method fit quite well with the exact solution. These figures demonstrate that the proposed method can successfully capture the transient behavior of the modified power grid network.

To further discuss the influence of modified block percentage,

---

[1]This heuristic OMP-like incremental solver is performed as follows. The OMP [8] is executed at each sampling time. As the residual exceeds the give threshold during the incremental transient analysis procedure, the incremental simulation is restarted from the beginning with a new basis set for avoiding the inconsistent basis problem.

Table 1: Comparison of the Proposed method, the Hierarchical method [1], GMRES [13], and the OMP-like incremental solver by modifying several regions.

Number of Nodes	Number of Blocks	Modified Blocks	Hierarchical [1] Runtime (sec)	GMRES [13] e_{max} (mV)	e_{avg} (mV)	Runtime (sec)	OMP-like e_{max} (mV)	e_{avg} (mV)	Runtime (sec)	Proposed Method e_{max} (mV)	e_{avg} (mV)	Runtime (sec)	Speedup [1] (×)	[13] (×)	OMP-like (×)
1.05M	160	6	426.88	0.11	1.97e-4	128.28	0.05	6.17e-4	31.91	0.04	9.0e-4	8.97	47.6	14.3	3.6
1.86M	180	7	1207.51	0.14	3.92e-3	197.16	0.27	2.82e-2	34.35	0.11	1.1e-3	15.24	79.2	12.9	2.3
2.54M	220	9	2005.05	0.99	1.81e-3	211.06	0.94	1.56e-2	58.92	0.94	1.2e-3	17.16	116.8	12.3	3.4
4.60M	220	9	3241.51	0.60	1.70e-3	291.23	0.56	1.07e-2	77.67	0.61	1.0e-2	29.04	111.6	10.0	2.7

† the number of sampling times is 50.

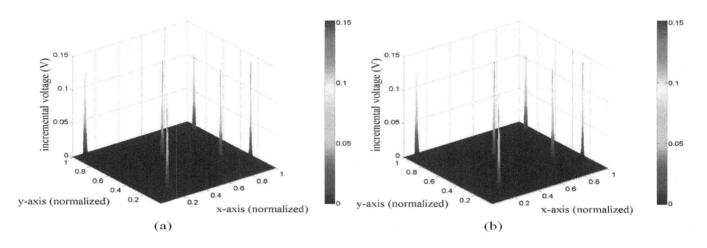

(a)   (b)

Figure 9: The distribution of incremental voltages at 420 ps for the 1.05M test case obtained by (a) the Hierarchical method [1] and (b) the Proposed method.

Table 2: Comparison of the Proposed method, the Hierarchical method [1], GMRES [13], and an OMP-like method with various percentages of modified blocks.

Modified Blocks	Hierarchical [1] Runtime (sec)	GMRES [13] e_{max} (mV)	e_{avg} (mV)	Runtime (sec)	OMP-like e_{max} (mV)	e_{avg} (mV)	Runtime (sec)	Proposed Method e_{max} (mV)	e_{avg} (mV)	Runtime (sec)	Speedup [1] (×)	[13] (×)	OMP-like (×)
1	430.57	0.13	2.50e-4	128.28	2.0e-3	8.8e-4	10.77	1.0e-3	1.0e-4	3.69	116.7	34.8	2.9
6	426.88	0.11	1.97e-4	128.28	5.2e-2	6.17e-4	31.91	4.0e-2	9.0e-4	8.97	47.6	14.3	3.6
29	427.10	0.20	7.71e-3	125.06	2.3e-1	4.88e-3	175.31	2.3e-1	3.0e-4	17.68	24.2	7.1	9.9
46	427.97	2.08	3.79e-2	119.04	3.5e-0	4.68e-2	722.66	2.4e-0	3.5e-2	28.02	15.3	4.2	25.8

† the number of blocks is 160, and the number of sampling times is 50.

Table 3: Comparison of the Proposed method, the Hierarchical method [1], and GMRES [13] with deleting/adding nodes and changing values of elements

Number of Nodes	Number of Blocks	Modified Blocks	Added Ports	Deleted Nodes	Hierarchical [1] Runtime (sec)	GMRES [13] e_{max} (mV)	e_{avg} (mV)	Runtime (sec)	Proposed Method e_{max} (mV)	e_{avg} (mV)	Runtime (sec)	Speedup [1] (×)	[13] (×)
1.05M	160	13	10	10	426.45	0.39	8.52e-3	123.00	0.35	2.10e-3	11.10	38.4	11.1
1.05M	160	15	20	20	427.04	3.70	4.53e-2	118.25	3.85	3.78e-2	14.15	30.2	8.4
4.60M	220	13	10	10	3241.88	2.48	1.75e-2	277.82	2.75	4.36e-2	46.02	70.4	6.0
4.60M	220	15	20	20	3167.51	2.59	1.89e-2	277.82	3.19	5.20e-2	51.01	62.1	5.4

† the number of sampling times is 50.

Table 4: Comparison of the Proposed method, the Hierarchical method [1], and GMRES [13] with various numbers of sampling times.

Number of Sampling Times	Hierarchical [1] Runtime (sec)	GMRES [13]			Proposed Method			Speedup	
		e_{max} (mV)	e_{avg} (mV)	Runtime (sec)	e_{max} (mV)	e_{avg} (mV)	Runtime (sec)	[1] (×)	[13] (×)
50	277.25	0.34	3.92e-3	32.4	0.46	6.36e-3	2.34	118.5	13.8
250	482.12	0.85	3.31e-2	132.0	1.25	3.10e-2	10.70	45.3	12.3
500	720.84	1.33	2.19e-2	257.1	2.16	3.61e-2	57.39	12.6	4.5
750	1007.94	2.32	3.09e-2	390.9	3.47	4.88e-2	84.98	11.9	4.6
1000	1242.23	3.13	7.13e-2	530.9	4.01	6.24e-2	112.57	11.0	4.7
1250	1751.19	3.99	9.66e-2	670.6	4.01	7.32e-2	140.32	12.5	4.8

† the number of nodes is 814K, and the number of blocks is 120.
† the number of modified blocks is 4, and the number of added nodes is 10
† the number of deleted nodes is 10.

the number of modified blocks of the test circuit with 1.05M nodes is varied from 1 to 46, and the results are illustrated in Table 2. The maximum percentage of modified blocks is about 30% of the original power grid network, and hundreds of element values are changed. As the percentage of modified blocks gets higher, the runtime becomes longer, and the maximum error becomes larger. However, the maximum absolute error is merely 2.4 mV that is about 0.24%, and the runtime is still an order of magnitude less than the hierarchical method [1] even one-third of blocks being modified. In addition, the proposed method maintains at least 4.2× speedup over GMRES [13] under the same level of accuracy. Furthermore, compared with the OMP-like incremental solver, the proposed method is much more robust and efficient while facing the significant modification of power grids.

To demonstrate the ability of the proposed method for simultaneously dealing with the adjusted values of elements and the modified topologies, we change several element values, delete nodes, and add nodes and ports in the test circuits with 1.05M and 4.6M nodes. Since the heuristic OMP-like incremental solver cannot deal with the topology change, the proposed method is only compared with the hierarchical method [1] and GMRES [13]. The results are shown in Table 3. It can be observed that the maximum absolute error is less than 4 mV that is about 0.4%, and the average absolute error is less than 0.1 mV for both cases. Furthermore, with a large portion change of topology and element values, the proposed method still keeps an order of magnitude speedup over the hierarchical method [1], and about 5 times faster than GMRES [13]. The proposed method is quite robust, efficient, and reliable.

Generally, the error might convey to the succeeding sampling times while doing the incremental transient analysis, so we test the proposed method with various numbers of sampling times. The test circuit has 814K nodes and is partitioned to 120 blocks. 4 blocks are modified, 10 nodes are added, 10 nodes are deleted, and the numbers of sampling times are 50, 250, 500, 750, 1000, and 1250. From Table 4, their maximum errors are at the same level while the average errors slightly grow. In addition, the speedup ratio still maintains a good level, which is about 11 compared with the hierarchical method [1] and about 5 compared with GMRES [13]. It shows that the proposed method is quite robust and reliable for capturing the transient behavior under long simulation time.

6. CONCLUSION

An efficient and reliable incremental transient simulator for the power grid was developed. The experimental results have shown that it can fast, accurately, and robustly capture the transient behavior of the power grid after modifying its topologies or/and the values of existing elements.

7. ACKNOWLEDGMENT

This work was supported in part by Industrial Technology Research Institute, and National Science Council of Taiwan under Grant NSC 102-2221-E-009-184.

8. REFERENCES

[1] M. Zhao, R. V. Panda, S. S. Sapatnekar, and D. Blaauw. Hierarchical analysis of power distribution networks. *IEEE TCAD*, 21(2):159–168, 2002.

[2] T. H. Chen and C. C. P. Chen. Efficient large-scale power grid analysis based on preconditioned Krylov-subspace iterative methods. In *DAC*, pages 559–562, 2001.

[3] C. H. Chou, N. Y. Tsai, H. Yu, C. R. Lee, Y. Shi, and S. C. Chang. On the preconditioner of conjugate gradient a power grid simulation perspective. In *ICCAD*, pages 494–497, 2011.

[4] H. Su, E. Acar, and S. R. Nassif. Power grid reduction based on algebraic multigrid principles. In *DAC*, pages 109–112, 2003.

[5] P. Y. Huang, H. Y. Chou, and Y. M. Lee. An aggregation-based algebraic multigrid method for power grid analysis. In *ISQED*, pages 159–164, 2007.

[6] H. F. Qian, S. R. Nassif, and S. S. Sapatnekar. Power grid analysis using random walks. *IEEE TCAD*, 24(8):1204–1224, 2005.

[7] X. Xiong and J. Wang. Vectorless verification of RLC power grids with transient current constraints. In *ICCAD*, pages 7–10, 2011.

[8] P. Sun, X. Li, and M. Y. Ting. Efficient incremental analysis of on-chip power grid via sparse approximation. In *DAC*, pages 676–681, 2011.

[9] Y. H. Lee, Y. M. Lee, L. C. Cheng, and Y. T. Chang. A robust incremental power grid analyzer by macromodeling approach and orthogonal matching pursuit. In *ASQED*, pages 64–70, 2012.

[10] Abhishek and F. N. Najm. Incremental power grid verification. In *DAC*, pages 151–156, 2012.

[11] Y. C. Pati, R. Rezaiifar, and P. S. Krishnaprasad. Orthogonal matching pursuit: recursive function approximation with applications to wavelet decomposition. In *ACSSC*, volume 1, pages 40–44, 1993.

[12] METIS. http://glaros.dtc.umn.edu/gkhome/views/metis/.

[13] Y. Saad and M. H. Schultz. GMRES: A generalized minimal residual algorithm for solving nonsymmetric linear systems. *SIAM J. Sci. Stat. Comput.*, 7:856–869, 1986.

Self-Aligned Double Patterning Aware Pin Access and Standard Cell Layout Co-Optimization

Xiaoqing Xu, Brian Cline[†], Greg Yeric[†], Bei Yu, David Z. Pan

ECE Department, Univ. of Texas at Austin, Austin, TX, USA

[†]ARM Inc, Austin, TX, USA

{xiaoqingxu, bei, dpan}@cerc.utexas.edu, {Brian.Cline, Greg.Yeric}@arm.com

ABSTRACT

Self-Aligned Double Patterning (SADP) is being considered for use at the $10nm$ technology node and below for routing layers with pitches down to ~$50nm$ because it has better LER and overlay control compared to other multiple patterning candidates. To date, most of the SADP-related literature has focused on enabling SADP-legal routing in physical design tools while few attempts have been made to address the impact SADP routing has on local, standard cell (SC) I/O pin access. In this paper, we present the first study on SADP-aware pin access and layout optimization at the SC level. Accounting for SADP-specific design rules, we propose a coherent framework that uses Mixed Integer Linear Programming (MILP) and branch and bound method to simultaneously optimize SADP-based local pin access and within-cell connections. Our experimental results show that, compared with the conventional approach, our framework effectively improves pin access of the standard cells and maximizes the pin access flexibility for routing.

Categories and Subject Descriptors

B.7.2 [**Hardware, Integrated Circuit**]: Design Aids

General Terms

Algorithms, Design, Performance

Keywords

Self-Aligned Double Patterning (SADP), Pin Access, Standard Cell Layout

1. INTRODUCTION

Due to the resolution limits of $193nm$ photolithography, double patterning techniques and regular layout have been widely used to extend semiconductor process technology scaling [1–3]. The design rules that enable double patterning (color decomposition, forbidden pitches, etc.) are much

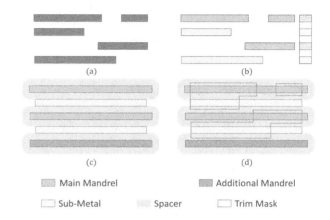

Figure 1: The line-space array decomposition, (a) target layout, (b) layout coloring, (c) mandrel mask design, (d) trim mask design.

more restrictive than the basic rules used previously in technology nodes >$20nm$. In addition, the expectation to continue Moore's Law translates to the same density and area scaling every node. That means the physical design tools need to access Standard Cell (SC) Input/Output (I/O) pins in more congested areas with increasingly restrictive rules.

One way that standard cell (SC) designers can assist physical design tools is through intelligent, optimized SC I/O pin design. Unfortunately, the complex design rules and neighbor interactions that exist due to various multiple patterning techniques like Litho-Etch-Litho-Etch (LELE) and Self-Aligned Double Patterning (SADP) make human-driven layout almost impossible at 14nm technologies and below. That means automated standard cell layout design and optimization are needed to provide flexible I/O pin access.

SADP, in particular, is a viable candidate for lower layer metallization with regular patterns at the 10nm technology node, due to better overlay and Line Edge Roughness (LER) control compared to LELE. To deploy the SADP technique for routing layers in practical designs, designers need to ensure that layout patterns are SADP-friendly to achieve successful layout decomposition. The SADP layout decomposition problem has been studied, as shown in [4–7]. For regular layout, the line-space array decomposition method can efficiently decompose SADP-based geometries and achieve good pattern fidelity and process margin [2], [8]. An example of line-space array decomposition is demonstrated in Fig. 1. Fig. 1(a) shows regular layout on horizontal tracks. We can assign different colors to patterns on neighbor tracks in

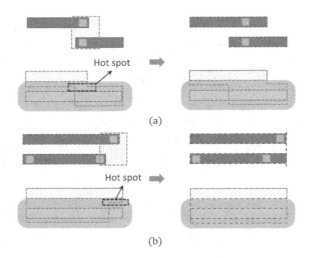

Figure 2: Line-end extension techniques, (a) anti-parallel line ends, (b) parallel line ends.

Fig. 1(b). Fig. 1(c) shows the mandrel mask design and spacer deposition. Then, the trim mask and spacer define the target layout as demonstrated in Fig. 1(d).

To incorporate SADP constraints into early design stages, there are several studies [9–12], dealing with the SADP-aware routing problem. However, to date, works studying how multiple patterning and decomposition impact SC I/O pin design are lacking, especially as pin congestion and routability become increasingly critical to the overall physical design results. Since most modern-day SC designs primarily use Metal-1 for local connections and I/O pins, Metal-2 design is essential for SC I/O pin access. SADP-based Metal-2 wires, in particular, present a new set of problems to SC I/O pin access. Specifically, because of the decomposition of SADP into the mandrel and trim masks, one cannot simply rely on via locations to determine line-end positions of Metal-2 wires. As shown in Fig. 2, SADP yield can be enhanced by simple line-end extensions that are dependent on both via placement and neighboring wire placement. For example, in Fig. 2(a) and (b) respectively, the extension of anti-parallel line ends and parallel line-end alignment both help to avoid hot spots on the trim masks [13].

In general, the ideal location of geometries is not as straightforward under SADP constraints and is more dependent on the neighborhood around the geometry in question. This means all SADP-based metal designs, including pin access and within-cell connections have to be optimized simultaneously during the I/O pin design phase.

In this work we formulate this issue as an SC I/O pin access problem and illustrate the usefulness of our methodology at the 10nm technology node. To solve this problem efficiently, this paper proposes a Mixed Integer Linear Programming (MILP) based technique that simultaneously optimizes the Metal-2 wires used for pin access and within-cell connections of standard cells. In addition, using the branch and bound method, we extend this technique to each pin access strategy and maximize pin accessibility for each cell in the 10nm library. Our main contributions are summarized as follows:

- To the best of our knowledge, this is the first work that addresses SC I/O pin access design at the SC level.

- We propose a MILP-based optimization methodology to enable SADP-aware Metal-2 layout design for pin access and within-cell connections.

- The pin access and cell layout co-optimization is proposed to systematically maximize the pin access flexibility for the entire standard cell library.

The rest of this paper is organized as follows: Section 2 introduces background material relevant to the pin access design issue. Section 3 shows the formulation of the SADP-aware pin access design problem, including several definitions and our design target. Section 4 presents our MILP-based methodology for Metal-2 layout optimization. Section 5 extends our optimization technique to the entire standard cell library based on the branch and bound method. Section 6 demonstrates the effectiveness of our optimization framework, and compares the SADP-aware pin access optimization to the conventional approach with the design rule checks. Section 7 concludes this paper.

2. PRELIMINARIES

2.1 Line-Space Array Decomposition

The continued geometric scaling of process technology depends on multiple patterning and increased layout regularity [2]. Thus, at the 10nm node and beyond, we assume that the Metal-2 layout will be extremely regular. Furthermore, in the 10nm commercial technology we used, the preferred direction of Metal-2 routing was horizontal. After studying the Metal-2 routing tracks, we made the following observation.

Observation 1 *There are no coloring conflicts between wires on even/odd Metal-2 routing tracks.*

In the 10nm technology node used, the Metal-2 pitch was assumed to be $M2_{pitch} = 48nm$, which corresponds to a 75% scaling from the 16nm node [14]. Thus, the pitch between even/odd routing tracks was $96nm$ ($2 \times M2_{pitch}$), which was larger than the resolution limit of $193nm$ photolithography. Hence, Metal-2 wires on even/odd routing tracks are free of SADP coloring conflicts. Moreover, if the Metal-2 wires on the same or neighbor routing tracks were carefully designed to be SADP-friendly, then the line-space array decomposition method [8] from Fig. 1 can be deployed. Basically, each wire on the same routing track is extended and merged to achieve the line-space array. As illustrated in Fig. 1(c), we place mandrel features on non-adjacent lines and add additional mandrels when necessary. In the *Spacer Is Dielectric* (SID) process, the final layout patterns are defined as *Trim mask NOT Spacer*. Hence, we can design the trim mask efficiently as shown in Fig. 1(d). After choosing to adhere to line-space array decomposition, a second observation follows.

Observation 2 *A single color is assigned to metal patterns on even routing tracks. The alternate color is then assigned to metal patterns on odd routing tracks.*

Metal-2 routing is becoming increasingly congested as we continue to scale towards the 10nm technology node because of the increasing density of transistors and SC I/O pins. Hence, increasing Metal-2 congestion leads to a higher likelihood of having Metal-2 wires on neighbor tracks at the same

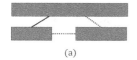 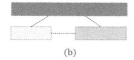

(a)   (b)

Figure 3: The potential odd-cycle conflicts of the coloring graph, (a) potential Metal-2 layout, (b) potential odd-cycle conflicts.

Table 1: SADP Related Notations

Metal-2 layer	MetalWidth	w
	MetalSpace	s
	minMetalArea	A_{min}
Spacer deposits	SpacerDepositWidth	w_{sp}
Trim mask	minResistWidth	w_r
	minResistSpace	s_r
	EtchBias	w_e
Design rules	minMetalLength (*Rule 0*)	l_0
	OnTrackSpace (*Rule 1*)	l_1
	OffTrackOverlap (*Rule 2*)	l_2
	OffTrackSpace (*Rule 3*)	l_3
	OffTrackOffset (*Rule 4*)	l_4

time, which leads to the layout patterns illustrated in Fig. 3. In Fig. 3(a), a solid edge denotes coloring conflict and a dashed edge denotes a potential coloring conflict. Fig. 3(b) demonstrates how a dashed edge changes to solid edge if we assign different colors to Metal-2 wires on the same track, which leads to an odd-cycle conflict in the coloring graph. SADP technique does not allow stitches during the layout decomposition stage, which means odd-cycle conflicts must be strictly forbidden in SADP-friendly layout patterns [5]. The color assignment strategy from observation 2 helps to avoid potential odd cycles in the coloring stage for SADP-friendly layout.

2.2 SADP-specific Design Rules

To enable layout design that is compatible with line-space array decomposition, we need to formulate SADP constraints into specific design rules. According to observations 1 and 2, we define the 4 design rules shown in Fig. 4 that enforce SADP-friendly layout using 1-D relationships.

Table 1 defines SADP-specific notations for the 10nm technology node [15]. First, the minimum area constraint of Metal-2 layout is converted to the minimum wire length design rule (l_0) due to the fixed width of Metal-2 wires. Then, we define the space between Metal-2 line ends on the same routing track as **OnTrackSpace**(l_1), as shown in Fig. 4(a). We use **OffTrackOverlap**(l_2) and **OffTrackSpace**(l_3) to define the prohibited region for the anti-parallel Metal-2 wires [15], as shown in Fig. 4(b) and Fig. 4(c), respectively. Finally, for parallel Metal-2 wires illustrated in Fig. 4(d), the line-end design constraint is defined as **OffTrackOffset**(l_4). Table 2 summarizes the design rules for Metal-2 layout patterns [13, 15].

3. PROBLEM FORMULATION

Our I/O pin access on the Metal-2 layer is based on practical layout of standard cells. For each cell in the library, we observe that I/O pins generally exist on either the Metal-1 or Metal-2 layer. To properly formulate the SADP-aware pin access design problem, we have the following definitions.

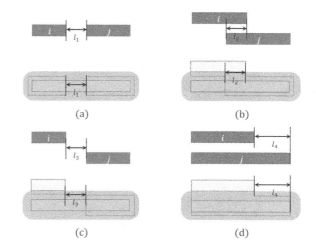

(a)   (b)

(c)   (d)

Figure 4: SADP-specific design rule formulation, **(a)** $OnTrackSpace \geq l_1$, **(b)** $OffTrackOverlap \geq l_2$, **(c)** $OffTrackSpace \geq l_3$, **(d)** $OffTrackOffset \geq l_4$ or $OffTrackOffset = l_4 = 0$.

Table 2: Design Rule Formulation

Rule 0	$l_0 \geq \frac{A_{min}}{w}$
Rule 1	$l_1 \geq w_r - 2 \cdot w_e$
Rule 2	$l_2 \geq s_r + 2 \cdot w_e$
Rule 3	$l_3 \geq \sqrt{(w_r - 2 \cdot w_e)^2 - {w_{sp}}^2}$
Rule 4	$l_4 \geq w_r$ or $l_4 = 0$

Definition 1 (Hit Point) *The intersection of a Metal-2 routing track (which is pre-determined by the place and route tool) and an I/O pin shape is defined as a Hit Point for that particular I/O pin.*

It can be observed that each hit point determines the range of positions for the corresponding Via-1 (the Metal-1 to Metal-2 connection). In the $10nm$ technology used, Metal-2 is uni-directional and runs horizontally. Thus, for each hit point, there are two accessing directions possible, either from left to right or from right to left. To access one hit point, we need to design the Metal-2 wire assuming one accessing direction for the hit point. Then, in order to connect to every I/O pin in a cell, we need to determine the accessing directions for a set of hit points. Hence, we have several definitions as follows.

Definition 2 (Hit Point Combination) *A set of hit points (with a defined access direction, left or right) where each I/O pin in the SC is accessed exactly once is defined as a Hit Point Combination for that cell.*

Definition 3 (Valid Hit Point Combination) *If a hit point combination induces zero design rule violations, it is considered a Valid Hit Point Combination. Otherwise, it is considered to be invalid.*

Definition 4 (Valid Hit Point) *If a hit point can be accessed from both directions within some valid hit point combinations for one cell, it is considered a valid hit point. Otherwise, it is considered to be invalid.*

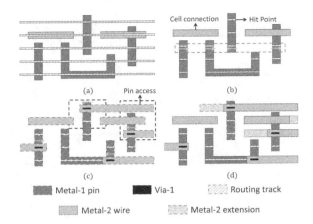

Table 3: Notations

c_L, c_R	left or right boundary of cell
c_W	cell width, $c_W = c_R - c_L$
S_m	set of Metal-2 wires
n	total number of Metal-2 wires
S_k	set of pairs of wires for rule k, $\forall k \in \{1, 2, 3, 4\}$
x_{iL}, x_{iR}	the left or right line end of i_{th} wire
x_{iL}^0, x_{iR}^0	the initial line ends of i_{th} wire

Figure 5: A simple example for pin access design, (a) Metal-2 tracks and cell layout, (b) hit points for each I/O pin, (c) Metal-2 wires for pin access, (d) line end extension.

A simple example of the I/O pin access design for one hit point combination is shown in Fig. 5. Fig. 5(a) demonstrates the Metal-1 I/O pin layout and Metal-2 routing tracks running horizontally above Metal-1. Fig. 5(b) shows how the hit points, which represent valid Via-1 locations for I/O pin access, are derived from the overlap of Metal-2 routing tracks and the Metal-1 I/O pins. It can be observed that, for most hit points, the length of the hit point is decided by the minimum width of Metal-1. However, if a Metal-1 wire runs horizontally, this leads to a long hit point, which allows more flexibility for the Via-1 position. The set of hit points within the dashed box in Fig. 5(b) shows one hit point combination and the pink arrows denote the arbitrary accessing directions chosen for the hit points. Fig. 5(c) illustrates another hit point combination and one way to access the cell using that hit point combination. After choosing one hit point for each I/O pin and the accessing direction for that hit point, the Metal-2 wires can be designed for pin access, accounting for the minimum enclosure design rule for Metal-2 over Via-1. However, the dashed boxes in Fig. 5(c) denote all pairs of line ends that cause hot spots in trim mask designs. Fig. 5(d) demonstrates that we can make use of line-end extension techniques to fix those hot spots in the trim mask.

However, in SC design, it is non-trivial to determine whether all hot spots are fixable via line-end extension techniques. Furthermore, the engineering efforts and iterations involved to fix all of the potential hot spots across the SC library is too large for the average layout design team. Therefore, a general methodology is needed to design the Metal-2 wires for pin access and within-cell connections simultaneously. We can now define the SADP-aware pin access optimization problem as follows.

Problem 1 (Pin Access Optimization (PAO)) *Given the standard cell layout and a specific hit point combination, determine whether or not it is possible to optimize the Metal-2 wires for pin access and within-cell connections under SADP constraints. If possible, show all SADP-friendly Metal-2 wires.*

Moreover, as shown in Fig. 5(b), we may have multiple hit points for one I/O pin, which leads to numerous hit point combinations for one cell. For one standard cell, we define the pin access and cell layout co-optimization problem as follows.

Problem 2 (PICO) *Given the standard cell layout, the Pin Access and Cell Layout Co-Optimization (PICO) problem is to show all Metal-2 wiring cases with successful PAO's and maximize the pin access flexibility under SADP constraints.*

4. SADP-AWARE PIN ACCESS

Given a specific hit point combination, we pre-design the Metal-2 wires for pin access. Then, we propose an MILP-based method to solve PAO problem efficiently.

4.1 Pin Access Pre-design

Given a hit point combination and the accessing direction for each hit point, we can determine the position of Via-1 and extend the line ends of the Metal-2 wires for pin access accordingly. Specifically, if we need to access the hit point from the right of cell, we will put the Via-1 as close to the right of the hit point as possible. Then, we can determine the line end position of the corresponding Metal-2 wire for pin access accounting for the minimum enclosure design rule for Metal-2 over Via-1.

For pin access design, we focus on SADP-aware layout optimization within a standard cell boundary. Hence, if one hit point is next to the right boundary of the cell and the access direction is from the right, the right line end of the corresponding Metal-2 wire will be extended to the right boundary. We have similar pre-design if the hit point is accessed from the left boundary of cell. Fig. 5(c) is an example of Metal-2 wires for pin access after the pre-design stage. The pre-design method induces the following observation.

Observation 3 *For Metal-2 wires after the pre-design stage, right line ends can only be extended to the right and left line ends can only be extended to the left.*

4.2 Pin Access Optimization

As illustrated in Fig. 5(c), if we simply use the hit point to determine the line end of Metal-2 wires, the SADP constraints may invalidate some hit point combinations. The line end extension techniques motivate us to legalize the Metal-2 layout to enable SADP-friendly design. The conventional layout migration issue has been formulated as a linear programming problem in [16]. A similar approach has also been deployed to deal with LELE double patterning layout decomposition in [17]. However, the linear programming technique used in [16] and [17] cannot be directly applied to SADP-aware I/O pin access design because the relative order of the metal line ends may change during the line end extension stage, as shown in Fig. 2(a). Instead, we propose an MILP-based optimization methodology to determine the Metal-2 wire design for each specific hit point combination. Table 3 shows the notations for the variables used in our formulation. We will first give the mathematical formulation for our Pin Access Optimization (PAO) problem. Then, we transfer the mathematical formulation to an MILP formulation. The results of the MILP can determine whether feasible solutions exist for the Metal-2 line ends of a particular hit point combination. If feasible solutions exist, the line end positions of each Metal-2 wire are decided while minimizing the total amount of line end extension.

4.2.1 *Mathematical Formulation*

Observation 3 allows us to quantify the total amount of extension in terms of line-end positions. It is known that line end extension techniques benefit SADP-based wires [13]. However, in next generation technology nodes, the routing resources are becoming increasingly limited, so line-end extensions of Metal-2 wires should be used judiciously. Additionally, line end extensions can potentially increase both coupling capacitance and ground capacitance on Metal-2 routes. Therefore, line-end extension minimization is a necessity for pin access optimization. The minimization of the total amount of line-end extensions is formulated as the objective function, as shown in (1).

Constraints (1a) - (1c) define the line-end extension limits and minimum wire length design rule (*Rule* 0 in Table 2) for each Metal-2 wire. The initial relative order can be determined for each pair of Metal-2 wires. Suppose the i_{th} wire is on the left of j_{th} wire, as demonstrated in Fig. 4(a). Constraint (1d) is formulated to define *Rule* 1. In set S_2, the line ends originally overlap each other and constraints (1e) and (1f) interpret *Rule* 2. In set S_3, the line ends initially have no overlap. After extension, the line ends may or may not overlap each other. Constraint (1g) satisfies *Rule* 2 or *Rule* 3. Then, constraints (1h) and (1i) are formulated to specify *Rule* 4 for each pair of Metal-2 wires in set S_4.

$$\min \sum_{i=0}^{n-1} (x_{iL}^0 - x_{iL}) + (x_{iR} - x_{iR}^0) \qquad (1)$$

$$\text{s.t.} \quad c_L \leq x_{iL} \leq x_{iL}^0 \qquad \forall i \in S_m \quad (1a)$$

$$x_{iR}^0 \leq x_{iR} \leq c_R \qquad \forall i \in S_m \quad (1b)$$

$$x_{iR} - x_{iL} \geq l_0 \qquad \forall i \in S_m \quad (1c)$$

$$x_{jL} - x_{iR} \geq l_1 \qquad \forall (i,j) \in S_1 \quad (1d)$$

$$x_{iR} - x_{jL} \geq l_2 \qquad \forall (i,j) \in S_2 \quad (1e)$$

$$x_{jR} - x_{iL} \geq l_2 \qquad \forall (i,j) \in S_2 \quad (1f)$$

$$x_{jL} - x_{iR} \geq l_3 \text{ or } x_{iR} - x_{jL} \geq l_2 \quad \forall (i,j) \in S_3 \quad (1g)$$

$$|x_{iL} - x_{jL}| \geq l_4 \text{ or } x_{iL} - x_{jL} = 0 \quad \forall (i,j) \in S_4 \quad (1h)$$

$$|x_{iR} - x_{jR}| \geq l_4 \text{ or } x_{iR} - x_{jR} = 0 \quad \forall (i,j) \in S_4 \quad (1i)$$

4.2.2 *MILP formulation*

Here, we show how to convert (1) into an MILP formulation. We can simplify the objective function by omitting item x_{iL}^0 and x_{iR}^0, which are constants for a specific hit point combination. In addition, we also need to convert constraints (1g)-(1i) to linear constraints based on the big-M transformation [18].

Note that $|x_{iL} - x_{jR}| \leq c_W, \forall i, j \in S_m$ and c_W is the width of the cell. Hence, in the SC level, the cell width c_W is an appropriate big-M parameter for our formulation. Constraint (1g) can be formulated as linear constraints (2a) - (2c) given below. s_k is an additional integer variable introduced so that both constraints can be satisfied at the same time.

$$x_{jL} - x_{iR} + (c_W + l_3) \cdot s_k \geq l_3 \qquad (2a)$$

$$x_{iR} - x_{jL} + (c_W + l_2) \cdot (1 - s_k) \geq l_2 \qquad (2b)$$

$$s_k \in \{0, 1\} \qquad \forall (i,j) \in S_3 \quad (2c)$$

Similarly, constraints (1h) and (1i) can also be converted to linear constraints by introducing integer variables as follows.

$$x_{jL} - x_{iL} + (c_W + l_4) \cdot s_{m1} \geq l_4 \cdot (1 - t_{n1}) \qquad (2d)$$

$$x_{iL} - x_{jL} + (c_W + l_4) \cdot (1 - s_{m1}) \qquad (2e)$$

$$\geq l_4 \cdot (1 - t_{n1}) + (c_W + l_4) \cdot t_{n1} \qquad (2f)$$

$$s_{m1} + t_{n1} \leq 1, s_{m1}, t_{n1} \in \{0, 1\} \qquad \forall (i,j) \in S_4 \quad (2g)$$

$$x_{jR} - x_{iR} + (c_W + l_4) \cdot s_{m2} \geq l_4 \cdot (1 - t_{n2}) \qquad (2h)$$

$$x_{iR} - x_{jR} + (c_W + l_4) \cdot (1 - s_{m2}) \qquad (2i)$$

$$\geq l_4 \cdot (1 - t_{n2}) + (c_W + l_4) \cdot t_{n2} \qquad (2j)$$

$$s_{m2} + t_{n2} \leq 1, s_{m2}, t_{n2} \in \{0, 1\} \qquad \forall (i,j) \in S_4 \quad (2h)$$

To summarize, the MILP formulation is shown in (2). The optimization results will decide whether it is possible to achieve a legal solution for the Metal-2 design of one hit point combination. In particular, the feasible solution of the MILP formulation consists of the legal line end position of each Metal-2 wire with the minimum amount of extension.

$$\min \sum_{i=0}^{n-1} (x_{iR} - x_{iL}) \qquad (2)$$

$$\text{s.t.} \quad (1a) - (1f)$$

$$\qquad (2a) - (2h)$$

5. PIN ACCESS AND CELL LAYOUT CO-OPTIMIZATION

Previously, we have shown that MILP-based optimization determines whether a single hit point combination is valid or not. If it is valid, we can achieve successful optimization of Metal-2 wires for pin access and cell connection simultaneously. However, as shown in Fig. 5, multiple hit points for one I/O pin lead to numerous hit point combinations for one standard cell. In general, the more valid hit point combinations we have for one cell, the more flexibility we can provide to the routing stage. Thus, we extend the MILP-based optimization to validate all hit point combinations of a standard cell.

The overall algorithm for the pin access and cell layout co-optimization (PICO) is given in Algorithm 1. First, as shown in lines 1-7, the preprocessing steps determine the set of hit points for each I/O pin. Then, in line 9, the branch and bound method is proposed to obtain a table of potential valid hit point combinations for the standard cell. From line 10 to line 15, we call the MILP-based optimization (2) for each entry in the table of potential hit point combinations. For each cell, all valid pin access designs are stored in a table, which can be incorporated into the standard cell library design. Hence, we have maximized the pin access flexibility of one cell for the routing stage.

Algorithm 1 PICO Algorithm

Require: Cell layout and Metal-2 routing tracks;
1: define C as set of Metal-2 wires for cell connection;
2: define IO as set of I/O pins;
3: define S_{IO} as the set of hit points for each I/O pin;
4: **for** each pin $p_k \in IO$ **do**
5:    get the set of hit points, P_k, for pin p_k;
6:    add P_k to S_{IO};
7: **end for**
8: define $MTable$ as table of Metal-2 layout design;
9: $MTable = $ Branch-and-Bound(S_{IO}, C);
10: **for** each entry H_k in $MTable$ **do**;
11:    **if** the pin access optimization for $H_k \cup C$ is feasible **then**
12:       replace H_k with the feasible solution;
13:    **else**
14:       delete H_k;
15:    **end if**
16: **end for**

Algorithm 2 illustrates the branch and bound method that yields a table of potential valid hit point combinations. In line 2, we construct a search tree out of all hit points for each I/O pin. Fig. 6 demonstrates the construction of the search tree from all hit points (p_i^k) of any standard cell. The root will be a virtual node for the tree. A path from root to leaf gives a hit point combination for the cell. The i_{th} level of the search tree contains the hit points for the i_{th} I/O pin of the cell. Lines 4-14 demonstrate the process of table construction. While traversing from root to node, before adding a new node to path, we should check the compatibility of this node with its ancestor nodes in path and Metal-2 wires for within-cell connections. We continue the traversal if the node is legal on path. Otherwise, we go to next node on the same level, which prunes the redundant hit point combinations relevant to that node.

Algorithm 2 Branch-and-Bound Algorithm

Require: a set of hit points (S_{IO}) and a set of Metal-2 wires (C);
1: **function** BRANCH-AND-BOUND(S_{IO}, C)
2:    construct search tree based on S_{IO};
3:    define list $Path$ for traversed nodes;
4:    **repeat**
5:       $Path = \emptyset$;
6:       **while** traverse from root to leaf **do**
7:          **if** Check($currentnode, Path, C$)=True **then**
            ▷ The check heuristics for branch and bound
8:             push($currentnode, Path$);
9:          **else**
10:            go to next node on the same level;
11:          **end if**
12:       **end while**
13:       add $Path$ to $Table$
14:    **until** all paths exhausted
15:    return $Table$;
16: **end function**

The following check heuristics help to prune out invalid hit point combinations.

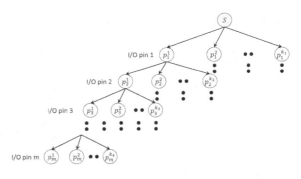

Figure 6: Search tree for the branch and bound method

1. Avoid two hit points that are close to each other and on the same track.

2. Existing Metal-2 wires used for within-cell connection invalidate the hit points they cover as well as hit points that are too close in proximity.

It shall be noted that we can further consider other pruning metrics during the branch and bound stage. For example, cell robustness metrics, such as pin density, are closely related to the pin access design at the standard cell level and it could be another metric used to prune out invalid hit point combinations.

6. EXPERIMENTAL RESULTS

We have implemented our algorithm in C++ and tested it using an industrial $14nm$ standard cell library that has been scaled and compacted to $10nm$-representative dimensions. We use CBC [19] as our MILP solver and all experiments are performed on a Linux machine with 3.33GHz Intel(R) Xeon(R) CPU X5680. The width and space of Metal-2 wires are assumed to be $24nm$. The spacer deposit width is set as $24nm$. For trim mask design, the minimum resist width and space are set as $44nm$ and $46nm$, respectively. The etch bias is set as $6nm$ [15].

Next, we demonstrate the strength of our optimization methodology by showing the results from pin access design for specific hit point combinations, standard cells and the entire standard cell library consisting of around 700 cells. Fig. 7 demonstrates a typical cell layout design in the 10nm technology node. The I/O pins for this cell are on the Metal-1 layer. Due to the complexity of this cell, Metal-2 wires are used for within-cell connections. Fig. 7(a) shows the Metal-2 layout design if we simply use hit point (Via-1) locations to determine the line end positions. A design rule check will reveal multiple violations in the dashed boxes. However, as illustrated in Fig. 7(b), the same Metal-2 wires for pin access and within-cell connections can be co-optimized to enable SADP-friendly layout. The MILP-based optimization ensures the minimum amount of line end extension and avoids potential engineering efforts from design rule violation fixes.

The PICO problem motivates us to extend the optimization technique to each hit point combination of the standard cell based on the branch and bound method. The pin access flexibility of each cell can be evaluated in terms of the number of hit point combinations or valid hit points for each I/O pin. As shown in Fig. 7, we may have various hit points for each I/O pin of the cell. We assume that

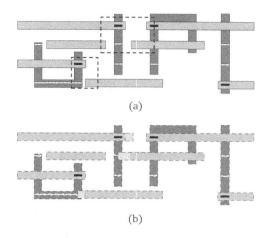

(a)

(b)

Figure 7: Pin access and cell connection co-optimization for one hit point combination. (a) design rule violations in layout, (b) MILP-based optimization result.

the hit point locations determine the line-end positions of Metal-2 wires in conventional pin access design. The design rule checks for conventional design have been implemented as the baseline. Fig. 8 shows the effectiveness of the PICO for 5 typical cells in the $10nm$ standard cell library. We observe that the improvement of the number of valid hit point combinations is cell dependent. For cell 1, the space between I/O pins is relatively large, which means pin access design can easily satisfy the SADP constraints but there is no significant improvement in terms of hit point combinations. However, we achieve a significant increase in the number of valid hit point combinations for other cells. Particularly, conventional design rule checking invalidates all of the hit point combinations for Cell 5, the layout of which is shown in Fig. 7. This invalidation is caused by the existing, within-cell connections in Metal-2, which illustrates why we need to simultaneously optimize the pin access wires along with the wires that already exist in a given cell's layout. Our optimization framework recovers nearly half of the total hit point combinations for Cell 5.

For both conventional and SADP-aware pin access design, we further evaluate the number of valid hit points based on the definition of the valid hit point shown in Section 3. Compared to the conventional approach, the SADP-aware pin access design achieves the increase of valid hit points for each I/O pin of the cells, as demonstrated in Table 4. We put a "-" in the entry of the table if the i_{th} I/O pin does not exist for that particular cell. For instance, Cell 1 only has 3 I/O pins, so pins #4 and #5 have a "-" in their entry since they do not apply. It is interesting to note that some cells like "Cell 3" show zero improvement in the number of valid hit points in Table 4, but show significant increases in the number of valid hit point combinations in Fig. 8. This example highlights the difference between hit points and hit point combinations, and the importance of enumerating and optimizing the combinations, not just the hit points themselves. This is due to the fact that hit points in a combination influence each other and can cause SADP violations in the combination. In isolation, a hit point may appear valid, but upon grouping into a combination, it may negatively impact other hit points.

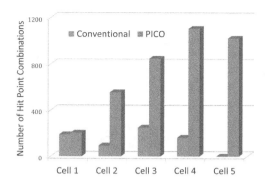

Figure 8: The increase in the number of valid hit point combinations

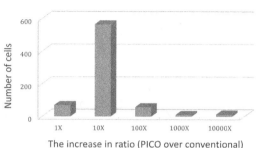

Figure 9: The increase in ratio on the number of valid hit point combinations across the entire cell library

To gauge the library-wide effectiveness of our optimization framework, we also applied the proposed technique to each cell in our 10nm library. We calculated the ratio of valid hit point combinations of PICO algorithm over the conventional approach for each cell. The histogram in Fig. 9 demonstrates the valid hit point combination ratio and the effectiveness of PICO technique. We obtain 10X or more improvement for most cells and some cells achieve up to a 10000X increase in the number of valid hit point combinations. This means that the PICO has significantly improved the pin access flexibility for the routing stage. We also evaluate the increase in the number of valid hit points for each I/O pin. The increase in percentage over total number of hit points is calculated for each cell in the library and shown in Fig. 10. In our $10nm$ experiments, we find that over 25 % of cells have 20 % improvement in the number of valid hit points.

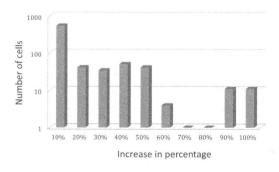

Figure 10: The increase in percentage on the number of valid hit points across the entire cell library

Table 4: The increase in the number of valid hit points for each I/O pin

pin index	Conventional					PICO				
	#1	#2	#3	#4	#5	#1	#2	#3	#4	#5
Cell 1	2	5	3	-	-	2	5	3	-	-
Cell 2	1	0	0	4	-	1	3	3	4	-
Cell 3	2	3	2	3	3	2	3	2	3	3
Cell 4	1	0	0	1	3	1	3	3	1	4
Cell 5	0	0	0	0	-	3	2	2	5	-

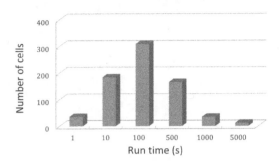

Figure 11: The run time of PICO algorithm for all cells across the entire cell library

Since the MILP-based optimization is implemented at the standard cell level, the optimization runtime for a specific hit point combination is < 0.1 sec. However, the majority of the total runtime is due to the branch and bound method used to enumerate all hit point combinations and the runtime of PICO algorithm for all cells across the library is given as a histogram in Fig. 11. For most cells in the library, the optimization can be finished within 500 sec. Since PICO is a one-time computation per cell, it is worthwhile to extend the framework to the entire library to avoid potential engineering efforts related to pin access design without SADP-aware optimization.

7. CONCLUSION

In this paper, we propose a systematic methodology and introduce two algorithms, PAO for a specific I/O hit point combination and PICO for a standard cell, which maximize the pin access flexibility for a $10nm$ standard cell library. To the best of our knowledge, this is the first work that addresses SADP-aware I/O pin access design. Compared to the conventional approach, we achieve significant improvement in pin accessibility of standard cells for the 10nm technology node, which is likely to use SADP for Metal-2 routing. Our pin access design results also provide maximized flexibility for the routing stage.

8. ACKNOWLEDGEMENTS

This work is supported in part by NSF and SRC.

9. REFERENCES

[1] B. Yu, J.-R. Gao, D. Ding, Y. Ban, J.-s. Yang, K. Yuan, M. Cho, and D. Z. Pan, "Dealing with IC Manufacturability in Extreme Scaling," in *Proceedings of the International Conference on Computer-Aided Design*. ACM, 2012, pp. 240–242.

[2] M. C. Smayling, K. Tsujita, H. Yaegashi, V. Axelrad, T. Arai, K. Oyama, and A. Hara, "Sub-12nm optical lithography with 4x pitch division and SMO-lite," in *SPIE Advanced Lithography*. International Society for Optics and Photonics, 2013, pp. 868 305–868 305.

[3] D. Z. Pan, B. Yu, and J.-R. Gao, "Design for Manufacturing With Emerging Nanolithography," *Computer-Aided Design of Integrated Circuits and Systems, IEEE Transactions on*, vol. 32, no. 10, pp. 1453–1472, 2013.

[4] H. Zhang, Y. Du, M. D. Wong, and R. Topaloglu, "Self-Aligned Double Patterning Decomposition for Overlay Minimization and Hot Spot Detection," in *IEEE/ACM Design Automation Conference (DAC)*, 2011.

[5] Y. Ban, K. Lucas, and D. Z. Pan, "Flexible 2D Layout Decomposition Framework for Spacer-type Double Patterning Lithography," in *IEEE/ACM Design Automation Conference (DAC)*, 2011, pp. 789–794.

[6] Z. Xiao. H. Zhang, Y. Du, and M. D. Wong, "A Polynomial Time Exact Algorithm for Self-Aligned Double Patterning Layout Decomposition," in *ACM International Symposium on Physical Design (ISPD)*, 2012.

[7] J.-R. Gao, B. Yu, and D. Z. Pan, "Self-aligned Double Patterning Layout Decomposition with Complementary E-Beam Lithography," in *IEEE/ACM Asia and South Pacific Design Automation Conference (ASPDAC)*, 2014.

[8] G. Luk-Pat, B. Painter, A. Miloslavsky, P. De Bisschop, A. Beacham, and K. Lucas, "Avoiding wafer-print artifacts in spacer is dielectric (SID) patterning," in *SPIE Advanced Lithography*. International Society for Optics and Photonics, 2013, pp. 868 312–868 312.

[9] M. Mirsaeedi, J. A. Torres, and M. Anis, "Self-aligned double-patterning (SADP) friendly detailed routing," in *Proc. of SPIE*, vol. 7974, 2011.

[10] J.-R. Gao and D. Z. Pan, "Flexible Self-aligned Double Patterning Aware Detailed Routing with Prescribed Layout Planning," in *ACM International Symposium on Physical Design (ISPD)*, 2012.

[11] C. Kodama, H. Ichikawa, K. Nakayama, T. Kotani, S. Nojima, S. Mimotogi, S. Miyamoto, and A. Takahashi, "Self-Aligned Double and Quadruple Patterning-Aware Grid Routing with Hotspots Control," in *IEEE/ACM Asia and South Pacific Design Automation Conference (ASPDAC)*, 2013.

[12] Y. Du, Q. Ma, H. Song, J. Shiely, G. Luk-Pat, A. Miloslavsky, and M. D. Wong, "Spacer-is-dielectric-compliant detailed routing for self-aligned double patterning lithography," in *Proceedings of the 50th Annual Design Automation Conference*. ACM, 2013, p. 93.

[13] Y. Ma, J. Sweis, H. Yoshida, Y. Wang, J. Kye, and H. J. Levinson, "Self-aligned double patterning (SADP) compliant design flow," in *SPIE Advanced Lithography*. International Society for Optics and Photonics, 2012, pp. 832 706–832 706.

[14] D. Nenni, "16nm FinFET versus 20nm Planar!" http://www.semiwiki.com/forum/content/1789-16nm-finfet-versus-20nm-planar.html.

[15] G. Luk-Pat, A. Miloslavsky, B. Painter, L. Lin, P. De Bisschop, and K. Lucas, "Design compliance for spacer is dielectric (SID) patterning," in *SPIE Advanced Lithography*. International Society for Optics and Photonics, 2012, pp. 83 260D–83 260D.

[16] F.-L. Heng, Z. Chen, and G. E. Tellez, "A VLSI artwork legalization technique based on a new criterion of minimum layout perturbation," in *Proceedings of the 1997 international symposium on Physical design*. ACM, 1997, pp. 116–121.

[17] R. S. Ghaida, K. B. Agarwal, S. R. Nassif, X. Yuan, L. W. Liebmann, and P. Gupta, "Layout Decomposition and Legalization for Double-Patterning Technology," *Computer-Aided Design of Integrated Circuits and Systems, IEEE Transactions on*, vol. 32, no. 2, pp. 202–215, 2013.

[18] A. Agarwal, S. Bhat, A. Gray, and I. E. Grossmann, "Automating mathematical program transformations," in *Practical Aspects of Declarative Languages*. Springer, 2010, pp. 134–148.

[19] "Cbc," http://www.coin-or.org/projects/Cbc.xml.

A Highly-Efficient Row-Structure Stencil Planning Approach for E-Beam Lithography with Overlapped Characters

Jian Kuang
Dept. of Computer Science and Engineering
The Chinese University of Hong Kong
Shatin, NT, Hong Kong
jkuang@cse.cuhk.edu.hk

Evangeline F. Y. Young
Dept. of Computer Science and Engineering
The Chinese University of Hong Kong
Shatin, NT, Hong Kong
fyyoung@cse.cuhk.edu.hk

ABSTRACT

Character projection is a key technology to enhance throughput of e-beam lithography, in which characters need to be selected and placed on the stencil. This paper solves the problem of planning for overlapping-aware row-structure stencil, and also considers multi-column cell system for further throughput improvement. We propose an integrated framework to solve the subproblems of character selection, row distribution, single-row ordering and inter-row swapping efficiently. Experiments show that our approach outperforms the existing methods on all the benchmarks. We can achieve significant throughput improvement and up to 1782× speedup comparing with previous works. The average speedup is 704×.

Categories and Subject Descriptors

B.7.2 [**Integrated Circuits**]: Design Aids

Keywords

Design for Manufacturability, E-Beam Lithography, Character Projection, the MCC System

1. INTRODUCTION

Manufacturability is one of the most critical issues in semiconductor industry. As technology advances and the minimum feature size keeps scaling down, it becomes even more challenging. The major printing technique, on the other hand, is still 193nm ArF immersion lithography. To handle the mismatch between current lithography capacity and the feature size in the sub-22nm technology node, double patterning lithography (DPL) and triple patterning lithography (TPL), that decompose one layer of layout into multiple masks, have been proposed for years [8, 11, 3, 7]. However,

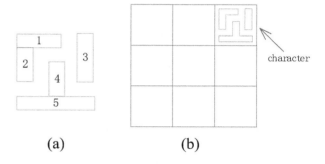

Figure 1: E-beam lithography. (a) The layout is printed by VSB. (b) The character is put on the stencil and printed by CP.

the cost of manufacturing will become much higher with more masks. As a consequence, the next generation lithography (NGL) technologies, such as extreme ultra-violet (EUV) and electron-beam lithography (EBL), are expected to be promising solutions in 14nm/10nm technology node.

However, both EUV and EBL are not ready for mass production yet. The availability of EUV is further delayed by the technological difficulties such as mask blank defects [13]. On the other hand, EBL suffers from the bottleneck of low throughput. Several key technologies, like character projection (CP) and multi-column cell (MCC) system, have been proposed to overcome this limitation.

EBL is a maskless lithography technology that shoots a beam of electrons onto a wafer and directly creates desired shapes there. Benefiting from this, EBL can achieve high resolution with relatively lower cost, compared with the cost of making masks. The total writing time of a layout is proportional to the number of shots that are made, thus fewer shots means higher throughput. Conventional EBL use variable shaped beam (VSB), by which every shot can only create one rectangle, hence the total number of shots will be unacceptable for high-volume manufacturing. CP is then proposed to handle this problem. With CP, various characters will be pre-designed. Each character is composed of some complex patterns. A limited number of characters can be selected and placed on the stencil. A character on the stencil needs only one shot to be printed, whereas a character not on the stencil still needs VSB. CP can improve

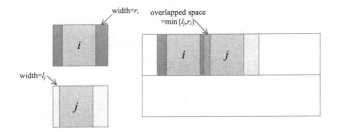

Figure 2: Overlapped characters and row-structure stencil.

the throughput of EBL greatly. For example, the patterns in Figure 1(a) needs 5 shots by VSB, but if a character is designed to contain the patterns and is put on the stencil, as shown in Figure 1(b), only 1 shot is needed. Note that a character may appear more than once in a layout, thus many more shots can actually be saved by CP.

There are a lot of optimization problems with CP. First of all, there will be restrictions on design rules to allow common CP patterns in the layout. Furthermore, character design is also a hard problem and attracts extensive research in these few years [6, 5, 2]. After the characters are ready, how to select appropriate characters and place them on the stencil (stencil planning) is another big challenge. In practice, each character has some blank areas surrounding it. By sharing the blank areas, the characters can be overlapped to save more stencil space and thus more characters can be placed on the stencil [4]. When CP is applied to standard cell design, each character usually contains the patterns of one cell. All characters have the same size and uniform top and bottom blank areas. Vertical overlapping can thus be optimized easily and only horizontal overlapping need to be considered [12, 10]. In this case, the stencil can be viewed as a set of rows, and the selected characters need to be packed into the rows. As shown in Figure 2, two characters i and j are placed in one row, overlapping with each other. Note that the uniform top and bottom blank areas are omitted *w.l.o.g* as in the previous work [10].

The MCC system [9] is a recent extension of EBL, in which a layout is divided into several regions, and several CPs print on these regions in parallel. The actual printing time of the layout is the maximum printing time among these regions, which is obviously shorter than conventional EBL. Because of the high complexity of designing stencil, the stencils for different CPs will contain the same set of characters and the characters will share the same placement. Therefore, for the MCC system, we still just have one stencil to design, but it is harder than that for conventional EBL, since the effects on different regions need to be considered simultaneously.

1.1 Previous Work

Overlapping-aware stencil planning (OSP) for row-structure stencil was referred as 1D-OSP problem. Yuan *et al.* [12] proposed the first systematic study on this topic, but the greedy and heuristic methods that were used are time consuming and lack of global view. E-BLOW [10] was then developed for OSP in the MCC system. The problem was formulated as an LP and solved iteratively by successive relaxation. However, the optimality loss because of rounding after LP is unavoidable and the iterative process will be

relatively slow. Furthermore, it failed to recognize the difference between conventional EBL and the MCC system. So, although the approach in [10] already performs much better than that in [12], the quality and efficiency can be further optimized for both types of EBL.

1.2 Our Contributions

In this paper, we propose a new approach to solve 1D-OSP, our main contributions can be summarized as follows:

- We propose an efficient and optimal algorithm to solve the single-row ordering problem under a condition. We will also present a simple way to distribute the characters into rows such that the condition can be satisfied.

- We present a greedy approach to solve the character selection problem and an accelerated ILP method to improve the solution quality.

- We propose an inter-row swapping algorithm to improve the result further. It is a deterministic algorithm instead of a random approach as in [12].

- Our approach performs very well in experiments, with remarkable reduction in shot numbers and up to $1782\times$ speedup comparing with the most updated result.

The rest of the paper is organized as follows. Section 2 introduces some preliminaries for the 1D-OSP problem. Section 3 describes the whole stencil planning approach. Section 4 reports experimental results and Section 5 concludes this paper.

2. PRELIMINARIES

First, some notations will be introduced. Suppose that the character design has already been done, and a set of n characters $C = \{c_1, c_2, ..., c_i, ..., c_n\}$ is given. The width of a character is w^1. The left and right blank length of c_i are l_i and r_i respectively. A stencil consisting of k rows is given. We need to select a set of characters $C' \subseteq C$ to put into the rows of the stencil. If c_i is not on the stencil and printed by VSB, it needs v_i shots, otherwise it will be printed by CP, and only 1 shot is needed. Suppose that character c_i appears t_i times in the layout. If only VSB is used, the original shot number for the whole layout will be:

$$S_o = \sum_{i=1}^{n} t_i \cdot v_i \qquad (1)$$

Putting c_i on the stencil will reduce the total number of shots, this reduction is called the *gain* of c_i. The gain can be calculated as:

$$gain_i = (v_i - 1) \cdot t_i \qquad (2)$$

Notice that in this paper we assume that CP shot and VSB shot have equal cost, as in the previous works[12, 10], but our approach can be easily extended to process CP shot that requires longer time. After putting the characters in C', the total shot number will be:

$$S = S_o - \sum_{c_i \in C'} gain_i = \sum_{i=1}^{n} t_i \cdot v_i - \sum_{c_i \in C'} (v_i - 1) \cdot t_i \qquad (3)$$

---

[1] Although in this paper we assume that all characters have the same with, which is also true in all the benchmarks given, our formulations and algorithms can be easily extended to handle characters with different width.

Characters can be overlapped when they are put into rows. Suppose character i is on the left of j, the overlapping space between them will be $\min\{l_j, r_i\}$ (Figure 2). The total length of the characters in a row after compacting cannot exceed the width of the stencil W.

The notations for the MCC system will be slightly different. The layout is divided into m regions: $R_1, R_2, ..., R_j, ...R_m$. Character c_i appears t_i^j times in the region R_j. The shot number of R_j after stencil design will be:

$$S_j = \sum_{i=1}^{n} t_i^j \cdot v_i - \sum_{c_i \in C'} (v_i - 1) \cdot t_i^j \qquad (4)$$

where $(v_i - 1) \cdot t_i^j$ is the gain of c_i in R_j. The total shot number of the layout that we want to minimize is:

$$S = \max_j \{S_j\} \qquad (5)$$

Now we can give the problem formulation of 1D-OSP.

PROBLEM 1. *Given a set C of characters, and a stencil of k rows and width W, select a subset of C and decide their positions in the rows of the stencil, such that the width of the stencil is not exceeded. The objective is to minimize the objective equation (3) for conventional EBL or to minimize the objective equation (5) for the MCC system.*

3. THE STENCIL PLANNING APPROACH

In this section, we give details of our approach for 1D-OSP. We first solve several subproblems, and then integrate them together.

3.1 Single-Row Ordering

After we select m characters into a particular row, we need to minimize their total length in order to make sure that all characters are within the row and try to put more characters into the row. This problem was formulated as a traveling salesman problem in [12], which is well-known to be NP-hard (This is also an important reason why the approach in [12] is much slower than that in [10] and our approach). However, we will show below that this problem can be solved optimally in a special case.

Suppose the characters in a row are $\{c_1, c_2, ..., c_i, ..., c_p\}$, then the total length of these characters with a specified order is

$$L = p \cdot w - TotalOverlappingSpace \qquad (6)$$

Since $p \cdot w$ is a constant, minimizing L is equivalent to maximizing $TotalOverlappingSpace$. To solve this problem, bipartite matching between the left and right blanks seems to be a good candidate approach. We describe our matching-based method that can find the optimal $TotalOverlappingSpace$ under a reasonable constraint as follows:

Step 1: Construct a bipartite graph $G=(U,V,E)$. Each character c_i has two nodes u_i and v_i in U and V, representing the left and right blank area of c_i respectively. Every node is weighted: $weight(u_i) = l_i$, $weight(v_i) = r_i$. Edge set $E = \{(u_i, v_j) : i \neq j\}$. Edges are also weighted: $weight(e(u,v)) = \min\{weight(u), weight(v)\}$. An example is shown in Figure 3(a), where there are 8 nodes representing the left and right blank areas of c_1, c_2, c_3 and c_4 respectively.

By now, one possible thought is to find a *maximum weighted bipartite matching* on G, which can be done in polynomial

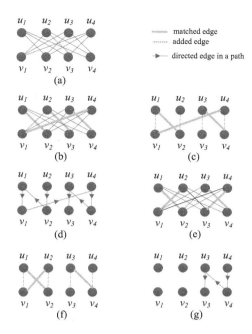

Figure 3: Illustration for the graph matching method. (a)Construction of the bipartite graph. (b)-(d) Successful matching. (e)-(g) Failed matching.

time. If u_i and v_j are matched, the left blank area of c_i and the right blank area of c_j should be put together (thus c_i is on the right of c_j) and an overlapping space with length $= weight(e(u_i, v_j))$ will be realized. For example, the matching solution in Figure 3(b) means that c_1 should be put on the right of c_2, *etc.* With the matching solution, we can modify the graph to find the order of placing the characters. First we can remove the edges in G that are not in the matching solution, and then add edges $E' = \{(u_i, v_i) : 1 \leq i \leq m\}$ to G. The resulting graph of our example is shown in Figure 3(c). The least-weighted edge in the matching solution should be removed, since the matching edges together with the edges in E' form a loop in this example but the characters are supposed to be placed in a row. Thus we choose to give up the smallest overlapping space to break the loop. For example, edge $e(u_2, v_3)$ is removed in Figure 3(c). Then we can check the directed path p from the degree-1 node in U to another degree-1 node in V. If p covers all the nodes in G, the optimal order of the characters can be derived from the order of the nodes appeared in p. For example, the path from u_2 to v_3 in Figure 3(d) implies the order $c_2 \rightarrow c_1 \rightarrow c_4 \rightarrow c_3$. However, this method will work only when p covers all the nodes. For example, if the maximum matching solution is as shown in Figure 3(e), the modified graph will be like the one shown in Figure 3(f). Here we cannot find any single path p that covers all the nodes in G (see Figure 3(g)), thus a full ordering of the characters cannot be obtained from the matching solution. Although the method above does not work in general, it can be modified to give the optimal solution effectively under some reasonable constraint on the left and right blanks as described below:

Step 2: Let $weight_{min}$ be the minimum weight among all the nodes in G. Update the weight of every node v as $weight(v) - weight_{min}$. This can simplify the graph and

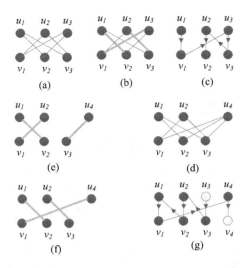

(a)   (b)   (c)

(e)   (d)

(f)   (g)

Figure 4: Illustration for the proof of Theorem 1. The legend is the same as Figure 3. (a)-(c) Case 1. (d)-(g) Case 2.

will not lose any optimality since the overlapping space of the minimum blank area can always be achieved between any two adjacent characters in any order.

Step 3: Remove those nodes with weight 0 and their corresponding edges. There is no need to consider the removed nodes and edges further.

Step 4: Update all the edge weights according the new node weights to obtain graph G'.

We have the following theorem about the maximum matching on the graph G'.

THEOREM 1. *When all the edges in G' are with equal weight, the maximum weighted matching on G' can always give a character ordering with the optimal overlapping space.*

PROOF. Let N_U and N_V be the numbers of nodes of G' in U and V respectively. Let DS be the set of characters that have corresponding nodes in both U and V, e.g., in Figure 4(d), $DS = \{c_1, c_2\}$. Suppose all the edges in G' are with the same weight w_e. There are two cases.

Case 1: $N_U = N_V = |DS|$. An example is shown in Figure 4(a). In this case, the maximum weighted matching $w_e \cdot DS$ can be easily achieved as shown in Figure 4(b). With the matching solution, just as what we did above (adding and removing some edges), we can get the path p and the order, e.g., we can get order $c_1 \to c_3 \to c_2$ as shown in Figure 4(c), which is resulted from the graph in Figure 4(b). Obviously, the optimal overlapping space $w_e \cdot (|DS| - 1)$ is achieved.

Case 2: $N_U \neq |DS|$ or $N_V \neq |DS|$. An example is shown in Figure 4(d). The optimal overlapping space in this case is $w_e \cdot \min\{N_U, N_V\}$. We first divide the nodes into two groups, the nodes corresponding to the characters in DS are in group A, others are in group B. Then we do two matchings on the two subgraphs induced from the two groups of nodes. The first matching is just like the matching in case 1, the second one is trivial since all the nodes in group B are independent from each other. Figure 4(e) shows a possible matching result on the graph in Figure 4(d), where only matched edges are shown and a loop between u_1, u_2, v_1 and v_2 exists. If we just remove one matched edge to break the loop like what

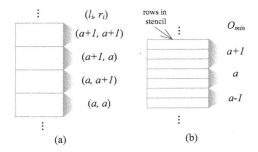

Figure 5: Row Distribution. (a) Sorted list of characters. (b) Groups of rows.

we did in case 1, we will get suboptimal solution. Actually, we can exchange one node in U (V) of group A and another node in U (V) of group B to break the loop and get the optimal overlapping space, e.g., we exchange u_2 and u_4 as shown in Figure 4(f). We can then add back the removed nodes and get the path. In this way the optimal order can be found (see Figure 4(g), where uncolored nodes are the ones that were removed previously). □

Note that there is no need to really call a matching solver. The matching solution can be obtained following the steps in our proof.

3.2 Row Distribution

3.2.1 Constraint Satisfaction

With Theorem 1, an immediate problem is how to ensure that the constraint will be satisfied. In the following, we will first present a simple sorting-based approach to solve this problem. We sort all the selected characters to be put on the stencil according to the following criteria: c_i is before c_j iff $l_i > l_j$ or $(l_i = l_j) \wedge (r_i > r_j)$. In practice, the length of the left and right blanks of a character c_i are integers and very similar to each other, typically we have $|l_i - r_i| \leq 1$[2]. Thus a sorted list of the characters will look like the one shown in Figure 5(a), in which characters are divided into clusters, e.g., characters with left blank of length $a+1$ and right blank of length a form a cluster. When we distribute the characters into rows following the sorted order, characters in clusters that are close to one another in the sorted list will be placed into a row. Let N_c and N_r be the numbers of characters in a cluster and in a row respectively. In practice, for any N_c and N_r, we always have $N_r \leq 2 \cdot N_c$, which means that there are not too many characters in a row, so characters in a row will be from at most three neighbouring clusters[3], e.g., the three clusters at the bottom of Figure 5(a). In this way, the constraint in our optimal row ordering method will be satisfied, which is, edges in the graph G' are of equal weight 1.

Beside satisfying the constraint, another advantage of our distribution method is that all the blank areas of the charac-

---

[2]This is also an observation in the real benchmarks.

[3]If the characters in a row come from four or more clusters, e.g., the four clusters shown in Figure 5(a), the characters in the middle 2 clusters must be fully used by this row, so we will have $N_r > N_{c1} + N_{c2}$, where N_{c1} and N_{c2} are N_c of the clusters $(a+1, a)$ and $(a, a+1)$ respectively, which is obviously a contradiction.

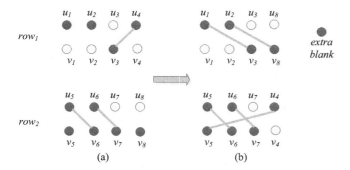

(a)   (b)

Figure 6: (a) Before redistribution, 3 pairs of extra blanks are overlapped in total. (b) After redistribution, 5 pairs of extra blanks are overlapped. Note that nodes corresponding to characters without extra blanks are not shown, so there may be more than 4 characters in each row.

ters are distributed regularly, thus there will be less wasting.

3.2.2 Redistribution

By the greedy distribution above, each row can be optimally ordered independently, but the relationships between rows are not considered, thus redistribution is needed. Let O_{min} denote the minimum blank area among the characters in a row. After the distribution, the rows of the stencil can be divided into groups according to different O_{min}, e.g., the group with O_{min} being a has 2 rows in Figure 5(b). We call the extra part of the blank area other than O_{min} of each character the *extra blank*. Following the steps in our proof of Theorem 1, N_U and N_V will be the numbers of left and right extra blanks in a row, respectively. Extra blanks are important for us to increase $TotalOverlappingSpace$ and thus to put more characters into a row, but they may be wasted because of unbalanced distribution, e.g., in a group, one row has $N_U = 3$ and $N_V = 1$, and another row has $N_U = 2$ and $N_V = 4$, as shown in Figure 6(a). After redistribution (exchanging c_4 and c_8 in this example), there will be more extra blanks overlapped (Figure 6(b)), and $TotalOverlappingSpace$ of both row_1 and row_2 will be increased.

To make full use of extra blanks, we will redistribute the characters among the rows in a group so as to maximize the number of extra characters (denoted as x) we can add to the group. This is not a trivial step. First of all, the value of x is constrained by the number of rows in the group. When a group has r_g rows, the maximum value of x we will test is $2 \cdot r_g$, because we found that one row can take at most 2 more characters through redistribution in practice. Secondly, as one row can only take a limited number of characters because the row length cannot be exceeded, so even if there are enough extra blanks available, we might not be able to distribute them as desired. For example, as shown in Figure 6, if we want to make 5 pairs of overlapped extra blanks in row_1 such that the $TotalOverlappingSpace$ of this row will be increased enough and one more character can be put in, one way is to put the 8 characters $c_1 \sim c_8$ into row_1, but doing this may violate the constraint of row width since row_1 can only take no more than 7 characters. Finally, the characters with extra blanks are with different types. Some have extra blanks only on the left or on the right, whereas the oth-

ers have extra blanks on both sides. As a result, they need to be combined and utilized carefully. For instance, when $r_g = 2$, to test whether x can be 3, we need to consider the extra blanks available and the extra blanks that we need, and check how the characters with different types of extra blanks in the group can be redistributed such that one row will have enough space to take two more characters and another row will have enough room to accommodate one more character, without any violation in the stencil width.

Notice that after redistribution within each group, characters in each row can still be ordered optimally as the constraint in Theorem 1 is still satisfied.

3.3 Inter-Row Swapping

After row distribution, there is still some room to improve the placement by swapping characters and putting in more characters. This is because a character in one group may be more useful in another group, e.g., character c_i with $l_i = r_i = a + 1$ has no extra blank in the group of $O_{min} = a + 1$, but it has two extra blanks if it is in the group of $O_{min} = a$.

There are two types of swapping: (1) The left (right) blank area of the leftmost (rightmost) character of a row is not used because there is no overlapping in the two ends of a row, so we can replace the leftmost (rightmost) character of a row by one with smaller left (right) blank area, and the length of the characters in this row will not be affected. (2) When the length L of the characters in a row is smaller than W, after we replace some characters in this row by some others with smaller blank areas, although $TotalOverlappingSpace$ will decrease and thus L will increase, L can still be not exceeding W.

After replacing, the replaced characters can be used in other groups such that these groups will have more extra blanks available to take more extra characters. Our swapping method will find the swapping candidates in a deterministic way, thus randomness as in the method of [12] is avoided.

3.4 Character Selection

The above three steps tell how to distribute characters into rows, how to order the characters in one row, and how to swap characters between rows. However, we still need to resolve a bigger problem of selecting a subset of C of characters to put on the stencil. To solve this problem, assuming that the average blank length among all the characters in C is b_{avg}, we first calculate the average number of characters n_r that can be put in a row by

$$w \cdot n_r - b_{avg} \cdot (n_r - 1) \leq W \qquad (7)$$

Then the number of characters to select (denoted as n_s) can be estimated by $k \cdot n_r$. However, this can be inaccurate and affect the performance. Therefore, we will first select n_s characters, try to put them onto the stencil, and then adjust n_s according to the actual number of characters that can be placed. After that, we will select again and repeat the whole process. Then we introduce our character selection methods for conventional EBL and the MCC system respectively, both of which are based on the gain of each character.

3.4.1 Selection for the Convention EBL

For conventional EBL, we calculate gains by Equation (3) and rank all characters by their gains in descending order.

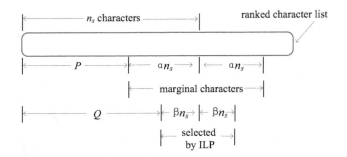

Figure 7: Illustration for marginal characters and ILP selecting characters.

Then we will select the highly ranked ones. This method is simple but effective for conventional EBL, in which the whole layout is considered as one region. It rarely happens that replacing a character with a higher gain by one with a lower gain can increase the number of characters in the stencil and reduce S.

3.4.2 Selection for the MCC System

For the MCC system, we first calculate the total gain of a character by summing up the gains of this character in all regions. However, we cannot simply use the same ranking method as above, because the objective now is to minimize the maximum shot number among several regions, and a character with high total gain may not be actually good. Thus, as shown in Figure 7, we first select a set P of characters with absolutely high total gains, and then identify a set of marginal characters next in the rank according to a parameter α called the *marginal character ratio*. After selecting P, we will update the gains of the marginal characters, with the information of the shot number in each region, assuming that the selected characters in P are already on the stencil. The gain of a character in a region with higher shot number will be considered more. The updated gain will be more accurate than the previous simple summation, and marginal characters can thus be chosen more effectively.

However, for large datasets, as the selection ratio $sr = n_s/|C|$ decreases, the selection process will become harder and the above marginal characters identification method is not sufficient. To handle these datasets with small sr, we present below an ILP based selection method. Similarly, we first select a set Q of characters, and then formulate the problem as an accurate ILP to select $\beta \cdot n_s$ characters out of $2\beta \cdot n_s$ ones (Figure 7). Since solving ILP is time-consuming, β is set to be smaller than α. The ILP formulation is as follows:

$$minimize\ S, \quad subject\ to$$

$$S \geq S_j, \quad 1 \leq j \leq m \tag{a}$$

$$S_j = S'_j - \sum_{i=1}^{2\beta \cdot n_s} y_i \cdot (v_i - 1) \cdot t_i^j, \quad 1 \leq j \leq m \tag{b}$$

$$\sum_{i=1}^{2\beta \cdot n_s} y_i \leq \beta \cdot n_s \tag{c}$$

$$y_i = 0\ or\ 1, \quad 1 \leq i \leq 2\beta \cdot n_s \tag{d}$$

In the formulation, y_i is a binary variable. It is 1 if c_i is selected, 0 otherwise. m is the number of regions. S'_j and S_j are the shot numbers of R_j before and after the ILP selection respectively. Equation (b) is used to update the shot numbers. Equation (c) is used to constrain the selected character number to be no more than $\beta \cdot n_s$. The number of variables is $O(\beta \cdot n_s)$. The ILP selection will be activated only when sr is smaller than a threshold γ. Parameters α, β and γ are set to 0.1, 0.05 and 0.8 respectively in our implementation.

We employ Gurobi Optimizer [1] as our ILP solver, which will terminate when the gap g between the lower and upper objective bound is achieved[4]. The solving process may be slow even for a small β, hence we use a larger parameter g (double of the original one in our implementation), by which the optimization process can be accelerated a lot but the quality loss is negligible in practice.

3.5 Overall Flow

Our algorithm can be summarized as follows. First, we calculate the number n_s and select n_s characters. Then, we distribute the selected characters into rows of the stencil. In each row, our optimal ordering method is applied. After that, we swap characters between rows to further improve the quality.

4. EXPERIMENTAL RESULTS

The proposed approach is implemented in C++, on a 2.39 GHz Linux machine with 48 GB memory. We test it on the benchmarks provided by the authors of the most updated work [10], and compare it with previous works. The shot numbers of [12] and [10] are taken from the published results. To compare runtime with [10], we run the executable file of [10] provided by the authors on our machine. We do not compare runtime with [12] because [10] is already very much faster than [12] as reported in [10].

Result comparisons are shown in Table 1, where r# is the number of rows, c# reports the number of characters on the stencil, s# denotes shot number, time is wall-clock time, reduce1 represents the reduction of shot number over [12] while reduce2 denotes the reduction over [10]. 1D-1~1D-4 are benchmarks for conventional EBL, while 1M-1~1M-8 are benchmarks for the MCC system. The region number is set as 10 for the MCC system. For the benchmarks 1D-1~1D-4 and 1M-1~1M-4, there are 1000 candidate characters, and the stencil size is set as $1000\mu m \times 1000\mu m$; for 1M-5~1M-8, there are 4000 candidate characters and the stencil size is set as $2000\mu m \times 2000\mu m$.

Character numbers on the stencil are just reported for reference because they are not necessarily related to the main objective, *i.e.*, shot numbers. For example, if the characters with the most blank space are selected, there will be more characters on the stencil, but the shot number will also be larger. So it is about trade-offs between blank spaces and gains of characters. There is no way to compare the character numbers on the stencil with previous works, because the selected characters are different.

As shown in the table, for shot numbers, we get the best results on all the benchmarks, and we can achieve 29.6% reduction on average compared with [12] and 9.9% reduction on average compared with [10], thus the throughput for both types of E-beam lithography can be improved significantly. For runtime, comparing with [10], we can attain up

---

[4]The details can be found in [1].

Table 1: Result comparisons

benchmark		TCAD'12[12]		DAC'13[10]			ours					
data	r#	c#	s#	c#	s#	time(s)	c#	s#	reduce1(%)	reduce2(%)	time(s)	speedup
1D-1	28	926	50809	934	29536	3.18	940	19095	62.4	35.4	0.005	636×
1D-2	27	854	93465	863	44544	3.31	864	35295	62.2	20.8	0.005	662×
1D-3	25	749	152376	758	78704	6.98	757	69301	54.5	11.9	0.005	1396×
1D-4	24	687	193494	699	107460	6.26	703	92523	52.2	13.9	0.005	1252×
1M-1	28	926	53333	938	45243	4.61	938	39026	26.8	13.7	0.01	461×
1M-2	27	854	95963	868	81636	6.79	864	77997	18.7	4.5	0.01	679×
1M-3	25	749	156700	769	140079	13.76	758	138256	11.8	1.3	0.56*	25×
1M-4	24	687	196686	707	179890	12.44	698	176228	10.4	2.0	0.36*	35×
1M-5	54	3629	255208	3650	227456	38.52	3660	204114	20.0	10.3	0.03	1284×
1M-6	52	3346	417456	3388	373324	53.45	3382	357829	14.3	4.2	0.03	1782×
1M-7	49	2986	644288	3044	570730	63.52	3016	568339	11.8	0.4	0.59*	108×
1M-8	47	2734	809721	2799	734411	55.27	2760	731483	9.7	0.4	0.42*	132×
Avg.	-	-	-	-	-	-	-	-	29.6	9.9	-	704×

* ILP selection is activated.

to 1782× speedup. Average speedup is 704×. Notice that runtime for 1M-3, 1M-4, 1M-7 and 1M-8 are longer than that for the others because ILP selection is activated for these benchmarks. However, since the ILP selection is only used to select a very small part of the characters and the number of variables is linearly related to the number of selected characters, the ILP formulation has a small size and can be solved very quickly.

For some of the benchmarks, although the numbers of shots are reduced significantly, the percentages of reductions are not that much compared with others. This is because in these benchmarks, there are relatively more characters that cannot be put on the stencil, and they contribute to the shot numbers a lot, so the the large shot numbers are inevitable.

For a stencil planning approach, speed is not so important as solution quality. However, as the design of circuits becomes increasingly complicated and the number of patterns explodes, the problem size of stencil planning will also gets larger, and efficiency and scalability of a approach is thus crucial. Furthermore, if we consider redesign of layout and characters, an efficient approach like ours is very beneficial and highly desirable.

5. CONCLUSIONS

In this paper, 1D-OSP problem for E-beam lithography is studied. Several efficient algorithms are proposed to solve the subproblems of 1D-OSP. Experiments verify that our approach is highly efficient and very effective, through which remarkable improvement of throughput can be achieved. As EBL is widely recognized as a promising solution of the next generation lithography, we expect that this result can benefit the industry on manufacturing and attract more research on EBL-related physical design.

6. REFERENCES

[1] Available online: http://www.gurobi.com.

[2] P. Du, W. Zhao, S.-H. Weng, C.-K. Cheng, and R. Graham. Character design and stamp algorithms for character projection electron-beam lithography. In *Proc. ASPDAC*, 2012.

[3] S. Fang, Y. Chang, and W. Chen. A novel layout decomposition algorithm for triple patterning lithography. In *Pro. DAC*, 2012.

[4] A. Fujimura, T. Mitsuhashi, K. Yoshida, S. Matsushita, L. L. Chau, T. D. T. Nguyen, and D. MacMillen. Stencil design and method for improving character density for cell projection charged particle beam lithography. U.S. Patent 20090325085, Jan. 2010.

[5] T. Fujino, Y. Kajiya, and M. Yoshikawa. Character-build standard-cell layout technique for high-throughput character-projection eb lithography. In *Proc. SPIE*, 2005.

[6] R. Inanami, S. Magoshi, S. Kousai, A. Ando, T. Nakasugi, I. Mori, K. Sugihara, and A. Miura. Maskless lithography: estimation of the number of shots for each layer in a logic device with character-projection-type low-energy electron-beam direct writing system. In *Proc. SPIE*, 2003.

[7] J. Kuang and E. F. Y. Young. An efficient layout decomposition approach for triple patterning lithography. In *Proc. DAC*, 2013.

[8] X. Tang and M. Cho. Optimal layout decomposition for double patterning technology. In *Proc. ICCAD*, 2011.

[9] A. Yamada, Y. Oae, T. Okawa, M. Takizawa, and M. Yamabe. Evaluation of throughput improvement by mcc and cp in multicolumn e-beam exposure system. In *Proc. SPIE*, 2010.

[10] B. Yu, K. Yuan, J. Gao, and D. Z. Pan. E-blow: e-beam lithography overlapping aware stencil planning for mcc system. In *Proc. DAC*, 2013.

[11] B. Yu, K. Yuan, B. Zhang, D. Ding, , and D. Z. Pan. Layout decomposition for triple patterning lithography. In *Proc. ICCAD*, 2011.

[12] K. Yuan, B. Yu, and D. Z. Pan. E-beam lithography stencil planning and optimization with overlapped characters. *TCAD*, 31(2):167–179, Feb 2012.

[13] H. Zhang, Y. Du, M. D. F. Wong, Y. Deng, and P. Mangat. Layout small-angle rotation and shift for euv defect mitigation. In *Proc. ICCAD*, 2012.

Carbon Nanotube Computer: Transforming Scientific Discoveries into Working Systems

Subhasish Mitra

Department of Electrical Engineering and Department of Computer Science
Stanford University
Stanford CA
subh@stanford.edu

ABSTRACT

Carbon Nanotube Field Effect Transistors (CNFETs) are excellent candidates for building highly energy-efficient future electronic systems. Unfortunately, carbon nanotubes (CNTs) are subject to substantial inherent imperfections that pose major obstacles to the design of robust and very large-scale CNFET digital systems:

- It is nearly impossible to guarantee perfect alignment and positioning of all CNTs. This limitation introduces stray conducting paths, resulting in incorrect circuit functionality.

- CNTs can be metallic or semiconducting depending on chirality. Metallic CNTs cause shorts resulting in excessive leakage and incorrect circuit functionality.

A combination of design and processing techniques overcomes these challenges by creating robust CNFET digital circuits that are immune to these inherent imperfections. This imperfection-immune design paradigm enables the first experimental demonstration of the carbon nanotube computer, and, more generally, arbitrary digital systems that can be built using CNFETs. Monolithically-integrated three-dimensional CNFET circuits will also be discussed.

This research was performed at Stanford University in collaboration with Prof. H.-S. Philip Wong and several graduate students.

Categories and Subject Descriptors

B.7 [**Hardware**]: Integrated Circuits

Keywords

Carbon Nanotube ; Imperfection-Immune Design ; Logic Design

ISPD'14, March 30–April 2, 2014, Petaluma, CA, USA.
ACM 978-1-4503-2592-9/14/03.
http://dx.doi.org/10.1145/2560519.2565872.

Making a Difference in EDA – A Thank You to Bryan Preas for His Contributions to the Profession

Michael J Lorenzetti
Mentor Graphics Corp
1811 Pike Road
Longmont CO 80501
720-494-1118
mike_lorenzetti@mentor.com

ABSTRACT

This presentation will review the numerous contributions that Bryan Preas has made to the EDA profession.

Categories and Subject Descriptors

A.0 [**General Literature**]: General Literature – *Biographies/autobiographies*

General Terms

Management, Standardization.

Keywords

Physical Design Automation, the EDA profession.

1. INTRODUCTION

I have had the privilege to serve with Bryan Preas on various EDA professional committees over the years, primarily the Design Automation Conference (DAC) Executive Committee and ACM SIGDA Board of Directors. Not only has he been tireless in his efforts with these endeavors, but he changed the direction of the group or activity and left it better off than when he found it.

For example, he recognized early on the need for a textbook for the numerous graduate courses being taught in the 1980's. He set out to recruit the experts needed to write the individual chapters and took on the editing task himself. The resulting textbook [1] became the required text for several graduate courses in Physical Design Automation Algorithms across the country and was the basis for one of the first DAC all-day tutorials.

As a member of the Design Automation Conference Program Committee, he helped assemble the first compendium of DAC papers [2] to help commemorate their 25th Anniversary. This volume provides a history of the seminal work first published at DAC.

Still not happy with the availability of DA literature to EDA researchers and practitioners, he pushed ACM SIGDA toward putting the entire 27 years of EDA literature on CD-ROM. Through tremendous effort he, along with his wife, Kathy, put all the DA literature on searchable CD-ROMs for anyone to access.

As an officer of ACM SIGDA, he enhanced the scholarship and travel grant programs within that organization and helped move those programs into to the Design Automation Conference itself so they could grow and expand with it.

As attendees to this event well know, he has been the primary force behind the effort to create a set of benchmarks to allow side-by-side comparisons of layout algorithms. He did this by recruiting professionals from industry to get real-life (committed to manufacture) circuits [3] from their companies and made them available to EDA researchers. He also helped devise a set of comparison metrics to make the discussions meaningful.

2. SUMMARY

Bryan has not only given time and tireless effort to the design automation profession, he has changed the profession for the better. He did this by helping others succeed through his advocacy of scholarships, workshops, benchmarks and accessibility of EDA literature. It is one thing to advance the state of the art through your own research and publications (and Bryan has certainly done that) but it really accelerates the advancement of the state of the art when you facilitate the work of others and grow the EDA community itself. There are, of course, countless individuals who were essential to these efforts as well, but it was often Bryan's vision that kept our eyes on the horizon.

3. REFERENCES

[1] Preas, B. and Lorenzetti, M. *Physical Design Automation of VLSI Systems*, 1988, The Benjamin/Cummings Publishing Company, Inc

[2] *25 Years of Electronic Design Automation*, 1988, The Association for Computing Machinery, ISBN 0-89791-267-5.

[3] Preas, B,."Benchmarks for Cell-Based layout Systems" In *24th Design Automation Conference Proceeding*, pages 319-320, 1987.

ISPD'14, March 30–April 2, 2014, Petaluma, California, USA.
ACM 978-1-4503-2592-9/14/03.
http://dx.doi.org/10.1145/2560519.2568051

From Design to Design Automation

Jason Cong
Computer Science Department and
Electrical Engineering Department
University of California, Los Angeles
cong@cs.ucla.edu

ABSTRACT

I had the pleasure to work at the Xerox Palo Alto Research Center (PARC) as a summer intern in 1987 with Dr. Bryan Preas. One of the many valuable lessons that I learned through that summer internship is that as a researcher in electronic design automation (EDA), there is a tremendous value to be had from an involvement in VLSI circuit and system designs. This involvement guarantees a first-hand opportunity to discover and formulate new and insightful EDA problems, and to develop practical and impactful solutions. This experience had a great influence on my career as an EDA researcher. In this paper, I would like to share several examples of research projects that I directed at UCLA which followed the principle of starting from design to gain insight and inspiration for design automation.

Categories and Subject Descriptors

B.5.2 [**Design Aids**]: Automatic synthesis, optimization

General Terms

Algorithms and Design

Keywords

Design, design automation, Boolean matching, buffer planning

1. INTRODUCTION

I began my graduate study at the University of Illinois at Urbana-Champaign in the winter of 1986, and my research area was in VLSI CAD (computer-aided design) or electronic design automation. In my second year as a graduate student, I received an offer to work at the Xerox Palo Alto Research Center (PARC) as a summer intern, and I was fortunate to have Dr. Bryan Preas as my mentor. He was already a highly respected researcher in design

automation at that time, with much pioneering work in IC placement and routing (e.g., [1][2][3][4][5][6]). Prior to my internship at PARC, I had just completed my first research project on three-layer channel routing; this became my MS thesis and was later published in ICCAD'87 [7]. I was in the process of looking for the next research problem, and although I had a paper accepted for publication in a top EDA conference, I had never done any VLSI design. Like many other graduate students in EDA, I was reading the leading journals and conference proceedings in the field and looking for opportunities for improvement of published results on some well-formulated problems. When I began my internship at PARC, the first assignment that Bryan gave me was to create some small circuit designs using the in-house VLSI design automation (DA) system developed at PARC, named DATools. It was a very advanced DA system at that time and allowed the designers to go from schematics to layout in a fairly automated fashion. This was a great learning experience for me, and I was exposed to many important concepts and problems that were totally new, such as the hierarchical design methodology, cell library design and selection, static timing analysis, and layout verification. It also gave me a clear perspective on the important factors that affect the chip area, which was the main optimization objective those days.

After I successfully completed the full design cycle, I was assigned to investigate whether one could improve the standard cell global routing package. At that time, the standard cell design methodology was just becoming popular. The Timberwolf placement package developed at UC Berkeley [9] based on simulated annealing was a big success, and it improved many in-house standard placement tools, including the one used inside of DATools. But there were relatively fewer studies on standard cell global routing. At that time, many standard cell based designs were done with one metal layer, and the two-metal-layer process had just become available. Feedthrough cells were needed to complete routing between cells in different rows. At that time, most of the standard cell global routing tools focused on wirelength minimization. Some considered feedthrough minimization. From my limited design experience gained at the beginning of that summer, I made the observations that (i) the chip area is determined by the maximum cell row length and the total channel density, (ii) the total channel density is a better metric to optimize than the total wirelength, and (iii) feedthrough assignment affects both the maximum row length and the total channel density. Based on these observations, I developed a new standard cell global routing algorithm that considered the interplay between feedthrough assignment and routing topology optimization, and we also proposed a novel optimization technique called iterative deletion for total channel density optimization[1]. This algorithm considerably outperforms both the standard cell global routing tool used in DATools and in the Timberwolf package [9]; it was selected as a highlighted paper for ICCAD'88 [10].

My summer internship with Bryan Preas was a great experience in multiple ways. First, I was able to publish another major research paper, which became a chapter in my PhD dissertation. Second, it was exciting to see my algorithm being used to generate real chip layout (as part of the Xerox PARC DATools System)—all of which was such a gratifying experience to a young PhD student. More importantly, I learned this valuable lesson: As a researcher in EDA, there is a tremendous benefit to be gained from an involvement in VLSI circuit and system designs. That involvement affords the opportunity for a first-hand experience in the discovery and formulation of new and insightful EDA problems, and the development of practical and impactful solutions. This experience has had a great influence on my career as an EDA researcher. In this paper, I will share several examples of the research projects that I directed at UCLA following this principle—from design to design automation.

2. BOOLEAN MATCHING FOR LUT-BASED FPGA SYNTHESIS

After I joined the faculty of UCLA in 1990, in addition to my research in VLSI physical designs, I soon developed a parallel interest in FPGA synthesis. Following the circuit model used in most FPGA synthesis papers in the early 1990s, my research team initially assumed that all the programmable logic blocks (PLBs) in SRAM-based FPGAs were uniform-size lookup tables (LUTs). We made significant progress on technology mapping LUT-based FPGAs, including the development of the first depth-optimal polynomial-time mapping algorithm [11]. Then, we began some FPGA design and prototyping efforts on commercial FPGAs. It was interesting to see, however, that some popular FPGAs, in fact, do not have uniform-size FPGAs. For example, the PLB in the widely successful Xilinx XC4K family consists of three LUTs of different sizes, as shown in Figure. 1.

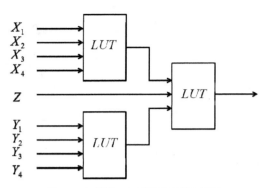

Figure 1. Xilinx XC4000 PLB [11].

It can implement some functions of up to nine inputs. But there is no theory or algorithm to decide what kind of logic can be mapped to such a PLB (not even by Xilinx, even though they designed and manufactured the chip with this PLB). To gain a better understanding of the efficiency of these PLBs, and more importantly to provide a tool to explore new PLBs in the future, we developed a theory and algorithm based on Boolean matching techniques to completely characterize the kind of logic functions that can be mapped to Xilinx XC4K PLBs ([12][13]). The result was exciting news (and surprising) to Xilinx. Overnight, Xilinx gave over 1,868 logic functions for testing. Our algorithm successfully mapped each of them to a Xilinx 4K PLB. It turned out that these test cases were actually customer complaints that had accumulated over the years (e.g., some customers reported that they could map the function manually to a XC4K PLB, but the automated mapping tool failed). Since our theory and algorithm provided the complete characterization of the set of Boolean functions implementable on the PLB[2], these were straightforward test cases for us [13]. This algorithm, together with other FPGA mapping algorithms that we developed at UCLA, is available for free download as part of the RASP system [16]. These algorithms were used by Aplus Design Technologies, a spin-off from the VLSI CAD Laboratory at UCLA. Aplus was among the first to provide FPGA architecture evaluation tools and physical synthesis tools. Aplus was acquired by Magma Design Automation (now part of Synopsys) in 2003.

3. 3D IC PHYSICAL DESIGN

In the early 2000s, my group was involved in a DARPA program to develop physical design automation tools for three-dimensional integrated circuits (3D ICs). As with most DARPA programs, this was very much a forward-looking project, as there were very few (if any) people doing 3D IC designs at that time. The first step of our research was an in-depth study of various IC design and fabrication technologies, and we worked with our partner CFDRC to come up with detailed technology and circuit

---

[1] The iterative deletion technique was also used for circuit partitioning [8]

[2] More general, but less efficient Boolean matching algorithms were later presented in [14] and [15].

models for 3D ICs. These studies gave us a more realistic understanding of the needs and challenges of 3D IC physical designs. We made two key observations. One observation focused on the thermal concerns due to both device stacking and low thermal conductivity of the dielectric layers (proposed or used in some 3D IC processes at that time). To address this problem, we were among the first to develop thermal-driven 3D floorplanning [17], placement [18], and routing [19] tools for 3D IC designs. Our second observation was that through-silicon-vias (TSVs) played a unique role in 3D IC designs. Once the TSV locations are determined, a 3D IC design can be decomposed into a sequence of 2D IC designs using standard 2D IC layout tools. Therefore, our research focused a lot on TSV planning and placement ([20][21]). Based on these research efforts, we jointly developed a 3D IC design environment with IBM and Penn State University. We released a complete 3D IC physical design tool, named 3D-Craft [22] (See Figure 2), in 2009 with interfaces to the OpenAccess design infrastructure [OA]. Our 3D placement tool was used by Prof. Paul Franzon's team at North Carolina State University for three 3D IC designs, including a 2-point FFT butterfly processing element (PE), an Advanced Encryption Standard (AES) encryption block, and a multiple-input and multiple-output wireless decoder (MIMO) [23].Their study showed that our 3D placement tool leads to significant wirelength and power reduction compared to manual 3D placement solutions.

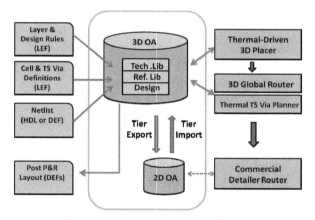

Figure 2. Overview of 3D-Craft [22].

4. HIGH-LEVEL SYNTHESIS

In the early 2000s, Xilinx introduced its Virtex-II Pro FPGAs with embedded IBM PowerPC 405 processor cores. Like many other researchers, we were very interested in using such a highly integrated field-programmable system-on-a-chip (FP-SoC) for prototyping and accelerated computing. After some initial exploration, it was evident to me that to design such an FP-SoC, one should raise the level of design abstraction so that the input language can specify both the function to be implemented on the FPGA fabric as well as the computation to be

executed on the embedded processors. For this reason, we selected C/C++ as the input languages (even though they were not ideal candidates for hardware synthesis) and started a research project on high-level synthesis (HLS) from C/C++ to cycle-accurate hardware descriptions in VHDL or Verilog. The concept of HLS was not new when we started, but prior HLS systems often failed to match the quality of human RTL designs. Therefore, we focused on optimization for a better quality of results and developed a number of novel algorithms to improve the quality of the HLS results, such as scheduling using systems of difference constraints [24],efficient pattern-mining [25], scheduling with soft constraints [26], optimization using behavior-level don't-cares ([27][28]), and automatic memory partitioning [29]. The project led to the development of xPilot, a novel platform-based HLS system [30] (See Figure 3), which was licensed to AutoESL Design Technologies, another spin-off from our lab at UCLA, for commercialization in 2006.

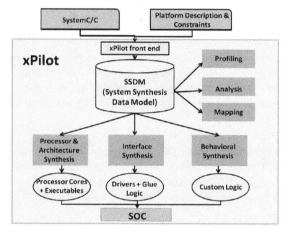

Figure 3. xPilot system-level synthesis framework [30].

Throughout the development of xPilot and AutoPilot (the HLS tool from AutoESL), my research group has been an active user of the HLS tools mainly for accelerated computing. In turn, these design activities helped to introduce interesting new research problems for HLS. One good example is memory partitioning. It is quite common for a HLS tool to map an array in the input C/C++ language to a memory block in the hardware implementation. However, most memory blocks have a very small number of ports (in fact, only two ports for most embedded memory blocks on FPGAs), which greatly limits the degree of parallelism in the final implementation. To overcome this limitation, the designer has to go through a tedious process to re-write the input C/C++ code to partition an array into a set of smaller arrays to enable multiple concurrent memory accesses [31]. To spare designers from such manual code rewriting, we quickly developed the theory and algorithms for automatic memory partitioning ([29][32]), and our work in [28] received a Best Paper Award from the ACM Transactions on Design Automation of Electronic Systems in 2013.

AutoESL's HLS tool was adopted by some of the world's largest software and semiconductor companies. AutoESL was acquired by Xilinx in 2011. The AutoESL's HLS tool was renamed as Vivado-HLS and is now available to tens of thousands of Xilinx FPGA designers worldwide, becoming the most widely deployed and used HLS tool in the history of EDA.

5. CONCLUDING REMARKS

I was very fortunate to have that summer research opportunity at Xerox PARC in 1987 and to have Bryan Preas as my mentor. I built up a long-term friendship with Bryan, and I benefited immensely from Bryan's vast experience, deep insight, and remarkable wisdom in the subsequent years. I considered Bryan as my second PhD advisor. The truly important lesson that I learned from Bryan is to go from design to design automation—always trying to gain first-hand knowledge and experience about needs from the designer's perspective, so that one can discover and formulate new and insightful EDA problems and develop practical and impactful solutions. This guiding principle led to multiple successes in my career as an EDA researcher, and I illustrated some of them in this paper. I am pleased to have the opportunity to share this experience with the EDA research community and to participate in the celebration of Bryan's ISPD Lifetime Achievement Award.

6. REFERENCES

[1] Preas, B. T., and C. W. Gwyn. "Architecture for contemporary computer aids to generate IC mask layouts," in *Record of 11th Asilomar Conf. on Circuits, Systems and Computers*, pp. 353-361, 1977.

[2] Preas, B. T., and Charles W. Gwyn. "Methods for hierarchical automatic layout of custom LSI circuit masks," in *Proc. of the 15th Design Automation Conf.*, pp. 206-212, 1978.

[3] Preas, B. T., and William M. vanCleemput. "Placement algorithms for arbitrarily shaped blocks." in *Proc. of the 16th Design Automation Conf.*, pp. 474-480, 1979.

[4] Preas, B. T. "*Placement and routing algorithms for hierarchical integrated circuit layout.*" Doctoral Dissertation, Department of Electrical Engineering, Stanford University, 1979.

[5] Preas, B. T., and C. S. Chow, "Placement and routing algorithms for topological integrated circuit layout," in *Proc. Of the Intl. Symposium on Circuits and Systems*, pp. 17-20, 1985.

[6] Preas, B. T., "An approach to placement for rectilinear cells," presented at Physical Design Workshop: Placement and Floorplanning, Hilton Head, South Carolina, April 1987.

[7] J. Cong, D. F. Wong and C. L. Liu. "A New Approach to the Three Layer Channel Routing,". *Int'l Conf. Computer-Aided Design*, pp. 378-381, 1987.

[8] Madden, Patrick H. "Partitioning by iterative deletion." *International Symposium on Physical Design*. ACM, 1999.

[9] Sechcn, C., and A. Sangiovanni-Vincentelli. "TimberWolf 3.2: A new standard cell placement and global routing package." *the 23rd Design Automation Conf.* 1986.

[10] J. Cong and Bryan Preas. "A new algorithm for standard cell global routing." *IEEE International Conference on Computer-Aided Design*, 1988.

[11] J. Cong and Yuzheng Ding. "FlowMap: An optimal technology mapping algorithm for delay optimization in lookup-table based FPGA designs." *IEEE Transactions on Computer-Aided Design of Integrated Circuits and Systems,* 13.1 (1994): 1-12.

[12] J. Cong and Yean-Yow Hwang. "Boolean matching for complex PLBs in LUT-based FPGAs with application to architecture evaluation." *International Symposium on Field Programmable Gate Arrays*. ACM, 1998.

[13] J. Cong and Yean-Yow Hwang. "Boolean matching for LUT-based logic blocks with applications to architecture evaluation and technology mapping." *IEEE Transactions on Computer-Aided Design of Integrated Circuits and Systems,* (2001): 1077-1090.

[14] Ling, Andrew, Deshanand P. Singh, and Stephen D. Brown. "FPGA technology mapping: a study of optimality." *the 42nd Annual Design Automation Conference*. ACM, 2005.

[15] J. Cong and Kirill Minkovich. "Improved SAT-based Boolean matching using implicants for LUT-based FPGAs." *15th International Symposium on Field Programmable Gate Arrays*. ACM, 2007.

[16] J. Cong, John Peck, and Yuzheng Ding. "RASP: A general logic synthesis system for SRAM-based FPGAs." *Fourth International Symposium on Field Programmable Gate Arrays*. ACM, 1996.

[17] J. Cong, Jie Wei, and Yan Zhang. "A thermal-driven floorplanning algorithm for 3D ICs." *International Conference on Computer Aided Design,* 2004.

[18] J. Cong, et al. "Thermal-aware 3D IC placement via transformation." *Asia and South Pacific Design Automation Conference*, 2007.

[19] J. Cong and Yan Zhang. "Thermal-driven multilevel routing for 3-D ICs." *Asia and South Pacific Design Automation Conference*, 2005.

[20] J. Cong and Yan Zhang. "Thermal via planning for 3-D ICs." *International Conference on Computer-Aided Design,* 2005.

[21] J. Cong, Guojie Luo, and Yiyu Shi. "Thermal-aware cell and through-silicon-via co-placement for 3D ICs." *Design Automation Conference (DAC)*, 2011.

[22] J. Cong and Guojie Luo. "A 3D physical design flow based on Open Access." *International Conference on Communications, Circuits and Systems,* 2009.

[23] Thorolfsson, Thorlindur, et al. "Logic-on-logic 3d integration and placement." *IEEE International 3D Systems Integration Conference (3DIC),* 2010.

[24] J. Cong and Zhiru Zhang. "An efficient and versatile scheduling algorithm based on SDC formulation." *the 43rd Annual Design Automation Conference.* 2006.

[25] J. Cong and Wei Jiang. "Pattern-based behavior synthesis for FPGA resource reduction." *International Symposium on Field Programmable Gate Arrays.* ACM, 2008.

[26] J. Cong, Bin Liu, and Zhiru Zhang. "Scheduling with soft constraints." *International Conference on Computer-Aided Design.* ACM, 2009.

[27] J. Cong, Bin Liu, and Zhiru Zhang. "Behavior-level observability don't-cares and application to low-power behavioral synthesis." *International Symposium on Low Power Electronics and Design.* ACM, 2009.

[28] J. Cong, et al. "Behavior-level observability analysis for operation gating in low-power behavioral synthesis." *ACM Transactions on Design Automation of Electronic Systems (TODAES)* 16.1 (2010): 4.

[29] J. Cong, et al. "Automatic memory partitioning and scheduling for throughput and power optimization." *ACM Transactions on Design Automation of Electronic Systems (TODAES)* 16.2 (2011): 15.

[30] J. Cong, et al. "Platform-based behavior-level and system-level synthesis." *IEEE International SOC Conference,* 2006.

[31] J. Cong and Yi Zou. "FPGA-based hardware acceleration of lithographic aerial image simulation." *ACM Transactions on Reconfigurable Technology and Systems (TRETS)* 2.3 (2009): 17.

[32] Wang, Yuxin, et al. "Memory partitioning for multidimensional arrays in high-level synthesis." *Proceedings of the 50th Annual Design Automation Conference.* ACM, 2013

Interconnect Length Estimation in VLSI Designs: A Retrospective

Massoud Pedram
University of Southern California
Dept. of Electrical Engineering
Los Angeles CA
pedram@usc.edu

ABSTRACT

A compilation of work related to a priori estimation of interconnect lengths in VLSI circuits is provided, with an emphasis on procedural wire length estimation methods that do not require knowledge of the circuit layout and instead rely on structural analysis of the circuit net list and stochastic modeling of the underlying placement and routing tools. Reviewed work includes references listed below.

Categories and Subject Descriptors

B.7.2 [**Integrated Circuits**]: Design Aids

Keywords

VLSI Layout, Wirelength Estimation, Place & Route, Average Interconnect Length

1. REFERENCES

[1] S. Balachandran and D. Bhatia. A-priori wirelength and interconnection estimation based on circuit characteristics. In *Workshop on System Level Interconnect Prediction*, 2003.

[2] S. Bodapati and F. N. Najm. Pre-layout estimation of individual wire lengths. In *Workshop on System Level Interconnect Prediction*, pages 91–96, 2000.

[3] J. Cong and S. K. Lim. Edge separability-based circuit clustering with application to multilevel circuit partitioning. *IEEE Transactions on Computer-Aided Design of Integrated Circuits and Systems*, 23(3):346–357, 2004.

[4] J. Dambre, D. Stroobandt, and J. V. Campenhout. Toward the accurate prediction of placement wire length distributions in vlsi circuits. *IEEE Transactions on Very Large Scale Integration (VLSI) Systems*, 12(4):339–348, 2004.

[5] A. E. Gamal and Z. Syed. A stochastic model for interconnections in custom integrated circuits. *IEEE Transactions on Circuits and Systems*, 28(2):888–894, 1981.

[6] T. Hamada, C.-K. Cheng, and P. M. Chau. A wire length estimation technique utilizing neighborhood density equations. In *Proceedings of the 29th ACM/IEEE Design Automation Conference*, pages 57–61, 1992.

[7] A. B. Kahng and S. Reda. Intrinsic shortest path length: a new, accurate a priori wirelength estimator. In *IEEE/ACM International Conference on Computer-Aided Design*, pages 173–180, 2005.

[8] Q. Liu and M. Marek-Sadowska. A study of netlist structure and placement efficiency. In *Proceedings of the 2004 International Symposium on Physical Design*, pages 198–203, 2004.

[9] T. Mak, P. Sedcole, P. Y. K. Cheung, and W. Luk. Interconnection lengths and delays estimation for communication links in fpgas. In *Workshop on System Level Interconnect Prediction*, 2008.

[10] M. Pedram, B. S. Nobandegani, and B. T. Preas. Design and analysis of segmented routing channels for row-based fpgas. *IEEE Transactions on Computer-Aided Design of Integrated Circuits and Systems*, 13(12):1470–1479, 1994.

[11] M. Pedram and B. Preas. Accurate prediction of physical design characteristics of random logic. In *Proceedings of the IEEE International Conference on Computer Design: VLSI in Computers and Processors*, pages 100–108, 1989.

[12] M. Pedram and B. T. Preas. Interconnection length estimation for optimized standard cell layouts. In *Proceedings of the IEEE International Conference on Computer-Aided Design*, pages 390–393, 1989.

[13] M. Pedram and B. T. Preas. Interconnection analysis for standard cell layouts. *IEEE Transactions on Computer-Aided Design of Integrated Circuits and Systems*, 18(10):1512–1518, 1999.

[14] C. Sechen. Average interconnection length estimation for random and optimized placements. In *Proceedings of the IEEE International Conference on Computer-Aided Design*, pages 190–193, 1988.

ISPD'14, March 30–April 2, 2014, Petaluma, CA, USA.
ACM 978-1-4503-2592-9/14/03.
http://dx.doi.org/10.1145/2560519.2568053.

Bryan Preas: Broad Contributions to System Engineering in the 2000's

Scott Elrod
PARC, a Xerox Company
3333 Coyote Hill Road
Palo Alto, CA 94304
(650) 812-5060
elrod@parc.com

ABSTRACT

For 10 years, until his retirement from PARC in 2012, I had the privilege of working with Bryan Preas on a broad set of projects in system engineering. From portable X-ray imaging systems, to parallel printing machines to bio-agent detection instruments, Bryan was the "go-to" person for the more complex aspects of hardware design and hardware/software integration across multiple labs at PARC. In this talk, I will share examples of Bryan's great skill, technical versatility and wonderful collaborative spirit.

ISPD'14, March 30–April 2, 2014, Petaluma, California, USA.
ACM 978-1-4503-2592-9/14/03.
http://dx.doi.org/10.1145/2560519.2568054

Smart Matter Systems, an Introduction through Examples

Bryan Preas
Battle Ground, WA 98604
bryan@preas.com

ABSTRACT

An important research theme at the Palo Alto Research Center was Smart Matter. We defined that to be integrating materials and mechanical hardware (matter) with computation, communications, sensors and actuators (smarts) to reduce the cost and improve the performance of systems and to enable entirely new functionalities. Increased functionality, reduced cost, and miniaturization of the smart components allowed us to demonstrate new systems and architectures that would have been unthinkable earlier. PARC demonstrated several Smart Matter systems. Three examples will be detailed: Air Jet Paper Mover, Tightly Integrated Parallel Printing, and an electrophretic display.

The Air Jet Paper Mover demonstrated that an array of air jets can levitate and move flexible media (for example, paper) without disturbing unfused toner or wet ink images. This approach allows high speed paper transport using individually addressed air jets with optical paper position sensing with tightly coupled, closed loop control. This architecture supports arbitrary paper trajectories with three degrees of freedom parallel to the array of jets. We built an example system using printed circuit board technology with 576 air jets controlled by electrostatic flap valves and an integrated array of 32000 optical position sensors. A high level control system ran on a PC, while integrated DSPs and FPGAs controlled the sensors and actuators.

High speed printers traditionally use a high speed print engine with a custom designed, highly tuned paper path. In this project we explored an opposite approach. We used several lower speed, lower cost print engines and a reconfigurable paper path constructed from a small number of part types (a bidirectional NIP assembly and a sheet director) called hypermodules. A paper path is constructed using tens to hundreds of hypermodules, each with its own computation, communication, sensing and actuation. Auto-identification is used to inform a system level controller of module capabilities and potential paths through the system. A sheet controller abstraction coordinates the actions of the hardware as a sheet moves through the system. Software/hardware co-design provided a system architecture that is scalable without requiring user relearning.

PARC developed an electrophretic material consisting of small, spherical, wax beads imbedded in a transparent, oily matrix. The beads are half white and half black (or any two colors). Positive and negative static electric charges are aligned with the two colors. Thus, the orientation of the beads can be controlled by an external electric field. Novel ways of decomposing and encoding images were developed to permit high-resolution images to be embedded in printed circuit artwork. As a result, display controllers can be implemented with very simple micro controllers and comparatively few pixel drivers. Addressing electronics and display controllers transform this material into interesting applications such as electric paper, active brochures and retail signage. Low power (some applications required that one small battery power the system for its entire life) and low cost (the electrophretic material cost so little that the electronics and packaging cost dominated the total cost) were constant themes.

ACM Classification

B. Hardware

Keywords

Air jets, smart matter, electrophoresis, electrostatic, printing, hypermodules, auto-identification, co-design

1. BIOGRAPHY

Bryan has more than 40 years of experience in systems and electronics design and design automation. He was Principal Scientist at the Palo Alto Research Center where he worked on low power electronics, high voltage systems, high speed communication, embedded systems and design automation. He was Chief Engineer for Gyricon Media, Inc., a PARC spin-out for commercializing large area, electric paper displays. Bryan was an Area Manager at PARC from 1983 until 1990.

He was also Vice President of Research and Development at VR Information Systems, a startup company which was developed physical design automation software for ASICs. Bryan has held research positions at Bell Telephone Laboratories, Sandia National Laboratories, and the CADLAB at the University of Paderborn in Paderborn, Germany.

Bryan received his BS with highest honors from Texas A&M University, his MS from Carnegie-Mellon University, and his PhD from Stanford University, all in Electrical Engineering.

Bryan was active in the Design Automation community. He is an ACM Fellow and was a member of ACM Council. He was awarded the Senior Scientist Prize from the Humboldt Foundation and was a Visiting Research Scientist at the Universities of Paderborn and Kaiserslautern. He was a long time member of the Executive Committees and Program committees for Design Automation Conference and Design Automation and Test in Europe. He was General Chair of the 32nd DAC. Bryan was an Associate Editor for the IEEE Transactions on CAD and served for several years on the SIGDA Executive committee.

ISPD'14, Mar 30 - Apr 02 2014, Petaluma, CA, USA
ACM 978-1-4503-2592-9/14/03.
http://dx.doi.org/10.1145/2560519.2567528

Bryan holds 38 patents and has published numerous papers and two encyclopedia articles. He is the co-author of a book on physical design automation.

2. REFERENCES

[1] Biegelsen, D. K. ; Berlin, A. ; Cheung, P.; Fromherz, M. P. J. ; Goldberg, D. ; Jackson, W. ; Preas, B .; Reich, J.; Swartz, L. E. Air-jet paper mover: an example of mesoscale MEMS. SPIE Proceedings, Micromachined Devices and Components VI; 2000 September; Santa Clara, CA. Bellingham, WA: SPIE; 2000; 4176: 122-129.

[2] Biegelsen, D. K.; Crawford, L. S.; Do, M. B.; Duff, D. G.; Eldershaw, C.; Fromherz, M. P. J.; Hindi, H.; Kott, G.; Larner, D. L.; Mandel, B.; Moore, S.; Preas, B. T.; Ruml, W.; Schmitz, G. P.; Swartz, L. E.; Zhou, R. Integrated parallel printing systems with hypermodular architecture. IS&T-SPIE Electronic Imaging Science & Technology; 2011 January 23-27; San Francisco, CA.

[3] Sheridon, N. K. ; Richley, E. A. ; Mikkelsen, J. C. ; Tsuda, D. ; Crowley, J. M. ; Oraha, K. A. ; Howard, M. E.; Rodkin, M. A.; Swidler, R. ; Sprague, R. A. The gyricon rotating ball display. Moreale, J. ed. Proceedings of the IEEE 1997 International Display Research Conference; 1997 September 15; Toronto, Canada. Santa Ana, CA. NY: IEEE; 1997: 82-85.

[4] B. Preas, F. Vest, E. Richley, N. Sheridon and R. Sprague. A Large Area, Tiled, Gyricon Display. SID Symposium Digest of Technical Papers, Volume 29, Issue 1, May 1998, 211–214.

Reliability-Driven Chip-Level Design for High-Frequency Digital Microfluidic Biochips

Shang-Tsung Yu, Sheng-Han Yeh, Tsung-Yi Ho
Department of Computer Science and Information Engineering
National Cheng Kung University, Tainan, Taiwan
{jidung, hardyyeh}@eda.csie.ncku.edu.tw
tyho@csie.ncku.edu.tw

ABSTRACT

Nowadays, electrowetting-on-dielectric (EWOD) chips have become the most popular actuator for droplet-based digital microfluidic biochips. As the complexity of biochemical assay increases, the chip-level design of EWOD chips which integrates electrode addressing and wire routing are widely adopted. Furthermore, to finish many time-sensitive bioassays such as incubation and emerging flash chemistry in a specific time, a high-frequency EWOD is used to satisfy the demand. However, the reliability of the EWOD chip degrades due to the contact angle reduction problem incurred by huge number of switching times of an electrode. Thus, the reliability issue, electrode addressing, and wire routing problem should be considered together in the chip-level design of an EWOD chips. In this paper, a graph-based chip-level design algorithm is presented. By setting the switching-time constraint, the number of switching times can be limited to minimize the impact of contact angle reductions problem. Also, a progressive addressing and routing approach is proposed to overcome the challenge of complex wire routing problem. Experimental results show that the influence of contact angle reduction problem can be effectively minimized by proposed algorithm. A reliable chip-level design with feasible wire routing solution can be generated with number of pins are satisfied.

Categories and Subject Descriptors

B.7.2 [**Integrated Circuits**]: Design Aids - Layout, Place and Route

Keywords

Biochip, microfluidics, chip level design

1. INTRODUCTION

In recent years, digital microfluidic biochips (DMFBs) [15] have become state-of-the-art portable devices for implementing laboratory procedures in biochemistry. On a

DMFB, droplets of nano-litter volume can be a sample carrier and manipulated as operating units. This approach offers advantages of high sensitivity, less consumption of bioassay, and lower probability of errors [6]. By precisely controlling the movement of droplets, various applications such as immunoassays, DNA sequencing, polymerase chain reaction (PCR) and point-of-care disease diagnostics can be successfully realized [16].

Nowadays, electrowetting-on-dielectric (EWOD) chips have emerged as the most widely used actuators particularly for DMFBs [14]. The general diagram of an EWOD chip is shown in Fig. 1. An EWOD chip consisted of two parallel plates including a top plate and a bottom plate. The top plate is a piece of electrode while the bottom plate comprises a two-dimensional (2D) array of electrodes. Under the bottom plate is a printed circuit board (PCB) where conduction wires are connected between electrodes and external electrical pads. The sample carriers (i.e., droplets) are sandwiched between the top plate and the bottom plate. By applying time-varying voltages to the electrodes, droplets can be manipulated to perform operations such as transportation, mixing, and splitting [2]. Besides, there are peripheral devices (e.g., dispensing port, optical detector) for dispensing the droplets from the reagent slots and detecting the outcome of the bioassay.

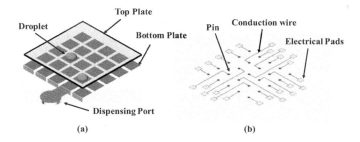

Figure 1: (a) The architecture of an EWOD chip (b) The routing layer in the downside

Recently, the chip-level design of an EWOD chip becomes important due to its high complexity. In order to drive electrodes correctly, all electrodes should be addressed with control pins to receive control signals from the external controller. This is referred to as *electrode addressing*. In electrode addressing scheme of conventional EWOD chips, each electrode is addressed with an independent control pin, which is named *direct addressing* [5]. In direct addressing scheme, all of the electrodes can be independently controlled. However, as the chip size increases, it is necessary to limit the number of control pins since these pins are controlled by external controller with a limited number of signal ports. This triggers the demands of pin-constrained EWOD chips. To solve this problem, a widely used approach, *broadcast addressing*, is proposed [17]. Broadcast addressing utilizes the concept of pin sharing to assign single control pin to multiple electrodes without affecting the execution of assay. Thus, the number of used control pins can be effectively reduced by broadcast addressing.

When running a bioassay on an EWOD chip, a sequence of electrode actuation vectors is sent to the external controller for assigning voltage to the electrodes. Each electrode is either being actuated or grounded at each time step. Because the droplet moves from one electrode to another adjacent electrode in each clock cycle, the completion time of many operations such as droplet transportation or dispensing, are determined by the clock frequency applied to the EWOD chip. These fluid-handling operations are referred to as frequency-sensitive operations [12]. In order to minimize the time required to complete a bioassay, a high-frequency EWOD chip with application of high clock frequency is introduced. With a high-frequency EWOD chip, the completion time of frequency-sensitive operations can be effectively decreased while the completion time of other frequency-insensitive operations can also be partially decreased [13]. However, for a high-frequency pin-constrained EWOD chip, although the number of control pins can be effectively reduced by broadcast addressing technique, reliability of the chip degrades if the signals are shared arbitrarily.

When a voltage is applied to an electrode, the sudden increase of current in the dielectric causes dielectric breakdown, which is called *electrolysis* [20]. The phenomenon of electrolysis decreases the contact angle reduction of the droplet, which affects the reliability of the EWOD chip. This problem is referred to as contact angle reduction problem. It has been reported that the effect of the contact angle reduction problem is highly related to the number of switching time of an electrode (i.e., the number of times an electrode is switched on and off) [10]. In direct addressing scheme, the actuation sequence of each electrode can be independently determined. Thus, the contact angle reduction problem can be simply avoided by minimizing the number of switching times of each electrode. However, when broadcast addressing is involved, the problem becomes severe. Arbitrary signal sharing results in huge number of switching times, which degrades the reliability of the chip. To deal with the contact angle reduction problem, electrodes should be carefully chosen when they are assigned to the same control pin.

In additional to the contact angle reduction problem, the wire routing also increases the design complexity. Wire routing is a critical step in the chip-level design of an EWOD chip. The target of wire routing is to route the conduction wires from bottom side of the electrode array, through the underlying substrate, to the surrounding electrical pads so as to transmit the control signal of each control pin. The connections may be infeasible if the electrodes are not addressed carefully (i.e., there is no existing routes between electrodes due to the blockage of existed conduction wires). In this situation, extra processes or even additional routing layer(s) are needed, which is undesirable for low-cost EWOD chips fabrication.

In the literature, there are lots of previous works focusing on the design of pin-constrained EWOD chips. Many previous works only focus the problem of electrode addressing [9, 11, 17, 21] and try to minimize the number of control pins. However, a feasible chip design cannot be generated without considering electrode addressing and wire routing together. The works in [1, 8, 18] consider both electrode addressing and wire routing. However, the solutions in these work are not reliable for a high-frequency EWOD chip. The influence of contact angle reduction problem degrades the reliability of the chip while the whole procedure is possibly ruined by the electric breakdown. Accordingly, to design a feasible and reliable chips, there is a urgent demand to develop a dedicated algorithm to generate a feasible EWOD chip design with appropriate electrode addressing and wire routing solution as well as minimize the impact of contact angle problem.

1.1 Contributions

In this work, by considering the contact angle reduction incurred by huge numbers of switching time, a chip-level design algorithm for high-frequency EWOD chips is proposed. To identify the reliability of the chip, a model considering the number of switching time is formulated. The contributions can be summarized as follows:

- We propose the first work that consider the reliability problem on a high-frequency EWOD chip. The contact angle reduction problem which degrades the reliability of the chip has been well studied and formulated.

- The algorithm not only maximizes the reliability of the chip but also provides a comprehensive routing solution for chip manufacturing. By taking both the reliability as well as routability issue into account, the corresponding wire routing result can be well obtained.

- We propose a progressive addressing and routing algorithm which addresses electrodes and route wires simultaneously. Accompanied by setting a switching time constraint and conducting effective maze routing, the addressing and routing problem can be efficiently and effectively solved.

Experimental results show the effectiveness of proposed chip-level design algorithm. By performing proposed algorithm on five real life applications, proposed algorithm can obtain the best electrode addressing and wire routing results to minimize the impact of contact angle reduction.

The remainder of this paper is organized as follows. Section 2 describes the related preliminaries including broadcast addressing, and the contact angle reduction problem. Then Section 3 formulates the problem in this paper. Section 4 details proposed algorithm to solve the pin-constrained high-frequency chip-level design problem. Section 5 and 6 demonstrate the experimental results and give the conclusions respectively.

2. PRELIMINARIES

This section describes the broadcast addressing technique, and the contact angle reduction problem which seriously degrades the reliability of EWOD chips.

2.1 Pin-constrained Broadcast Addressing

As mentioned above, the number of control pin is limited by the external controller in a pin-constrained EWOD chip. We denote the number of control pins provided by the external controller as P_{max}. To overcome this challenge, an efficient approach, broadcast addressing technique [17], is proposed to reduce the number of control pins.

2.1.1 Electrode Actuation Sequence

In an application-specified biochip, each electrode has their own status demanded at each time step to have droplets behave in an intended or anticipated manner. Electrode actuation sequences show control signals of electrodes at each time step. An electrode actuation sequence is a sequence containing 0, 1, X. A "0" term represents that electrode should be grounded, a "1" term represents that electrode should be actuated, and a "X" term (don't care term) represents that electrode could be grounded or actuated.

For example, the actuation sequence is "10X01X", which means that the electrode must be actuated at 5-th time, and grounded at 4-th time. It can be either actuated or grounded at 3-th time. By observing the actuation sequence, it can be found that multiple actuation sequences can share an identical sequence by replacing "don't care" terms with "1" or "0". AS_i is used to denote the actuation sequence of Electrode i. We say Electrode e_x and e_y are compatible if and only if they can be assigned to the same control pin, which also means that actuation sequences AS_x and AS_y are compatible.

2.1.2 Broadcast Addressing

To identify the compatibility between electrodes and do broadcast addressing, a compatibility graph is constructed. In the compatibility graph, each node stands for an electrode, and each edge between two nodes stands for the compatibility between two electrodes. If Electrode e_a and e_b is compatible, an edge is constructed between Electrode e_a and e_b. By checking each pair of the electrodes, the compatibility graph can be simply built.

By observing the compatibility graph, broadcast addressing can be done easily. Because an edge stands for a compatible relationship, that is, a clique stands for an electrode group where all electrodes are mutually compatible and can be addressed to the same control pin. Thus, the broadcast addressing technique can be seen as finding a clique partition in the compatibility graph.

2.2 Contact Angle Reduction Problem

The contact angle is the angle between droplet and bottom plate, which is an important issue in a high-frequency EWOD chip. When the electrode is actuated, the contact angle of a droplet on this electrode changes from Fig. 2(a) to 2(b). [10] shows that contact angle change ($\Delta\theta$) is directly related to degradation of an electrode, and the number of switching times of actuation affects contact angle change ($\Delta\theta$) as shown in Fig. 3.

Fig. 3 shows that reduction of the number of switching times implies better reliability of the EWOD device. In other words, when the number of switching times of an electrode increases, the contact angle change ($\Delta\theta$) decreases, and thus the reliability of the chip decreases. This is an important issue of reliability for a high-frequency EWOD chip.

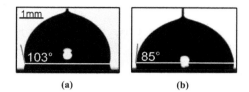

Figure 2: [10] shows the photo of contact angle change ($\Delta\theta$). (a) The contact angle before the electrode is actuated. (b) The contact angle after the electrode is actuated.

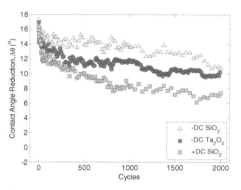

Figure 3: Contact angle reduction problem, [10] reveals that the number of switching times of an electrode affects the contact angle change ($\Delta\theta$), which also implies the reliability of EWOD device.

2.2.1 Switching Times

ST_i denotes the number of switching times of Electrode i. When the actuation sequence AS_i^* of Electrode e_i are determined without any don't care term, the number of switching times ST_i of the actuation sequence can be calculated by counting switching on and switching off. For example, the number of switching times of actutation sequence "001100101101" is 7.

2.2.2 Reliability Problem in Broadcast Addressing

As mentioned above, broadcast addressing is used to reduce the number of pins. However, arbitrary results of broadcast addressing have a huge influence on the reliability of the chip. The contact angle reduction problem should be avoided in broadcast For example, there are three electrodes, e_1, e_2 and e_3 with actuation sequences AS_1=10X0X0, AS_2=1X0X00, and AS_3=X01X1X respectively. By observing these actuation sequences, Electrode e_1 and e_2 are compatible. Electrode e_1 and e_3 are compatible. Hence, if broadcast addressing is used to reduce the number of pins, for Electrode e_1, there are two choices that can be merged with the same pin. If Electrode e_1 and e_2 are merged with the same pin, the actuation sequence of Electrode e_1 becomes the actuation sequence AS_{1+2}=100000. On the other hand, if Electrode e_1 and e_3 are merged with the same pin, the actuation sequence of Electrode e_1 becomes the actuation sequence AS_{1+3}=101010. It can be seen that the number of switching times of AS_{1+3} is bigger than the number of switching times of AS_{1+2}. Therefore, how to perform broadcast addressing and take the maximum number of switching times into consideration simultaneously is a very important issue.

3. PROBLEM FORMULATION

Regarding above discussions, the problem of reliability-driven chip-level design for a high-frequency EWOD chip can be formulated as follows:

Input:

- A set of electrodes $E = \{e_1, e_2, ..., e_n\}$ with corresponding actuation sequences $AS = \{AS_1, AS_2, ..., AS_n\}$, and coordinates.

- A pin-constrained number P_{max}.

- A specified chip with fixed-outline.

Output:

- A set of pins $P = \{P_1, P_2, ..., P_m\}$ where $m \leq P_{max}$.

- Each electrode $e_i \in E$ is assigned to exactly one pin $P_j \in P$ satisfying the broadcast-addressing constraint with corresponding actuation sequences AS_i^*.

- Feasible escape routing and wire routing results.

Due to the contact angle reduction problem, the global effect of contact angle reduction can be reduced by minimizing ST_{max}, which is the maximum of ST_i (see Eq.1).

$$ST_{max} = max\{ST_i | \forall e_i \in E\} \tag{1}$$

Objective:

- Minimize ST_{max} to achieve a good reliability of an EWOD chip.

4. ALGORITHM

In this section, the algorithm is described in detail. First, we will briefly introduce the whole procedure by the flow chart in Fig. 4. First, we will briefly introduce the whole procedure. Then, four subsections are used to discuss the detail of proposed algorithm, which includes *(1) incremental search technique (2) switching-time constrained compatibility graph (3) merge pins and electrodes (4) wire routing and escape routing*.

Fig. 4 shows the overview of proposed algorithm. The basic idea of proposed algorithm is to reduce maximum number of switching times in incremental search and obtain a good broadcast-addressing result by *minimum-cost maximum-flow* (**MCMF**). In the beginning, we set the initial switching-time constraint, select a set of electrodes as an initial pin set, let each pin contains exactly one electrode, and make the rest of electrodes be an unaddressed electrode set. Next, we start to keep matching current unaddressed electrodes and current pins according to the resulting flow of MCMF. In each matching process, routability of routing is checked. If it is a successful routing, then the unaddressed electrode is assigned into the corresponding current pin in the matching process. For pin-constrained restriction, during iterations, an unaddressed electrode should only be brought into a new pin if the executing matching process demands extra one (i.e., all of unaddressed electrodes cannot be assigned into a current pin any more). For example in Fig. 5, there is an initial pin set containing four pins, and each pin contains exactly one electrode. Compatible electrodes-pins matching pairs are selected appropriately by proposed matching mechanism. According to the pairs obtained, each one of selected unaddressed Electrodes e_2, e_3,

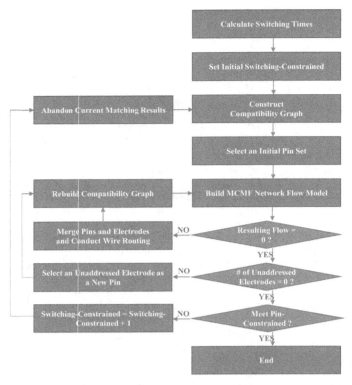

Figure 4: Flow chart of proposed algorithm.

e_6, and e_7 is assigned into a current pin and becomes an addressed electrode respectively. Electrodes e_4 and e_9 left cannot be assigned into any current pin due to incompatible or failed check of routing, and thus all of unaddressed electrodes cannot be assigned into a current pin any more. Hence, a new pin is added and e_4 is assigned into this new pin. Then, e_9 can be assigned into the new pin and the whole procedure is finished successfully. Instead of solving the original problem directly, the original problem is split into a lot of sub-problems and solved progressively, which is well-manipulated. If the result is not an available solution finally (i.e., it violates the pin-constraint when all electrodes are addressed), then the switching-time constraint is relaxed and the procedure mentioned above is repeated until finding an available solution.

4.1 Incremental Search Technique

Given an actuation sequence AS_i, the number of switching times ST_i cannot be decreased without limits. There is a lower bound of the switching time (BST_{ASi}) in the actuation sequence of Electrode e_i. After eliminating all the don't care terms, BST_{ASi} can be calculated by counting switching on and switching off of the actuation sequence AS_i. In other words, after broadcast addressing, the number of switching times ST_i is greater or equal to its lower bound BST_{ASi} as shown in Eq.2. Hence, the maximum switching time ST_{max} which should be minimized as possible can be induced by Eq.2, as shown in Eq.3

$$ST_i \geq BST_{ASi} \quad (\forall e_i \in E) \tag{2}$$

$$ST_{max} \geq max(BST_{ASi}) \quad (\forall e_i \in E) \tag{3}$$

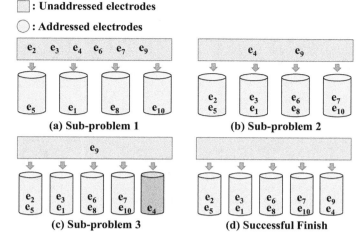

□ : Unaddressed electrodes

○ : Addressed electrodes

(a) Sub-problem 1

(b) Sub-problem 2

(c) Sub-problem 3

(d) Successful Finish

Figure 5: Progressive addressing to solve original problem which can be transformed into several sub-problems. (a) After setting initial pin set (b) After a successful 4 matches (c) After adding extra one pin when there are no successful matching (d) Successful finish.

The maximum number of switching-time constraint is defined as S_{max}. To minimize ST_{max}, an incremental search technique is conducted by setting the switching-time constraint S_{max}. The switching-time constraint is the upper bound of tolerable switching times in a round of iteration. Because of Eq.3, incremental search of S_{max} starts searching from $max(BST_{ASi})$ instead of zero. Therefore, at first, the initial value of switching-time constraint S_{max} is set as $max(BST_{ASi})$. If a solution with feasible addressing and routing cannot be obtained at this switching-time constraint, then the switching-time constraint S_{max} is increased by one and recheck whether there is a solution with feasible addressing and routing under this restriction. By keeping relaxing S_{max}, the maximum switching times ST_{max} can be as small as possible when there is a feasible solution.

4.2 Switching-time Constrained Compatibility Graph

To satisfy the switching-time constraint S_{max} of incremental search, a switching-time constrained compatibility graph is introduced. In switching-time constrained compatibility graph, electrodes e_x, e_y are compatible if and only if (1) actuation sequences AS_x and AS_y are compatible and (2) the actuation sequence AS' that can control both e_x and e_y, $BST_{AS'} \leq S_{max}$. For example, under the switching-time constraint of 3, there are three electrodes, e_1, e_2, and e_3 with their own actuation sequence AS_1=1XX1X1, AS_2=1X1101, and AS_3=XX0X01 respectively. Although e_1 and e_3 are compatible in their actuation sequence, the actuation sequence "1X0101" which can control both e_1 and e_3 violates the switching-time constraint because its bound of switching time is 4 which is bigger than 3. The bound of switching time of the actuation sequence "1X1101" which can control both e_1 and e_2 is 2 which is equal or smaller than 3. Thus, in this switching-time constrained compatibility graph, there is an edge between Electrode e_1 and e_2 and there is no edge between Electrode e_1 and e_3. Therefore, by using switching-

time constrained compatibility graph to implement broadcast addressing, the $max(BST_{ASi})$ can be controlled easily.

4.3 Merge Pins and Electrodes

After getting the switching-time constrained compatibility graph, mutually incompatible electrodes are selected to be the initial pins. Next, the following sub-problem is solved by network flow.

Network flow model:

- Create a source node S, and a sink node T.
- For each existing pin, create a node P_i.
- For each unaddressed electrode, create a node UE_i.
- For each node P_i, add an edge $S \rightarrow P_i$ with unit capacity and zero cost.
- For each node UE_i, add an edge $UE_i \rightarrow T$ with unit capacity and zero cost.
- Add edges $P_i \rightarrow UE_j$ according to compatibility graph with unit capacity and $\Delta HPWL(P_i, UE_j)$ cost.

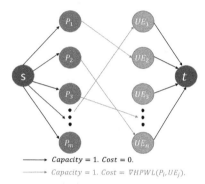

→ Capacity = 1. Cost = 0.

→ Capacity = 1. Cost = $\nabla HPWL(P_i, UE_j)$.

Figure 6: Network flow model of minimum-cost maximum-flow.

By this network flow model, for example in Fig. 6, we can get better matches according to the resulting flows. When there is a resulting flow $S \rightarrow P_i \rightarrow UE_j \rightarrow T$, both wire routing and escape routing of (P_i, UE_j) is checked. If (P_i, UE_j) can be routed successfully, UE_j will be added into the pin P_i and both wire routing and escape routing will be executed simultaneously. For the consideration of routability, the cost of edge (P_i, UE_j) is set as the variation of half-perimeter wire length, $\Delta HPWL(P_i, UE_j)$.

By setting $\Delta HPWL(P_i, UE_j)$ as the cost of $P_i \rightarrow UE_j$, a matching with better routability is obtained as possible decreasing the probability of failed electrodes routing. However, whenever an unaddressed electrode is added into a current pin, the actuation sequence of the electrode may change (don't care term "X" becomes "1" or "0") to fit the actuation of the pin. That is, it brings the change of compatibility graph. Hence, a pin should only merge one unaddressed electrode at most in a round of network flow, and each capacity of all edges is set as one to implement it. Also, the switching-time constrained compatibility graph and network flow model will be regenerated before the next round of network flow. Finally, the procedure keep merging unaddressed electrodes and current pins by network flow based matching mechanism until there is no unaddressed electrode.

4.4 Wire Routing and Escape Routing

After a round of network flow matching, several matching pairs may be obtained from resulting flows. When there is a matching pair (P_i, UE_j) with very high $\Delta HPWL$, it means that it is hard to route UE_j to the nets of pin P_i, and it will cost a lot of extra space to finish the routing. Hence, these matching pairs will be checked for routing and routed in the increasing order of their $\Delta HPWL$ to have more pairs of successful routing.

There are two parts of routing, (1) wire routing and (2) escape routing. Wire routing is the routing between electrodes, and escape routing is to route each individual terminal pin to the boundary of the chips. In our algorithm, wire routing is done by breadth-first search (BFS) based algorithm, and escape routing is done by a classic approach which models the original routing problem into maximum-flow problem [19].

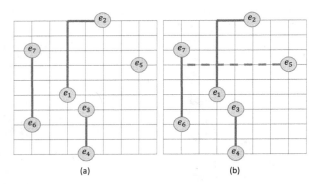

Figure 7: An example of wire routing. (a) Ready for wire routing (b) Failed wire routing between e_5 and the net containing e_6 and e_7.

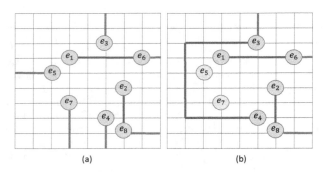

Figure 8: An example of escape routing. (a) A successful escape routing (b) Failed escape routing since e_5 and e_7 cannot reach boundary simultaneously without overlapping.

However, both wire routing and escape routing may fail. For example, in Fig. 7(a), routing between e_5 and a net (also a pin) which contains e_6 and e_7 will fail due to no feasible path as shown in Fig. 7(b). In Fig. 8(a), it is a successful escape routing. However, if Electrode e_3 and Electrode e_4 are merged together and perform wire routing between them, then it becomes the situation of Fig. 8(b), which may cause failed escape routing. If both e_5 and e_6 are individual pins finally, then they cannot perform escape routing simultaneously without overlapping because there is only an indepedent way out. It cannot be sure that e_5

Table 1: STATISTICS OF ALL CASES

Chip	Size	#E	P_{max}	BST
amino	6 X 8	20	16	12
multiplex	15 x 15	59	32	4
PCR	15 X 15	62	32	6
multifunctional	15 X 15	91	64	12
DNA preparation	13 X 21	77	32	12

and e_7 can reach boundary without overlapping. Hence, in the procedure, both wire routing and escape routing will be checked completely before an unaddressed electrode is added into a current pin. Although routing check takes a lot of execution time, it can absolutely guarantee that escape routing will be successful in the end because we check escape routing whenever there is a wire routing one by one.

5. EXPERIMENTAL RESULTS

We implement the proposed algorithm with C++ language on a 3.40-GHz 64-bit Linux machine with 8GB memory. There are five test cases, including amino acid synthesis, multiplexed assay, PCR amplification, multifunctional chip, and DNA sample preparation to evaluate efficiency of our algorithm. Table 1 lists the specification containing the size of the chips, number of electrodes, pin-constraints, and each initial lower bound of switching time $BST_{initial}$ of all test cases.

We compare the electrode addressing results with a baseline algorithm in Table 2. We implement the identical progressive addressing and wire routing technique in baseline algorithm without limiting the number of switching times. ST_{max} denotes the maximum number of switching times. BST denotes the maximum number of initial bound of switching time. To evaluate the reliability of the chips, $ST_{max}/BST(\%)$ is calculated to represents the growth rate of ST_{max}. Compared with the baseline, although proposed algorithm has slightly overhead on pins and CPU times, the average growth rate can be decreased from 76.67% to 1.67%. Furthermore, the growth rate of most test cases can be successfully minimized to 0%. Besides, for DNA preparation, although the pin-constraint is the strictest one among all test cases, the growth rate can still be minimized from 83.33% to 8.33%. To further evaluate the reliability, the distribution of switching times among all test cases is shown in Fig. 9. In Fig. 9(a), for baseline, it can be found that large number of electrodes are actuated by huge number of switching times. It represents that many electrodes suffer the contact angle reduction problem after broadcast addressing. On the other hand, in Fig. 9(b), most electrodes are actuated by few number of switching times, which represents the impact of the contact angle reduction problem can be well-controlled by proposed algorithm. Most important of all, the pin-constraints of all test cases are satisfied with feasible routing solutions.

6. CONCLUSIONS

In this paper, an algorithm of reliability-driven chip-level design for high-frequency EWOD chips is presented. A network flow based progressive addressing and routing approach is proposed to overcome the challenge of reliability issue and complex wire routing problem. Experimental result shows

Table 2: ELECTRODE ADDRESSING COMPARISON BETWEEN BASELINE AND OURS

Chip	BASELINE				OURS			
	ST_{max}	#Pin	$ST_{max}/BST(\%)$	CPU(s)	ST_{max}	#Pin	$ST_{max}/BST(\%)$	CPU(s)
amino	14	13	16.67%	0.19	12	14	0%	0.15
multiplex	10	18	150%	29.6	4	23	0%	21.95
PCR	12	29	100%	33.2	6	32	0%	34.09
multifunctional	16	58	33.33%	39.81	12	61	0%	37.62
DNA preparation	22	28	83.33%	41.54	13	31	8.33%	70.78
Average			76.67%				1.67%	

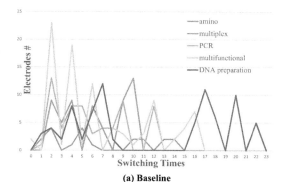

(a) Baseline

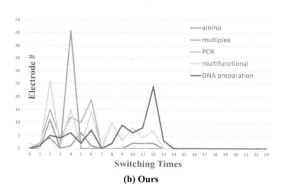

(b) Ours

Figure 9: Distribution of electrodes numbers and switching times.

that our algorithm is effective that the influence of the contact angle reduction problem is minimized. A reliable chip-level design satisfying the pin-constraint can be generated with feasible wire routing solution by our algorithm.

7. REFERENCES

[1] J.-W. Chang, T.-W. Huang, and T.-Y. Ho, "An ILP-based obstacle-avoiding Routing algorithm for pin-constrained EWOD chips," *Proc. IEEE/ACM ASPDAC*, pp. 67–72, 2012.

[2] K. Chakrabarty, "Towards fault-tolerant digital microfluidic lab-on-chip: defects, fault modeling, testing, and reconfiguration," *Proc. IEEE ICBCS*, pp. 329–332, 2008.

[3] R. B. Fair, "Digital microfluidics: is a true lab-on-a-chip possible?," *Microfluidics and Nanofluidics*, vol. 3, no. 3, pp. 245–281, 2007.

[4] Shih-Kang Fan, Tsung-Han Hsieh and Di-Yu Lin "General digital microfluidic platform manipulating dieletric and conductive droplets by dielectrophoresis and electrowetting," *Lab on chip*, pp. 1236–1242, 2009

[5] J. Gong and C. J. Kim, "Direct-referencing two-dimensional-array digital microfluidics using multilayer printed circuit board," *IEEE J. MEMS*, no. 2, pp. 257–264, 2008.

[6] T.-Y. Ho, J. Zeng, and K. Chakrabarty, "Digital microfluidic biochips: A vision for functional diversity and more than Moore," *IEEE/ACM ICCAD*, pp. 578–585, 2010.

[7] T.-W. Huang, S.-Y. Yeh, and T.-Y. Ho, "A network-flow based pin-count aware routing algorithm for broadcast electrode-addressing EWOD chips," *Proc. IEEE/ACM ICCAD*, pp. 425–431, 2010.

[8] T.-W. Huang, H.-Y. Su and T.-Y. Ho, "Progressive Network-Flow Based Power-Aware Broadcast Addressing for Pin-Constrained Digital Microfluidic Biochips," *Proc. IEEE/ACM DAC*, pp. 741–746, 2011.

[9] T.-W. Huang, K. Chakrabarty, and T.-Y. Ho, "Reliability-oriented broadcast electrode-addressing for pin-constrained digital microfluidic biochips," *Proc. IEEE/ACM ICCAD*, pp. 448–455, 2011.

[10] L. Huang, B. Koo, and C. J. Kim, "Evaluation of anodic Ta2 O5 as the dielectric layer for EWOD devices," *IEEE MEMS*, pp. 428-431, 2012.

[11] C. C.-Y. Lin and Y.-W. Chang, "ILP-based pin-count aware design methodology for microfluidic biochips," *Proc. ACM/IEEE DAC*, pp. 258–263, 2009.

[12] Y. Luo, K. Chakrabarty, and T.-Y. Ho "Design of cyberphysical digital microfluidic biochips under Completion-Time Uncertainties in Fluidic Operations," *Proc. ACM/IEEE DAC*, 2013

[13] P. Paik, V. Pamula, and R. Fair, "Rapid droplet mixers for digital microfluidic systems", *Lab on a Chip*, vol.3, pp. 253–259, 2003.

[14] M. G. Pollack, A. D. Shenderov, and R. B. Fair, "Electrowetting-based actuation of droplets for integrated microfluidics," *Lab on chip*, pp. 96–101, 2002.

[15] J. H. Song, R. Evans, Y. Y. Lin, B. N. Hsu, and R. B. Fair, "A scaling model for electrowetting-on-dielectric microfluidic actuators," *Microfluidics and Nanofluidics*, pp. 75–89, 2009.

[16] F. Su, K. Chakrabarty, and R. B. Fair, "Microfluidics based biochips: technology issues, implementation platforms, and design-automation challenges," *IEEE Trans. on CAD*, pp. 211–223, 2006.

[17] T. Xu and K. Chakrabarty, "Broadcast electrode-addressing for pin-constrained multi-functional digital microfluidic biochips," *Proc. ACM/IEEE DAC*, pp. 173–178, 2008.

[18] S.-H. Yeh, J.-W. Chang, T.-W. Huang, T.-Y. Ho, "Voltage-aware chip-level design for reliability-driven pin-constrained EWOD chips", *Proc. IEEE/ACM ICCAD*, pp. 353–360, 2012.

[19] T. Yan and M. D. F. Wong, "A correct network flow model for escape routing", *Proc. ACM/IEEE DAC*, pp. 332–335, 2009.

[20] L. Young, "Anodic oxides films," New York, NY: Academic Press Inc., 1961.

[21] Y. Zhao and K. Chakrabarty, "Co-optimization of droplet routing and pin assignment in disposable digital microfluidic biochips," *Proc. ACM ISPD*, pp. 69–76, 2011.

Design Synthesis and Optimization for Automotive Embedded Systems

Qi Zhu
Department of Electrical Engineering
University of California, Riverside

Peng Deng
Department of Electrical Engineering
University of California, Riverside

ABSTRACT

Embedded software and electronics are major contributors of values in vehicles, and play a dominant role in vehicle innovations. The design of automotive embedded systems has become more and more challenging, with the rapid increase of system complexity and more requirements on various design objectives. Methodologies such as model-based design are being adopted to improve design quality and productivity through the usage of functional models. However, there is still a significant lack of design automation tools, in particular synthesis and optimization tools, that can turn complex functional specifications to correct and optimal software implementations on distributed embedded platforms. In this paper, we discuss some of the major technical challenges and the problems to be solved in automotive embedded systems design, especially for the synthesis and optimization of embedded software.

Categories and Subject Descriptors

C.3 [**Special-purpose and Application-based Systems**]: [Real-time and embedded systems]

Keywords

automotive embedded systems; design automation; software synthesis and optimization

1. TRENDS AND CHALLENGES

The fast advancement of embedded software and electronics in vehicles presents tremendous technical and business challenges for automotive systems design. These challenges are discussed in [57, 55, 21]. In below, we highlight the major technical challenges in design synthesis and optimization.

1.1 Complexity

The complexity of automotive embedded systems has been increasing dramatically in terms of both scale and features. From year 2000 to 2010, embedded software development

cost increased from 2% to 13% of a vehicle's total value, and the number of lines of code increased from 1 million to 100 million. In a premium car, there are 2000 to 3000 singular functions that are related to software, which are combined into 250 to 300 functions used by the driver and passengers to operate the car [16]. On the hardware side, electronics increased from 13% to 24% of a vehicle's total value, and is closer to 45% in hybrid vehicles. The number of ECUs (electronic control units) in a standard car has gone from 20 to over 50 in past decade, and is closer to 100 ECUs in a premium car [57].

Moving forward, software and electronics will play a dominant role in vehicle innovation. Approximately 90% of automotive innovations in 2012 featured software and electronics, especially in active safety and infotainment systems [40], and it is predicted that this will continue to be the trend in the future. With this trend, the complexity of automotive embedded systems, in particular the complexity of embedded software, will continue to rise rapidly.

1.2 Multicore and distributed platforms

The rapid increase of functional complexity, the potential cost saving from system integration, and the changes in the supply chain have lead to a fundamental shift in system architecture of automotive embedded systems [21]. The traditional *federated architecture*, where each function is deployed to one ECU and provided as a black-box by Tier-1 supplier, is shifting to the *integrated architecture*, where one function can be distributed over multiple ECUs and multiple functions can be supported by one ECU. There is also the trend to deploy multicore ECUs to support the increasing functional complexity and to reduce the number of ECUs in the system (therefore reduce the costs for ECUs and their connection wires). With the shift to integrated architecture and the usage of multicore ECUs, there is significantly more sharing and contention among software functions over computation and communication resources.

1.3 Design objectives

In the design of automotive embedded systems, in addition to guarantee the functional correctness of the system, there are greater and more diverse demands on a variety of non-functional design objectives. Many of those objective are timing related, such as control performance, safety, timing extensibility and robustness. *Performance* of a control path is affected by sampling period and end-to-end latency [58, 13, 53, 24]. *Safety* relates to whether end-to-end latency deadlines along functional paths can be met, and to whether faults can be tolerated and in what fashion (e.g. fail safety versus fail operational). *Timing extensibility* as defined in [69, 70, 71] measures how much the execution time of each task can be increased without violating design constraints. This metric reflects the capability of a system to accommodate future upgrades and modifications, which is imperative for large-volume and long-lifetime systems such as vehicle and airplanes. *Timing robustness* as defined in [69] measures the maximum scaling factor of the execution times of all tasks that allows to retain feasibility, and is called breakdown factor. Intuitively, a larger breakdown factor allows a wider selection of implementation platforms (e.g. different processor speeds for cost/performance trade-off) and makes the system more robust with respect to timing variations.

In addition to timing related objectives, objectives such as *reusability* and *modularity* have become more and more important for improving design productivity and reducing design cost. *Memory usage*, which relates to program code size, data memory usage, and communication buffers, is an important metric as well. There are also emerging design objectives such as *security*. Automotive security has become critical as the vehicles are more networked and more connected with the environment, infrastructure, and other systems. Researchers demonstrated that modern vehicles can be attacked from a variety of interfaces including physical access, short-range wireless, and long-range wireless channels [17, 31, 32]. To protect against the attacks, not only the various interfaces of the systems need to be secured, the internal embedded software and hardware architectures need to be hardened with security mechanisms as well.

It is important and challenging to address various non-functional objectives during the design process, while guaranteeing the functional correctness of the system. Different objectives typically lead to different design choices, and careful trade-offs need to be made during the design space exploration. For instance, allocating tasks evenly across processors usually improves timing extensibility, however puts more messages on the buses and may be detrimental to system safety and security.

2. DESIGN METHODOLOGIES AND FRAMEWORKS

Various methodologies and frameworks are proposed to address the design challenges for real-time embedded systems and cyber-physical systems, including automotive embedded systems. Model-based design (MBD) is increasingly used in the development of complex embedded systems due to its capabilities to support early design verification/validation through formal functional models and the capabilities to generate software implementations from those functional models [56, 1]. Among many functional modeling tools, the Simulink/Stateflow toolset [62] is popular in control systems design, and is based on the synchronous reactive (SR) semantics. There are a number of other languages/tools based on SR models, such as Signal, Lustre and Esterel languages [11], and the SCADE suite [5]. Esterel and Lustre models are implemented as a single event-server software task. The need to depart from the monolithic code generation and allow for multiple functions for each module is acknowledged in [12]. The Simulink/Embedded Coder code generators allow a single software task and a fixed-priority multi-task code generation options, in which one

task is generated for each period in the model and tasks are scheduled by Rate Monotonic policy. The single-task implementations preserve the model semantics at the cost of a very strong condition on task schedulability, while the multi-task solutions provided by Simulink do not consider many non-functional objectives and do not target multicore and distributed platforms. Overall, there is a lack of support for defining the software task and hardware resource model in the model-based design flow [57], and consequently a lack of modeling and optimization in task generation with respect to non-functional objectives such as timing (which may further affect functional correctness).

There are many other model-based (or meta-model based) design frameworks and methodologies proposed for real-time embedded systems. The platform-based design (PBD) [30, 15, 55] paradigm is based on the separation of functionality and architecture in modeling, and the mapping of functional model onto architectural platform for design space exploration. The previous design space exploration work based on PBD [46, 68, 19, 72, 70] focuses on the mapping between software tasks and hardware platform, including work for hard real-time automotive embedded systems. Model-integrated computing (MIC) [63, 29, 4] refines and facilitates model-based development of complex software systems by providing a comprehensive set of tools – GME [33], UDM, GReAT – for building, analyzing, managing and transforming domain-specific models. It also provides a domain independent tool DESERT for generic constraint-based design space exploration [44]. The work in [64] decouples software design from platform uncertainties based on the Embedded Systems Modeling Language (ESMoL) [48, 49]. Ptolemy is a design environment for heterogeneous and hybrid systems that supports modeling with a number of common models of computation [23]. It is well designed for modeling real-time embedded systems, and mostly focuses on functional modeling of the algorithms. Giotto is a time-triggered language that provides an abstract programmer's model for the implementation of embedded control systems with hard real-time constraints [28]. A compositional real-time scheduling framework is proposed in [59, 60, 22] for supporting the compositionality of timing requirements in complex embedded systems. The framework is supported by the CARTS tool [3] and the Real-Time Xen visualization platform [35, 65]. BIP (Behavior, Interaction, Priority) is a general framework that supports a rigorous model-based and component-based design flow [8, 9, 14]. It provides the BIP language for building complex systems by coordinating the behavior of atomic components, and a tool set including translators, source-to-source transformers and compilers. Other frameworks include Compaan/Laura [61], ForSyDe [52], MESH [45], Mescal [6], MILAN [7], etc.

3. SOFTWARE SYNTHESIS AND OPTIMIZATION

To fully unleash the power of model-based approaches and improve the design quality, it is important to have an automated software synthesis flow that turns functional models to correct, predictable, and optimal software task implementations on various embedded platforms. As shown in Fig. 1, such flow should optimize the generation of software tasks from the functional model, and optimize the mapping from those tasks onto the embedded platform by exploring the allocation and scheduling of tasks on ECUs and the communication mechanisms among tasks.

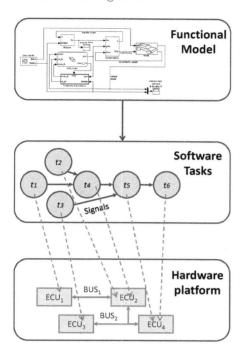

Figure 1: Model-based software synthesis flow for automotive embedded systems

Task generation and task mapping should not be treated as isolated steps, but rather in an *integrated fashion*, e.g., through solving integrated formulations or using iterative algorithms, since the two aspects are highly interdependent. The first requirement for task generation and mapping is to preserve the functional correctness by guaranteeing the consistency of data values (for communication and state variables) and the preservation of data flows (i.e. for any flow of data in the system, both the values and the order should be consistent between the task implementation and the functional model specification).

While guaranteeing the functional correctness, task generation and mapping are optimized with respect to a variety of non-functional objectives that may include timing-related objectives (performance, safety, extensibility, robustness), software engineering related objectives (reusability, modularity, memory usage), reliability, security, etc. The target embedded platforms may be single-core, multicore, time-triggered distributed platforms, or asynchronous distributed platforms without a global clock.

In the AUTOSAR (AUTomotive Open System ARchitecture) standard [2], which defines open standards for automotive Electrics/Electronics (E/E) architectures, task generation can be regarded as a process that first maps functional blocks in *software components (SWC)* to *runnables* and then maps runnables to tasks.

Next, we will discuss more details about task generation and task mapping in synthesizing functional models.

3.1 Task generation

The generation of tasks strongly depends on the *semantics* of the initial functional models. In automotive domain, the synchronous reactive (SR) semantics is widely used in functional modeling, with popular tools such as Simulink/Stateflow.

An SR models is typically represented by a synchronous block diagram (SBD), where links connect functional blocks through their input and output ports. Blocks can be of two types: dataflow blocks or extended finite state machine (FSM) blocks – called regular blocks and Stateflow blocks in Simulink, respectively. *Dataflow blocks* can be of three types: discrete, continuous, and triggered. Discrete blocks are activated at periodic time instants to process input signals and produce output signals and state updates. Continuous blocks process continuous signals, and triggered blocks are only activated on the occurrences of a given event. Each *FSM block* has a set of trigger (activation) events that, when active, may result in the execution of a set of actions. Each trigger event is associated with a period, and may or may not be active at each period instant. An extended FSM allows internal concurrency and hierarchy, and may be transformed into an equivalent regular (flat) FSM in many cases[27, 34].

In an SBD, some blocks may be *macro blocks* that include lower-level blocks and captured by lower-level SBDs. A block that does not include other blocks is an atomic block. During task generation, an atomic dataflow block cannot be decomposed further and is implemented in one task (may be with other blocks). A macro block or an FSM block can be implemented in multiple tasks. Most of the existing approaches, however, conduct only single-task generation for FSM blocks, and either single-task or limited multi-task generation without much optimization for macro blocks. This might lead to suboptimal solutions, as demonstrated in work such as [69] for FSM blocks.

3.1.1 Task generation for FSM blocks

In SR models, synchronous FSMs are commonly used to capture changes of the system state under trigger events. Each FSM block has a set of trigger (activation) events that, when active, may result in the execution of a set of actions. Each trigger event is associated with a period, and it is common for an FSM to have multiple trigger events with different periods. In current tools such as the Embedded Coder/Simulink Coder [62], a single periodic task is generated for each FSM block. Every time this task is activated, it checks for active trigger events and processes them. To make sure it will not miss any trigger event, the task is executed at the greatest common divisor (GCD) of the periods of its trigger events. In [43], it is observed that such single-task implementations may lead to unnecessary activations, and therefore reduce the system schedulability and cause memory overhead on communication buffers. By generating multiple software tasks according to a *partitioning* of the FSM based on the periods of the trigger events, the system schedulability and memory usage may be improved.

Formally, an FSM is defined by a tuple $(\mathbf{S}, S_0, \mathbf{I}, \mathbf{O}, \mathbf{E}, \mathbf{T})$, where $\mathbf{S} = \{S_0, S_1, S_2, \ldots S_l\}$ is a set of states, $S_0 \in \mathbf{S}$ is the initial state, $\mathbf{I} = \{i_1, i_2, \ldots i_p\}$ and $\mathbf{O} = \{o_1, o_2, \ldots o_q\}$ are the input and output signals. $\mathbf{E}$ is a set of trigger events. Each event e_j is generated by the value change of a signal, and may only occur with a period t_{e_j} that is an integer multiple of a system base period t_{base} (i.e. $t_{e_j} = k_{e_j} \cdot t_{base}$). At each time instant $k \cdot t_{e_j}$, the event may or may not present (in which case the system may stutter). Finally, $\mathbf{T}$ is a set of transition rules. Each transition $\theta_j \in \mathbf{T}$ is a tuple

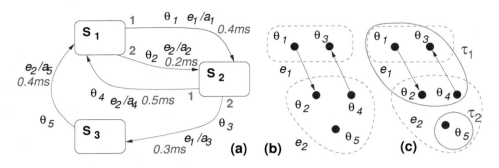

Figure 2: (a) an FSM example; e_1 has $2ms$ period and e_2 has $3ms$ period, (b) a transition partition of the FSM (in dotted lines) that does not lead to feasible multi-task implementation, (c) another partition (in red, solid lines) that leads to a feasible multi-task implementation (τ_1 and τ_2).

$\theta_j = \{S_{s_j}, S_{d_j}, e_{\theta_j}, g_j, a_j, \gamma_j\}$, where S_{s_j} is the source state, S_{d_j} is the destination state, $e_{\theta_j} \in \mathbf{E}$ is the trigger event (different transitions may be triggered by the same event), g_j is the guard condition, a_j is the action, and γ_j is the priority among the transitions that start from the same state (the lower the number, the higher the priority). When two or more transitions from the same source state are enabled at the same time, the priority associated with the transition is used to determine which transition should be performed.

Fig. 2(a) shows an example FSM. The periods of e_1 and e_2 are $2ms$ and $3ms$ respectively. For each transition, the associated trigger event and action are shown, along with the transition priority (in red and bold) and the execution time of the action (in blue and italic). The guard condition is omitted.

During task generation, an FSM F may be implemented by a set of tasks $\mathcal{T} = \{\tau_1, \tau_2, \ldots \tau_n\}$. In a *single-task implementation*, all transitions from the same FSM F are implemented in a single task τ. The period of τ is the GCD of the periods of all trigger events. For the example in Fig. 2(a), the task period is the GCD of event periods $2ms$ and $3ms$, i.e. $1ms$. All transitions must complete within this task period to ensure it will not miss the next trigger event so as to guarantee functional correctness.

A *multi-task implementation* depends on the partitioning of the transitions to different tasks, however not every partition leads to a feasible implementation. Because of the fixed priority scheduling among tasks (common scenario in automotive systems), the task priorities in a feasible multi-task implementation needs to be consistent with the transition priorities, i.e. τ_i has higher priority than τ_j if a transition in τ_i has higher priority than a transition in τ_j. During execution, τ_i sends an inhibition signal to all lower priority tasks τ_j generated from the same FSM, if one of its transitions executes. When this happens, τ_j skips. It is easy to see that the transition partition in Fig. 2(b) does not lead to a feasible implementation because θ_1 has higher priority than θ_2 and θ_4 has higher priority than θ_3 (denoted by uni-directional edges). Fig. 2(c) demonstrates a partition that leads to a feasible multi-task implementation. The four transitions $\{\theta_1, \theta_2, \theta_3, \theta_4\}$ are implemented in task τ_1 with period $1ms$, while θ_5 is implemented in τ_2 with period $3ms$.

There may exist many feasible multi-task implementations for an FSM. In [69], a *general partitioned model* is proposed for formalizing multi-task implementations of a synchronous FSM and defined two metrics for quantitatively measuring

the quality of different task implementations: a *breakdown factor* that measures the timing robustness, and an *action extensibility* metric that measures the capability to accommodate upgrades. For the example in Fig. 2(a), the action extensibility of the multi-task implementation in Fig. 2(c) is better than the single-task implementation, and there are other multi-task implementations that may improve both action extensibility and breakdown factor. An algorithm is proposed in [69] to generate a correct and efficient task implementation of synchronous FSMs for these two metrics on single-core platforms, while guaranteeing the functional correctness and satisfying schedulability constraints.

3.1.2 Task generation for macro blocks

An SR model is represented by a network of functional blocks in an SBD, and organized in hierarchy through macro blocks that themselves are described by SBDs. Therefore, task generation for macro blocks (subsystems in Simulink) is one of the key aspects in synthesizing SR models.

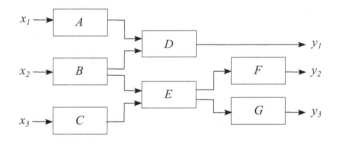

Figure 3: An SBD example

Fig. 3 shows an SBD example, with three inputs, three outputs, and seven blocks. Each block has an activation period. If all blocks have the same period, it is a *single-rate* SBD, otherwise it is a *multi-rate* SBD. During task generation, the functionality of the SBD is implemented by a set of tasks. Each task implements a subset of blocks, and each block is implemented in at least one task. If a block is implemented in multiple tasks, the corresponding code is only executed once within one synchronous instant (e.g. through a modulo counter as in [38]). Each task has an activation period, which is the GCD of the periods of the blocks that are implemented in the task.

Various non-functional objectives may be considered during the task generation from SBDs. *Modularity, reusability*

144

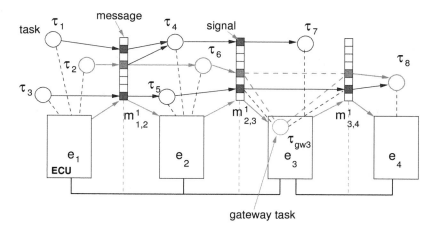

Figure 4: Mapping of tasks onto embedded hardware platform. The design space typically includes task allocation, signal packing and message allocation, and task and message scheduling.

and code size are software engineering related objectives, and can be evaluated based on the definitions in [38, 37]. Modularity is measured by the number of tasks, and optimum modularity is achieved when the number of tasks is minimum. Optimum reusability is achieved when no false input-output dependency is introduced in the task generation. In the example of Fig. 3, if the SBD is implemented in a single task and reused as a black-box, false dependencies would exist between y_1 and x_3, y_2 and x_1, and y_3 and x_1. The feedback connections between those pairs (e.g., y_1 and x_3) are not allowed, leading to limitations in its reuse. In reality, there are no dependencies among those pairs, and the corresponding feedback connections are safe. Optimum (minimum) code size is achieved when no block is included in more than one task.

The work in [38] addresses the problem of clustering synchronous blocks for modular reuse by avoiding false input-output dependencies, quantifies the modularity in terms of the number of clusters and interface functions, and explores the trade-off between modularity and reusability. In [37] the trade-off between modularity and code size is further explored. In [50], an efficient symbolic representation is proposed to simplify the modularity optimization. In [42], a branch-and-bound algorithm is presented for buffer optimization in multi-task implementation of Simulink models. In [20], an MILP (Mixed Integer Linear Programming) formulation is provided for similar problem.

Timing related objectives can be defined based on output latencies. For each output y_i, the worst case latency within a synchronous instant is the latest possible time when the task that generates y_i completes. Some outputs may be control signals that are sensitive to latencies, and a control performance metric can be defined to minimize such latencies. Extensibility and robustness can also be defined similarly as for FSMs but based on blocks (instead of actions).

3.2 Task mapping

The tasks generated from functional models are mapped onto embedded hardware platforms for execution. The design space to be explored typically includes the allocation of tasks onto ECUs, the packing of signals into messages and the allocation of messages on buses, the scheduling of

tasks and messages (e.g. through priority assignment) and possibly the assignment of their periods, as shown in Fig. 4.

There is a large body of work in the literature that address various aspects of mapping for real-time embedded systems. Design objectives such as timing, utilization, reliability, fault tolerance, extensibility, and security have been optimized during mapping. Platforms with various communication protocols are addressed, such as CAN (Controller Area Network, currently the most used protocol for safety critical applications in cars) and FlexRay. We will review some of the work in below.

The problem of optimal packing of periodic signals into CAN frames while minimizing bus utilization is proven to be NP-hard in [54], where a heuristic solution is provided. A similar problem for FlexRay time-triggered bus is discussed in [39]. In [51], genetic algorithms are used for optimizing priority and period assignments with respect to a number of constraints, including end-to-end deadlines and jitter. In [47] a heuristic optimization algorithm for mixed time-triggered and event-triggered systems is proposed. In [41], a SAT-based approach for task and message allocation is proposed. In [10], task allocation and priority assignment are defined with the purpose of optimizing the extensibility with respect to changes in task computation times. In [26, 25], a generalized definition of extensibility on multiple dimensions is presented, and a randomized optimization procedure based on a genetic algorithm is proposed to solve the optimization problem.

In [72, 68], an MILP formulation is presented to minimize end-to-end path latencies by exploring task allocation, signal packing and message allocation, and task and message scheduling. A two-stage MILP based algorithm is presented to reduce the complexity. In [18], a geometric programming based algorithm is proposed to explore task and message periods for meeting constraints on end-to-end latencies and resource utilization. In [70, 71], a multi-step algorithm with an MILP front-end and a heuristic back-end is proposed to optimize task extensibility. In [66, 67], algorithms are proposed to minimize stack and communication memory usage during mapping. In [36], an approach is proposed to address security together with performance and schedulability during task mapping on CAN based automotive systems.

4. CONCLUSION

The design of automotive embedded systems is very challenging, especially with the fast increase of software complexity and the move to integrated architecture and multicore platforms. While methodologies such as model-based design provide functional modeling capabilities for early design verification/validation, there is an urgent need for design automation methodologies and tools to synthesize those functional models to correct and optimal task implementations on embedded hardware platforms. In this paper, we discuss this aspect of the automotive design and review some of the relevant work. Other aspects, such as code generation, hardware architectural exploration, formal verification and testing, are also in great need of design automation methods and tools, and in many cases should be addressed together with the software synthesis aspect.

References

[1] Automakers opting for model-based design. http://www.designnews.com.

[2] Autosar. http://www.autosar.org.

[3] Carts (compositional analysis of real-time systems). http://rtg.cis.upenn.edu/carts/index.php.

[4] Model integrated computing. http://www.isis.vanderbilt.edu/research/MIC.

[5] Scade. http://www.esterel-technologies.com/products/scade-suite/.

[6] K. K. A. Mihal. Mapping Concurrent Applications onto Architectural Platforms. pages 39–59. Kluwer Academic Publishers, 2003.

[7] A. Bakshi, V. Prasanna, and A. Ledeczi. MILAN: A model based integrated simulation framework for design of embedded systems. In *Proceedings of Workshop on Languages, Compilers, and Tools for Embedded Systems*, June 2001.

[8] A. Basu, B. Bensalem, M. Bozga, J. Combaz, M. Jaber, T. Nguyen, and J. Sifakis. Rigorous component-based system design using the bip framework. *Software, IEEE*, 28(3):41 –48, may-june 2011.

[9] A. Basu, M. Bozga, and J. Sifakis. Modeling heterogeneous real-time components in BIP. In *Proceedings of the Fourth IEEE International Conference on Software Engineering and Formal Methods (SEFM06)*, pages 3–12, Washington, DC, USA, 2006.

[10] I. Bate and P. Emberson. Incorporating scenarios and heuristics to improve flexibility in real-time embedded systems. In *12th IEEE RTAS Conference*, pages 221–230, April 2006.

[11] A. Benveniste, P. Caspi, S. Edwards, N. Halbwachs, P. Le Guernic, and R. de Simone. The synchronous languages 12 years later. *Proceedings of the IEEE 91(1)*, pages 64–83, 2003.

[12] A. Benveniste, P. Le Guernic, and P. Aubry. Compositionality in dataflow synchronous languages: specification and code generation. In *Technical Report 3310, Irisa - Inria*, 1997.

[13] E. Bini and A. Cervin. Delay-aware period assignment in control systems. In *Real-Time Systems Symposium, 2008*, pages 291 –300, 30 2008-dec. 3 2008.

[14] S. Bliudze and J. Sifakis. The algebra of connectors – structuring interactions in BIP. In *Proceedings of the 7th ACM & IEEE International conference on Embedded Software (EMSOFT07)*, Salzburg, Austria, September 30–October 3 2007.

[15] L. Carloni, F. D. Bernardinis, C. Pinello, A. Sangiovanni-Vincentelli, and M. Sgroi. Platform-Based Design for Embedded Systems. In *The Embedded Systems Handbook*. CRC Press, 2005.

[16] R. N. Charette. This car runs on code. *IEEE Spectrum*, February 2009.

[17] S. Checkoway, D. McCoy, B. Kantor, D. Anderson, H. Shacham, S. Savage, K. Koscher, A. Czeskis, F. Roesner, and T. Kohno. Comprehensive experimental analyses of automotive attack surfaces. In *Proceedings of the 20th USENIX Conference on Security*, SEC'11, pages 6–6, Berkeley, CA, USA, 2011. USENIX Association.

[18] A. Davare, Q. Zhu, M. D. Natale, C. Pinello, S. Kanajan, and A. Sangiovanni-Vincentelli. Period Optimization for Hard Real-time Distributed Automotive Systems. In *Design Automation Conference (DAC'07)*, June 2007.

[19] D. Densmore, A. Simalatsar, A. Davare, R. Passerone, and A. Sangiovanni-Vincentelli. Umts mpsoc design evaluation using a system level design framework. In *Proceedings of the Conference on Design, Automation and Test in Europe*, DATE '09, pages 478–483, 3001 Leuven, Belgium, Belgium, 2009. European Design and Automation Association.

[20] M. Di Natale, L. Guo, H. Zeng, and A. Sangiovanni-Vincentelli. Synthesis of multi-task implementations of simulink models with minimum delays. *IEEE Transactions on Industrial Informatics 6(4)*, pages 637–651, 2010.

[21] M. Di Natale and A. Sangiovanni-Vincentelli. Moving from federated to integrated architectures in automotive: The role of standards, methods and tools. *Proceedings of the IEEE*, 98(4):603 –620, april 2010.

[22] A. Easwaran, M. Anand, and I. Lee. Compositional analysis framework using edp resource models. In *Real-Time Systems Symposium, 2007. RTSS 2007. 28th IEEE International*, pages 129 –138, dec. 2007.

[23] J. Eker, J. Janneck, E. Lee, J. Liu, X. Liu, J. Ludvig, S. Neuendorffer, S. Sachs, and Y. Xiong. Taming heterogeneity - the ptolemy approach. *Proceedings of the IEEE*, 91(1):127 – 144, jan 2003.

[24] D. Goswami, M. Lukasiewycz, R. Schneider, and S. Chakraborty. Time-triggered implementations of mixed-criticality automotive software. In *Design, Automation Test in Europe Conference Exhibition (DATE), 2012*, pages 1227 –1232, march 2012.

[25] A. Hamann, R. Racu, and R. Ernst. Methods for multi-dimensional robustness optimization in complex embedded systems. In *Proc. of the ACM EMSOFT Conference*, September 2007.

[26] A. Hamann, R. Racu, and R. Ernst. Multi-dimensional robustness optimization in heterogeneous distributed embedded systems. In *Proc. of the 13th IEEE RTAS Conference*, April 2007.

[27] D. Harel. Statecharts: A visual formalism for complex systems. *Sci. Comput. Program.*, 8(3):231–274, June 1987.

[28] T. Henzinger, B. Horowitz, and C. Kirsch. Giotto: a time-triggered language for embedded programming. *Proceedings of the IEEE*, 91(1):84–99, 2003.

[29] G. Karsai, J. Sztipanovits, A. Ledeczi, and T. Bapty. Model-integrated development of embedded software. *Proceedings of the IEEE*, 91(1):145 – 164, jan 2003.

[30] K. Keutzer, S. Malik, A. R. Newton, J. Rabaey, and A. Sangiovanni-Vincentelli. System Level Design: Orthogonolization of Concerns and Platform-Based Design. *IEEE Transactions on Computer-Aided Design of Integrated Circuits and Systems*, 19(12), December 2000.

[31] P. Kleberger, T. Olovsson, and E. Jonsson. Security aspects of the in-vehicle network in the connected car. In *Intelligent Vehicles Symposium (IV), 2011 IEEE*, pages 528–533, 2011.

[32] F. Koushanfar, A.-R. Sadeghi, and H. Seudie. Eda for secure and dependable cybercars: Challenges and opportunities. In *Design Automation Conference (DAC), 2012 49th ACM/EDAC/IEEE*, pages 220–228, 2012.

[33] A. Ledeczi, M. Maroti, A. Bakay, G. Karsai, J. Garrett, C. Thomason, G. Nordstrom, J. Sprinkle, and P. Volgyesi. The generic modeling environment. In *IEEE Workshop on Intelligent Signal Processing*, May 2001.

[34] E. A. Lee and P. Varaiya. *Structure and Interpretation of Signals and Systems, Second Edition*. LeeVaraiya.org, 2011.

[35] J. Lee, S. Xi, S. Chen, L. Phan, C. Gill, I. Lee, C. Lu, and O. Sokolsky. Realizing compositional scheduling through virtualization. In *Real-Time and Embedded Technology and Applications Symposium (RTAS), 2012 IEEE 18th*, pages 13 –22, april 2012.

[36] C.-W. Lin, Q. Zhu, C. Phung, and A. Sangiovanni-Vincentelli. Security-aware mapping for can-based real-time distributed automotive systems. In *Computer-Aided Design (ICCAD), 2013 IEEE/ACM International Conference on*, pages 115–121, 2013.

[37] R. Lublinerman, C. Szegedy, and S. Tripakis. Modular code generation from synchronous block diagrams: modularity vs. code size. In *Proceedings of the 36th annual ACM SIGPLAN-SIGACT symposium on Principles of programming languages*, POPL '09, pages 78–89, New York, NY, USA, 2009. ACM.

[38] R. Lublinerman and S. Tripakis. Modularity vs. reusability: code generation from synchronous block diagrams. In *Proceedings of the conference on Design, automation and test in Europe*, DATE '08, pages 1504–1509, New York, NY, USA, 2008. ACM.

[39] M. Lukasiewycz, M. Glass, P. Milbredt, and J. Teich. Flexray schedule optimization of the static segment. In *CODES+ISSS Conference*, June 2009.

[40] McKinsey&Company. The road to 2020 and beyond: What's driving the global automotive industry? September 2013.

[41] A. Metzner and C. Herde. RTSAT– an optimal and efficient approach to the task allocation problem in distributed architectures. In *RTSS '06: Proceedings of the 27th IEEE International Real-Time Systems Symposium*, pages 147–158, Washington, DC, USA, 2006. IEEE Computer Society.

[42] M. D. Natale and V. Pappalardo. Buffer optimization in multitask implementations of simulink models. *ACM Trans. Embed. Comput. Syst.*, 7(3):23:1–23:32, May 2008.

[43] M. D. Natale and H. Zeng. Task Implementation and Schedulability Analysis of Synchronous Finite State Machines. In *DATE '12: Proceedings of the Conference on Design, Automation and Test in Europe*, 2012.

[44] S. Neema, J. Sztipanovits, and G. Karsai. Constraint-based design-space exploration and model synthesis. In *IN PROCEEDINGS OF EMSOFTâĂŹ03, VOLUME 2855 OF LNCS*, pages 290–305. Springer, 2003.

[45] J. Paul and D. Thomas. A Layered, Codesign Virtual Machine Approach to Modeling Computer Systems. In *Proceedings of the conference on Design, automation and test in Europe*, page 522. IEEE Computer Society, 2002.

[46] A. Pinto, A. Bonivento, A. L. Sangiovanni-Vincentelli, R. Passerone, and M. Sgroi. System level design paradigms: Platform-based design and communication synthesis. *ACM Trans. Des. Autom. Electron. Syst.*, 11(3):537–563, June 2004.

[47] T. Pop, P. Eles, and Z. Peng. Design optimization of mixed time/event-triggered distributed embedded systems. In *CODES+ISSS '03: Proceedings of the 1st IEEE/ACM/IFIP International Conference on Hardware/Software Codesign and System Synthesis*, pages 83–89, New York, NY, USA, 2003. ACM Press.

[48] J. Porter, G. Hemingway, H. Nine, C. vanBuskirk, N. Kottenstette, G. Karsai, and J. Sztipanovits. The esmol language and tools for high-confidence

distributed control systems design. part 1: Language, framework, and analysis. 09/2010 2010.

[49] J. Porter, G. Karsai, P. Völgyesi, H. Nine, P. Humke, G. Hemingway, R. Thibodeaux, and J. Sztipanovits. Models in software engineering. chapter Towards Model-Based Integration of Tools and Techniques for Embedded Control System Design, Verification, and Implementation, pages 20–34. Springer-Verlag, Berlin, Heidelberg, 2009.

[50] M. Pouzet and P. Raymond. Modular static scheduling of synchronous data-flow networks: An efficient symbolic representation. In *Proceedings of the Seventh ACM International Conference on Embedded Software*, EMSOFT '09, pages 215–224, New York, NY, USA, 2009. ACM.

[51] R. Racu, M. Jersak, and R. Ernst. Applying sensitivity analysis in real-time distributed systems. In *Proceedings of the 11th Real Time and Embedded Technology and Applications Symposium*, pages 160–169, San Francisco (CA), U.S.A., Mar. 2005.

[52] T. Raudvere, I. Sander, A. K. Singh, and A. Jantsch. Verification of Design Decisions in ForSyDe. In *Proceedings of the 1st IEEE/ACM/IFIP international conference on Hardware/software codesign and system synthesis*, pages 176–181. ACM Press, 2003.

[53] S. Samii, A. Cervin, P. Eles, and Z. Peng. Integrated scheduling and synthesis of control applications on distributed embedded systems. In *Design, Automation Test in Europe Conference Exhibition, 2009. DATE '09.*, pages 57 –62, april 2009.

[54] K. Sandstrom, C. Norstom, and M. Ahlmark. Frame packing in real-time communication. *Seventh International Conference on Real-Time Computing Systems and Applications*, pages 399–403, 2000.

[55] A. Sangiovanni-Vincentelli. Quo Vadis, SLD? Reasoning About the Trends and Challenges of System Level Design. *Proceedings of the IEEE*, 95(3):467–506, March 2007.

[56] A. Sangiovanni-Vincentelli, W. Damm, and R. Passerone. Taming dr. frankenstein: Contract-based design for cyber-physical systems*. *European Journal of Control*, 18(3):217 – 238, 2012.

[57] A. Sangiovanni-Vincentelli and M. Di Natale. Embedded system design for automotive applications. *Computer*, 40(10):42 –51, 2007.

[58] D. Seto, J. Lehoczky, L. Sha, and K. Shin. On task schedulability in real-time control systems. In *Real-Time Systems Symposium, 1996., 17th IEEE*, pages 13 –21, dec 1996.

[59] I. Shin and I. Lee. Compositional real-time scheduling framework. In *Real-Time Systems Symposium, 2004. Proceedings. 25th IEEE International*, pages 57 – 67, dec. 2004.

[60] I. Shin and I. Lee. Compositional real-time scheduling framework with periodic model. *ACM Trans. Embed. Comput. Syst.*, 7(3):30:1–30:39, May 2008.

[61] T. Stefanov, C. Zissulescu, A. Turjan, Bart, and E. Deprettere. System Design Using Kahn Process Networks: The Compaan/Laura Approach. In *Proceedings of the conference on Design, automation and test in Europe*, page 10340. IEEE Computer Society, 2004.

[62] M. Stigge, P. Ekberg, N. Guan, and W. Yi. The digraph real-time task model. In *Real-Time and Embedded Technology and Applications Symposium (RTAS), 2011 17th IEEE*, pages 71 –80, april 2011.

[63] J. Sztipanovits and G. Karsai. Model-integrated computing. *Computer*, 30(4):110 –111, apr 1997.

[64] J. Sztipanovits, X. Koutsoukos, G. Karsai, N. Kottenstette, P. Antsaklis, V. Gupta, B. Goodwine, J. Baras, and S. Wang. Toward a science of cyber-physical system integration. *Proceedings of the IEEE*, 100(1):29 –44, jan. 2012.

[65] S. Xi, J. Wilson, C. Lu, and C. Gill. Rt-xen: Towards real-time hypervisor scheduling in xen. In *Embedded Software (EMSOFT), 2011 Proceedings of the International Conference on*, pages 39 –48, oct. 2011.

[66] H. Zeng, M. D. Natale, and Q. Zhu. Minimizing stack and communication memory usage in real-time embedded applications. *to appear in the ACM Transactions on Embedded Computing Systems*.

[67] H. Zeng, M. D. Natale, and Q. Zhu. Optimizing stack memory requirements for real-time embedded applications. In *Proceedings of the 17th IEEE International Conference on Emerging Technologies and Factory Automation (ETFA)*, 2012.

[68] W. Zheng, Q. Zhu, M. D. Natale, and A. Sangiovanni-Vincentelli. Definition of Task Allocation and Priority Assignment in Hard Real-Time Distributed Systems. In *RTSS '07: Proceedings of the 28th IEEE International Real-Time Systems Symposium*, pages 161–170, 2007.

[69] Q. Zhu, P. Deng, M. D. Natale, and H. Zeng. Robust and Extensible Task Implementations of Synchronous Finite State Machines. *the 16th IEEE/ACM Conference on Design, Automation and Test in Europe (DATE)*, 2013.

[70] Q. Zhu, Y. Yang, M. D. Natale, E. Scholte, and A. Sangiovanni-Vincentelli. Optimizing the Software Architecture for Extensibility in Hard Real-Time Distributed Systems. *the IEEE Transactions on Industrial Informatics*, 6(4):621–636, 2010.

[71] Q. Zhu, Y. Yang, E. Scholte, M. D. Natale, and A. Sangiovanni-Vincentelli. Optimizing Extensibility in Hard Real-Time Distributed Systems. In *RTAS '09: Proceedings of the 2009 15th IEEE Real-Time and Embedded Technology and Applications Symposium*, pages 275–284, 2009.

[72] Q. Zhu, H. Zeng, W. Zheng, M. D. Natale, and A. Sangiovanni-Vincentelli. Optimization of task allocation and priority assignment in hard real-time distributed systems. *ACM Trans. Embed. Comput. Syst.*, 11(4):85:1–85:30, 2012.

Opportunities in Power Distribution Network System Optimization: From EDA Perspective

Gi-Joon Nam
IBM Research
11501 Burnet Road
Austin TX 78750
gnam@us.ibm.com

Sani Nassif
Radyalis LLP
7000 N. Mopac Expressway Suite 200
Austin, TX 78731
sani.r.nassif@ieee.org

ABSTRACT

Smart Grid refers to the technology that uses computer-based remote control and automation on electricity delivery systems. In recent years, the industry is going through rather dramatic transformations thanks to the quite significant scale of shifts in energy policy, technology and consumer focus. The current situation is dire however. It was reported that the United States loses $150 billion per year due to power interruptions for example and the energy companies lag behind in adopting these new trends. Hence, there are urgent urges for them to act on a number of critical challenges and opportunities in order to build and manage the electric power systems in more efficient manners. In this presentation, we first provide a brief introduction of energy distribution system design and show how much energy distribution problem resembles that of EDA optimization. Then, we claim that there exist ample opportunities for the traditional VLSI design automation techniques to play a critical role in this relatively new domain of problems. As a proof of concept, a few real world power distribution problems are formulated and solved via advanced simulation, analysis and optimization techniques that are adapted from the EDA field. Finally the potential future research directions are discussed where further innovations are possible via EDA-like thinking process.

Categories and Subject Descriptors

J.6 [**Computer-Aided Engineering**], G.1.6 [**Optimization**]

General Terms

Algorithms, Management, Measurement, Performance, Design, Reliability, Experimentation.

Keywords

Smart Grid, Power distribution networks, Simulation, Optimization, Analytics, EDA.

ISPD'14, March 30–April 2, 2014, Petaluma, California, USA.
ACM 978-1-4503-2592-9/14/03.
http://dx.doi.org/10.1145/2560519.2565875

Indoor Localization Technology and Algorithm Issues

[Extended Abstract]

Fan Ye

EECS School, Peking University, Beijing, China 100871

yefan@pku.edu.cn

Categories and Subject Descriptors

C.2.m [**Computer Systems Organization**]: Computer-communication networks

Keywords

Indoor Localization, Physical Feature, Floor Plan

1. INTRODUCTION

Localization [2, 4] is the basis for novel features in various location based applications. Despite more than a decade of research, localization service is still far from pervasive indoors. The latest industry state-of-the-art, Google Indoor Maps [1], covers about 10,000 locations in 18 countries, which are only a fraction of the millions of shopping centers, airports, train stations, museums, hospitals and retail stores on the planet.

There are two major obstacles behind the sporadic availability. First, current mainstream indoor localization technologies largely rely on RF (Radio Frequency) signatures from certain IT infrastructure (e.g., WiFi access points [2] and cellular towers)Obtaining the *signature map* usually requires dedicated labor efforts to measure the signal parameters at fine grained grid points. Because they are susceptible to intrinsic fluctuations and external disturbances, the signatures have to be re-calibrated periodically to ensure accuracy. Some recent research has started to leverage crowdsourcing to reduce site survey efforts, but incentives are still lacking for wide user adoption. Thus the progress is inevitably slow.

Second, the floor plans of most indoor environments are not easily accessible to localization service providers. Google Indoor Maps has a web page where building owners or operators can upload their floor plans. However, the floor plan itself is a valuable business asset. Unless there are compelling business gain, the owners and operators may not necessarily want to share it with service providers. That is why explicit business negotiation and arrangement are usually required to have the coordination of the building owners or operators.

Such manually process inevitably incurs high cost and long latency.

We present two pieces of work towards addressing the two obstacles. First, we explore an alternative approach that has comparable performance to the industry state-of-the-art but without relying on the RF signature. Specifically, we leverage environmental physical features, such as logos of stores, paintings on the walls. Users use the smartphone to measure their relative positions to physical features, and the coordinates of these reference points are used to compute user locations. This has a few advantages: 1) Physical features are part of and abundant in the environment; they do not require dedicated deployment and maintenance efforts like IT infrastructure; 2) They seldom move and usually remain static over long periods of time. They are not affected by and thus impervious to electromagnetic disturbances from microwaves, cordless phones or wireless cameras. Once measured, their coordinates do not change, thus eliminating the need for periodic re-calibration.

Second, we describe a mobile crowdsensing [3] based approach to build indoor floor plans, such that service providers can leverage various kinds of data (such as images and motion) collected from common users without the need of business negotiation with building owners or operators. Given enough number of images of an indoor element (e.g., a store), one may infer the sizes and relative positions of the element to the locations where images are taken. Users may also provide additional input from inertial sensors about the relation between different locations, such as the angle rotated or distance traveled. Such input constitutes various constraints about the relative positions among elements. By formulating and solving an optimization problem that takes into consideration the sizes, relative positions among elements and image locations, we can produce a global map with the absolute coordinates of all elements in the floor plan.

2. REFERENCES

[1] Google indoor maps
http://maps.google.com/help/maps/indoormaps/.

[2] P. Bahl and V. N. Padmanabhan. RADAR: An in-building RF-based user location and tracking system. In *IEEE INFOCOM*, 2000.

[3] R. Ganti, F. Ye, and H. Lei. Mobile crowdsensing: current state and future challenges. *Communications Magazine, IEEE*, 49(11):32–39, 2011.

[4] H. Liu, Y. Gan, J. Yang, S. Sidhom, Y. Wang, Y. Chen, and F. Ye. Push the limit of wifi based localization for smartphones. In *ACM Mobicom 2012*.

ISPD'14, March 30–April 2, 2014, Petaluma, CA, USA.
ACM 978-1-4503-2592-9/14/03.
http://dx.doi.org/10.1145/2560519.2565874.

TAU 2014 Contest on Removing Common Path Pessimism during Timing Analysis

Jin Hu, Debjit Sinha, Igor Keller†

IBM Systems and Technology Group, Hopewell Junction, USA

†Cadence Design Systems, San Jose, USA

tau.contest@gmail.com

ABSTRACT

To margin against modeling limitations in considering design and electrical complexities (e.g., crosstalk coupling, voltage drops) as well as variability (e.g., manufacturing process, environmental), "early" and "late" signal propagation delays in static timing analysis are often made pessimistic by addition of extra guard bands. While these forced "early-late splits" provide desired margins, the splits applied across the entire design introduce excessive and undesired pessimism. To this end, "common path pessimism removal (CPPR)" eliminates the redundant pessimism during timing analysis.

The aim of the TAU 2014 timing contest is to seek novel ideas for fast CPPR by: (*i*) introducing the concept and importance of common path pessimism removal while highlighting the exponential run-time complexity of an optimal solution, (*ii*) encouraging novel parallelization techniques (including multi-threading), and (*iii*) facilitating the creation of a timing analysis and CPPR framework with benchmarks to further advance research in this area.

Categories and Subject Descriptors

B.8.2 [**Hardware**]: Performance and Reliability—
Performance Analysis and Design Aids

Keywords

Timing analysis; Common path pessimism removal; Algorithms; Design; Experimentation; Performance

1. INTRODUCTION

Static timing analysis is a key component of any integrated circuit (IC) chip design-closure flow, and is employed to obtain bounds on the fastest (*early*) and slowest (*late*) signal transition times for various timing tests and paths in the chip design. Growing chip design sizes and complexities (e.g., increased number of clock domains, increased significance of crosstalk coupling, voltage islands), as well as more complex and accurate timing models (e.g., current source models) lead to longer timing analysis run-times, thereby hindering designer productivity.

ISPD'14, March 30–April 2, 2014, Petaluma, California, USA.
Copyright 2014 ACM 978-1-4503-2592-9/14/03 ...$15.00.
http://dx.doi.org/10.1145/2560519.2565876

Variability in the deep sub-micron chip manufacturing process adds another dimension of timing analysis complexity, and ideally necessitates variation aware timing analysis. Manufacturing sources of variability include device front-end variability (e.g., variations in channel length, oxide thickness, dopant concentration) and back-end-of-line variability (e.g., metal). In addition, environmental sources of variation (e.g., voltage, temperature) impact circuit timing. While variation aware timing analysis approaches like statistical timing analysis and multi-corner timing analysis have been proposed to model variability, not all sources of variability are accurately modeled either due to increased modeling complexity or increased number of multi-corner runs.

Trade-offs are naturally performed on timing model complexity to achieve practical turn-around-times for chip static timing analysis. To margin against the ignored (or traded-off or uncertain) modeling limitations that are not explicitly and accurately modeled in the native timing models, *early* and *late* signal propagation delays (for both gates and wires) are made further pessimistic by the addition of extra guard bands. While these forced *early-late splits* provide the desired safety margins, applying the splits for the full path of some timing test introduces excessive and undesired pessimism if the data path shares an overlap with the clock path. *Common path pessimism removal (CPPR)* [1] attempts to remove this pessimism by tracing these potentially problematic paths and discarding some of the early-late difference along the common sub-path. An optimal solution to CPPR may require analysis of all paths in the design. For modern multi-million gate designs, this exponential performance complexity is impractical, and demands an intelligent selective analysis on only a sub-set of paths.[1]

This paper describes the TAU 2014 timing contest on common path pessimism removal, which seeks novel ideas for fast and accurate CPPR. The TAU 2014 timing contest (*i*) introduces the concepts and importance of CPPR while highlighting its challenges, such as exhibiting an exponential run-time complexity of an optimal solution, (*ii*) encourages novel parallelized analysis techniques, including the use of multiple threads, and (*iii*) provides a publicly available timing analysis and CPPR framework with benchmarks.

The paper is organized as follows. Section 2 provides a conceptual understanding of static timing analysis. Section 3 introduces the basic concept of CPPR. Section 4 discusses commonly-used filters in CPPR. Section 5 provides an example illustrating CPPR. Section 6 outlines the file formats of the TAU 2014 contest. Section 7 tabulates the benchmarks used in the contest. Section 8 describes the evaluation process. Section 9 concludes the paper.

---

[1]CPPR is alternatively known as clock reconvergence pessimism removal (CRPR).

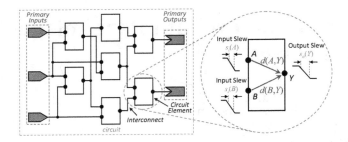

Figure 1: Generic circuit (left) and delay model representation of a combinational element (right).

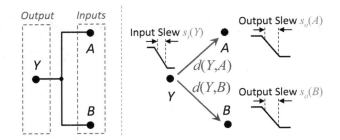

Figure 2: Generic output to input connection (left) and delay model (right).

2. STATIC TIMING ANALYSIS

A static timing analysis of a design typically provides a profile of the design's performance by measuring the timing propagation from inputs to outputs. This analysis provides a pessimistic bound, and thus facilitates further analysis of only problematic portions of the design.

2.1 Definitions

Timing analysis of a circuit computes the amount of time required for signals to propagate from *primary inputs (PIs)* to *primary outputs (POs)* through various *circuit elements* and *interconnect*. Signals arriving at an input of an element will be available at its output(s) at some later time; each pin-to-pin connection therefore introduces a *delay* during signal propagation. For example, as shown in Figure 1 (right), the delay across the circuit element from input A to output Y is designated by $d(A, Y)$. A *timing path* is a set of directed connections through circuit elements and interconnect, and its delay is quantified by the sum of those components' delays.

A signal transition is characterized by its *input slew* and *output slew*, where slew is defined as the amount of time for the signal to transition from *high-to-low* or *low-to-high*.[2] For example, in Figure 1, the input slew at A is denoted by $s_i(A)$, and the output slew at Y is denoted by $s_o(Y)$.

To account for timing modeling limitations in considering design and electrical complexities, as well as multiple sources of variability, such as manufacturing variations, temperature fluctuation, voltage drops, and electromigration, timing analysis is typically done using an *early-late split*, where each circuit node has an early (lower) bound and a late (upper) bound on its time.[3] By convention, if the mode (early or late) is not explicitly specified, both modes should be considered. Both slew and delay are computed separately on early and late modes. For example, in early mode, an output slew s_o^E is computed using the input slew taken from the early mode, s_i^E, and, similarly, in late mode, the output slew s_o^L is computed using s_i^L.

Circuit elements. A *combinational* circuit element (e.g., OR gate) and interconnect propagate signals from input to output. Each combinational element has a defined delay d and output slew s_o for an input/output pin-pair. A *sequential* circuit element (e.g., flip-flop (FF)) captures data from the output(s) of a combinational block, and injects it into the input(s) of the combinational block in the next stage (Figure 3). This operation is synchronized by *clock signals*

generated by one or multiple clock sources. Clock signals that reach distinct flip-flops (e.g., sinks in the clock tree), are delayed from the clock source by a *clock latency*.

A (D) flip-flop captures a given logic value at its input data pin D, when a given clock edge is detected at its clock pin CK, and subsequently presents the captured value[4] at the output pin Q. For correct operation, a flip-flop requires the logic value of the input data pin to be stable for a specific period of time *before* the capturing clock edge, and is denoted by *setup time* (t^S). Additionally, the logic value of the input data pin must also be stable for a specific period of time *after* the capturing clock edge. This period of time is designated by the *hold time* (t^H). These constraints are modeled by timing *setup* and *hold* tests (denoted as T_S and T_H, respectively), between the data and clock pins of the flip-flop, as shown in Figure 3 (left).

2.2 Timing Propagation

Starting from the primary input(s), the instant that a signal reaches an input or output of a circuit element is quantified as the *arrival time (at)*. Similarly, starting from the primary output(s), the limits imposed for each arrival time to ensure proper circuit operation is quantified as the *required arrival time (rat)*. Given an arrival time and a required arrival time, the *slack* at a circuit node quantifies how well timing constraints are met. That is, a positive slack means the required time is satisfied, and a negative slack means the required time is in violation.

Actual arrival time. Starting from the primary inputs, arrival times (at) are computed by adding delays across a path, and performing the minimum (in early mode) or maximum (in late mode) of such accumulated times at a convergence point. This establishes bounds on the time that a signal transition can reach any given circuit node. For example, let $at^E(A)$ and $at^E(B)$ denote the early arrival times at pins A and B, respectively, in Figure 1 (right). The most pessimistic early mode arrival time at the output pin Y is:

$$at^E(Y) = \min \left(at^E(A) + d^E(A, Y), \atop at^E(B) + d^E(B, Y) \right). \tag{1}$$

Conversely, in late mode, the latest time that a signal transition can reach any given circuit node is computed. Following the same example in Figure 1 (right), the most pessimistic late mode arrival time at Y is:

$$at^L(Y) = \max \left(at^L(A) + d^L(A, Y), \atop at^L(B) + d^L(B, Y) \right). \tag{2}$$

---

[2]A *low (high)* signal is defined as 10% (90%) of the voltage.
[3]This is commonly accomplished by *derating* an existing delay value (e.g., by ±5%).

[4]The complement output $\overline{Q}$, is usually available as well.

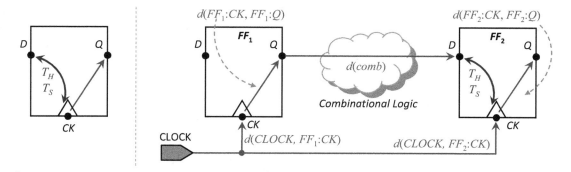

Figure 3: Generic D FF and its timing model (left), and two FFs in series and their timing models (right).

Required arrival time. Starting from the primary outputs, required arrival times (*rat*) are computed by subtracting the delays across a path, and performing the maximum (minimum) in early (late) mode of such accumulated times at a convergence point. That is, in early mode, the earliest time that a signal transition must reach any circuit node is computed. For example, in Figure 2, the most pessimistic early mode required arrival time at the output pin Y is:

$$rat^E(Y) = \max \left(rat^E(A) - d^E(Y, A), \\ rat^E(B) - d^E(Y, B) \right). \tag{3}$$

Conversely, in late mode, the earliest time that a signal transition must reach a given circuit node is computed. Following the example in Figure 2, the most pessimistic late mode required arrival time at the input pin Y is:

$$rat^L(Y) = \min \left(rat^L(A) - d^L(Y, A), \\ rat^L(B) - d^L(Y, B) \right). \tag{4}$$

Slack. For proper circuit operation, the following conditions *must* be met:

$$at^E \geq rat^E, \tag{5}$$
$$at^L \leq rat^L. \tag{6}$$

To quantify how well timing constraints are met at each circuit node, slacks (*slack*) can be computed based on the aforementioned conditions. That is, slacks are positive when the required times are met, and negative otherwise.

$$slack^E = at^E - rat^E \tag{7}$$
$$slack^L = rat^L - at^L \tag{8}$$

Slew propagation. As circuit element delays and interconnect delays are functions of input slew (s_i), subsequent output slew (s_o) must be propagated. One approach to slew propagation at a convergence point is *worst-slew* propagation, wherein the smallest (largest) slew in early (late) mode is propagated. Following the example in Figure 1 (right), the early and late output slew at output pin Y, respectively, are:

$$s_o^E(Y) = \min \left(s_o^E(A, Y), s_o^E(B, Y) \right), \tag{9}$$
$$s_o^L(Y) = \max \left(s_o^L(A, Y), s_o^L(B, Y) \right), \tag{10}$$

where $s_o^E(A, Y)$ is a function of $s_i^E(A)$, $s_o^E(B, Y)$ is a function of $s_i^E(B)$, $s_o^L(A, Y)$ is a function of $s_i^L(A)$, and $s_o^L(B, Y)$ is a function of $s_i^L(B)$.

Sequential signal propagation. Signal transition between two flip-flops is illustrated in Figure 3 (right). Assuming that the clock edge is generated at the source at time 0, it reaches the injecting (launching) flip-flop FF_1 at time $d(CLOCK, FF_1{:}CK)$, making the data available at the input of the combinational block $d(FF_1{:}CK, FF_1{:}Q)$ time later. If the propagation delay in the combinational block is $d(comb)$, then the data is available at the input of the capturing flip-flop FF_2 at time:

$$d(CLOCK, FF_1{:}CK) + d(FF_1{:}CK, FF_1{:}Q) + d(comb).$$

Assuming the clock period to be a constant P, the next clock edge reaches FF_2 at time $P + d(CLOCK, FF_2{:}CK)$. For correct operation, the data must be be available at the input pin $(FF_2{:}D)$ t^S time units before the next clock edge. Therefore, the late arrival time and the late required arrival time at the data pin are:

$$at^L(FF_2{:}D) = d^L(CLOCK, FF_1{:}CK) \\ + d^L(FF_1{:}CK, FF_1{:}Q) + d^L(comb), \tag{11}$$

$$\begin{aligned} rat^{Setup}(FF_2{:}D) &= rat^L(FF_2{:}D) \\ &= P + at^E(FF_2{:}CK) - t^S \tag{12} \\ &= P + d^E(CLOCK, FF_2{:}CK) - t^S. \end{aligned}$$

A similar condition is derived for ensuring that the hold time is respected. The data input pin D of FF_2 must remain stable for at least t^H time after the clock edge reaches the corresponding CK pin. Therefore, the early arrival time and early required arrival time at the data pin are:

$$at^E(FF_2{:}D) = d^E(CLOCK, FF_1{:}CK) \\ + d^E(FF_1{:}CK, FF_1{:}Q) + d^E(comb), \tag{13}$$

$$\begin{aligned} rat^{Hold}(FF_2{:}D) &= rat^E(FF_2{:}D) \\ &= at^L(FF_2{:}CK) + t^H \tag{14} \\ &= d^L(CLOCK, FF_2{:}CK) + t^H. \end{aligned}$$

The aforementioned arrival times from Equations (11) and (13) and required arrival times from Equations (12) and (14) induce hold and setup slacks, which are derived from Equations (7) and (8), respectively.

The timing model used for this contest is a simplified derivation of the model employed in the TAU 2013 variation-aware timing contest. Additional details are provided in [2].

3. COMMON PATH PESSIMISM REMOVAL (CPPR)

The early-late split based timing analysis effectively accounts for modeling limitations at the cost of added *pessimism*. Consequently, this can lead to an overly conservative design. Consider the slack computation example in Figure 4. The early (late) data's arrival time is compared with the late (early) clock's arrival time for the hold (setup) test. However, along the physically-common portion of the data path and clock path, the signal cannot simultaneously experience all the effects accounted for during early and late mode operation, (e.g., the signal cannot be both at high voltage and low voltage). As a result, this unnecessary pessimism can lead to tests being marked as failing (having negative slack), when in actuality, they could be passing (having positive slack). This unnecessary pessimism should thus be avoided when reporting final timing results.

Generally, the amount of pessimism for a given test can be approximated by the difference in the early and late arrival times at the *common point* (Figure 4). The common point is found by backwards tracing from the data and clock for the *path with the worst slack*. In the general case, there are multiple paths converging at the data input of a flip-flop, and every path will have its own amount of undue pessimism. Therefore, to find the correct *credit* or slack, the minimum credit found across all paths needs to be computed.

Hold tests. For tests that compare the data arrival against the clock arrival in the *same clock cycle* (e.g., data must be stable *after* the clock signal arrives at the capturing flip-flop in this case), the total pessimism incurred is the difference between the early and late arrival times at the last meeting point between the data path and clock path. That is, the signal propagation to this common point is identical for both clock and data, and thus does not warrant any early-late split. Thus, the credit for a hold test with one data path dp sharing a sub-path with clock path cp is:

$$C^{Hold}(dp) = at^L(CP) - at^E(CP), \qquad (15)$$

where CP is the point when cp and dp diverge (Figure 4).

Setup tests. For tests that compare the data arrival against the clock arrival in *different clock cycles* (e.g., data must be stable *before* the subsequent cycle clock-signal arrives at the capturing flip-flop in this case), the total pessimism incurred is the sum of the partial difference of late and early delays upstream of the common point. While the data and clock path share the same physical components, they are launched at different clock cycles. Therefore, only cycle-independent contributors to the early-late split can be removed (e.g., due to global chip-to-chip variation), while cycle-dependent ones cannot be removed (e.g., due to crosstalk coupling adjusts, clock primary input arrival times, and intra-chip voltage variation). If the early-late split is limited to cycle-independent variation,[5] the credit for a setup test with one data path dp sharing a sub-path with clock path cp is:

$$C^{Setup}(dp) = \sum_{p \in \{cp \cap dp\}} d^L(p) - d^E(p), \qquad (16)$$

Test slack. As removing pessimism could require analyzing many paths, the post-CPPR test slack is the minimum slack of all paths that converge at the data point of the test.[6]

---

[5]Considering crosstalk noise is out of scope for this contest.
[6]Only hold and setup tests are considered in the contest.

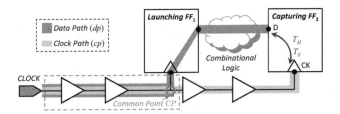

Figure 4: Pessimism due to early-late timing split.

4. CPPR RUN-TIME IMPROVEMENTS

A complete common path pessimism removal analysis necessitates investigating all paths for every (failing) test in this design. This naive procedure, however, is not used in practice by commercial timing analysis tools due to the impractical run-time for modern chip designs. As alluded to in Section 2, performing an upfront static timing analysis to find a guaranteed lower bound for all test slacks is instrumental to quickly narrow the analysis space to specific paths that causing timing failures.

A set of filters or *fast-outs* is then employed by CPPR algorithms to further prune the search space. Among common filters used in CPPR, (i) *path-limit*, (ii) *pre-CPPR slack-limit*, and (iii) *post-CPPR path-slack-limit*, contribute to the largest run-time savings without significantly impacting the final solution accuracy. This condition applies to the scope of this paper wherein CPPR can only improve the test slack by application of non-negative common-path credits.

Path-limit filters. Path-limit filters enforce tracing at most a given threshold number of paths for each timing test analyzed by CPPR. Ideally, if there were a known correspondence between pre- and post-CPPR paths and slacks, this filter would be able to guarantee tracing and analysis of the most critical path(s) for each test. However, such a correspondence does not always exist, and only heuristically over a representative set of designs, can a threshold for the path-limit filter be determined (which is "likely" to trace and analyze critical paths for tests). This filter is primarily used for reducing CPPR run-time while taking some risk of an incorrect test slack being reported. It should be noted that any reported test slack in this case is guaranteed to be an upper bound of the ideal test slack (Figure 5). For any given test with slack $slack_{pre}$ prior to CPPR,

$$slack_{pre} \leq slack^* \leq slack^j_{inCPPR}, \qquad (17)$$

where $slack^j_{inCPPR}$ denotes the worst slack among the post-CPPR path slacks for j paths traced by CPPR, and $slack^*$ denotes the golden (correct) answer. If CPPR traces all N paths for the test, the following is guaranteed:

$$slack^N_{inCPPR} = slack^*. \qquad (18)$$

It can be observed from the figure that it is not essential to trace all N paths to obtain $slack^*$. However, it is not trivial to determine if the worst post-CPPR path has already been traced, and this is what necessitates tracing all paths.

Slack-limit filters. The goal of the pre-CPPR slack-limit and *post-CPPR path-slack-limit* filters is to predict if timing tests meet specified requirements (non-negative slacks). That is, if the slack of a test is guaranteed to be above a threshold (e.g., 0), the test is considered passing and the actual value of the slack is no longer relevant. This forms

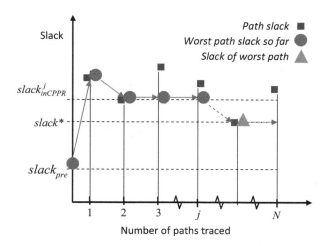

Figure 5: Illustration of worst path slack as function of paths traced during CPPR.

the basis of the *pre-CPPR slack-limit*, which denotes the threshold above which a test is considered passing. CPPR is performed on a test only if the test slack is smaller than this threshold, since it is known that CPPR can only increase the final slack. This filter can also be used during CPPR, wherein if paths are being traced in a non-decreasing order of pre-CPPR path slacks, tracing is performed only as long as for each path traced, the pre-CPPR path slack is smaller than the *pre-CPPR slack-limit* threshold.

In contrast, a post-CPPR path slack that is smaller than a threshold *post-CPPR path-slack-limit* may indicate a design problem that forces a designer to perform design updates or optimization. In such cases, the precise worst slack value is likewise irrelevant.[7] For such a test, it is commonly no longer beneficial to trace additional paths since that test's slack is guaranteed to be at most the last encountered post-CPPR path slack (which is indicating a failing test).

Commercial timing analysis tools employ a large number of similar filters to improve CPPR run-time. In this contest, a *pre-CPPR slack-limit* filter threshold of 0 is used for generation of golden results as well as for output comparisons. While useful in controlling run-time, filters should be used in CPPR with discretion to avoid optimistic results wherein the true critical path(s) is (are) not traced.

Other important factors (e.g., crosstalk, waveform effects) that impact timing and CPPR are considered by commercial timing analysis tools, but are ignored for simplicity in the contest. In addition, the topology of the clock structure is limited to a tree; clock path reconvergence and clock-grid structures are not considered for the contest.

Path tracing under variability is a considerably more difficult problem. In statistical timing, the concept of a critical path becomes less well-defined; there is now a probability p that a path is critical (e.g., $0 \le p \le 1$). Path ordering in this situation is a difficult problem, and destroys the properties that facilitate the use of the aforementioned slack filters in deterministic timing analysis. Statistical common path pessimism reduction is out of scope of this contest and could be a natural extension of the contest in the future.

---

[7]It should be noted that the pre-CPPR slack is still a slack lower bound.

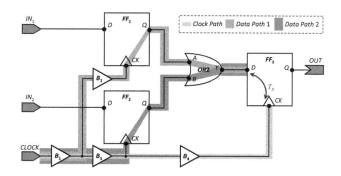

Figure 6: Example sequential circuit.

5. EXAMPLE

Consider a sample circuit as shown in Figure 6, where two data paths feed a common flip-flop (FF_3). Using the following timing information, the final CPPR credit calculation for the setup test T_S at FF_3 is illustrated. Assume that all wire delays and all primary input arrival times are zero.

$$
\begin{aligned}
d^E(B_1) &= 20, & d^L(B_1) &= 25 \\
d^E(B_2) &= 10, & d^L(B_2) &= 30 \\
d^E(B_3) &= 10, & d^L(B_3) &= 45 \\
d^E(B_4) &= 10, & d^L(B_4) &= 30 \\
d^L(FF_1{:}CK, FF_1{:}Q) &= d^L(FF_2{:}CK, FF_2{:}Q) = 40 \\
d^L(OR2{:}A, OR2{:}Y) &= d^L(OR2{:}B, OR2{:}Y) = 50 \\
P &= 120 \\
t^S(FF_3) &= 30
\end{aligned}
$$

Pre-CPPR test slack computation. The pre-CPPR test slack is computed as follows:

$$
slack_{pre}^L(FF_3{:}D) = rat^L(FF_3{:}D) - at^L(FF_3{:}D). \quad (19)
$$

Using Equation (12) in Equation (19),

$$
\begin{aligned}
slack_{pre}^L(FF_3{:}D) &= P + at^E(FF_3{:}CK) - t^S(FF_3) \\
&\quad - at^L(FF_3{:}D) \quad (20) \\
&= 120 + 40 - 30 - \max(145, 160) = -30.
\end{aligned}
$$

Pre-CPPR path slack computation. Consider data path 1 (dp_1):

$$
CLOCK \rightarrow B_1 \rightarrow B_2 \rightarrow FF_1 \rightarrow OR2 \rightarrow FF_3.
$$

Using Equations (20) and (11), its pre-CPPR path slack is:

$$
\begin{aligned}
slack_{pre}^L(FF_3{:}D)|_{dp_1} &= P + \Big(d^E(B_1) + d^E(B_3) + d^E(B_4)\Big) \\
&\quad - t^S(FF_3) \\
&\quad - \big(d^L(OR2{:}A, OR2{:}Y) \\
&\quad + d^L(FF1{:}CK, FF1{:}Q) + \\
&\quad + d^L(B_2) + d^L(B_1)\big) \\
&= 120 + (40) - 30 - (145) = -15.
\end{aligned}
$$

Similarly, consider data path 2 (dp_2):

$$
CLOCK \rightarrow B_1 \rightarrow B_3 \rightarrow FF_2 \rightarrow OR2 \rightarrow FF_3.
$$

The pre-CPPR path slack for this path is:

$$
\begin{aligned}
slack^L_{pre}(FF_3{:}D)|_{dp_2} = {} & P + \Big(d^E(B_1) + d^E(B_3) + d^E(B_4) \Big) \\
& - t^S(FF_3) \\
& - \big(d^L(OR2{:}B, OR2{:}Y) \\
& + d^L(FF_2{:}CK, FF_2{:}Q) \\
& + d^L(B_3) + d^L(B_1) \big) \\
= {} & 120 + (40) - 30 - (160) = -30.
\end{aligned}
$$

Post-CPPR path slack computation. Without loss of generality, paths are traced in order of criticality, i.e., most negative to least negative. Starting with dp_2, its common portion with the clock path contains B_1 and B_3. Therefore, its credit is:

$$
\begin{aligned}
C^{Setup}(dp_2) &= \Big(d^L(B_1) - d^E(B_1) \Big) + \Big(d^L(B_3) - d^E(B_3) \Big) \\
&= (25 - 20) + (45 - 10) = 40.
\end{aligned}
$$

Similarly for dp_1, its CPPR credit is computed by finding the common portion, i.e., B_1:

$$
C^{Setup}(dp_1) = \Big(d^L(B_1) - d^E(B_1) \Big) = (25 - 20) = 5.
$$

The post-CPPR path slacks for dp_1 and dp_2 are:

$$
\begin{aligned}
slack^L_{post}(FF_3{:}D)|_{dp_1} &= slack^L_{pre}(FF_3{:}D)|_{dp_1} \\
&\quad + C^{Setup}(dp_1) \\
&= -15 + 5 = -10, \\
slack^L_{post}(FF_3{:}D)|_{dp_2} &= slack^L_{pre}(FF_3{:}D)|_{dp_2} \\
&\quad + C^{Setup}(dp_2) \\
&= -30 + 40 = 10.
\end{aligned}
$$

Post-CPPR test slack computation. The post-CPPR test slack for the setup test T_S between $FF_3{:}D$ and $FF_3{:}CK$ is the minimum post-CPPR path slack across all (data) paths through $FF_3{:}D$:

$$
\begin{aligned}
slack^S_{post}(FF_3{:}D) = \min \big(& slack^L_{post}(FF_3{:}D)|_{dp_1}, \\
& slack^L_{post}(FF_3{:}D)|_{dp_2} \big) \\
= \min \big({-10}, & \, 10 \big) = -10.
\end{aligned}
$$

Final CPPR credit computation. The final CPPR credit for the test is the difference between the post- and pre-CPPR test slacks:

$$
\begin{aligned}
C^{Setup} &= slack^S_{post}(FF_3{:}D) - slack^S_{pre}(FF_3{:}D) \\
&= -10 - (-30) = 20.
\end{aligned}
$$

Three observations are made from this example. (i) The most critical path *pre*-CPPR is not necessarily reflective of the true critical path. This emphasizes the importance of CPPR analysis, and highlights its impact on chip performance. (ii) During CPPR, analyzing the single-most critical path can be insufficient. In the example, if CPPR was only performed on the most critical pre-CPPR path dp_2, the final test slack would incorrectly seem positive, i.e., passing. In actuality, the next-most critical path is still failing. (iii) The final CPPR credit for the test need not match the credit for any one path traced during CPPR.

6. FILE FORMATS

Given a set of input files, the TAU 2014 contest requests development of a timer that reports post-CPPR critical tests and paths. The number of tests and paths to be reported is controlled via a set of pre-defined inputs to the tool.

6.1 User-def ned Parameters

The command line for the timer allows the following user-defined parameters: (i) the types of relevant tests (`<test-Type>`), (ii) the number of tests (`-numTests`), and (iii) the number of paths for each test (`-numPaths`).

- `-hold`, `-setup`, `-both`: input command switches that specify which set of tests to report in the output file. The option `-hold` indicates only hold tests, the option `-setup` indicates only setup tests, and the option `-both` indicates both hold and setup tests.
- `-numTests (int)`: input command where `(int)` is the number of *most critical* tests to be reported for each type of test. A test is considered critical if it has a non-positive *pre-CPPR* slack. The ordering of criticality, however, should be based on its *post-CPPR* slack. Non-critical tests should not be printed.
- `-numPaths (int)`: input command where `(int)` is the number of *most critical* paths per test to be reported for each type of test. The ordering of criticality is based on the *post-CPPR* slack, i.e., consistent with the test slack. Non-critical paths should not be printed.

6.2 Input Files

Each design consists of (i) a delay and (ii) a timing input file. The former describes the timing behavior of the circuit; the latter asserts the initial operating conditions.

Delay file. The delay file contains the description of the circuit cells as well as the delays and constraints for direct connection. Circuit topology is implicitly derived from this file, which has the following format.

```
input <PI>
output <PO>
<source> <sink> dᴱ dᴸ
hold <data> <clock> tᴴ
setup <data> <clock> tˢ
```

Keywords:
- `input` (`output`): primary input (output).
- `setup` (`hold`): setup (hold) test.

Variable fields:
- `<PI> <PO> <source> <sink> <data> <clock>` specify a node or pin name. `<PI>` (`<PO>`) is a primary input (output) of the design. `<source>` and `<sink>` specify a directed connection between a source pin and sink pin of a delay segment; `<data>` and `<clock>` specify the data and clock pins of a flip-flop.
- d^E (d^L) specify the early (late) delays between `<source>` and `<sink>`.
- t^H (t^S) specify the hold (setup) test time between `<data>` and `<clock>`.

Timing file. The timing file contains the relevant timing information needed to start signal propagation. The format of this file is as follows.

```
clock <PI> P
at <PI> at^E(<PI>) at^L(<PI>)
```

Keywords:
- clock: clock pin.
- at: arrival time.

Variable fields:
- P is the clock period.
- <PI> is a primary input node.
- at^E(<PI>) $(at^L$(<PI>)) is the early (late) arrival time of <PI>.

6.3 Output File

The output file contains the paths for each type of test specified in accordance with the input commands. The format for each critical test T with critical paths $DP = \{dp_1, dp_2, \ldots\}$, where $slack_{post}(dp_i) < slack_{post}(dp_j)$, $i < j$, is as follows.

```
<type> slack_pre^<type>(T) slack_post^<type>(T) |DP|
slack_pre(dp_1) slack_post(dp_1) |dp_1|
dp_1
slack_pre(dp_2) slack_post(dp_2) |dp_2|
dp_2
...
```

Variable fields:
- <type> is the test type, either **hold** or **setup**.
- $slack_{pre}^{<type>}(T)$ ($slack_{post}^{<type>}(T)$) is the pre- (post-)CPPR test slack for <type> test T.
- $|DP|$ is the number of reported data paths in DP.
- $slack_{pre}(p_i)$ ($slack_{post}(p_i)$) is the pre- (post-)CPPR path slack for path dp_i, $1 \leq i \leq |DP|$.
- $|dp_i|$ is the length of dp_i.
- dp_i is the node by node trace of the critical path, originating from the data pin of the FF and terminating at a primary input.

7. CONTEST BENCHMARKS

Table 1 presents the list of all benchmarks used in the TAU 2014 timing contest. The table shows number of primary inputs (PIs), primary outputs (POs), timing segments or arcs, and the number of timing tests for each benchmark. The larger benchmarks have close to a million (M) segments and several thousand (K) timing tests. Benchmark *Combo6* has 3.8M segments and 128.2K timing tests. A subset of the larger benchmarks are used for the final contest evaluation.

Figure 7 illustrates the impact of CPPR on some setup and hold test slacks for benchmarks *des_perf* and *vga_lcd*. The horizontal and vertical axes in the plots denote the pre-CPPR and post-CPPR slacks, respectively. Using the line indicating identical slack (with slope = 1.0) as reference, it is observed that each post-CPPR slack is at least the pre-CPPR slack value. Slack improvements of up to 100 picoseconds are seen from the figure. The plots indicate the importance of CPPR during design closure from a designer's perspective.

Table 1: Contest benchmarks and statistics.

Design	Number of:			
	PIs	POs	Segments	Tests
s27	6	1	112	6
s344	11	11	658	30
s349	11	11	682	30
s386	9	7	701	12
s400	5	6	813	42
s510	21	7	1091	12
s526	5	6	1097	42
s1196	16	14	2.4K	36
s1494	10	19	2.9K	12
systemcdes	132	65	13.3K	380
wb_dma	217	215	17.4K	1374
tv80	14	32	23.7K	838
systemcaes	260	129	29.6K	2.5K
mem_ctrl	115	152	45.0K	3.7K
ac97_ctrl	84	48	55.7K	9.3K
usb_funct	128	121	66.1K	4.3K
pci_bridge32	162	207	78.2K	16.4K
aes_core	260	129	86.7K	2.5K
des_perf	235	64	404.2K	19.7K
vga_lcd	89	109	525.6K	50.1K
Combo2	170	218	284.4K	29.5K
Combo3	353	215	216.2K	8.2K
Combo4	260	169	866.3K	53.5K
Combo5	432	164	2229.6K	79.0K
Combo6	486	174	3843.9K	128.2K
Combo7	459	148	3012.3K	109.6K

8. EVALUATION

A timer is evaluated on its (i) accuracy relative to the "golden" reference and (ii) relative run-time. Each output file o is uniquely identified by the benchmark design and the command-line settings of -numTests, -numPaths, and <testType>. The final score is the average across the set of all output files O.

Test and path accuracy. The slack accuracy $A(T)$ ($A(dp)$) for each reported test (path) with negative post-CPPR slack in o is compared with the golden. The accuracy score is a function of the slack difference, where if the difference falls outside of a specified threshold, no score is awarded.

Design accuracy. Given all test and path accuracy scores, the (raw) accuracy measurement $A(o)$ for an output file is the average of the following five terms:
- average of $A(T)$ of $T \in TEST$, where $TEST$ is bounded by -numTests
- average of $A(dp)$ of $dp \in DP$, where DP is bounded by -numPaths
- average of $A(critDP(T))$ of $T \in TEST$, where $critDP(T)$ is the most critical path for T
- $A(critT)$ of $critT \in TEST$, where $critT$ is the most critical test in the design
- minimum of $A(T)$ of $T \in TEST$

The first three terms quantify the overall accuracy quality, while the last two terms quantify the worst accuracy quality.

Run-time. Timer run-time is used as a modifier to $A(o)$.

Final ranking. A timer's overall score is the average across each output's weighted accuracy. For each benchmark design, multiple output files that emphasize both the importance of finding the most critical tests, and the set of paths that cause each test's timing violations, are generated.

159

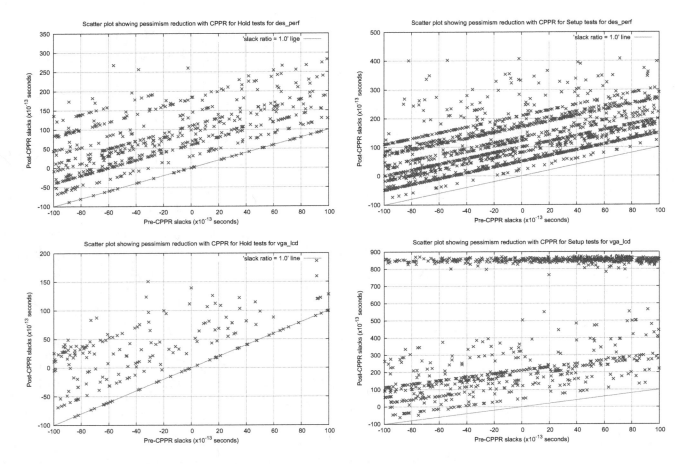

Figure 7: Impact of CPPR on test slacks.

9. SUMMARY

Common path pessimism reduction is an essential step during static timing analysis which reduces undesired pessimism from forced "early-late splits" in the common data and clock portion of timing tests' paths. An exhaustive approach may required analysis of all paths in the design, which is run-time impractical for modern large designs. This paper describes the TAU 2014 timing contest on common path pessimism reduction.

The aim of the TAU 2014 timing contest is to seek novel ideas for fast common path pessimism removal (CPPR) by: (*i*) introducing the concept and importance of common path pessimism removal while highlighting its associated challenges, (*ii*) encouraging novel parallelization techniques, and (*iii*) facilitating the creation of a publicly available timing analysis and CPPR framework, along with a set of benchmarks. Simplified delay models are used in the contest to steer focus towards algorithm development that aim to reduce run-time (including parallelization or multi-threading). Additional important factors for CPPR (e.g., crosstalk, waveform effects, and clock-grid structures) are ignored for simplicity in the contest.

Acknowledgments

The netlist and library formats used in the contest are simplified derivations of those used in the TAU 2013 variation aware timing analysis contest [2]. The authors acknowledge the help and support of the TAU 2013 contest committee for providing sample benchmarks and library.

The authors also acknowledge Jobin Jacob Kavalam, Sudharshan V, Prof. Nitin Chandrachoodan and Prof. Shankar Balachandran (IITimer team) from the Indian Institute of Technology, Madras, India for sharing the source code of their timing analysis tool (winners of [2]) with the participants of the TAU 2014 timing contest, and helping with the initial benchmark conversion from the prior year's contest.

10. REFERENCES

[1] J. Bhasker and R. Chadha, *Static timing analysis for nanometer designs: A practical approach*, Springer, 2009.

[2] D. Sinha, L. Guerra e Silva, J. Wang, S. Raghunathan, D. Netrabile and A. Shebaita, "TAU 2013 variation aware timing analysis contest", *Proc. International Symposium on Physical Design*, 2013, pp. 171-178.

ISPD 2014 Benchmarks with Sub-45nm Technology Rules for Detailed-Routing-Driven Placement

Vladimir Yutsis   Ismail S. Bustany   David Chinnery   Joseph R. Shinnerl

Mentor Graphics Corporation
Fremont, California, USA
{Vladimir_Yutsis, Ismail_Bustany, David_Chinnery, Joseph_Shinnerl}@mentor.com

Wen-Hao Liu
Department of Computer Science
National Tsing Hua University, Hsinchu, Taiwan
dnoldnol@gmail.com

ABSTRACT

The public release of realistic industrial placement benchmarks by IBM and Intel Corporations from 1998–2013 has been crucial to the progress in physical-design algorithms during those years. Direct comparisons of academic tools on these test cases, including widely publicized contests, have spurred researchers to discover faster, more scalable algorithms with significantly improved quality of results.

Nevertheless, close examination of these benchmarks reveals that the removal of important physical data from them prior to release now presents a serious obstacle to any accurate appraisal of the detailed routability of their placements. Recent studies suggest that academic placement algorithms may lack sufficient awareness of the pin geometry and routing rules missing from these benchmarks to adequately address the challenge of computing routable placements at 28nm-process technologies and below.

In this article, the reconstitution of the existing benchmarks via the injection of realistic yet fictitious pin data and routing rules is described. The enhanced benchmarks enable more meaningful comparisons of new placement algorithms by industrial detailed routing, beginning with the 2014 ISPD placement contest.

Categories and Subject Descriptors

B.7.2 [**Integrated Circuits**]: Design Aids - Placement and Routing; D.2.8 [**Software Engineering**]: Metrics—*complexity measures, performance measures*

General Terms

Algorithms, Design

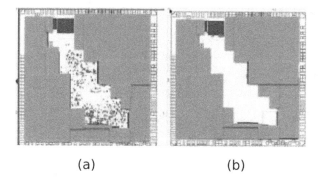

Figure 1: Sample GR/DR miscorrelation: (a) errors predicted by GR (b) actual DR errors.

Keywords

Placement; routability; placement evaluation; global routing; detailed routing

1. INTRODUCTION

As design rules continue to proliferate with downward scaling in the fabrication technology of integrated circuits, the importance of accuracy in routability modeling at the placement stage continues to increase. Numerous recent studies [1, 8, 10, 17] and contests [12, 15, 16] indicate a growing gap between the predictions of global-routing (GR) models traditionally employed in placement and the actual violations encountered by detailed routing (DR); an example is illustrated in Figure 1.

Highly accurate local modeling of routability throughout global placement, however, seems unlikely to be computationally efficient. As design sizes grow to tens of millions of movable objects or more, and the design cycle itself grows ever more complex, demand on the speed and scalability of placement continues to increase. Fine-grain design rules may hold little or no relevance to the coarse-grain cell-area density targets typically employed at the earliest iterations of global placement. Thus, one of the more pressing challenges to placement developers is the formulation of routability models which (a) provide high enough scale-appropriate accuracy when needed and (b) demand low computational overhead when irrelevant.

Existing benchmarks [12, 13, 15, 16] originated in industry and do illustrate much of the modern placement challenge, especially with respect to complex floorplan geometry, placement utilization, and global netlist structure. However, a large fraction of the technical specifications for these benchmarks has been removed for proprietary reasons. In addition to all timing-related data, pin shapes and their locations on cells are gone. These missing details impose hard limits on the testability of academic algorithms developed without access to proprietary design data.

The release of improved global-placement test suites constructed from publicly available benchmarks is the primary contribution of our work. Reducing the gap between routability estimates used by global placement [3, 4, 5, 7] and errors revealed only by detailed routing [8, 9, 14, 18] requires test suites that better expose inadequate consideration of design rules most frequently violated during placement. While actual proprietary information cannot be released, it is not difficult for an experienced physical-design engineer to create fictitious geometry reproducing the essential challenges of real fabrication geometry. Details of our construction are listed in the remaining sections of this paper along with simplified descriptions of some design rules they expose. Without our enhancements, the existing test cases lack sufficient detail to fully reveal the miscorrelation between global routing and detailed routing seen on actual industrial designs.

A brief description of the evaluation metric used for the ISPD 2014 Detailed-Routability-Driven Placement Contest is presented in the last section.

2. SAMPLE DESIGN RULES

General routability challenges for placement include the following.

- **Netlist:** high-fanout nets, data paths, timing objectives
- **Floorplan:** low or high placement utilization, irregular placeable area, narrow channels between fixed blocks
- **Routing constraints:** routing blockages and restrictions by layer, pin access, boundary-pin placement, power/ground(PG)-grid avoidance
- **Design rules:** minimum spacing, pin geometry, edge-type, end-of-line, non-default routing (NDR)

As is customary, we label routing layers from lowest to highest as M1 (Metal 1), M2, ... Standard cells typically have pins connecting to routing wires directly on M1 but frequently have pins directly connecting to routes on M2 and, in some technologies, even up to M4. Connections to highly dense M1 pins are subject to complex design rules related to cut space, minimum metal area, end-of-line rules, double patterning rules, etc. These rules make it challenging to pre-calculate routable combinations of placed objects. Figure 2 illustrates how the availability of routing tracks within a cell, as determined by pin geometry, influences the ease of routing to the cell.

For 65nm technology and below, many design rules are imposed to ensure a printable GDSII mask [2], and contemporary industrial detailed routers typically issue reports on 40 or more distinct types of design-rule-check (DRC) violations. However, we view a handful of the most commonly violated of these as generally representative: minimum spacing, end-of-line, non-default routing (NDR), edge-type, and

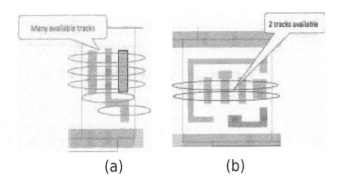

(a)   (b)

Figure 2: Pin layout in a cell affects routability: (a) easier (b) harder.

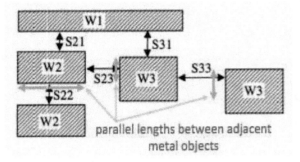

Figure 3: Minimum spacing design rule.

blocked pin. These are described in the remainder of this section.

2.1 Minimum-Spacing Rule

There is a required minimum spacing between any two metal edges. This minimum spacing requirement depends on both the widths of the two adjacent metal objects and the *parallel length* of one object's neighboring edge projected on to the other object's edge facing it. See Figure 3.

2.2 End-of-Line Rule (EOL)

EOL is another spacing rule between objects, but more than two shapes can be involved, and various distance metrics can be used. A 3-object EOL between the top of Object 1 and the bottom of Object 2 is illustrated in Figure 4. EOL is a function of these four parameters:

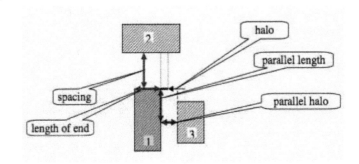

Figure 4: EOL-spacing rule terms defined.

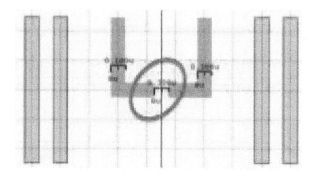

Figure 5: EOL-spacing violations can occur if cells with L-shaped pins are abutted.

Figure 6: Example violations of (a) minimum spacing and (b) EOL spacing restrictions between routing objects within over-congested areas. Most of these violations occur in the vicinity of pins assigned with an NDR.

Length of end: A minimum width for Object 1 to avoid a violation.

Parallel length: Vertical distance below the top of Object 1 within which Object 3 will increase the minimum spacing between Objects 1 and 2.

Halo: Area around corner of Object 1 where Object 2 may trigger the EOL rule.

Parallel halo: Minimum spacing between Object 1 and Object 3 to avoid a violation. The parallel halo is a second spacing requirement triggered by the EOL spacing.

See Figures 5 and 6 for example EOL violations.

2.3 Non-Default Routing Rule (NDR)

Non-default routing rules may specify by routing layer increased wire spacing for a net, increased wire width for a net, or increased via cut number at selected junctions [2]. Via cut number is the number of vias connected to a wire at a single junction. In practice, such rules might be imposed to avoid electromigration or to reduce wire delay.

An NDR may be assigned to a cell pin for wires or vias connecting to it. An NDR may or may not accompany increased pin width or specific non-rectangular pins. NDRs are specified in the floorplan DEF file but may be assigned to a pin in the cell LEF file. See Figure 7.

2.4 Edge-Type Rule

While the preceding rules apply uniformly to all shapes based on geometry alone, an *edge-type rule* is specific to neighboring vertical-edge pairs of particular cell instances.

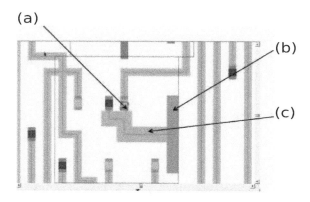

Figure 7: EOL violations due to NDR. (a) EOL spacing violation for routing objects within over-congested areas; (b) Double-width magenta pin with NDR assigned; (c) Double-width wires in accordance with the NDR assigned to magenta pin.

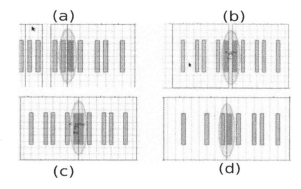

Figure 8: Four edge-type violations. Double width M2 is used for the red pins. An edge-type double-spacing constraint is also enforced at the adjacent cell edge.

These spacings may be required to improve yield, for spacing between different implant dosages, to ensure pin reachability, etc. Examples:

- The left edge of every `ao22s01` cell must be placed at least 0.600μm away from the *right* edge of every `a034s01` cell adjacent to it.
- The left edge of every `ao22s01` cell must be placed at least 0.400μm away from the *left* edge of every other `ao22s01` cell.
- The left edge of every `ao22s01` cell must be placed at least 0.800μm away from the *right* edge of every other `ao22s01` cell adjacent to it.

See Figure 8.

2.5 Blocked Pin

A *blocked pin* cannot be reached by a via or wire without violations. See Figure 9.

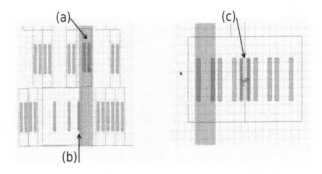

Figure 9: Blocked pins. (a) M1 pins (blue) under M2 power stripe (pink) are not accessible by vias. (b) M2 pin (red) overlaps M2 stripe. (c) M2 pins with NDR assigned are placed too close to each other.

3. BENCHMARKS

Two separate benchmark suites,[1] A and B, have been adapted from public suites used in previous contests. Both suites have been translated [8] from Bookshelf Format [6] to LEF/DEF format [2] so that industrial routers can parse and route the benchmarks. Neither suite has region constraints, and all standard-cell rows in each design are the same height. There are no fixed standard cells or movable macros in any of the test cases. Each suite presents routability challenges in different ways, as described below.

Some characteristic data for the benchmarks are presented in Tables 3 and 5, following notation in Table 1. The statistics on cell widths, pin areas per cell, and boundary perimeter provide some crude, aggregated proxies for routability complexity. Smaller average cell widths will tend to amplify routability congestion caused by high cell-area density. Higher pin density per cell may obstruct routing tracks inside cells (Figure 2) and make pins harder to reach. The placement boundary includes contours around all interior fixed macros (Figure 11) as well as the primary contour enclosing the entire placement region. A relatively longer boundary indicates more concave corners in the placement region, increased likelihood of narrow channels, and increased complexity in the estimation of wirelength and routing congestion due to fixed obstructions along signal paths.

3.1 Suite A

Suite A consists of eight test cases adapted from benchmarks released by Intel Corporation for the ISPD 2013 discrete cell-sizing contest [13]. These test cases have essentially the simplest possible floorplan geometry. Each of the test cases has a rectangular placement region without fixed macros or any other fixed obstructions. All movable objects are standard cells of comparable sizes. Thus, routability challenges in these test cases arise only from cell sizes, pin geometry, power/ground (PG) grid geometry, design rules, and cell placements. Suite A PG grid geometry is listed in Table 2.

---

[1] As of this writing, some specifications of these benchmarks are being adjusted and may still change, in order to provide an appropriate level of difficulty. Additional test-case variants are also being considered. All such changes and additional test cases, if any, will be collected and posted on the ISPD 2014 contest web site as an addendum to this article.

Table 1: Benchmark data notation

#cells	number of movable standard cells
#nets	number of nets
#I/Os	number of fixed I/O pins
#macs	number of fixed macros
util	(cell area) / (placeable region area)
$\bar{w}$	average standard-cell width (μm)
$\sigma(w)$	std. deviation in standard cell widths (μm)
$\bar{\rho}$	average per-cell of (pin area)/(cell area)
$\sigma(\rho)$	std. deviation of (per-cell pin area)/cell area
λ	(number L-shaped pins)/(total number of pins)
π	(boundary perimeter)/(bounding-box perimeter)

Table 2: Suite A PG-grid geometry (μm) by layer

	M1	M2	M3	M4	M5
rail width w_r	0.51	0.58	3.50	4.00	4.00
rail spacing s_r	1.49	20.0	14.0	20.0	14.0

The test cases have the following additional characteristics; most of these are modifications made to the original data in order to increase expected routing difficulty.

1. Each cell instance is down-sized to the minimum area available for it in the associated 65nm cell library.[2]
2. The routing pitch (minimum track height) is 0.2μm.
3. There are 10 routing tracks per standard cell row; hence, each such row is 2.0μm high.
4. All movable cells are single-row high.
5. Except for L-shaped pins, all pins are uniformly shaped rectangles 1μm high by 0.1μm wide.
6. Approximately 7.7 % of all cell instances of test case `edit_dist` and 0.02% of the 2nd variant of test case `pci_bridge32` are given exactly one L-shaped output pin each, placed as shown in Figure 5.
7. The rectangular pins on each cell are grouped in pairs uniformly spaced 0.3μm apart, including the spacing between the left-most pair and the left cell edge. Pins in each pair are placed the minimum-spacing distance from each other.
8. The I/O pins have been placed by OLYMPUS-SoC™ [11] along the boundaries of the M3, M4, and M5 layers and marked fixed.
9. Most cell pins are located on layer M1.
10. NDR with double wire width and double wire spacing is assigned to all nets with fanout > 10.
11. The driving pin of standard cell `ms00f80` is promoted to layer M2 to check the ability of placement to prevent its intersection with PG rails.
12. Standard cell `ao22s01` has output pin near edge on M1 but has edge-type constraint with 2× spacing, i.e., 0.2μm.
13. There are 5 routing layers, but only 4 routing layers are available: M2, M3, M4, and M5.
14. Cells have signal pins only, no power or ground pins. M1 may be used only for vias to M1 pins. M1 is otherwise excluded from routing.

---

[2] Despite the 65nm cell library, the modified routing dimensions and additional design rules do present challenges typical of sub-45nm designs.

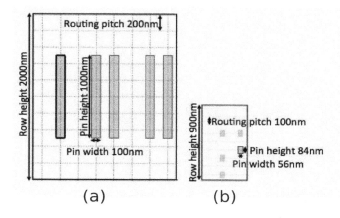

Figure 10: Example standard cells from Suites A (a) and B (b).

Table 4: Suite B PG-grid geometry (μm) by layer

	M2	M3	M4	M5	M6	M7
rail width w_r	0.10	0.86	0.80	0.90	0.90	1.0
rail spacing s_r	9.0	18.0	9.0	18.0	9.0	18.0

15. On some designs, M5 is also blocked to increase routing difficulty. This is representative of designs where fewer routing layers are used to reduce fabrication cost.

16. More conservative minimum-spacing, edge-type, and end-of-line design rules have been added.

17. Non-default routing rules — double width, double spacing, double-cut vias, layer restrictions — are assigned to medium-fanout nets and to some cell pins.

Figure 10 shows example standard cell layouts.

The design rules listed above were applied uniformly across all the test cases in Benchmark Suite A. However, Design Rule 1 below was applied in two different ways to each of the following designs only: **des_perf**, **edit_dist**, and **pci_bridge32**. Hence, each of these test cases has two variants, as listed in Table 3.

DESIGN RULE 1. *Standard cell* **oa22f01** *has output pin 'o' promoted to* M2 *and imposed 2× width, 2× spacing, double-cut vias* NDR. *This restriction should be observed within 1.0μm, i.e., 5 pitches of the output pin; beyond that, only default spacing rules apply.*

VARIANT 1. *Double width (0.2μm) for pin 'o' and edge-type spacing 0.2μm assigned to edge next to pin 'o' with* NDR *double wire width and double wire spacing.*

VARIANT 2. *Single-width L-shaped pin for 'o'.*

3.2 Suite B

Suite B consists of three cases adapted from benchmarks released by IBM Corporation for the DAC 2012 placement contest [15]. In contrast to the test cases in Suite A, the test cases in Suite B have many fixed macros and hence more complicated floorplan geometry; see Figure 11. Suite B power/ground (PG) grid geometry is listed in Table 4. The standard cells in Suite B have been left at their given sizes.

To enable detailed routing, the translator [8] has been adapted to modify the benchmarks as follows.

1. Wire width and wire spacing rules are set based on the 28nm technology node. The minimum wire width and via size are set respectively to 50 nm and 50×50 nm². The minimum-spacing and EOL spacing rules are set respectively to 50nm and 65nm. In addition, based on the default settings in the DAC 2012 benchmarks, metal layers 1–4 and 5–7 have respectively 1× and 2× the minimum wire width, via size, and wire spacing.

2. The routing pitch (minimum track height) is 0.1μm.

3. There are 9 routing tracks per standard cell row; hence, each such row is 0.9μm high.

4. All pins are uniformly sized rectangles 0.056×0.084μm² and have been left at their given locations on cells and macros, except where their placements cause DRC violations for all placements. In such cases, the offending pins have been moved minimally to prevent such DRC violations.

5. Pins rendered inaccessible by routing blockages have been promoted to the top layer of the blockages to make them accessible.

6. Some I/O pins were originally located at the same position, which would cause routing violations. The translator retains only the I/O pin that appears first in the benchmark files and removes the others located at the same position.

7. All cells without any pins were removed; these amounted to less than 0.25% of total cell area. Cells with one output pin and no input pins were retained, with an input pin added but left unconnected.

8. There are between 6 and 7 routing layers available on these designs: either M1–M6 or M1–M7. In contrast to Suite A, M1 *is* available for routing on all test cases in Suite B.

9. A PG grid has been inserted into metal layers 2–7 following the geometry in Table 4. PG rails on M2 are spaced 10 rows apart instead of just one row apart.

10. There are neither M1 PG pins on cells nor M1 PG rails, because M1 cell signal pins are too close to their cells' horizontal-edge boundaries and would overlap with any realistic M1 PG rails.

11. About 0.02% of standard-cell pins in the original benchmarks are at the same location and thus short the nets connecting to these pins. These shorts have been corrected by retaining only the cell pin connected to the last such net.

12. The I/O pins for the testcases in Suite B were placed by OLYMPUS-SoC [11] on either (a) layers M6 and M7, for the test cases with M1–M7 allowed for routing, or (b) layers M5 and M6, for the test cases with M1–M6 allowed for routing. The placed I/O pins were then marked fixed.

13. Double-width-double-spacing non-default rules are assigned to nets with $60 \leq$ fanout ≤ 128.

4. PLACEMENT CONTEST EVALUATION

Submitted DEF placement solutions were evaluated in the OLYMPUS-SoC™ place and route system subject to system memory limits and a 24-hour run-time limit. A script was used to check the placed designs for the following in-

Table 3: Benchmark Suite A characteristics, following notation in Table 1

test case	#cells	#nets	#I/Os	#macs	util	$\bar{w}$	$\sigma(w)$	$\bar{\rho}$	$\sigma(\rho)$	λ	π
mgc_des_perf_1	112644	112878	374	0	0.90	0.794	0.389	0.199	0.045	0	1.0
mgc_des_perf_2	112644	112878	374	0	0.85	0.794	0.389	0.199	0.045	0	1.0
mgc_edit_dist_1	130661	133223	2574	0	0.40	0.799	0.521	0.210	0.048	0.0265	1.0
mgc_edit_dist_2	130661	133223	2574	0	0.43	0.799	0.521	0.210	0.048	0.0265	1.0
mgc_fft	32281	33307	3010	0	0.83	0.905	0.428	0.191	0.044	0	1.0
mgc_matrix_mult	155325	158527	4802	0	0.80	0.781	0.368	0.203	0.037	0	1.0
mgc_pci_bridge32_1	30675	30835	361	0	0.84	0.830	0.369	0.191	0.044	0	1.0
mgc_pci_bridge32_2	30675	30835	361	0	0.85	0.830	0.369	0.191	0.044	0.0001	1.0

Table 5: Benchmark Suite B characteristics, following notation in Table 1

test case	#cells	#nets	#I/Os	#macs	util	$\bar{w}$	$\sigma(w)$	$\bar{\rho}$	$\sigma(\rho)$	λ	π
mgc_superblue11	925616	935731	27371	1458	0.44	1.196	0.964	0.027	0.019	0	6.08
mgc_superblue12	1286948	1293436	5908	89	0.48	0.871	0.729	0.034	0.016	0	3.39
mgc_superblue16	680450	697458	17498	419	0.49	1.014	0.882	0.031	0.018	0	5.25

validating features: cells out of bounds, netlist changes, and movement of fixed objects. Valid placements were legalized and routed in OLYMPUS-SOC.

Each placement's score S was computed as a sum of four category scores: cell legalization displacement, detailed-routing violations, detail-routed wire length, and run time:

$$S = S_{dp} + S_{dr} + S_{wl} + S_{cpu}. \qquad (1)$$

The better the placement, the *lower* the score. Each category score is normalized and scaled to lie in $[0, 25]$. An invalid placement receives the worst possible score of $S = 100$.

With the exception of the detailed routing score, all categories make use of simple affine scaling $f_{as} : [a, \ b] \to [0, \ 25]$ defined as

$$f_{as}(t) = 25 \cdot (t - a)/(b - a) \qquad (2)$$

for every $t \in [a, \ b]$.

4.1 Placement-Legalization Score

All placement submissions were run through OLYMPUS-SOC placement legalization prior to routing, in order to support wide participation by global-placement teams not necessarily having access to DRC-aware legalization. The OLYMPUS-SOC placement legalization was used to fix the following defects in the submitted global placements.

1. Overlaps, both cell-to-cell and cell-to-blockage
2. Edge-type violations
3. Cells not aligned on standard-cell rows
4. Cells with incorrect orientation
5. Cell pins that short to the PG grid
6. Cell pins inaccessible due to the PG grid
7. DRC *placement* violations between standard cells

Significant cell displacement in legalization was penalized as follows. First, a raw legalization score DP was calculated as the average Manhattan displacement of the 10% most displaced of all cells in units of standard-cell row height (SCRH).[3] From DP, the legalization-displacement category

---

[3]For well-spread placements, many cells in this 10% might have zero displacement.

Table 6: Routing violation weights

Design Violation Type i	Weight w_i
Routing open	1.0
Routing blocked pin	1.0
Routing short	1.0
Design-Rule-Check (DRC) violation	0.2

score S_{dp} was computed as

$$S_{dp} = \begin{cases} 0 & \text{if} & \text{DP} \leq 0.25 \text{ SCRH} \\ \text{DP} - 0.25 & \text{if} & 0.25 < \text{DP} < 25.25 \text{ SCRH} \\ 25 & \text{if} & \text{DP} \geq 25.25 \text{ SCRH}. \end{cases} \qquad (3)$$

A placement for which $S_{dp} = 25$ is considered invalid and hence receives score $S = 100$.

4.2 Detailed-Routing Score

Weighted sum

$$\text{DR} = \text{DR}(p) = w_1 v_1 + w_2 v_2 + w_3 v_3 + w_4 v_4$$

is computed from the number of violations v_i of routing violation type i and weight w_i in Table 6. Let DR_{med} denote the median of these unscaled sums DR over valid placements p, and let

$$\text{DR}_{rel} = \sqrt{\frac{\text{DR}}{1 + \text{DR}_{med}}}.$$

Then

$$S_{dr} = \begin{cases} 2.5 \cdot \text{DR}_{rel} & \text{if} & \text{DR}_{rel} \leq 10 \\ 25 & \text{if} & \text{DR}_{rel} > 10. \end{cases}$$

In all cases, $0 \leq S_{dr} \leq 25$. Square root is taken, as there may be a wide range in violation counts.

4.3 Detail-Routed Wirelength Score

Unscaled score WL is simply the final detail-routed wirelength reported by the router. Over all valid placements p on a benchmark with $S_{dp}(p) < 25$, let

$$\begin{aligned} wl_{med} &= \text{the median of the WL}(p). \\ wl_{min} &= \text{the minimum of the WL}(p). \end{aligned}$$

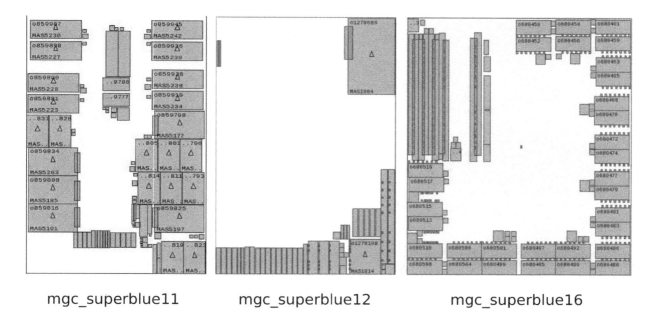

| mgc_superblue11 | mgc_superblue12 | mgc_superblue16 |

Figure 11: Floorplans for the test cases in Suite B; all macros are fixed.

Then

$$S_{wl} = \begin{cases} f_{as}(\text{WL}) & \text{if WL} < 5 \times wl_{med} \\ 25 & \text{if WL} \geq 5 \times wl_{med}, \end{cases}$$

where f_{as} denotes affine scaling (2) from $[wl_{min}, 5 \cdot wl_{med}]$ into $[0, 25]$.

4.4 Run-time Score

Let CPU denote total wall-clock time for placement, legalization, global routing, and detailed routing on one benchmark, on an unloaded machine with 8 cores. Each benchmark suite has a hard run-time limit per test case, CPU_{max}. For Benchmark Suite A, $\text{CPU}_{max} = 24$ hours per test case. If $\text{CPU} > \text{CPU}_{max}$, then the placement is disqualified, $S_{cpu} = 25$, and $S = 100$.

Over all valid placements p on the benchmark, let

$$\text{CPU}_{min} = \text{minimum of the CPU}(p).$$

Then

$$S_{cpu} = f_{as}(\text{CPU}),$$

where f_{as} denotes affine scaling (2) from $[\text{CPU}_{min}, \text{CPU}_{max}]$ into $[0, 25]$.

5. CONCLUSIONS

Constructive collaboration between academic and industrial researchers in physical design depends on the ability of both groups to share useful test data and results. The challenge of computing routable placements in sub-45nm technology has increased with the proliferation of complex geometries and design rules, yet publicly available benchmarks to date have generally lacked the detail needed for researchers to evaluate new placement techniques accurately.

The constructions described here, while far from restoring full physical realism, represent an important improvement in the test data used to quantify placement quality. Artificial reconstructions of pin geometry and routing rules in conjunction with enhanced translation [8] to LEF/DEF format

have enabled more realistic detailed routing on those placements and a higher standard against which proposed new methods for physical design can be judged. Future enhancements can be expected to include more diverse pin geometry and routing rules and, ultimately, the incorporation of realistic timing constraints.

6. ACKNOWLEDGMENTS

We thank the following people for their insight and help: Charles J. Alpert, Yao-Wen Chang, William Chow, Chris Chu, Azadeh Davoodi, Andrew B. Kahng, Shankar Krishnamoorthy, Igor L. Markov, Alexandre Matveev, Mustafa Ozdal, Cliff Sze, Prashant Varshney, Natarajan Viswanathan, Alexander Volkov, Benny Winefeld, Evangeline F.Y. Young.

7. REFERENCES

[1] C. J. Alpert, Z. Li, M. D. Moffitt, G.-J. Nam, J. A. Roy, and G. Tellez. What makes a design difficult to route. In *Proceedings of the 19th International Symposium on Physical Design*, pages 7–12, New York, NY, USA, 2010. ACM.

[2] Cadence, Inc. LEF/DEF 5.3 to 5.7 exchange format. 2009. www.si2.org/openeda.si2.org/projects/lefdef.

[3] J. Cong, G. Luo, K. Tsota, and B. Xiao. Optimizing routability in large-scale mixed-size placement. In *ASP-DAC*, pages 441–446, 2013.

[4] X. He, T. Huang, L. Xiao, H. Tian, G. Cui, and E. F. Y. Young. Ripple: An effective routability-driven placer by iterative cell movement. In *Proceedings of the International Conference on Computer-Aided Design*, pages 74–79, Piscataway, NJ, USA, 2011. IEEE Press.

[5] M.-K. Hsu, S. Chou, T.-H. Lin, and Y.-W. Chang. Routability-driven analytical placement for mixed-size circuit designs. In *Proceedings of the International Conference on Computer-Aided Design*, pages 80–84, Piscataway, NJ, USA, 2011. IEEE Press.

[6] A. B. Kahng and I. L. Markov. VLSI CAD Bookshelf 2. 1999. vlsicad.eecs.umich.edu/BK/.

[7] M.-C. Kim, J. Hu, D.-J. Lee, and I. L. Markov. A SimPLR method for routability-driven placement. In *Proceedings of*

the *International Conference on Computer-Aided Design*, ICCAD '11, pages 67–73, Piscataway, NJ, USA, 2011. IEEE Press.

[8] W.-H. Liu, C.-K. Koh, and Y.-L. Li. Case study for placement solutions in ISPD11 and DAC12 routability-driven placement contests. In *Proceedings of the 2013 ACM International Symposium on International Symposium on Physical Design*, pages 114–119, New York, NY, USA, 2013. ACM.

[9] W.-H. Liu, C.-K. Koh, and Y.-L. Li. Optimization of placement solutions for routability. In *Proceedings of the 50th Annual Design Automation Conference*, pages 153:1–153:9, New York, NY, USA, 2013. ACM.

[10] I. L. Markov, J. Hu, and M.-C. Kim. Progress and challenges in VLSI placement research. In *Proceedings of the International Conference on Computer-Aided Design*, pages 275–282, New York, NY, USA, 2012. ACM.

[11] Mentor Graphics, Inc. Olympus-SoC place and route for advanced node designs. 2014. `www.mentor.com/products/ic_nanometer_design/place-route/olympus-soc`.

[12] G.-J. Nam. ISPD 2006 placement contest: Benchmark suite and results. In *Proceedings of the 2006 International Symposium on Physical Design*, pages 167–167, New York, NY, USA, 2006. ACM.

[13] M. M. Ozdal, C. Amin, A. Ayupov, S. M. Burns, G. R. Wilke, and C. Zhuo. An improved benchmark suite for the ISPD-2013 discrete cell sizing contest. In *Proceedings of the 2013 ACM International Symposium on International Symposium on Physical Design*, pages 168–170, New York, NY, USA, 2013. ACM.

[14] H. Shojaei, A. Davoodi, and J. Linderoth. Planning for local net congestion in global routing. In *Proceedings of the 2013 ACM International Symposium on International Symposium on Physical Design*, pages 85–92, New York, NY, USA, 2013. ACM.

[15] N. Viswanathan, C. Alpert, C. Sze, Z. Li, and Y. Wei. The DAC 2012 routability-driven placement contest and benchmark suite. In *Proceedings of the 49th Annual Design Automation Conference*, pages 774–782, New York, NY, USA, 2012. ACM.

[16] N. Viswanathan, C. J. Alpert, C. Sze, Z. Li, G.-J. Nam, and J. A. Roy. The ISPD-2011 routability-driven placement contest and benchmark suite. In *Proceedings of the 2011 International Symposium on Physical Design*, pages 141–146, New York, NY, USA, 2011. ACM.

[17] Y. Wei, C. Sze, N. Viswanathan, Z. Li, C. J. Alpert, L. Reddy, A. D. Huber, G. E. Tellez, D. Keller, and S. S. Sapatnekar. Glare: Global and local wiring aware routability evaluation. In *Proceedings of the 49th Annual Design Automation Conference*, pages 768–773, New York, NY, USA, 2012. ACM.

[18] Y. Zhang and C. C. Chu. GDRouter: interleaved global routing and detailed routing for ultimate routability. In *Proceedings of the 49th Annual Design Automation Conference*, pages 597–602, New York, NY, USA, 2012. ACM.

Author Index